The Dickens Critics

The Dickens Critics

Edited by

George H. Ford

University of Rochester

AND

Lauriat Lane, Jr.

*University of New Brunswick,
Canada*

GREENWOOD PRESS, PUBLISHERS
WESTPORT, CONNECTICUT

The Library of Congress has catalogued this publication as follows:

Library of Congress Cataloging in Publication Data

Ford, George Harry, 1914-   ed.
     The Dickens critics.

     Bibliography: p.
     1. Dickens, Charles, 1812-1870--Criticism and
interpretation.   I. Lane, Lauriat, joint ed.
II.   Title.
[PR4588.F63 1972]   823'.8   72-152596
ISBN 0-8371-6029-4

First published in 1961
by Cornell University Press, Ithaca

Reprinted with the permission
of Cornell University Press

First Greenwood Reprinting 1972

Library of Congress Catalogue Card Number 72-152596

ISBN 0-8371-6029-4

Printed in the United States of America

#267032

Preface

TO aid the many readers and students of Dickens' fiction many books have been published, among them dictionaries of characters, encyclopedias of place names, bibliographies, and biographies. The present volume offers a new and different kind of aid. It brings together a selection of the important essays, articles, and chapters, from 1841 to now, that critically examine Dickens' fiction. With this collection the modern reader can test his own responses to Dickens against those of others—sometimes hostile, sometimes friendly, but always lively and suggestive.

All the essays in this collection were chosen because they made a serious critical statement about Dickens' fiction in general or about a single work. Some were chosen as necessary examples of the work of well-known critics of Dickens; some were chosen to bring to the reader essays or articles less widely known. One of the most important essays on Dickens, that by Edmund Wilson, unfortunately could not be included, as a note in the collection indicates, but the essay is readily available. Another important essay, F. R. Leavis' *"Hard Times:* An Analytic Note," could not be included because, in Dr. Leavis' words, "it's a very special piece of work with a special context." This essay is also readily available in Dr. Leavis' *The Great*

Tradition. Many excellent essays have had to be omitted for lack of space, but they and others will be found in the bibliography.

Except for correcting a few obvious slips of the pen and regularizing printing style slightly, we have printed all essays as they appeared, making no attempt to make standard such things as British and American usage or the specific text of Dickens' novels quoted.

GEORGE H. FORD
LAURIAT LANE, JR.

Rochester, New York
Fredericton, New Brunswick
April 1961

Acknowledgments

ACKNOWLEDGMENT is gratefully made to the following for permission to reproduce copyrighted essays or selections from the books and magazines that are named below: to Librairie Gallimard for "Alain," *En lisant Dickens* (Paris, 1945); to A. P. Watt and Son and to Dodd, Mead and Co. for G. K. Chesterton, *Charles Dickens, A Critical Study* (New York, 1906); to Faber and Faber, Ltd., and to Harcourt, Brace and World, Inc., for T. S. Eliot, *Selected Essays* (London, 1932); to Houghton Mifflin Co. for George H. Ford, "Introduction" to the Riverside Edition of *David Copperfield* (Cambridge, 1958), and for Morton D. Zabel, "Introduction" to the Riverside Edition of *Bleak House* (Cambridge, 1956); to Laurence Pollinger, Ltd., and to the Viking Press, Inc., for Graham Greene, *The Lost Childhood* (London, 1951); to Rupert Hart-Davis, Ltd., for Humphry House, *All in Due Time* (London, 1955); to Chatto and Windus, Ltd., and to Harper and Brothers for Aldous Huxley, *Vulgarity in Literature* (London, 1930); to Simon and Schuster, Inc., and to Laurence Pollinger, Ltd., for Edgar Johnson, *Charles Dickens* (New York, 1952); to the Hutchinson Group for Arnold Kettle, *An Introduction to the English Novel* (London, 1951); to Andrew Dakers, Ltd., and to the Philosophical Library, Inc., for Jack Lindsay, *Charles Dickens* (New York, 1950); to Harvard University Press for J. Hillis Miller, *Charles Dickens: The World of His Novels* (Cambridge, 1958); to the editor of *Partisan Review* for Robert Morse, *"Our Mutual Friend"* (*Partisan Review*, March 1949); to A. M. Heath and Co. and to Harcourt, Brace and World, Inc., for George Orwell, *Inside the Whale* (London, 1940); to Harold Matson Co. and to A. D. Peters, Esq., for V. S. Pritchett, "The Humour of Dickens" (*The Listener*, June 3, 1954); to Constable and Co., Ltd., and to Daniel C. Cory for George Santayana, *Soliloquies in England* (New York, 1922); to the Society of Authors for G. B. Shaw, Introduction to *Hard Times* (London, 1911); to the editor of *College English* for Robert Stange, "Expectations Well Lost" (*College English*, October 1954); to the Viking Press, Inc., and to Martin Secker and Warburg, Ltd., for Lionel Trilling, *The Opposing Self* (New York, 1955); to the editor of the *Sewanee Review* for Dorothy Van Ghent, "The View from Todgers's" (*Sewanee Review*, Summer 1950); to John Lane, The Bodley Head, Ltd., for Rex Warner, *The Cult of Power* (Philadelphia, 1947); to the editor of the *Critical Quarterly* for Angus Wilson, "Charles Dickens: A Haunting" (*Critical Quarterly*, Summer 1960).

Contents

The Dickens Critics

Introduction: Dickens and Criticism

WHAT do we apprehend from the novels of Dickens, and how do we respond to his artistry? Essentially, all criticism of Dickens asks in some form these questions. To put these questions another way, what meaning or "message" do Dickens' novels have, and by what artistic method does he bring this meaning or message to the reader? Or, to ask the second question still another way, out of what uniting of matter and manner does Dickens create literary meaning? Criticism asks, and tries to answer, these questions.

Certain things the Dickens critics do not do; certain questions they do not, primarily, ask. They do not ask how Dickens directly reflects his own age—that is for the cultural historian, who has found Dickens a good source for his work. They do not ask how Dickens' works reveal his life—that is for the biographer, who has probably done his task more thoroughly and more finally than has any other species of Dickensian. Nor do they search too closely into exactly how Dickens' novels were published, and how illustrated—that is for the bibliographer, whose serious work is just beginning. They do not ask what were the real originals of character and place—that is for the literary antiquarian, whose energy and enthusiasm they can nevertheless admire and whose satisfaction they can share. Nor, finally, do they trace the process of creation and revision too closely, except as knowledge of it sharpens awareness of the exact nature of the final effect. Yet the Dickens critics do not scorn but eagerly borrow the work of all of these—the cultural historian, the biographer, the bibliographer, the literary antiquarian, and the close student of the evolving text—when it can help to solve critical problems.

Many critics have attacked or rejected Dickens—often by implication or innuendo—for three clearly unjustifiable reasons. Some critics have really attacked not Dickens but the Dickensians, not his writings but the excessive adulation of them. No doubt the admirer and student of Dickens will find himself in strange company at times, amid not only responsible historians and critics but also obsessed antiquarians, enthusiastic name droppers, and sentimental rhapsodizers. Not all readers of Dickens also read Dostoevsky or Henry James, nor need they. But enough readers have taken Dickens seriously as an artist to answer such objection. Moreover, some of his defenders would claim with good cause that Dickens' double appeal to a popular as well as a sophisticated audience gives his genius an extra dimension and his novels an extra artistic strength.

Other critics have looked not for Dickens' strengths but only for his weaknesses. They have condemned him for those of his early works in which he often either relied too fully on the cruder conventions of earlier fiction or gave too much freedom to his own still imperfect genius. They have condemned him for overobvious irony and satire, and clumsy picaresque plots; or for oversimple morality and melodrama, and false emotionalizing and uncontrolled verbal fancy. Dickens undeniably had these faults, especially at first, but they are the faults of his creative ambition and imagination. They are the faults of a novelist who never feared to take chances artistically to say what he wished to say, who never had the artistic discretion of Jane Austen, who knew her limitations and made her successes within them. When Dickens failed artistically he failed greatly, but as he matured and as he perfected his special genius, he then succeeded more greatly than had he disciplined himself too soon.

Still other critics have set up a limited definition of the novel and by it have determined that Dickens was no novelist and therefore no artist. They have decided that the novel is not romance but reality, not myth but history; that it is not symbolic but literal and not poetic but prosaic. Hence they would have action always probable, behavior always explainable in everyday terms; they would have style decorous and restrained, speech the speech of normal men and women, and characters moved only by the ordinary springs of human behavior, by the ordinary human desires for fame and fortune, money and matrimony.

Judged wholly by any or all of these views, Dickens fails artistically. But they are all one-sided, they all take too limited a view of Dickensians, of Dickens, and of prose fiction. A roll call of past and present criticism of Dickens shows that his work has seriously engaged the minds of many important critics and writers of the last hundred years, and the range and depth of their reaction to Dickens show how much more there is to him than the obvious faults of his early work, or the obvious merits of that work. Also, recent theorists of fiction—for example, Northrop Frye, who in *Anatomy of Criticism* sees prose fiction as having four forms: novel, romance, confession, and anatomy—demand either a more generous definition of the novel or, more usefully, a sharper sense of the different types of prose fiction, of which the novel is only one. Seen through the work of such critics and of such theorists of fiction, Dickens stands as a meaningful and critically challenging creative artist in prose.

A last preliminary critical issue but a crucial one is: which Dickens is the critic talking about, which of the fifteen novels and the shorter tales does he choose to praise or to blame or simply to analyze and comment on? Critical choice within the body of Dickens' work has varied as much as has Dickens' general reputation and has more affected that general reputation than any other single cause. Dickens was as much to blame for this as his readers. *Pickwick Papers,* by its artistic force and its popularity, has impressed on its readers the image of a Pickwickian Dickens that not only colored their reactions to those novels written directly after *Pickwick Papers,* but caused many readers to reject the later novels wholly or to accept them only grudgingly. A good example is Chesterton, who in his general studies of Dickens can never bring himself to give the later novels the due he gives them in his prefaces to the individual books. Also, many readers and even serious critics have found greater solace and less troublesome complexity in the earlier novels. Even Dickens himself seems to have been—for various biographical and psychological reasons—more at ease with his earlier work, though not therefore more caught up in it. Thus until very recently it was almost possible to divide Dickens critics into those who felt that *David Copperfield* was Dickens' last great novel and those who felt that *Bleak House* was his first great one. The former looked into the later novels for saving remnants of Dickensian "character" and of what Chesterton called "the great gusto." The latter—for whom Edmund Wilson may stand as the type—looked into the earlier novels for foreshadowings of the "darker" Dickens and of the elaborate symbolic techniques of the later, greater novels. In the end, perhaps, criticism may resolve this issue by finding that Dickens' works, like Shakespeare's, range across the full individual and cultural cycle from youth through maturity to age, from life and "gusto" through doubt, darkness, and near despair to final resolution.

II

Literature, especially prose fiction, imposes a meaningful moral pattern on the complexities of real life. If the pattern imposed is too false to our sense of reality, the result is melodrama, and we reject it. But a more subtle artistic vision, ordered enough to be morally meaningful, yet complex enough to suggest that, though not life itself, it is a true reading of life, is one quality of all good literature. This complexity need not be direct and literal, for a work of transparent simplicity on one level may express through its symbols and its allegory a much more complex reading of life. Many critics have charged Dickens, especially in his early novels, with writing melodrama; however, even in Dickens' weakest novels the plots and personages of melodrama are rarely an end in themselves but, when extended and developed through a novel's length, often carry more than their literal meaning. In Dickens' major novels, moreover, such plots and personages lose all taint of melodrama and become vital parts of a unified moral vision.

To speak of Dickens' meaning apart from his method is in theory the worst of critical acts, but in practice it can be one of the most helpful. Moreover, although to consider Dickens' meaning before considering the artistic methods by which he created that meaning may seem backwards, we gain in two ways by so doing. We take up first what, for most readers, remains the more obvious kind of literary awareness, awareness of meaning, and what has hitherto got more attention from criticism. And we give final emphasis to effects of method that readers too often do not sense fully, and criticism has too often overlooked or avoided. First, then, what meanings and what kinds of meaning can critics find in Dickens' work? In what ways do Dickens' novels, in Kenneth Burke's phrase, equip us for living?

Dickens' special way of achieving and communicating meaning—a way obviously the result of his special method—has, it must be granted, helped to pose critical problems for the analyzers and interpreters of that meaning. Prose commentary, at least academic prose commentary, often finds dissection more presentable, and more publishable, than delight. Yet delight, or some equally intense and empathic response to Dickens' artistry, must be part of an awareness of his meaning. For more than other English novelists Dickens does not so much present his meaning to us as demand that we experience it. In those critical quarters which insist, as has been said, that all literature would be *Middlemarch* if it could, Dickens' version of literary meaning and of literary experience has often been turned aside for more intellectual and analytical ones. Yet Dr. Leavis has found in *Hard Times* "a profound inspiration," "a comprehensive vision." And Dr. Leavis' coupling of Dickens with Shakespeare reminds us that whenever and whatever Dickens' novels "mean," they do so not assertively but imaginatively and poetically. Dickens forces us not to think but, in the highest sense, to feel; severed from artistic expression and embodiment, his ideas become truisms. It is our experience of the literary expression of these ideas that matters.

Thus what Dickens' novels lack in intellectual clarity they more than make up in emotional richness. But critics who seek the meaning of Dickens' novels find in this emotional richness a complexity and ambiguity that, if they do not mislead the critic, at least challenge any too explicit generalization he may make. Although short segments of Dickens' art are morally decipherable and identifiable—one can usually tell if a single action, or a minor character, is good or bad, just or unjust—the total moral world is less clear. Often in the earlier novels (*Oliver Twist*, for example), moral and literary emphases contend for the reader's response. Even in the mature novels the reader, if he give himself freely and fully to the now-unified literary and moral experience, feels not an explicit meaning or "message" but a pervasive moral atmosphere and weight, a moral pressure not a moral.

Of one level of meaning, of course, there is little doubt. Most of Dickens' novels—some critics would say all—begin with or contain an attack on a specific abuse. Dickens attacks these abuses directly, often in his prefaces as well. No critics deny that such attacks take place, and only those critics such as Lord Denman or Fitzjames Stephen—who felt that the attacks were aimed at themselves—have objected seriously to them. But such satiric assaults, limited in time, place, and scope, hardly make Dickens a universally meaningful novelist, or a great one. The reader might read the opening chapters of *Oliver Twist* once as an attack on the New Poor Law of 1834, but he would hardly reread them as such. The Court of Chancery stands at the center of the action of *Bleak House* but only points toward the heart of the meaning. If to the reader Dickens' novels are merely topical, then they are so merely.

But once criticism moves beyond the topical, and in a few cases even before it does so, it comes up against the complexity and ambiguity already mentioned. To take just one example: Dickens is a radical, even revolutionary, writer. Directly and symbolically he expresses a pressure for social change and even upheaval, although at the same time fearing the unleashed violence they seem to carry with them. Most critics would accept this preliminary statement of meaning. But change how, and in what direction? Here, critics disagree. For Dickens arouses the revolutionary impulse but seems to most critics to do little to direct the revolutionary purpose toward a specific constructive program. But this, it might be answered, is the revolutionary role of literature, of imaginative art: to stir the sympathy and imaginative identification that vitalize conscious, reconstructive reform. To make us repelled by the Circumlocution Office, in short, not to show us how to reorganize it.

Yet our sympathies are stirred to one purpose; Dickens does exert moral pressure in one direction. Both the abuses he attacks and the society he angrily calls to our attention are organized, impersonal, institutionalized. They are great, unhuman, inhuman social forces or webs by which the weak or vulnerable individual is crushed, in which he is entangled unto death. In such a world, of hypocrisy, pride, and folly, of Chancery, dust heaps, and the Fleet, of death by violence and death by ignorance, men can

survive and can aid others to survive only as individuals caring
about other individuals. "Love thy brother"—as Orwell notes,
this is not such a platitude as it sounds; practiced rather than
preached it could, says Dickens, save the world.

But the world, in Dickens' novels, is not saved. Criticism, no
longer misled by the conventional endings of certain novels or
by the escape into idyllic security of a select few characters,
sees this. And as criticism sees this of the world of Dickens'
novels, more and more it feels, apparent, insistent, oppressive
even, the meaningful weight of Dickens' revolutionary art.

What meaning, in turn, can the individual characters in
Dickens' novels achieve, meaning at times contained within, at
times counterpointed against the meaning of Dickens' total
world-in-fiction? First, the meaning of Dickens' characters lies
in what happens to them. By this simple test, to take *Bleak House*
for an example, some characters, such as Jo or Gridley, are
victims of social oppression or personal violence and are destroyed unjustly. Some, such as the various lawyers from Mr.
Tulkinghorn to Conversation Kenge, do evil indirectly by carrying out their proper roles in society and are either punished
(often comically) or left to prosper. Some, such as Mlle Hor-
tense, do evil actively and personally and are punished wholly,
usually by death. Some combat evil by armed or armored virtue,
as do Inspector Bucket and John Jarndyce, and some escape it
by cloistered virtue, as does George; both of these seem, at the
end of the novel, to live happily ever after. To a large group of
characters, finally, nothing much happens; they have no destinies.
Many of them, the little people, the Snagsbys and Bagnets, hide
from fate down alleys and up courtways; others, often the great
Dickens "characters," transcend fate by gigantic, inspired folly,
as does Boythorn, or by simple madness, as does Miss Flite.

Over what happens to these and other figures critics argue
little. But over why it happens, over "meaning" in the fuller
sense, critics have argued, do argue, and will no doubt go on

arguing. For Dickens' characters engage the critic's interest and even his loyalty and demand some kind of moral judgment. But Dickens' meaning, as we have already seen, although so insistent as to call forth interpretation, is rarely so explicit as to dictate the exact form interpretation must take.

Characters, in literary art, we may take to have four kinds of meaning: psychological, social, ethical, and "spiritual." (By "spiritual" meaning, for want of a better term, we signify how characters add to or fix the author's total moral view: his vision, call it religious or mythic, of how and why the world is.) Some authors of fiction succeed or fail by allowing their characters only some or one of these kinds of meaning. Dickens, like Shakespeare, often succeeds or fails by attempting all.

What special meaning the critic finds in any Dickens character may depend on a choice or decision many critics seem unaware of having made. For before he can search out meaning, by analysis, by comparison, by intuition, by identification—all presumably in contexts of the real and the ideal—the critic must choose to what degree he will take the characters in a Dickens novel as human beings and to what degree as fictional characters. To what degree, that is, he will read complex characters such as Skimpole or Bucket as life and to what degree as literature— a question compounded, with Skimpole, by the frequent Dickensian problem of a real-life model, in this case Leigh Hunt.

Literature can, by its flexibility of method, create characters, Jo, for example, that are both human and artificial. Thereby literature can, in its complexity of meaning, have its characters taken both directly and indirectly, both actually and symbolically. Criticism errs if, in reading Dickens, it chooses one or the other of these ways to meaning exclusively. It also errs if it loses sight of the tension and balance between them in a given work, when speaking of that work. Finally, if criticism finds these two ways to meaning, the actual and the symbolic, to diverge too far, the author has failed. But if criticism forces them to diverge, then the critic has become obsessed, and has failed.

Thus a full critical act may find that a given Dickens character achieves, in two ways, four kinds of meaning. As a human being, first, he or she may exemplify an actual psychological state, may be evidence of some social situation, may behave badly or virtuously, and may reveal by some human fate what power oversees mankind. Psychologically, the Dickens character gives form to some feeling or fantasy within or around the author, in the case of Jo the helplessness and endurance of childhood and innocence, and thereby brings the reader to fuller awareness of the psychological world within or around him. Socially, the Dickens character exhibits some phase of that tyranny of institutions over individuals already cited—Jo is obviously a victim of social and economic forces. Ethically, the Dickens character acts out the traditional, even proverbial, wisdom of the Bible, above all of the New Testament—Jo is a moral touchstone, bringing out the good Samaritan in many of the characters he encounters. Spiritually, the Dickens characters, by their existences and fates, show the world to be infested by disease, violence, and oppression, foes from which characters may escape for a time into some idyllic unreality, from which they escape finally only by death—as does Jo. For some critics, however, the Dickens characters affirm by their fates that the weak and the self-deluded may fall but that the good and the strong and the self-aware may pass through the valley of the shadow of the law or of other shadows and be redeemed in this world. Yet in either case the world from which or in which the characters are saved seems little changed by their salvation. Dickens' vision of social reality remains a dark one.

Also, characters may represent or suggest other, further degrees and dimensions of meaning. A character or group of characters may not so much demonstrate the effect of psychological forces as embody these forces in a kind of allegory of the mind's division or progress, the most obvious example of this being the many allegorical pairs of characters in Dickens' novels, from Pickwick and Weller to Jaggers and Wemmick. The victim of a social evil may come to stand for a class of victims, just as the doer of that evil may come to stand for the institution he directly acts for—beadledom become Bumbledom. The good and the bad deeds men and women do to one another in Dickens' novels may become melodramatically heightened into ethical parables; characters may become Vices and Virtues and their lives a kind of continuing morality play. Critics may even choose to see Dickens' world of imagination as closer to Bunyan's and Blake's than often granted, as a world whose creator is, literally, visionary.

One final point about the meaning of Dickens' fiction. To Dickens' biographer and closest friend, John Forster, Dickens was "one of the greatest humourists England has produced." And the face George Orwell sees "behind the page" is that of a man "laughing, with a touch of anger in his laughter." Criticism loses sight of Dickens' sense of humor only at the risk of losing sight of its own—the worst fate for a critic of Dickens. Dickens' humor is part of his artistic method, of course, but humor is so strong and so universal in Dickens' novels that it becomes part of his meaning as well. In "A Free Man's Worship" Bertrand Russell sees man, in a godless, naturalistic world, dignified by his awareness of Fate, of Tragedy, and of the Past. To these three Dickens would add Humor, by which, if man may not keep his dignity, he may keep his sympathy and his sanity. Humor—of style, of situation, of action, and of character—is not the least part of Dickens' meaning. To grasp Dickens' meaning wholly, critics must grasp the meaning of his humor.

III

Dickens' humor is part of his method. And Dickens' whole method, his choice of material and his manner of rendering that material in prose fiction, may also be regarded under the four headings of style, situation, action, and character.

In the largest sense all of Dickens' artistic method is his "style," his special form of self-expression in prose fiction. And in a lesser sense the other parts of Dickens' art, his situations, actions, and characters, and the meaning that they carry, rest upon style and take their essence from it. But style in the narrowest and directest sense remains words responded to primarily for their own sakes, for their artistically effective arrangement felt as such. "Style," in this sense, criticism feels at those places in Dickens' novels where style becomes end as well as means, where it becomes eloquence.

Dickens' characteristic style, as seen for example in *Great Expectations*, is at its strongest organic, at its richest poetic, at its most intense both organic and poetic. Organically it grows out of the imaginative moment it renders, and it re-creates that moment almost physically by every artistic resource of diction, syntax, and rhythm; poetically it takes upon itself as much added meaning and effect as it can and still provide the needed sense of situation, action, or character, thus becoming, in Ezra Pound's phrase, "language charged with meaning to the utmost possible degree." To be organic or poetic this style does not fear to extend or even break the bounds of grammatical or verbal decorum, narrowly plotted. It is clear, but it is never content to be "correct." Many critics have objected to this incorrectness or extravagance of style; many others have simply yielded to its eloquence. Above all, Dickens' style is intent on satisfying the internal needs of the fictional moment, whether they be mimetic or interpretive. Thus, although Dickens' style does heed the most basic restraints of convention, it stays relatively free of other external demands. It does not consciously rebel against and revise established methods, nor does it conform to the author's special personality or philosophy—unless its intentness on the demands of the fictional moment be taken as such. The personality sometimes ascribed to Dickens by students of his style more often proves to be a persona assumed to fulfill an artistic requirement, or at the least the characteristic mixture of personal involvement and artistic detachment also revealed by Dickens' comments about his writing.

Critics have already singled out many elements of this style for descriptive comment. For example, they have noted Dickens' "animism," his way of imparting life to objects in a passing image, an elaborated fantasy, or even a symbolic pattern that dominates a whole novel. They have noted, at times with pain, Dickens' comments on the action he is presenting, his apostrophes to the reader, failing often to realize that such apostrophes are not to excite the reader's emotions but to release them. They have noted how the special style of his first-person narrators develops from David Copperfield's traditional autobiographical manner, through Esther's somehow obligatory testimony, to the perfected eloquence of Pip's revelations, "that sense of a mind speaking to itself with no one there to listen," as Graham Greene calls it. They have noted how aptly Dickens fits verbal movement to the action described, as in the opening scene of *Great Expectations*, and dramatic indications to the drama. Above all, they have noted the range of Dickens' dialogue from the idiosyncratic humorous dialect of "character" such as Joe's "Which I meantersay," to the universal rhetoric of an archetypal human response, verbally idealized into art: Pip's "when I loved Estella with the love of a man, I loved her simply because I found her irresistible."

Often, as critics have noted, Dickens creates situation out of pure description, out of an atmosphere so intense that something must come of it, such as the first three paragraphs of *Great*

Expectations. Often, again as critics have noted, a situation grows potentially dramatic, even melodramatic, preparing the reader for a confronting, a conflict, a revelation, a resolution, as does the scene of Magwitch's return at the end of the second stage of Pip's expectations. On the whole, criticism has noted only the most obvious of such situations, only the most conspicuous mood pieces and the most tense moments. It has overlooked, as Dickens never did, the reader's expectations, great and small. It has perhaps feared to find out how much Dickens had in common with such plot spinners as Wilkie Collins for fear of losing sight of how much greater an artist Dickens was, for fear of not finding how much profounder and more enriching were the kinds of "interest" Dickens drew on by his creation of the sense of situation. Criticism, that is, has not always realized that to have moved the reader's emotions by means of situation is not necessarily to have manipulated them.

In Dickens' world-in-fiction the characteristic act, action, or activity, although observed so acutely and rendered so vividly as to seem actual to the reader, has weight, importance, significance, beyond this actuality. In varying ways and with varying intensity or insistence, action in Dickens' novels becomes at the least representative, at the most symbolic. Earlier critics have recognized this symbolic action as part of Dickens' "poetry"; recent critics have often recognized it as part of his creation of allegory, or myth. Dickens probably came to this mode of writing by way of his special genius, but he may have learned it from such sources as Carlyle, folk or traditional literature, or the Bible. Such indebtednesses are hard to prove. Yet if criticism cannot prove them, it may at least suggest them so as to show, by analogy, when and how action in Dickens' novels becomes symbolic.

In Dickens' novels a single act is a gesture rather than a motion, movement, or deed. It intends to catch the reader's eye and gain his response just as it would on an actual stage and even sometimes in reality. This is why it is both vivid and symbolic. The reader sees it as clearly and directly as the medium of the printed page allows, but also sees that it speaks to him about something beyond its actual self. By its special intensity and its special appropriateness, the gesture demands a further reading, insists on its further meaning. Too often criticism has blamed action in Dickens' novels for ignoring narrow probabilities while itself ignoring potentialities for other, richer artistic effects than mere lifelikeness. Yet at the same time criticism can never ignore the literal weight and direction of Dickens' words; it must read for symbolic action closely and imaginatively but not eccentrically or esoterically. The more extended and complex patterns of action and activity in Dickens' novels, the linear, evolving plots and the reiterated, fixed comic or tragic rites, also demand this generously double response to their actuality and to their further significance. One obvious example of this further significance is the number of single acts and extended actions in Dickens' novels that prove to exemplify proverbial wisdom—Sikes is given enough rope to hang himself—thereby adding a special aptness and rightness to Dickens' ordering of the fictional world in which these acts and actions occur.

Dickens' characters are "flat" not "round": Dickens' characters are, somehow, Shakespearean. These two statements recur in some form throughout criticism of Dickens' novels. By one Dickens is condemned, by the other raised to the highest place. As implied value judgments both cannot be true. But both, properly defined, qualified, and explored, tell us important things about Dickens' art of characterization and about how criticism has regarded that art.

First, an important distinction. In a very real sense no character in a work of literature is less flat than the printed page on which it appears. Literature may last longer than life, it may be more eloquent, more vivid, more meaningful than life, but it can hardly be more alive than life. Literally, and literarily, all char-

acters are flat; no character is round. If those critics who con-
demn Dickens for creating "unalive" characters mean anything
by their statements, they mean it metaphorically. Those, and
there have been some, who seem to have spoken literally, spoke
nonsense. They affirmed a willful self-delusion not at all the
same as Coleridge's "willing suspension of disbelief," the latter
a far more complex and rewarding form of literary experience.

Metaphorically then, what does criticism mean when it says
that a character is flat not round? The term may be merely
descriptive. In literature as in life persons may show more or
less of their inner selves; those who give us only their surface do
appear to lack depth, do have a kind of flatness. Also some persons, again in literature as in life, have only a surface self to
show. To see their flatness is to see their essential being. But the
term "flat"—as used, for example, by E. M. Forster—may imply
a value judgment. For to assume that literature must give us
life and to assume that life is "round" is to assign flat characters
to an inferior order of literary craft and meaning. By such a
process Dickens' characters, his art of characterization, have
often been charged, tried, and found guilty.

To answer this charge one may appeal to life or to art. Some
defenders of Dickens' characterization answer the charge of
flatness, or caricature, by appealing to life. They say that this is
really the way life is—that those who fail to recognize this as
life either do not know enough of life or do not look at life
closely enough. For such critics even Dickens' grossest fools
are not grotesques or gargoyles but simply a more perceptive
vision of human reality. Dickens himself often defended his
characters by some such appeal to real life as a standard. But
such appeals limit the authority of art as no other kind of defense
does, limit it in time, in place, and in kind. Dickens can be defended on surer grounds than these.

Many critics seem to accept the flatness of Dickens' characters
and glory in it. For these Dickens has simply raised caricature to

a high level of art. Dickens is a great caricaturist, and caricature can be great art. For others, in the words of Chesterton, "it is a caricature of Dickens to call him a caricaturist." "The very criticism itself," says Chesterton, "has exactly the oversimplification of a caricature." For Chesterton such characters are instead a form of "poetry." Gissing, in turn, sees them as "idealism." And other critics have found other terms. Yet of course all of them, Chesterton, Gissing, and the many others, do not really accept flatness as such, but deny the metaphor wholly, or at least see flatness as somehow translucent or even transparent, opening up into depth and awareness far beyond mere surface exaggeration of outline and shape. Thus for Gissing it is because Dickens is a "supreme idealist" that he can be ranked with Shakespeare.

One other piece of evidence often cited for the flatness of Dickens' characters is that they are static, unchanging; that they do not grow, and that thereby they violate both living reality and the artistic rule exemplified by George Eliot's "character is a process and an unfolding." But critics who argue thus have failed to notice the differing types of character and the shifting perspectives in a Dickens novel. For even in the earlier novels we have degrees of flatness and roundness, extending outward from the "rounder" character or characters whose point of view we share, and whose inner change and growth we are therefore party to, to those whose entire role in the novel and relation to the central figures is external—though not necessarily less meaningful. By their obviousness such external "flat" characters catch attention first and may, for the naïve reader, hold it too long. Hence the often-noted gap between the Dickens of everyone's childhood and the Dickens adult criticism wishes to take so seriously. For the perceptive critic, however, even Pickwick gains in wisdom from his adventures, and in the novels from *David Copperfield* on Dickens always details, amid some recurring, unchanging social problem, the rise or fall, the corruption or education, of selected individual characters.

In ranking Dickens with Shakespeare most critics obviously
have in mind the Shakespeare of Falstaff and Bottom, not of
Hamlet or Lear—even if Jeffrey did think Little Nell as moving
as Cordelia. They see Dickens and Shakespeare as great humorists, creating characters of wit, vivacity, earthiness, gusto, above
all unforgettability, that embody and appeal to certain basic
human needs and desires and at the same time charm us toward
moral sympathy and awareness. Yet the best of such critics also
see both Dickens and Shakespeare as great poets, whose art
encloses but transcends reality, above all by imagination of style
and subject matter, by what Bagehot calls "irregular genius."
For these critics not just Dickens' humorous "flat" characters
but his "rounder" ones become poetic, by eloquence of speech,
by dramatic intensity, by stylization of action, and by extension
of significance. In such terms, not just Dickens' great fools but
his major ironic or tragic characters are Shakespearean as well.
Criticism may without fear set not only Mrs. Gamp beside Mrs.
Quickly and Pecksniff beside Malvolio, but also Pip beside Hamlet, Jaggers beside Prospero, Dorrit beside Lear, and feel something of the same sense of the ironic mysteries of human nature,
of the tragic dilemmas of existence.

EDGAR ALLAN POE: 1841

The Old Curiosity Shop

THIS plot is the best which could have been constructed for
the main object of the narrative. This object is the depicting of
a fervent and dreamy love for the child on the part of the grandfather—such a love as would induce devotion to himself on the
part of the orphan. We have thus the conception of a childhood,
educated in utter ignorance of the world, filled with an affection
which has been, through its brief existence, the sole source of its
pleasures, and which has no part in the passion of a more mature
youth for an object of its own age—we have the idea of this
childhood, full of ardent hopes, leading by the hand, forth from
the heated and wearying city, into the green fields, to seek for
bread, the decrepid imbecillity of a doting and confiding old
age, whose stern knowledge of man, and of the world it leaves
behind, is now merged in the sole consciousness of receiving love
and protection from that weakness it has loved and protected.

This conception is indeed most beautiful. It is simply and
severely grand. The more fully we survey it, the more thoroughly
are we convinced of the lofty character of that genius which
gave it birth. That in its present simplicity of form, however,
it was first entertained by Mr. Dickens, may well be doubted.
That it was *not*, we are assured by the title which the tale bears.

From *Graham's Magazine*, May 1841, pp. 248–251.

When in its commencement he called it "The Old Curiosity Shop," his design was far different from what we see it in its completion. It is evident that had he now to name the story he would not so term it; for the shop itself is a thing of an altogether collateral interest, and is spoken of merely in the beginning. This is only one among a hundred instances of the disadvantage under which the periodical novelist labors. When his work is done, he never fails to observe a thousand defects which he might have remedied, and a thousand alterations, in regard to the book as a whole, which might be made to its manifest improvement.

But if the conception of this story deserves praise, its execution is beyond all—and here the subject naturally leads us from the generalisation which is the proper province of the critic, into details among which it is scarcely fitting that he should venture.

The Art of Mr. Dickens, although elaborate and great, seems only a happy modification of Nature. In this respect he differs remarkably from the author of *Night and Morning*. The latter, by excessive care and by patient reflection, aided by much rhetorical knowledge, and general information, has arrived at the capability of producing books which might be mistaken by ninety-nine readers out of a hundred for the genuine inspirations of genius. The former, by the promptings of the truest genius itself, has been brought to compose, and evidently without effort, works which have effected a long-sought consummation—which have rendered him the idol of the people, while defying and enchanting the critics. Mr. Bulwer, through art, has almost created a genius. Mr. Dickens, through genius, has perfected a standard from which Art itself will derive its essence, in rules.

When we speak in this manner of *The Old Curiosity Shop*, we speak with entire deliberation, and know quite well what it is we assert. We do not mean to say that it is perfect, as a whole— this could not well have been the case under the circumstances of its composition. But we know that, in all the higher elements which go to make up literary greatness, it is supremely excellent. We think, for instance, that the introduction of Nelly's brother (and here we address those who have read the work) is supererogatory—that the character of Quilp would have been more in keeping had he been confined to petty and grotesque acts of malice—that his death should have been made the *immediate* consequence of his attempt at revenge upon Kit; and that after matters had been put fairly in train for this poetical justice, he should not have perished by an accident inconsequential upon his villany. We think, too, that there is an air of *ultra*-accident in the finally discovered relationship between Kit's master and the bachelor of the old church—that the sneering politeness put into the mouth of Quilp, with his manner of commencing a question which he wishes answered in the affirmative, with an affirmative interrogatory, instead of the ordinary negative one— are fashions borrowed from the author's own Fagin—that he has repeated himself in many other instances—that the practical tricks and love of mischief of the dwarf's boy are too nearly consonant with the traits of the master—that so much of the propensities of Swiveller as relate to his inapposite appropriation of odds and ends of verse, is stolen from the generic loafer of our fellow-townsman, Neal—and that the writer has suffered the overflowing kindness of his own bosom to mislead him in a very important point of art, when he endows so many of his *dramatis personae* with a warmth of feeling so very rare in reality. Above all, we acknowledge that the death of Nelly is excessively painful—that it leaves a most distressing oppression of spirit upon the reader—and should, therefore, have been avoided.

But when we come to speak of the excellences of the tale these defects appear really insignificant. It embodies more *originality* in every point, but in character especially, than any single work within our knowledge. There is the grandfather—a truly profound conception; the gentle and lovely Nelly—we have discoursed of her before; Quilp, with mouth like that of the panting dog—(a bold idea which the engraver has neglected to embody) with his hilarious antics, his cowardice, and his very petty and spoilt-child-like malevolence; Dick Swiveller, that prince of good-hearted, good-for-nothing, lazy, luxurious, poetical, brave, romantically generous, gallant, affectionate, and not over-and-above honest, "glorious Apollos"; the marchioness, his bride; Tom Codlin and his partner; Miss Sally Brass, that "fine fellow"; the pony that had an opinion of its own; the boy that stood upon his head; the sexton; the man at the forge; not forgetting the dancing dogs and baby Nubbles. There are other admirably drawn characters—but we note these for their remarkable originality, as well as for their wonderful keeping, and the glowing colors in which they are painted. We have heard some of them called caricatures—but the charge is grossly ill-founded. No critical principle is more firmly based in reason than that a certain amount of exaggeration is essential to the proper depicting of truth itself. We do not paint an object to be true, but to appear true to the beholder. Were we to copy nature with accuracy the object copied would seem unnatural. The columns of the Greek temples, which convey the idea of absolute proportion, are very considerably thicker just beneath the capital than at the base. We regret that we have not left ourselves space in which to examine this whole question as it deserves. We must content ourselves with saying that caricature seldom exists (unless in so gross a form as to disgust at once) where the component parts are *in keeping;* and that the laugh excited by it, in any case, is radically distinct from that induced by a properly artistical *incongruity*—the source of all mirth. Were these creations of Mr. Dickens' really caricatures they would not live in public estimation beyond the hour of their first survey. We regard them as *creations*—(that is to say as original combinations of character) only not all of the highest order, because the elements employed are not always of the highest. In the instances of Nelly, the grandfather, the Sexton, and the man of the furnace,

the force of the creative intellect could scarcely have been engaged with nobler material, and the result is that these personages belong to the most august regions of the *Ideal*.

In truth, the great feature of the *Curiosity Shop* is its chaste,
vigorous, and glorious *imagination*. This is the one charm, all
potent, which alone would suffice to compensate for a world
more of error than Mr. Dickens ever committed. It is not only
seen in the conception, and general handling of the story, or in
the invention of character; but it pervades every sentence of the
book. We recognise its prodigious influence in every inspired
word. It is this which induces the reader who is at all ideal, to
pause frequently, to re-read the occasionally quaint phrases, to
muse in uncontrollable delight over thoughts which, while he
wonders he has never hit upon them before, he yet admits that
he never has encountered. In fact it is the wand of the enchanter.

Had we room to particularise, we would mention as points
evincing most distinctly the ideality of the *Curiosity Shop*—the
picture of the shop itself—the newly-born desire of the worldly
old man for the peace of green fields—his whole character and
conduct, in short—the schoolmaster, with his desolate fortunes,
seeking affection in little children—the haunts of Quilp among
the wharf-rats—the tinkering of the Punch-men among the
tombs—the glorious scene where the man of the forge sits por-
ing, at deep midnight, into that dread fire—again the whole
conception of this character; and, last and greatest, the stealthy
approach of Nell to her death—her gradual sinking away on the
journey to the village, so skilfully indicated rather than described—her pensive and prescient meditation—the fit of strange
musing which came over her when the house *in which she was
to die* first broke upon her sight—the description of this house,
of the old church, and of the churchyard—every thing in rigid
consonance with the one impression to be conveyed—that deep
meaningless well—the comments of the Sexton upon death, and
upon his own secure life—this whole world of mournful yet

peaceful idea merging, at length, into the decease of the child Nelly, and the uncomprehending despair of the grandfather. These concluding scenes are so drawn that human language, urged by human thought, could go no farther in the excitement of human feelings. And the pathos is of that best order which is relieved, in great measure, by ideality. Here the book has never been equalled,—never approached except in one instance, and that is in the case of the *Undine* of De La Motte Fouqué. The imagination is perhaps as great in this latter work, but the pathos, although truly beautiful and deep, fails of much of its effect through the material from which it is wrought. The chief character, being endowed with purely fanciful attributes, cannot command our full sympathies, as can a simple denizen of earth. In saying, a page or so above, that the death of the child left too painful an impression, and should therefore have been avoided, we must, of course, be understood as referring to the work as a whole, and in respect to its general appreciation and popularity. The death, as recorded, is, we repeat, of the highest order of literary excellence—yet while none can deny this fact, there are few who will be willing to read the concluding passages a second time.

Upon the whole we think the *Curiosity Shop* very much the best of the works of Mr. Dickens. It is scarcely possible to speak of it too well. It is in all respects a tale which will secure for its author the enthusiastic admiration of every man of genius.

DAVID MASSON: 1859

Dickens and Thackeray

PROSE FICTION in Britain—nay, in the rest of Europe and in America too—has received a fresh impulse, and has taken on a new set of characteristics, since Dickens and Thackeray became, for us, its chief representatives. These two writers belong to the classic roll; they are now in their living activity, and the buzz of critics is about them; but a time will come when they shall have their settled places, and, the buzz having transferred itself to others whose turn of penance it will then be, they shall be seen in their full proportions relatively to the Fieldings and Smolletts and Sternes that went before them, and men, noting their differences in comparison with these, may assert also, more boldly than we, what shall seem their superiorities. Dickens, as you are aware, was the first in the field. His *Sketches by Boz* appeared in 1837 followed, within the next ten years, by his *Pickwick*, his *Nicholas Nickleby*, his *Oliver Twist* (previously published in magazine parts), his *Humphrey's Clock* (including *The Old Curiosity Shop* and *Barnaby Rudge*), his *Martin Chuzzlewit*, and several of his Christmas Stories. It was not till after these ten years of Dickens's established popularity, or till about the year 1847, that Mr. Thackeray—whose extraordinary powers had already, however, been long recognized within a

From *British Novelists and Their Styles* (Cambridge, Eng., 1859).

limited circle of intellectual men, in virtue of his numerous scattered publications and papers—stepped forth into equally extensive celebrity. His *Vanity Fair* was the first efficient proclamation to the public at large of the existence of this signal British talent, increasingly known since by the republication of those *Miscellanies* which had been buried in magazines and other periodicals, and by the successive triumphs of the *Snob Papers, Pendennis, Esmond*, the *Newcomes*, and various Christmas Books. Parallel with these had been running later fictions from Mr. Dickens's pen—*Dombey and Son, David Copperfield*, and *Bleak House*. Mr. Dickens also had the last word in his *Little Dorrit*, until the other day, when Mr. Thackeray recommenced in his *Virginians*. For, with the two writers, according to the serial system, it seems to be, whether by arrangement or by necessity, as with Castor and Pollux; both cannot be above the horizon of the publishing world at once, and when the one is there, the other takes his turn in Tartarus. But whether simultaneously visible or alternate, the two are now so closely associated in the public mind, that whenever the one is mentioned the other is thought of. It is now Dickens and Thackeray, Thackeray and Dickens, all the world over. Nay, not content with associating them, people have got into the habit of contrasting them and naming them in opposition to each other. There is a Dickens faction, and there is a Thackeray faction; and there is no debate more common, wherever literary talk goes on, than the debate as to the respective merits of Dickens and Thackeray.

Perhaps there is a certain ungraciousness in our thus always comparing and contrasting the two writers. We ought to be but too glad that we have such a pair of contemporaries, yet living and in their prime, to cheer on against each other. I felt this strongly once when I saw the two men together. The occasion was historic. It was in June, 1857; the place was Norwood Cemetery. A multitude had gathered there to bury a man known to both of them, and who had known both of them well—a man

whom we have had incidentally to name as holding a place, in
some respects peculiar, in the class of writers to which *they*
belong, though his most effective place was in a kindred department of literature; a man, too, of whom I will say that, let the
judgment on his remaining writings be permanently what it may,
and let tongues have spoken of him this or that awry, there
breathed not, to my knowledge, within the unwholesome bounds
of what is specially London, any one in whose actual person
there was more of the pith of energy at its tensest, of that which
in a given myriad anywhere distinguishes the one. How like
a little Nelson he stood, dashing back his hair, and quivering for
the verbal combat! The flash of his wit, in which one quality
the island had not his match, was but the manifestation easiest
to be observed of a mind compact of sense and information, and
of a soul generous and on fire. And now all that remained of
Jerrold was enclosed within the leaden coffin which entered the
cemetery gates. As it passed, one saw Dickens among the bearers
of the pall, his uncovered head of genius stooped, and the wind
blowing his hair. Close behind came Thackeray; and, as the slow
procession wound up the hill to the chapel, the crowd falling
into it in twos and threes and increasing its length, his head was
to be seen by the later ranks, towering far in the front above
all the others, like that of a marching Saul. And so up to the little
chapel they moved; and, after the service for the dead, down
again to another slope of the hill, where, by the side of one of
the walks, and opposite to the tombstone of Blanchard, Jerrold's
grave was open. There the last words were read; the coffin was
lowered; and the two, among hundreds of others, looked down
their farewell. And so, dead at the age of fifty-four, Jerrold was
left in his solitary place, where the rains were to fall, and the
nights were to roll overhead, and but now and then, on a summer's day, a chance stroller would linger in curiosity; and back
into the roar of London dispersed the funeral crowd. Among
those remitted to the living were the two of whom we speak,

aged, the one forty-five, the other forty-six. Why not be thankful that the great city had two such men still known to its streets; why too curiously institute comparisons between them?

And yet, in instituting such comparisons, the public are guided by a right critical instinct. There can be no doubt that the two writers bring out and throw into relief each other's peculiarities—that they are, in some respects, the opposites of each other; and that each is most accurately studied when his differences from the other are noted and scrutinized.

But, first, as to their general resemblances. Both novelists belong, in the main, though by no means exclusively, to the order of Humorists, or writers of Comic Fiction. Moreover, under this distinction, both stand very much in the same relation to their predecessors in respect of the kind or kinds of fiction, previously in use, to which they have attached themselves, and in respect of the extension of range which that kind or those kinds of fiction have received at their hands. The connections of both at first were chiefly with that which we have distinguished as the Novel of English Life and Manners; and both, in working this kind of Novel, have added immensely to its achievements and capabilities in one particular field—that of the Metropolis. The Novels of Dickens and Thackeray are, most of them, novels of London; it is in the multifarious circumstance of London life, and its peculiar humors, that they move most frequently and have their most characteristic being;—a fact not unimportant in the appreciation of both. As the greatest aggregate of human beings on the face of the earth, as a population of several millions crushed together in one dense mass on a space of a few square miles—this mass consisting, for the most part, of Englishmen, but containing also as many Scotchmen as there are in Edinburgh, as many Irishmen as there are in Dublin, and a perfect Polyglott of other nations in addition—London is as good an epitome of the world as anywhere exists, presenting all those phenomena of interest, whether serious or humorous, which result from great numbers, heterogeneousness of composition, and close social packing; besides which, as the metropolis of the British Empire, it is the centre whither all the sensations of the Empire tend, and whence the motive currents issue that thrill to the extremities. If any city could generate and sustain a species of Novel entirely out of its own resources, it might surely be London; nor would ten thousand novels exhaust it. After all the mining efforts of previous novelists in so rich a field, Dickens and Thackeray have certainly sunk new shafts in it, and have come upon valuable veins not previously disturbed. So much is this the case that, without injustice to Fielding and others, Dickens and Thackeray might well be considered as the founders of a peculiar sub-variety of the Novel of English Life and Manners, to be called "The British Metropolitan Novel." As Londoners, however, do not always stay in London, or, while in London, are not always engrossed by what is passing there, so our two novelists both range, and range about equally, beyond the bounds of the kind of fiction thus designated. They do give us English life and manners out of London; nay, they have both, as we have seen, given us specimens also of their ability in at least two varieties of the Novel distinct from that of English life and manners—the Traveller's Novel, and the Historical Novel. If, in this respect of external range, either has the advantage, it is perhaps Dickens—who, in his Christmas stories, and in stories interspersed through his larger fictions, has given us specimens of his skill in a kind of prose phantasy which Thackeray has not attempted.

In addition to the difference just indicated, critics have pointed out, or readers have discovered for themselves, not a few other differences between Dickens and Thackeray.

In the mere matter of literary style, there is a very obvious difference. Mr. Thackeray, according to the general opinion, is the more terse and idiomatic, and Mr. Dickens the more diffuse and luxuriant writer. There is an Horatian strictness and strength

in Thackeray which satisfies the most cultivated taste, and wins
the respect of the severest critic; but Dickens, if he is the more
rapid and careless on the whole, seems more susceptible to passion, and rises to a keener and wilder song. Referring the difference of style to its origin in difference of intellectual constitution,
critics are accustomed to say that Thackeray's is the mind of
closer and harder, and Dickens the mind of looser and richer
texture—that the intellect of the one is the more penetrating and
reflective, and that of the other the more excursive and intuitive.

Passing to the substance of their novels, as composed of
incident, description, and character, we are able to give more
definiteness to the popularly felt differences between the two
novelists in this respect, by attending to the analogies between
novel-writing and the art of painting. In virtue of his descriptions,
or imaginations of scenery, the Novelist may be considered along
with Landscape and Object painters; and, in virtue of his
characters and his incidents, along with Figure and Action
painters. So, on the whole, we find the means of indicating a
novelist's range and peculiarities by having recourse to the
kindred craft for names and terms. On this plan we should have
to say that, while both our novelists are masterly artists, the art
of Dickens is the wider in its range as to object and circumstance.
I may here use a sentence or two on this subject which I wrote
for another occasion. "Dickens," I then said, "can give you a
landscape proper—a piece of the rural English earth in its
summer or in its winter dress, with a bit of water and a village
spire in it; he can give you, what painters seldom attempt, a
great patch of flat country by night, with the red trail of a
railway-train traversing the darkness; he can succeed in a sea-
piece; he can describe the crowded quarter of a city, or the
main street of a country town, by night or by day; he can paint
a garden, sketch the interior of a cathedral, or photograph the
interior of a hut or of a drawing-room; he can even be minute

in his delineations of single articles of dress or of furniture. Take him again in the Figure department. Here he can be an animal painter, with Landseer, when he likes, as witness his dogs, ponies, and ravens; he can be a historical painter, as witness his description of the Gordon Riots; he can be a caricaturist, like Leech; he can give you a bit of village life with Wilkie; he can paint a haggard scene of low city life, so as to remind one of some of the Dutch artists, or a pleasant family scene, gay or sentimental, reminding one of Maclise or of Frank Stone; he can body forth romantic conceptions of terror or beauty that have arisen in his imagination; he can compose a fantastic fairy piece; he can even succeed in a dream or allegory, where the figures are hardly human. The range of Thackeray, on the other hand, is more restricted. In the landscape department, he can give you a quiet little bit of background, such as a park, a clump of trees, or the vicinity of a country house, with a village seen in the sunset; a London street also, by night or by day, is familiar to his eye; but, on the whole, his scenes are laid in those more habitual places of resort, where the business or the pleasure of aristocratic or middle-class society goes on—a pillared clubhouse in Pall Mall, the box or pit of a theatre, a brilliant reception-room in Mayfair, a public dancing-room, a newspaper office, a shop in Paternoster Row, the interior of a married man's house, or a bachelor's chambers in the Temple. And his choice of subjects from the life corresponds. Men and women as they are, and as they behave daily in the charmed circles of rank, literature, and fashion, are the objects of Mr. Thackeray's pencil; and in his delineations of them, he seems to unite the strong and fierce characteristics of Hogarth, with a touch both of Wilkie and Maclise, and not a little of that regular grace and bloom of coloring which charm us in the groups of Watteau." Within his range, the merit of superior care, clearness, and finish, may be assigned to Thackeray; but there are passages in Dickens—

such as the description of the storm on the East Coast in his
Copperfield—to which, for visual weirdliness, there is nothing
comparable in the pages of his rival.

As to the difference of ethical spirit, or of general philosophy,
between the two writers, the public have come to a very definite
conclusion. Dickens, it is said, is the more genial, kindly, cheerful, and sentimental; Thackeray, the more harsh, caustic, cynical,
and satirical writer. And, proceeding on this distinction, the two
factions argue, consistently with it, in behalf of their respective
favorites—the adherents of Dickens objecting to what they call
Thackeray's merciless views of human life, and his perception
of the mean at the roots of everything; and the adherents of
Thackeray, on the other hand, maintaining the wholesome effect
of his bracing sense in comparison with what they call Dickens's
sickly sentimentalism. For us, joining neither of the factions,
it is enough to recognize the fact of the difference on which
they agree so constantly. The philosophy of Dickens certainly
is the professed philosophy of kindliness, of a genial interest in
all things great and small, of a light English joyousness, and a
sunny universal benevolence; whereas, though I do not agree
with those that represent Thackeray's writings as mainly cynical,
but think that, in such characters as his Warrington, he has
shown his belief in manly nobleness, and his power of representing it—yet it seems clear that the pervading philosophy of his
writings, far more than those of Dickens, is that of a profoundly
reasoned pococurantism, of a skeptical acquiescence in the
world as it is; or, to use his own words in describing the state of
mind of his hero Pendennis, "of a belief, qualified with scorn,
in all things extant." The difference is perhaps best seen, and
with most advantage to Thackeray, when it is expressed nega-
tively—that is, with reference not to what the two writers
respectively inculcate, but to what they respectively attack and
oppose. Stated so (but such a method of statement, it should
be remembered, is not the fairest for all purposes), the philosophy

of Dickens may be defined as Anti-Puritanism, whereas that of
Thackeray may be defined as Anti-Snobbism. Whatever practice,
institution, or mode of thinking is adverse, in Mr. Dickens's
view, to natural enjoyment and festivity, against that he makes
war; whereas that which Mr. Thackeray hunts out and hunts
down everywhere is Snobbism. Although, in their positive forms,
both philosophies are good, perhaps in their negative applications
Mr. Thackeray's is the least liable to exception. Anti-Snobbism,
it may indeed be admitted, is not a perfect summary of the whole
decalogue; but, in the present day, and especially in and about
London, it is that which most nearly passes for such a summary;
and, seeing that there is no question anywhere but that Snobbism
is a bad thing, and little difficulty anywhere in knowing what it
is, Mr. Thackeray's doctrine is one to which there needs be less
hesitation in wishing universal good speed than to the correspond-
ing doctrine of his rival—a doctrine which would too hastily
extinguish that, about the nature of which, and its proper
varieties, there may well be much controversy. Farther, it is to
Mr. Thackeray's advantage, in the opinion of many, that in his
satires in behalf of Anti-Snobbism, or of any other doctrine that
he may hold, it is men and their modes of thinking and acting
that he attacks, and not social institutions. To do battle with the
vanity, the affectation, the insincerity, the Snobbism, that lies
under each man's own hat, and actuates each man's own gestures
and conduct, is Mr. Thackeray's way; and rarely or never does he
concern himself with social anomalies or abuses. In this respect he
is singularly acquiescent and conservative for a man of such general strength of intellect. Mr. Dickens, on the other hand, is singularly aggressive and opinionative. There is scarcely a social
question on which he has not touched; and there are few of his
novels in which he has not blended the functions of a social and
political critic with those of the artist, to a degree detrimental, as
many think, to his genius in the latter capacity. For Mr. Dickens's
wonderful powers of description are no guarantee for the

correctness of his critical judgments in those particulars to which
he may apply them. "We may owe one degree of respect," I
have said, "to Dickens, as the describer of Squeers and Creakle,
and quite another degree of respect when he tells us how he
would have boys educated. Mr. Spenlow may be a capital likeness of a Doctors' Commons lawyer; and yet this would not be
proper ground for concluding Mr. Dickens's view of a reform
in the Ecclesiastical Courts to be right. No man has given more
picturesque illustrations of London criminal life; yet he might
not be equally trustworthy in his notions of prison-discipline.
His Dennis, the hangman, is a powerfully conceived character;
yet this is no reason for accepting his opinion on capital punish-
ments." And yet, how much we owe to Mr. Dickens for this
very opinionativeness! With his real shrewdness, his thoughtful-
ness, his courage, what noble hits he has made! The Adminis-
trative Reform Association might have worked for ten years
without producing half of the effect which Mr. Dickens has
produced in the same direction, by flinging out the phrase, "The
Circumlocution Office." He has thrown out a score of such
phrases, equally efficacious for social reform; and it matters little
that some of them might turn out on inquiry to be ludicrous
exaggerations.

All these differences, however, between Dickens and Thackeray, and still others that might be pointed out, resolve themselves into the one fundamental difference, that they are artists
of opposite schools. Thackeray is a novelist of what is called
the Real school; Dickens is a novelist of the Ideal, or Romantic
school. (The terms Real and Ideal have been so run upon of
late, that their repetition begins to nauseate; but they must be
kept, for all that, till better equivalents are provided.) It is
Thackeray's aim to represent life as it is actually and historically
—men and women, as they are, in those situations in which they
are usually placed, with that mixture of good and evil and of
strength and foible which is to be found in their characters, and

liable only to those incidents which are of ordinary occurrence. He will have no faultless characters, no demigods—nothing but men and brethren. And from this it results that, when once he has conceived a character, he works downwards and inwards in his treatment of it, making it firm and clear at all points in its relations to hard fact, and cutting down, where necessary, to the very foundations. Dickens, on the other hand, with all his keenness of observation, is more light and poetic in his method. Having once caught a hint from actual fact, he generalizes it, runs away with this generalization into a corner, and develops it there into a character to match; which character he then transports, along with others similarly suggested, into a world of semi-fantastic conditions, where the laws need not be those of ordinary probability. He has characters of ideal perfection and beauty, as well as of ideal ugliness and brutality—characters of a human kind verging on the supernatural, as well as characters actually belonging to the supernatural. Even his situations and scenery often lie in a region beyond the margin of everyday life. Now, both kinds of art are legitimate; and each writer is to be tried within his own kind by the success he has attained in it. Mr. Thackeray, I believe, is as perfect a master in his kind of art as is to be found in the whole series of British prose writers; a man in whom strength of understanding, acquired knowledge of men, subtlety of perception, deep philosophic humor, and exquisiteness of literary taste, are combined in a degree and after a manner not seen in any known precedent. But the kinds of art are different; and I believe some injustice has been done to Mr. Dickens of late, by forgetting this when comparing him with his rival. It is as if we were to insist that all painters should be of the school of Hogarth. The Ideal or Romantic artist must be true to nature, as well as the Real artist; but he may be true in a different fashion. He may take hints from Nature in her extremest moods, and make these hints the germs of creations fitted for a world projected imaginatively beyond the real one, or inserted into the midst of the real one, and yet imaginatively moated round from it. Homer, Shakespeare, and Cervantes, are said to be true to nature; and yet there is not one of their most pronounced characters exactly such as ever was to be found, or ever will be found in nature—not one of them which is not the result of some suggestion snatched from nature, in one or other of her uttermost moments, and then carried away and developed in the void. The question with the Real artist, with respect to what he conceives, is, "How would this actually be in nature; in what exact setting of surrounding particulars would it appear?" and, with a view to satisfy himself on this question, he dissects, observes, and recollects all that is in historical relation to his conception. The question with the Ideal artist is, "What can be made out of this; with what human conclusions, ends, and aspirations can it be imaginatively interwoven, so that the whole, though attached to nature by its origin, shall transcend or overlie nature on the side of the possibly existent—the might, could, or should be, or the might, could, or should have been?" All honor to Thackeray and the prose fiction of social reality; but much honor, too, to Dickens, for maintaining among us, even in the realm of the light and the amusing, some representation in prose of that art of ideal phantasy, the total absence of which in the literature of any age would be a sign nothing short of hideous. The true objection to Dickens is, that his idealism tends too much to extravagance and caricature. It would be possible for an ill-natured critic to go through all his works, and to draw out in one long column a list of their chief characters, annexing in a parallel column the phrases or labels by which these characters are distinguished, and of which they are generalizations—the "There's some credit in being jolly here" of Mark Tapley; the "It isn't of the slightest consequence" of Toots; the "Something will turn up" of Mr. Micawber, etc., etc. Even this, however, is a mode of art legitimate, I believe, in principle, as it is certainly most effective in fact. There never was a Mr. Micawber in nature, exactly as he appears in the pages of Dickens; but Micawberism pervades nature through and through; and to have extracted this quality from nature, embodying the full essence of a thousand instances of it in one ideal monstrosity, is a feat of invention. From the incessant repetition by Mr. Dickens of this inventive process openly and without variation, except in the results, the public have caught what is called his mannerism or trick; and hence a certain recoil from his later writings among the cultivated and fastidious. But let any one observe our current table-talk or our current literature, and, despite this profession of dissatisfaction, and in the very circles where it most abounds, let him note how gladly Dickens is used, and how frequently his phrases, his fancies, and the names of his characters come in, as illustration, embellishment, proverb, and seasoning. Take any periodical in which there is a severe criticism of Dickens's last publication; and, ten to one, in the same periodical, and perhaps by the same hand, there will be a leading article, setting out with a quotation from Dickens that flashes on the mind of the reader the thought which the whole article is meant to convey, or containing some allusion to one of Dickens's characters which enriches the text in the middle and floods it an inch round with color and humor. Mr. Thackeray's writings also yield similar contributions of pithy sayings applicable to the occasions of common talk, and of typical characters serving the purpose of luminous metonymy —as witness his Becky Sharps, his Fokers, his Captain Costigans, and his Jeameses; but, in his case, owing to his habit rather of close delineation of the complex and particular as nature presents it, than of rapid fictitious generalization, more of the total effect, whether of admiration or of ethical instruction, takes place in the act of reading him.

SIR JAMES FITZJAMES STEPHEN: 1859
A Tale of Two Cities

THERE are few more touching books in their way than the last
of the *Waverly Novels*. The readers of *Castle Dangerous* and
Count Robert of Paris can hardly fail to see in those dreary
pages the reflection of a proud and honourable man redeeming
what he looked upon as his honour at the expense of his genius.
Sir Walter Scott's desperate efforts to pay his debts by extracting
the very last ounce of metal from a mine which had long been
substantially worked out, deserve the respect and enlist the
sympathy which is the due of high spirit and unflinching courage.
The novels, to be sure, are as bad as bad can be; but to pay debts
is a higher duty than to write good novels, and as monuments
of what can be done in that direction by a determined man, they
are not without their interest and value. They have, moreover,
the negative value of being only bad. They are not offensive or
insulting. The usual strong men, the usual terrific combats, and
the usual upholstery are brought upon the stage. They are no
doubt greatly the worse for wear; but if they were good of their
kind, there would be nothing to complain of. The soup is cold,
the mutton raw, and the fowls tough; but there are soup, mutton,
and fowls for dinner, not puppy pie and stewed cat.

In the *Tale of Two Cities*, Mr. Dickens has reached the *Castle
Dangerous* stage without Sir Walter Scott's excuse; and instead

Saturday Review, 17 December 1859, pp. 741–743.

of wholesome food ill-dressed, he has put before his readers dishes of which the quality is not disguised by the cooking. About a year ago, he thought proper to break up an old and to establish a new periodical, upon grounds which, if the statement —and, as far as we are aware, the uncontradicted statement—of Messrs. Bradbury and Evans is true, were most discreditable to his character for good feeling, and we might almost say for common decency, and in order to extend the circulation of the new periodical he published in it the story which now lies before us. It has the merit of being much shorter than its predecessors, and the consequence is, that the satisfaction which both the author and his readers must feel at its conclusion was deferred for a considerably less period than usual. It is a most curious production, whether it is considered in a literary, in a moral, or in an historical point of view. If it had not borne Mr. Dickens's name, it would in all probability have hardly met with a single reader; and if it has any popularity at all, it must derive it from the circumstance that it stands in the same relation to his other books as salad dressing stands in towards a complete salad. It is a bottle of the sauce in which *Pickwick* and *Nicholas Nickleby* were dressed, and to which they owed much of their popularity; and though it has stood open on the sideboard for a very long time, and has lost a good deal of its original flavour, the philosophic inquirer who is willing to go through the penance of tasting it will be, to a certain extent, repaid. He will have an opportunity of studying in its elements a system of cookery which procured for its ingenious inventor unparalleled popularity, and enabled him to infect the literature of his country with a disease which manifests itself in such repulsive symptoms that it has gone far to invert the familiar doctrines of the Latin Grammar about ingenuous arts, and to substitute for them the conviction that the principal results of a persistent devotion to literature are an incurable vulgarity of mind and of taste, and intolerable arrogance of temper.

As, notwithstanding the popularity of its author, it might be an error to assume that our readers are at all acquainted with the *Tale of Two Cities*, it may be desirable to mention shortly the points of the story. The Two Cities are London and Paris. A French physician, who has just been released after passing many years in the Bastille, is brought over to England, where he lives with his pretty daughter. Five years elapse, and the doctor and his daughter appear as witnesses on the trial for treason of a young Frenchman, who is suspected of being a French spy, and acquitted. A year or two more elapses, and the doctor's daughter marries the acquitted man, refusing two barristers, one of whom had defended him, whilst the other was devil to the first. Then ten years elapse, and as the Revolution is in full bloom in Paris, all the characters go over there on various excuses. The Frenchman turns out to be a noble who had given up his estate because he was conscience-stricken at the misery of the population around him, and thought he had better live by his wits in London than have the responsibility of continuing to be a landowner in France. He gets into prison, and is in great danger of losing his head, but his father-in-law, on the strength of his Bastille reputation, gets him off. He is, however, arrested a second time, and turns out to be the son of the infamous Marquis who had put the father-in-law into the Bastille for being shocked at his having murdered a serf. On this discovery he is condemned to death, and his wife goes through the usual business—"If I might embrace him once," "My husband—No! A moment," "Dear darling of my soul," and so forth. Next day, before the time fixed for his execution, the rejected barrister—the devil, not the counsel for the prisoner—gets into the prison, changes clothes with the husband, stupefies him with something in the nature of chloroform, gets him passed out of the prison by a confederate before he revives, and is guillotined in his place.

Such is the story, and it would perhaps be hard to imagine a clumsier or more disjointed framework for the display of the tawdry wares which form Mr. Dickens's stock-in-trade. The broken-backed way in which the story maunders along from 1775 to 1792 and back again to 1760 or thereabouts, is an excellent instance of the complete disregard of the rules of literary composition which have marked the whole of Mr. Dickens's career as an author. No portion of his popularity is due to intellectual excellence. The higher pleasures which novels are capable of giving are those which are derived from the development of a skilfully constructed plot, or the careful and moderate delineation of character; and neither of these are to be found in Mr. Dickens's works, nor has his influence over his contemporaries had the slightest tendency to promote the cultivation by others of the qualities which produce them. The two main sources of his popularity are his power of working upon the feelings by the coarsest stimulants, and his power of setting common occurrences in a grotesque and unexpected light. In his earlier works, the skill and vigour with which these operations were performed were so remarkable as to make it difficult to analyse the precise means by which the effect was produced on the mind of the reader. Now that familiarity has deprived his books of the gloss and freshness which they formerly possessed, the mechanism is laid bare; and the fact that the means by which the effect is produced are really mechanical has become painfully apparent. It would not, indeed, be matter of much difficulty to frame from such a book as the *Tale of Two Cities* regular recipes for grotesque and pathetic writing, by which any required quantity of the article might be produced with infallible certainty. The production of pathos is the simpler operation of the two. With a little practice and a good deal of determination, it would really be as easy to harrow up people's feelings as to poke the fire. The whole art is to take a melancholy subject, and rub the reader's nose in it, and this does not require any particular amount either of skill or knowledge. Every one knows, for example, that death is a solemn and affecting thing. If, therefore, it is wished to make a pathetic impression on the reader, the proper course is to introduce a death-bed scene, and to rivet attention to it by specifying all its details. Almost any subject will do, because the pathetic power of the scene lies in the fact of the death; and the artifice employed consists simply in enabling the notion of death to be reiterated at short intervals by introducing a variety of irrelevant trifles which suspend attention for the moment, and allow it after an interval to revert to death with the additional impulse derived from the momentary contrast. The process of doing this to almost any conceivable extent is so simple that it becomes, with practice, almost mechanical. To describe the light and shade of the room in which the body lies, the state of the bedclothes, the conversation of the servants, the sound of the undertaker's footsteps, the noise of driving the coffin-screws, and any number of other minutiae, is in effect a device for working on the feelings by repeating at intervals, Death—death—death—death—death, just as feeling of another class might be worked upon by continually calling a man a liar or a thief. It is an old remark, that if dirt enough is thrown some of it will stick; and Mr. Dickens's career shows that the same is true of pathos.

To be grotesque is a rather more difficult trick than to be pathetic; but it is just as much a trick, capable of being learned and performed almost mechanically. One principal element of grotesqueness is unexpected incongruity; and inasmuch as most things are different from most other things, there is in nature a supply of this element of grotesqueness which is absolutely inexhaustible. Whenever Mr. Dickens writes a novel, he makes two or three comic characters just as he might cut a pig out of a piece of orange-peel. In the present story there are two comic characters, one of whom is amusing by reason of the facts that his name is Jerry Cruncher, that his hair sticks out like iron spikes, and that, having reproached his wife for "flopping down on her knees" to pray, he goes on for seventeen years speaking of praying as "flopping." If, instead of saying that his hair was like iron spikes, Mr. Dickens had said that his ears were like mutton-chops, or his nose like a Bologna sausage, the effect would have been much the same. One of his former characters was identified by a habit of staring at things and people with his teeth, and another by a propensity to draw his moustache up under his nose, and his nose down over his moustache. As there are many members in one body, Mr. Dickens may possibly live long enough to have a character for each of them, so that he may have one character identified by his eyebrows, another by his nostrils, and another by his toe-nails. No popularity can disguise the fact that this is the very lowest of low styles of art. It is a step below Cato's full wig and lacquered chair which shook the pit and made the gallery stare, and in point of artistic merit stands on precisely the same level with the deformities which inspire the pencils of the prolific artists who supply valentines to the million at a penny a-piece.

One special piece of grotesqueness introduced by Mr. Dickens into his present tale is very curious. A good deal of the story relates to France, and many of the characters are French. Mr. Dickens accordingly makes them talk a language which, for a few sentences, is amusing enough, but which becomes intolerably tiresome and affected when it is spread over scores of pages. He translates every French word by its exact English equivalent. For example, "Voilà votre passeport" becomes "Behold your passport"— "Je viens de voir," "I come to see," &c. Apart from the bad taste of this, it shows a perfect ignorance of the nature and principles of language. The sort of person who would say in English, "Behold," is not the sort of person who would say in French "Voilà"; and to describe the most terrible events in this misbegotten jargon shows a great want of sensibility to the real requirements of art. If an acquaintance with Latin were made the excuse for a similar display, Mr. Dickens and his disciples would undoubtedly consider such conduct as inexcusable pedantry. To show off familiarity with a modern language is not very different from similar conduct with respect to an ancient one.

The moral tone of the *Tale of Two Cities* is not more wholesome than that of its predecessors, nor does it display any nearer approach to a solid knowledge of the subject-matter to which it refers. Mr. Dickens observes in his preface— "It has been one of my hopes to add something to the popular and picturesque means of understanding that terrible time, though no one can hope to add anything to the philosophy of Mr. Carlyle's wonderful book." The allusion to Mr. Carlyle confirms the presumption which the book itself raises, that Mr. Dickens happened to have read the History of the French Revolution, and, being on the look-out for a subject, determined off-hand to write a novel about it. Whether he has any other knowledge of the subject than a single reading of Mr. Carlyle's work would supply does not appear, but certainly what he has written shows no more. It is exactly the sort of story which a man would write who had taken down Mr. Carlyle's theory without any sort of inquiry or examination, but with a comfortable conviction that "nothing could be added to its philosophy." The people, says Mr. Dickens, in effect, had been degraded by long and gross misgovernment, and acted like wild beasts in consequence. There is, no doubt, a great deal of truth in this view of the matter, but it is such very elementary truth that, unless a man had something new to say about it, it is hardly worth mentioning; and Mr. Dickens supports it by specific assertions which, if not absolutely false, are at any rate so selected as to convey an entirely false impression. It is a shameful thing for a popular writer to exaggerate the faults of the French aristocracy in a book which will naturally find its way to readers who know very little of the subject except what he chooses to tell them; but it is impossible not to feel that the melodramatic story which Mr. Dickens tells about the wicked Marquis who violates one of his serfs and murders another, is a grossly unfair representation of the state of society in France in the middle of the eighteenth century. That the French *noblesse* had much to answer for in a thousand ways, is a lamentable truth; but it is by no means true that they could rob, murder, and ravish with impunity. When Count Horn thought proper to try the experiment under the Regency, he was broken on the wheel, notwithstanding his nobility; and the sort of atrocities which Mr. Dickens depicts as characteristic of the eighteenth century were neither safe nor common in the fourteenth.

England as well as France comes in for Mr. Dickens's favours. He takes a sort of pleasure, which appears to us insolent and unbecoming in the extreme, in drawing the attention of his readers exclusively to the bad and weak points in the history and character of their immediate ancestors. The grandfathers of the present generation were, according to him, a sort of savages, or very little better. They were cruel, bigoted, unjust, ill-governed, oppressed, and neglected in every possible way. The childish delight with which Mr. Dickens acts Jack Horner, and says What a good boy am I, in comparison with my benighted ancestors, is thoroughly contemptible. England some ninety years back was not what it now is, but it was a very remarkable country. It was inhabited and passionately loved by some of the greatest men who were then living, and it possessed institutions which, with many imperfections, were by far the best which then existed in the world, and were, amongst other things, the sources from which our present liberties are derived. There certainly were a large number of abuses, but Mr. Dickens is not content with representing them fairly. He grossly exaggerates their evils. It is usually difficult to bring a novelist precisely to book, and Mr. Dickens is especially addicted to the cultivation of a judicious vagueness; but in his present work he affords an opportunity for instituting a comparison between the facts on which he relies, and the assertions which he makes on the strength of them. In the early part of his novel he introduces the trial of a man who is accused of being a French spy, and does his best to show how utterly corrupt and unfair everybody was who took part in the proceedings. The counsel for the Crown is made to praise the Government spy, who is the principal witness, as a man of exalted virtue, and is said to address himself with zeal to the task of driving the nails into the prisoner's coffin. In examining the witnesses he makes every sort of unfair suggestion which can prejudice the prisoner, and the judge shows great reluctance to allow any circumstance to come out which would be favourable to him, and does all in his power to get him hung, though the evidence against him is weak in the extreme. It so happens that in the State Trials for the very year (1780) in which the scene of Mr. Dickens's story is laid, there is a full report of the trial of a French spy—one De la Motte—for the very crime which is imputed to Mr. Dickens's hero. One of the principal witnesses in this case was an accomplice of very bad character; and in fact it is difficult to doubt that the one trial is merely a fictitious "rendering" of the other. The comparison between them is both curious and instructive. It would be perfectly impossible to imagine a fairer trial than De la Motte's, or stronger evidence than that on which he was convicted. The counsel for the Crown said not one word about the character of the approver, and so far was the judge from pressing hard on the prisoner, that he excluded evidence offered against him which in almost any other country would have been all but conclusive against him. It is surely a very disgraceful thing to represent such a transaction as an attempt to commit a judicial murder.

We must say one word in conclusion as to the illustrations. They are thoroughly worthy of the text. It is impossible to imagine faces and figures more utterly unreal, or more wretchedly conventional, than those by which Mr. Browne represents Mr. Dickens's characters. The handsome faces are caricatures, and the ugly ones are like nothing human.

JOHN RUSKIN: 1860

A Note on *Hard Times*

THE essential value and truth of Dickens's writings have been unwisely lost sight of by many thoughtful persons merely because he presents his truth with some colour of caricature. Unwisely, because Dickens's caricature, though often gross, is never mistaken. Allowing for his manner of telling them, the things he tells us are always true. I wish that he could think it right to limit his brilliant exaggeration to works written only for public amusement; and when he takes up a subject of high national importance, such as that which he handled in *Hard Times*, that he would use severer and more accurate analysis. The usefulness of that work (to my mind, in several respects, the greatest he has written) is with many persons seriously diminished because Mr. Bounderby is a dramatic monster, instead of a characteristic example of a worldly master; and Stephen Blackpool a dramatic perfection, instead of a characteristic example of an honest workman. But let us not lose the use of Dickens's wit and insight, because he chooses to speak in a circle of stage fire. He is entirely right in his main drift and purpose in every book he has written; and all of them, but especially *Hard Times*, should be studied with close and earnest care by

Cornhill Magazine, II (1860), 159; also, *Unto This Last* (London, 1862).

persons interested in social questions. They will find much that
is partial, and, because partial, apparently unjust; but if they
examine all the evidence on the other side, which Dickens seems
to overlook, it will appear, after all their trouble, that his view
was the finally right one, grossly and sharply told.

HENRY JAMES: 1865

The Limitations of Dickens

OUR MUTUAL FRIEND is, to our perception, the poorest
of Mr. Dickens's works. And it is poor with the poverty not of
momentary embarrassment, but of permanent exhaustion. It is
wanting in inspiration. For the last ten years it has seemed to us
that Mr. Dickens has been unmistakeably forcing himself. *Bleak
House* was forced; *Little Dorrit* was laboured; the present work
is dug out as with a spade and pickaxe.

Of course—to anticipate the usual argument—who but Dickens could have written it? Who, indeed? Who else would have
established a lady in business in a novel on the admirably solid
basis of her always putting on gloves and tying a handkerchief
around her head in moments of grief, and of her habitually
addressing her family with "Peace! hold!" It is needless to say
that Mrs. Reginald Wilfer is first and last the occasion of considerable true humour. When, after conducting her daughter to

The Nation, I (1865), 786–787; also, *Views and Reviews* (Boston,
1908).

Mrs. Boffin's carriage, in sight of all the envious neighbours, she is described as enjoying her triumph during the next quarter of an hour by airing herself on the doorstep "in a kind of splendidly serene trance," we laugh with as uncritical a laugh as could be desired of us. We pay the same tribute to her assertions, as she narrates the glories of the society she enjoyed at her father's table, that she has known as many as three copper-plate engravers exchanging the most exquisite sallies and retorts there at one time. But when to these we have added a dozen more happy examples of the humour which was exhaled from every line of Mr. Dickens's earlier writings, we shall have closed the list of the merits of the work before us.

To say that the conduct of the story, with all its complications, betrays a long-practised hand, is to pay no compliment worthy the author. If this were, indeed, a compliment, we should be inclined to carry it further, and congratulate him on his success in what we should call the manufacture of fiction; for in so doing we should express a feeling that has attended us throughout the book. Seldom, we reflected, had we read a book so intensely *written*, so little seen, known, or felt.

In all Mr. Dickens's works the fantastic has been his great resource; and while his fancy was lively and vigorous it accomplished great things. But the fantastic, when the fancy is dead, is a very poor business. The movement of Mr. Dickens's fancy in Mr. Wilfer and Mr. Boffin and Lady Tippins, and the Lammles and Miss Wren, and even in Eugene Wrayburn, is, to our mind, a movement lifeless, forced, mechanical. It is the letter of his old humour without the spirit. It is hardly too much to say that every character here put before us is a mere bundle of eccentricities, animated by no principle of nature whatever.

In former days there reigned in Mr. Dickens's extravagances a comparative consistency; they were exaggerated statements of types that really existed. We had, perhaps, never known a Newman Noggs, nor a Pecksniff, nor a Micawber; but we had known

persons of whom these figures were but the strictly logical consummation. But among the grotesque creatures who occupy the
pages before us, there is not one whom we can refer to as an
existing type. In all Mr. Dickens's stories, indeed, the reader has
been called upon, and has willingly consented, to accept a
certain number of figures or creatures of pure fancy, for this
was the author's poetry. He was, moreover, always repaid for
his concession by a peculiar beauty or power in these exceptional
characters. But he is now expected to make the same concession,
with a very inadequate reward.

What do we get in return for accepting Miss Jenny Wren as
a possible person? This young lady is the type of a certain class
of characters of which Mr. Dickens has made a specialty, and
with which he has been accustomed to draw alternate smiles and
tears, according as he pressed one spring or another. But this
is very cheap merriment and very cheap pathos. Miss Jenny
Wren is a poor little dwarf, afflicted as she constantly reiterates,
with a "bad back" and "queer legs," who makes doll's dresses,
and is for ever pricking at those with whom she converses in the
air, with her needle, and assuring them that she knows their
"tricks and their manners." Like all Mr. Dickens's pathetic
characters, she is a little monster; she is deformed, unhealthy,
unnatural; she belongs to the troop of hunchbacks, imbeciles,
and precocious children who have carried on the sentimental
business in all Mr. Dickens's novels; the little Nells, the Smikes,
the Paul Dombeys.

Mr. Dickens goes as far out of the way for his wicked people
as he does for his good ones. Rogue Riderhood, indeed, in the
present story, is villainous with a sufficiently natural villainy;
he belongs to that quarter of society in which the author is
most at his ease. But was there ever such wickedness as that of
the Lammles and Mr. Fledgeby? Not that people have not been
as mischievous as they; but was any one ever mischievous in that
singular fashion? Did a couple of elegant swindlers ever take

such particular pains to be aggressively inhuman?—for we can find no other word for the gratuitous distortions to which they are subjected. The word *humanity* strikes us as strangely discordant, in the midst of these pages; for, let us boldly declare it, there is no humanity here.

Humanity is nearer home than the Boffins, and the Lammles, and the Wilfers, and the Veneerings. It is in what men have in common with each other, and not what they have in distinction. The people just named have nothing in common with each other, except the fact that they have nothing in common with mankind at large. What a world were this world if the world of *Our Mutual Friend* were an honest reflection of it! But a community of eccentrics is impossible. Rules alone are consistent with each other; exceptions are inconsistent. Society is maintained by natural sense and natural feeling. We cannot conceive a society in which these principles are not in some manner represented. Where in these pages are the depositaries of that intelligence without which the movement of life would cease? Who represents nature?

Accepting half of Mr. Dickens's persons as intentionally grotesque, where are those exemplars of sound humanity who should afford us the proper measure of their companions' variations? We ought not, in justice to the author, to seek them among his weaker—that is, his mere conventional—characters; in John Harmon, Lizzie Hexam, or Mortimer Lightwood; but we assuredly cannot find them among his stronger—that is, his artificial creations.

Suppose we take Eugene Wrayburn and Bradley Headstone. They occupy a half-way position between the habitual probable of nature and the habitual impossible of Mr. Dickens. A large portion of the story rests upon the enmity borne by Headstone to Wrayburn, both being in love with the same woman. Wrayburn is a gentleman, and Headstone is one of the people. Wrayburn is well-bred, careless, elegant, sceptical, and idle: Headstone is a high-tempered, hard-working, ambitious young schoolmaster. There lay in the opposition of these two characters a very good story. But the prime requisite was that they should *be* characters: Mr. Dickens, according to his usual plan, has made them simply figures, and between them the story that was to be, the story that should have been, has evaporated. Wrayburn lounges about with his hands in his pockets, smoking a cigar, and talking nonsense. Headstone strides about, clenching his fists and biting his lips and grasping his stick.

There is one scene in which Wrayburn chaffs the schoolmaster with easy insolence, while the latter writhes impotently under his well-bred sarcasm. This scene is very clever, but it is very insufficient. If the majority of readers were not so very timid in the use of words we should call it vulgar. By this we do not mean to indicate the conventional impropriety of two gentlemen exchanging lively personalities; we mean to emphasise the essentially small character of these personalities. In other words, the moment, dramatically, is great, while the author's conception is weak. The friction of two *men*, of two characters, of two passions, produces stronger sparks than Wrayburn's boyish repartees and Headstone's melodramatic commonplaces.

Such scenes as this are useful in fixing the limits of Mr. Dickens's insight. Insight is, perhaps, too strong a word; for we are convinced that it is one of the chief conditions of his genius not to see beneath the surface of things. If we might hazard a definition of his literary character, we should, accordingly, call him the greatest of superficial novelists. We are aware that this definition confines him to an inferior rank in the department of letters which he adorns; but we accept this consequence of our proposition. It were, in our opinion, an offence against humanity to place Mr. Dickens among the greatest novelists. For, to repeat what we have already intimated, he has created nothing but figure. He has added nothing to our understanding of human character. He is master of but two alternatives: he reconciles us to what is commonplace, and he reconciles us to what is odd. The value of the former service is questionable; and the manner in which Mr. Dickens performs it sometimes conveys a certain impression of charlatanism. The value of the latter service is incontestable, and here Mr. Dickens is an honest, an admirable artist.

But what is the condition of the truly great novelist? For him there are no alternatives, for him there are no oddities, for him there is nothing outside of humanity. He cannot shirk it; it imposes itself upon him. For him alone, therefore, there is a true and a false; for him alone, it is possible to be right, because it is possible to be wrong. Mr. Dickens is a great observer and a great humourist, but he is nothing of a philosopher.

Some people may hereupon say, so much the better; we say, so much the worse. For a novelist very soon has need of a little philosophy. In treating of Micawber, and Boffin, and Pickwick, *et hoc genus omne,* he can, indeed, dispense with it, for this— we say it with all deference—is not serious writing. But when he comes to tell the story of a passion, a story like that of Headstone and Wrayburn, he becomes a moralist as well as an artist. He must know *man* as well as *men,* and to know man is to be a philosopher.

The writer who knows men alone, if he have Mr. Dickens's humour and fancy, will give us figures and pictures for which we cannot be too grateful, for he will enlarge our knowledge of the world. But when he introduces men and women whose interest is preconceived to lie not in the poverty, the weakness, the drollery of their natures, but in their complete and unconscious subjection to ordinary and healthy human emotions, all his humour, all his fancy, will avail him nothing if, out of the fullness of his sympathy, he is unable to prosecute those generalisations in which alone consists the real greatness of a work of art.

This may sound like very subtle talk about a very simple

matter. It is rather very simple talk about a very subtle matter. A story based upon those elementary passions in which alone we seek the true and final manifestation of character must be told in a spirit of intellectual superiority to those passions. That is, the author must understand what he is talking about. The perusal of a story so told is one of the most elevating experiences within the reach of the human mind. The perusal of a story which is not so told is infinitely depressing and unprofitable.

GEORGE HENRY LEWES: 1872

Dickens in Relation to Criticism

THE old feud between authors and critics, a feud old as literature, has not arisen on the ground of chariness in praise, but rather on the ground of deficient sympathy, and the tendency to interpret an author's work according to some standard which is not his. Instead of placing themselves at his point of view, and seeing what he has attempted, how far he has achieved the aim, and whether the aim itself were worthy of achievement, critics have thrust between his work and the public some vague conception of what they required, and measured it by an academic or conventional standard derived from other works. Fond as an author necessarily is of praise, and pained as he must always be by blame, he is far more touched by a sympathetic recognition of his efforts, and far more hurt by a misrepresentation of

Fortnightly Review, February 1872, pp. 141–154.

them. No hyperbole of laudation gives a tithe of the delight which is given by sympathetic insight. Unhappily for the author, this can but sparingly be given by critics, who trust less to their emotions than to their standards of judgment; for the greater the originality of the writer, and the less inclination he has for familiar processes and already-trodden tracks, the greater must be the resistance he will meet with from minds accustomed to move in those tracks, and to consider excellence confined within them. It is in the nature of the critical mind to judge according to precedent; and few minds have flexibility enough to adopt at once a novelty which is destined in its turn to become a precedent.

There is another source of pain. Besides the very great difficulties of independent judgment, of adjusting the mental focus to new objects under new perspectives, and the various personal considerations which trammel even open minds—considerations of friendship, station, renown, rivalry, etc.—there is the immense difficulty which all men find in giving anything like an adequate expression to their judgments. It is easy for us to say that a book has stirred, or instructed us; but it is by no means easy to specify the grounds of our pleasure, or profit, except in a very general way; and when we attempt to do so we are apt to make ludicrous mistakes. Thus it is that the criticism which begins with a general expression of gratitude to the author, will often deeply pain him by misplaced praise, or blame misdirected.

Longinus declares that criticism is the last result of abundant experience; he might have added that even the amplest experience is no safeguard against utter failure. For it is true in Art as in the commonest details of life, that our perceptions are mainly determined by our pre-perceptions, our conceptions by our preconceptions. Hence I have long maintained the desirability of preserving as far as possible the individual character of criticism. The artist in his work gives expression to his individual feelings and conceptions, telling us how Life and Nature are mirrored in his mind; we may fairly state how this affects us, whether it accords with our experience, whether it moves or instructs us; but we should be very chary of absolute judgments, and be quite sure of our ground before venturing to assume that the public will feel, or ought to feel, as we feel. Now it is the tendency of criticism to pronounce absolute verdicts, to speak for all; and the exasperation of the artist at finding individual impressions given forth as final judgments is the main cause of the outcry against criticism. The writer who would feel little irritation on hearing that A. and B. were unmoved by his pathos, dead to his humour, unenlightened by his philosophy, may be excused if he writhe under the authoritative announcement that his pathos is maudlin, his humour flat, his philosophy shallow. He may be convicted of bad grammar, bad drawing, bad logic; and if the critic advances reasons for particular objections, these reasons may be weighed, and perhaps accepted with resignation if not without pain; but no verdict which does not distinctly carry its evidence can be accepted as more than an individual judgment; and in matters of Art there is always great difficulty, sometimes a sheer impossibility, in passing from the individual to the universal. It is impossible to resist feeling. If an author makes me laugh, he is humourous; if he makes me cry, he is pathetic. In vain will any one tell me that such a picture is not laughable, not pathetic; or that I am wrong in being moved.

While from these and other causes, especially from the tendency to exaggerate what is painful, authors have deeply resented "the malevolence" of critics—a malevolence which has been mostly incompetence, or inconsiderateness—it is not less true that there has been much heartfelt gratitude given by authors to critics who have sympathised with and encouraged them; and many lasting friendships have been thus cemented. It was thus that the lifelong friendship of Dickens and his biographer began, and was sustained. Nor is it just to object to Mr. Forster's enthusiasm on the ground of his friendship, since he may fairly answer, "Dickens was my friend because I so greatly admired him." One thing is certain: his admiration was expressed long before all the world had acknowledged Dickens's genius, and was continued through the long years when the majority of writers had ceased to express much fervour of admiration, preferring rather to dwell on his shortcomings and exaggerations.

And this brings me to the noticeable fact that there probably never was a writer of so vast a popularity whose genius was so little *appreciated* by the critics. The very splendour of his successes so deepened the shadow of his failures that to many eyes the shadows supplanted the splendour. Fastidious readers were loath to admit that a writer could be justly called great whose defects were so glaring. They admitted, because it was indisputable, that Dickens delighted thousands, that his admirers were found in all classes, and in all countries; that he stirred the sympathy of masses not easily reached through Literature, and always stirred healthy, generous emotions; that he impressed a new direction on popular writing, and modified the Literature of his age, in its spirit no less than in its form; but they nevertheless insisted on his defects as if these outweighed all positive qualities; and spoke of him either with condescending patronage, or with sneering irritation. Surely this is a fact worthy of investigation? Were the critics wrong, and if so, in what consisted their error? How are we to reconcile this immense popularity with this critical contempt? The private readers and the public critics who were eager to take up each successive number of his works as it appeared, whose very talk was seasoned with quotations from and allusions to these works, who, to my knowledge, were wont to lay aside books of which they could only speak in terms of eulogy, in order to bury themselves in the "new number" when the well-known green cover made its appearance—were nevertheless at this very time niggard in their praise, and lavish in their scorn of the popular humorist. It is not long since I heard a very distinguished man express measureless contempt for

Dickens, and a few minutes afterwards, in reply to some representations on the other side, admit that Dickens had "entered into his life."

Dickens has proved his power by a popularity almost unexampled, embracing all classes. Surely it is a task for criticism to exhibit the sources of that power? If everything that has ever been alleged against the works be admitted, there still remains an immense success to be accounted for. It was not by their defects that these works were carried over Europe and America. It was not their defects which made them the delight of grey heads on the bench, and the study of youngsters in the counting-house and school-room. Other writers have been exaggerated, untrue, fantastic, and melodramatic; but they have gained so little notice that no one thinks of pointing out their defects. It is clear, therefore, that Dickens had powers which enabled him to triumph in spite of the weaknesses which clogged them; and it is worth inquiring what those powers were, and their relation to his undeniable defects.

I am not about to attempt such an inquiry, but simply to indicate two or three general points of view. It will be enough merely to mention in passing the primary cause of his success, his overflowing fun, because even uncompromising opponents admit it. They may be ashamed of their laughter, but they laugh. A revulsion of feeling at the preposterousness or extravagance of the image may follow the burst of laughter, but the laughter is irresistible, whether rational or not, and there is no arguing away such a fact.

Great as Dickens is in fun, so great that Fielding and Smollett are small in comparison, he would have been only a passing amusement for the world had he not been gifted with an imagination of marvellous vividness, and an emotional, sympathetic nature capable of furnishing that imagination with elements of universal power. Of him it may be said with less exaggeration than of most poets, that he was of "imagination all compact";

if the other higher faculties were singularly deficient in him, this faculty was imperial. He was a seer of visions; and his visions were of objects at once familiar and potent. Psychologists will understand both the extent and the limitation of the remark, when I say that in no other perfectly sane mind (Blake, I believe, was not perfectly sane) have I observed vividness of imagination approaching so closely to hallucination. Many who are not psychologists may have had some experience in themselves, or in others, of that abnormal condition in which a man hears voices, and sees objects, with the distinctness of direct perception, although silence and darkness are without him; these *revived* impressions, revived by an internal cause, have precisely the same force and clearness which the impressions originally had when produced by an external cause. In the same degree of vividness are the images *constructed* by his mind in explanation of the voices heard or objects seen: when he imagines that the voice proceeds from a personal friend or from Satan tempting him, the friend or Satan stands before him with the distinctness of objective reality; when he imagines that he himself has been transformed into a bear, his hands are seen by him as paws. In vain you represent to him that the voices he hears have no external existence; he will answer, as a patient pertinently answered Lélut: "You believe that I am speaking to you because you hear me, is it not so? Very well, I believe that voices are speaking to me because I hear them." There is no power of effacing such conviction by argument. You may get the patient to assent to any premises you please, he will not swerve from his conclusions. I once argued with a patient who believed he had been transformed into a bear; he was quite willing to admit that the idea of such a transformation was utterly at variance with all experience; but he always returned to his position that God being omnipotent there was no reason to doubt his power of transforming men into bears: what remained fixed in his mind was the image of himself under a bear's form.

The characteristic point in the hallucinations of the insane, that which distinguishes them from hallucinations equally vivid in the sane, is the coercion of the image in *suppressing comparison* and all control of experience. Belief always accompanies a vivid image, for a time; but in the sane this belief will not persist against rational control. If I see a stick partly under water, it is impossible for me not to have the same feeling which would be produced by a bent stick out of the water—if I see two plane images in the stereoscope, it is impossible not to have the feeling of seeing one solid object. But these beliefs are rapidly displaced by reference to experience. I know the stick is not bent, and that it will not appear bent when removed from the water. I know the seeming solid is not an object in relief, but two plane pictures. It is by similar focal adjustment of the mind that sane people know that their hallucinations are unreal. The images may have the vividness of real objects, but they have not the properties of real objects, they do not preserve consistent relations with other facts, they appear in contradiction to other beliefs. Thus if I see a black cat on the chair opposite, yet on my approaching the chair feel no soft object, and if my terrier on the hearthrug looking in the direction of the chair shows none of the well-known agitation which the sight of a cat produces, I conclude, in spite of its distinctness, that the image is an hallucination.

Returning from this digression, let me say that I am very far indeed from wishing to imply any agreement in the common notion that "great wits to madness nearly are allied"; on the contrary, my studies have led to the conviction that nothing is less like genius than insanity, although some men of genius have had occasional attacks; and further, that I have never observed any trace of the insane temperament in Dickens's works, or life, they being indeed singularly free even from the eccentricities which often accompany exceptional powers; nevertheless, with all due limitations, it is true that there is considerable light shed upon his works by the action of the imagination in hallucination.

To him also *revived* images have the vividness of sensations; to him also *created* images have the coercive force of realities, excluding all control, all contradiction. What seems preposterous, impossible to us, seemed to him simple fact of observation. When he imagined a street, a house, a room, a figure, he saw it not in the vague schematic way of ordinary imagination, but in the sharp definition of actual perception, all the salient details obtruding themselves on his attention. He, seeing it thus vividly, made us also see it; and believing in its reality however fantastic, he communicated something of his belief to us. He presented it in such relief that we ceased to think of it as a picture. So definite and insistent was the image, that even while knowing it was false we could not help, for a moment, being affected, as it were, by his hallucination.

This glorious energy of imagination is that which Dickens had in common with all great writers. It was this which made him a creator, and made his creations universally intelligible, no matter how fantastic and unreal. His types established themselves in the public mind like personal experiences. Their falsity was unnoticed in the blaze of their illumination. Every humbug seemed a Pecksniff, every nurse a Gamp, every jovial improvident a Micawber, every stinted serving-wench a Marchioness. Universal experiences became individualised in these types; an image and a name were given, and the image was so suggestive that it seemed to *express* all that it was found to *recall*, and Dickens was held to have depicted what his readers supplied. Against such power criticism was almost idle. In vain critical reflection showed these figures to be merely masks,—not characters, but personified characteristics, caricatures and distortions of human nature,—the vividness of their presentation triumphed over reflection: their creator managed to communicate to the public his own unhesitating belief. Unreal and impossible as these types were, speaking a language never heard in life, moving like pieces of simple mechanism always in one way (instead of moving with the infinite fluctuations of organisms, incalculable yet intelligible, surprising yet familiar), these unreal figures affected the uncritical reader with the force of reality; and they did so in virtue of their embodiment of some real characteristic vividly presented. The imagination of the author laid hold of some well-marked physical trait, some peculiarity of aspect, speech, or manner which every one recognised at once; and the force with which this was presented made it occupy the mind to the exclusion of all critical doubts: only reflection could detect the incongruity. Think of what this implies! Think how little the mass of men are given to reflect on their impressions, and how their minds are for the most part occupied with sensations rather than ideas, and you will see why Dickens held an undisputed sway. Give a child a wooden horse, with hair for mane and tail, and wafer-spots for colouring, he will never be disturbed by the fact that this horse does not move its legs, but runs on wheels—the general suggestion suffices for his belief; and this wooden horse, which he can handle and draw, is believed in more than a pictured horse by a Wouvermanns or an Ansdell. It may be said of Dickens's human figures that they too are wooden, and run on wheels; but these are details which scarcely disturb the belief of admirers. Just as the wooden horse is brought within the range of the child's emotions, and dramatizing tendencies, when he can handle and draw it, so Dickens's figures are brought within the range of the reader's interests, and receive from these interests a sudden illumination, when they are the puppets of a drama every incident of which appeals to the sympathies. With a fine felicity of instinct he seized upon situations having an irresistible hold over the domestic affections and ordinary sympathies. He spoke in the mother-tongue of the heart, and was always sure of ready listeners. He painted the life he knew, the life every one knew; for if the scenes and manners were unlike those we were familiar with, the feelings and motives, the joys and griefs, the mistakes and efforts of the actors were universal, and therefore universally intelligible; so that even critical spectators who complained that these broadly painted pictures were artistic daubs, could not wholly resist their effective suggestiveness. He set in motion the secret springs of sympathy by touching the domestic affections. He painted nothing ideal, heroic; but all the resources of the bourgeois epic were in his grasp. The world of thought and passion lay beyond his horizon. But the joys and pains of childhood, the petty tyrannies of ignoble natures, the genial pleasantries of happy natures, the life of the poor, the struggles of the street and back parlour, the insolence of office, the sharp social contrasts, east-wind and Christmas jollity, hunger, misery, and hot punch—these he could deal with, so that we laughed and cried, were startled at the revelation of familiar facts hitherto unnoted, and felt our pulses quicken as we were hurried along with him in his fanciful flight.

Such were the sources of his power. To understand how it is that critics quite competent to recognise such power, and even so far amenable to it as to be moved and interested by the works in spite of all their drawbacks, should have forgotten this undenied power, and written or spoken of Dickens with mingled irritation and contempt, we must take into account two natural tendencies—the bias of opposition, and the bias of technical estimate.

The bias of opposition may be illustrated in a parallel case. Let us suppose a scientific book to be attracting the attention of Europe by the boldness, suggestiveness, and theoretic plausibility of its hypotheses; this work falls into the hands of a critic sufficiently grounded in the science treated to be aware that its writer, although gifted with great theoretic power and occasional insight into unexplored relations, is nevertheless pitiably ignorant of the elementary facts and principles of the science; the critic noticing the power, and the talent of lucid exposition, is yet perplexed and irritated at ignorance which is inexcusable, and a reckless twisting of known facts into impossible relations, which seems wilful; will he not pass from marvelling at this inextricable web of sense and nonsense, suggestive insight and mischievous error, so jumbled together that the combination of this sagacity with this glaring inefficiency is a paradox, and be driven by the anger of opposition into an emphatic assertion that the belauded philosopher is a charlatan and an ignoramus? A chorus of admirers proclaims the author to be a great teacher, before whom all contemporaries must bow; and the critic observes this teacher on one page throwing out a striking hypothesis of some geometric relations in the planetary movements, and on another assuming that the hypothenuse is equal to its perpendicular and base, because the square of the hypothenuse is equal to the squares of its sides—in one chapter ridiculing the atomic theory, and in another arguing that carbonic acid is obtained from carbon and nitrogen—can this critic be expected to join in the chorus of admirers? and will he not rather be exasperated into an opposition which will lead him to undervalue the undeniable qualities in his insistence on the undeniable defects?

Something like this is the feeling produced by Dickens's works in many cultivated and critical readers. They see there human character and ordinary events portrayed with a mingled verisimilitude and falsity altogether unexampled. The drawing is so vivid yet so incorrect, or else is so blurred and formless, with such excess of *effort* (as of a showman beating on the drum) that the doubt arises how an observer so remarkably keen could make observations so remarkably false, and miss such very obvious facts; how the rapid glance which could swoop down on a peculiarity with hawk-like precision, could overlook all that accompanied and was organically related to that peculiarity; how the eye for characteristics could be so blind to character, and the ear for dramatic idiom be so deaf to dramatic language; finally, how the writer's exquisite susceptibility to the grotesque could be insensible to the occasional grotesqueness of his own attitude. Michael Angelo is intelligible, and Giotto is intelligible; but a critic is nonplussed at finding the invention of Angelo with the drawing of Giotto. It is indeed surprising that Dickens should have observed man, and not been impressed with the fact that man is, in the words of Montaigne, *un être ondoyant et diverse*. And the critic is distressed to observe the substitution of mechanisms for minds, puppets for characters. It is needless to dwell on such monstrous failures as Mantalini, Rosa Dartle, Lady Dedlock, Esther Summerson, Mr. Dick, Arthur Gride, Edith Dombey, Mr. Carker—needless, because if one studies the successful figures one finds even in them only touches of verisimilitude. When one thinks of Micawber always presenting himself in the same situation, moved with the same springs, and uttering the same sounds, always confident of something turning up, always crushed and rebounding, always making punch—and his wife always declaring she will never part from him, always referring to his talents and her family—when one thinks of the "catchwords" personified as characters, one is reminded of the frogs whose brains have been taken out for physiological purposes, and whose actions henceforth want the distinctive peculiarity of organic action, that of fluctuating spontaneity. Place one of these brainless frogs on his back and he will at once recover the sitting posture; draw a leg from under him, and he will draw it back again; tickle or prick him and he will push away the object, or take *one* hop out of the way; stroke his back, and he will utter *one* croak. All these things resemble the actions of the unmutilated frog, but they differ in being *isolated* actions, and *always the same:* they are as uniform and calculable as the movements of a machine. The uninjured frog may or may not croak, may or may not hop away; the result is never calculable, and is rarely a single croak or a single hop. It is this complexity of the organism which Dickens wholly fails to conceive; his characters have nothing fluctuating and incalculable in them, even when they embody true observations; and very often they are creations so fantastic that one is at a loss to understand how he could, without hallucination, believe them to be like reality. There are dialogues bearing the traces of straining effort at effect, which in their incongruity painfully resemble the absurd and eager expositions which insane patients pour into the listener's ear when detailing their wrongs, or their schemes. Dickens once declared to me that every word said by his characters was distinctly *heard* by him; I was at first not a little puzzled to account for the fact that he could hear language so utterly unlike the language of real feeling, and not be aware of its preposterousness; but the surprise vanished when I thought of the phenomena of hallucination. And here it may be needful to remark in passing that it is not because the characters are badly drawn and their language unreal, that they are to be classed among the excesses of imagination; otherwise all the bad novelists and dramatists would be credited with that which they especially want—powerful imagination. His peculiarity is not the incorrectness of the drawing, but the vividness of the imagination which while rendering that incorrectness insensible to him, also renders it potent with multitudes of his fellowmen. For although his weakness comes from excess in one direction, the force which is in excess must not be overlooked; and it is overlooked or undervalued by critics who, with what I have called the bias of opposition, insist only on the weakness.

This leads me to the second point, the bias of technical estimate. The main purpose of Art is delight. Whatever influences may radiate from that centre,—and however it may elevate or modify,—the one primary condition of influence is stirred emotion. No Art can teach which does not move; no Art can move without teaching. Criticism has to consider Art under two aspects, that of emotional pleasure, and that of technical pleasure. We all—public and critics—are susceptible of the former, are capable of being moved, and are delighted with what stirs the emotions, filling the mind with images having emotional influence; but only the critics are much affected by technical skill, and the pleasure it creates. *What* is done, what is suggested, constitutes the first aspect; *how* it is done the second. We all delight in imitation, and in the skill which represents one object in another medium; but the refinements of skill can only be appreciated by study. To a savage there is so little suggestion of a human face and form in a painted portrait that it is not even recognised as the representation of a man; whereas the same savage would delight in a waxwork figure, or a wooden Scotchman at the door of a tobacconist. The educated eye sees exquisite skill in the portrait, a skill which gives exquisite delight; but this eye which traces and estimates the subtle effects of colour and distribution of light and shade in the portrait, turns with disgust from the wax figure, or the wooden Highlander. In the course of time the pleasure derived from the perception of difficulty overcome, leads to such a preponderance of the technical estimate, that the sweep of the brush, or the composition of lines, becomes of supreme importance, and the connoisseur no longer asks, What is painted? but How is it painted? The *what* may be a patch of meadow, the bend of a river, or a street boy munching bread and cheese, and yet give greater delight by its *how*, than another picture which represented the Andes, Niagara, or a Madonna and Child. When the critic observes technical skill in a picture, he pronounces the painter to be admirable, and is quite unmoved by any great subject badly painted. In like manner a great poet is estimated by the greatness of his execution of great conceptions, not by the greatness of his intention.

How easily the critic falls into the mistake of overvaluing technical skill, and not allowing for the primary condition, how easily he misjudges works by applying to them technical rules derived from the works of others, need not here be dwelt on. What I wish to indicate is the bias of technical estimate which, acting with that bias of opposition just noted, has caused the critics to overlook in Dickens the great artistic powers which are proved by his immense success; and to dwell only on those great artistic deficiencies which exclude him from the class of exquisite writers. He worked in delf, not in porcelain. But his prodigal imagination created in delf forms which delighted thousands. He only touched common life, but he touched it to "fine issues"; and since we are all susceptible of being moved by pictures of children in droll and pathetic situations, and by pictures of common suffering and common joy, any writer who can paint such pictures with sufficient skill to awaken these emotions is powerful in proportion to the emotion stirred. That Dickens had this skill is undisputed; and if critical reflection shows that the means he employs are not such as will satisfy the technical estimate, and consequently that the pictures will not move the cultivated mind, nor give it the deep content which perfect Art continues to create, making the work a "joy for ever," we must still remember that in the present state of Literature, with hundreds daily exerting their utmost efforts to paint such pictures, it requires prodigious force and rare skill to impress images that will stir the universal heart. Murders are perpetrated without stint, but the murder of Nancy is unforgettable. Children figure in numberless plays and novels, but the deaths of little Nell and little Paul were national griefs. Seduction is one of the commonest of tragedies, but the scene in Peggotty's boat-house burns itself into the memory. Captain Cuttle and Richard Swiveller, the Marchioness and Tilly Slowboy, Pecksniff and Micawber, Tiny Tim and Mrs. Gamp, may be imperfect presentations of human character, but they are types which no one can forget. Dr. Johnson explained the popularity of some writer by saying, "Sir, *his* nonsense suited *their* nonsense"; let us add, "and his sense suited their sense," and it will explain the popularity of Dickens. Readers to whom all the refinements of Art and Literature are as meaningless hieroglyphs, were at once laid hold of by the reproduction of their own feelings, their own experiences, their own prejudices, in the irradiating splendour of his imagination; while readers whose cultivated sensibilities were alive to the most delicate and evanescent touches were, by virtue of their common nature, ready to be moved and delighted at his pictures and suggestions. The cultivated and uncultivated were affected by his admirable *mise en scène*, his fertile invention, his striking selection of incident, his intense vision of physical details. Only the cultivated who are made fastidious by cultivation paused to consider the pervading commonness of the works, and remarked that they are wholly without glimpses of a nobler life; and that the writer presents an almost unique example of a mind of singular force in which, so to speak, sensations never passed into ideas. Dickens sees and feels, but the logic of feeling seems the only logic he can manage. Thought is strangely absent from his works. I do not suppose a single thoughtful remark on life or character could be found throughout the twenty volumes. Not only is there a marked absence of the reflective tendency, but one sees no indication of the past life of humanity having ever occupied him; keenly as he observes the objects before him, he never connects his observations into a general expression, never seems interested in general relations of things. Compared with that of Fielding or Thackeray, his was merely an *animal* intelligence, *i.e.*, restricted to perceptions. On this ground his early education was more fruitful and less injurious than it would have been to a nature constructed on a more reflective and intellectual type. It furnished him with rare and valuable experience, early developed his sympathies with the lowly and struggling, and did not starve any intellectual ambition. He never was and never would have been a student.

My acquaintance with him began soon after the completion of "Pickwick." Something I had written on that book pleased him, and caused him to ask me to call on him. (It is pleasant for me to remember that I made Thackeray's acquaintance in a similar way.) He was then living in Doughty Street; and those who remember him at that period will understand the somewhat disturbing effect produced on my enthusiasm for the new author by the sight of his bookshelves, on which were ranged nothing but three-volume novels and books of travel, all obviously the presentation copies from authors and publishers, with none of the treasures of the bookstall, each of which has its history, and all giving the collection its individual physiognomy. A man's library expresses much of his hidden life. I did not expect to find a bookworm, nor even a student, in the marvellous "Boz"; but nevertheless this collection of books was a shock. He shortly came in, and his sunny presence quickly dispelled all misgivings. He was then, as to the last, a delightful companion, full of sagacity as well as animal spirits; but I came away more impressed with the fulness of life and energy than with any sense of distinction. I believe I only saw him once more before I went to Germany, and two years had elapsed when next we met. While waiting in his library (in Devonshire Terrace) I of course glanced at the books. The well-known paper boards of the three-volume novel no longer vulgarised the place; a goodly array of standard works, well-bound, showed a more respectable and conventional ambition; but there was no physiognomy in the collection. A greater change was visible in Dickens himself. In these two years he had remarkably developed. His conversation turned on graver subjects than theatres and actors, periodicals and London life. His interest in public affairs, especially in social questions, was keener. He still remained completely outside philosophy, science, and the higher literature, and was too unaffected a man to pretend to feel any interest in them. But the vivacity and sagacity which gave a charm to intercourse with him had become weighted with a seriousness which from that time forward became more and more prominent in his conversation and his writings. He had already learned to look upon the world as a scene where it was the duty of each man in his own way to make the lot of the miserable Many a little less miserable;

and, having learned that his genius gave him great power, he was bent on using that power effectively. He was sometimes laughed at for the importance he seemed to attach to everything relating to himself, and the solemnity with which he spoke of his aims and affairs; but this belonged to his quality. *Il se prenait au sérieux,* and was admirable because he did so. Whatever faults he may have committed there were none attributable to carelessness. He gave us his best. If the effort were sometimes too strained, and the desire for effect too obtrusive, there was no lazy indulgence, no trading on a great renown, no "scumbling" in his work. "Whatever I have tried to do in life," he said, speaking through Copperfield, "I have tried with all my heart to do well. Never to put one hand to anything on which I could throw my whole self, and never to affect depreciation of my work, whatever it was, I now find to have been my golden rules."

Since I have been led in the course of argument to touch upon my personal acquaintance with Dickens, I may take advantage of the opening to introduce a point not mentioned in Mr. Forster's memoir, though he most probably is familiar with it. Mr. Forster has narrated Dickens's intense grief at the death of his sister-in-law, Mary—a grief which for two months interrupted the writing of "Pickwick," and which five years afterwards thus moves him in a letter to Mr. Forster on the death of her grandmother. The passage itself is in every way interesting, displaying a depth and delicacy of feeling, combined with a tenderness towards the sacredness due to the wishes of the dead, which is very noticeable:—

It is a great trial to me to give up Mary's grave; greater than I can possibly express. I thought of moving her to the catacomb, and saying nothing about it; but then I remembered that the poor old lady is buried next her at her own desire, and could not find it in my heart directly she is laid in the earth to take her grandchild away. The desire to be buried next her is as strong upon me now as it was five years ago; and I *know* (for I don't think there ever was love like that I bear her) that it will never diminish. I cannot bear the thought of being excluded from her dust; and yet I feel that her brothers and sisters and her mother have a better right than I to be placed beside her. It is but an idea. I neither hope nor think (God forbid) that our spirits would ever mingle *there*. I ought to get the better of it, but it is very hard. I never contemplated this; and coming so suddenly, and after being ill, it disturbs me more than it ought. It seems like losing her a second time.

Again, when writing from America and describing his delight at the Niagara Falls, he says:—

What would I give if you and Mac were here to share the sensations of this time! I was going to add, what would I give if the dear girl whose ashes lie in Kensal Green had lived to come so far along with us; but she has been here many times, I doubt not, since her sweet face faded from my earthly sight.

Several years afterwards, in the course of a quiet chat over a cigar, we got on a subject which always interested him, and on which he had stored many striking anecdotes—dreams. He then narrated, in his quietest and most impressive manner, that after Mary's death her image not only haunted him by day, but for twelve months visited his dreams every night. At first he had refrained from mentioning it to his wife; and after deferring this some time, felt unable to mention it to her. He had occasion to go to Liverpool, and as he went to bed that night, there was a strong hope that the change of bed might break the spell of his dreams. It was not so however. That night as usual the old dream was dreamt. He resolved to unburthen his mind to his wife, and wrote that very morning a full account of his strange experience. From that time he ceased to dream of her. I forget whether he said he had never dreamt of her since; but I am certain of the fact that the spell had been broken then and there.

Here is another contribution to the subject of dreams, which I had from him shortly before his death. One night after one of his public readings, he dreamt that he was in a room where every one was dressed in scarlet. (The probable origin of this was the mass of scarlet opera-cloaks worn by the ladies among the audience, having left a sort of *afterglow* on his retina). He stumbled against a lady standing with her back towards him. As he apologised she turned her head and said, quite unprovoked, "My name is Napier." The face was one perfectly unknown to him, nor did he know any one named Napier. Two days after he had another reading in the same town, and before it began, a lady friend came into the waiting-room accompanied by an unknown lady in a scarlet opera cloak, "who," said his friend, "is very desirous of being introduced." "Not Miss Napier?" he jokingly inquired. "Yes; Miss Napier." Although the face of his dream-lady was not the face of this Miss Napier, the coincidence of the scarlet cloak and the name was striking.

In bringing these detached observations to a close, let me resume their drift by saying that while on the one hand the critics seem to me to have been fully justified in denying him the possession of many technical excellencies, they have been thrown into unwise antagonism which has made them overlook or undervalue the great qualities which distinguished him; and that even on technical grounds their criticism has been so far defective that it failed to recognise the supreme powers which ensured his triumph in spite of all defects. For the reader of cultivated taste there is little in his works beyond the stirring of their emotions—but what a large exception! We do not turn over the pages in search of thought, delicate psychological observation, grace of style, charm of composition; but we enjoy them like children at a play, laughing and crying at the images which pass before us. And this illustration suggests the explanation of how learned and thoughtful men can have been almost as much delighted with the works as ignorant and juvenile readers; how Lord Jeffrey could have been so affected by the presentation of Little Nell, which most critical readers pronounce maudlin and unreal. Persons unfamiliar with theatrical representations, consequently unable to criticise the acting, are stirred by the suggestions of the scenes presented; and hence a great philosopher, poet, or man of science, may be found applauding an actor whom every play-going apprentice despises as stagey and inartistic.

ANTHONY TROLLOPE: 1882
Charles Dickens

THERE can be no doubt that the most popular novelist of my time—probably the most popular English novelist of any time—has been Charles Dickens. He has now been dead nearly six years, and the sale of his books goes on as it did during his life. The certainty with which his novels are found in every house—the familiarity of his name in all English-speaking countries—the popularity of such characters as Mrs. Gamp, Micawber, and Pecksniff, and many others whose names have entered into the English language and become well-known words—the grief of the country at his death, and the honours paid to him at his funeral,—all testify to his popularity. Since the last book he wrote himself, I doubt whether any book has been so popular as his biography by John Forster. There is no withstanding such testimony as this. Such evidence of popular appreciation should

From *Autobiography* (London, 1882).

go for very much, almost for everything, in criticism on the work of a novelist. The primary object of a novelist is to please; and this man's novels have been found more pleasant than those of any other writer. It might of course be objected to this, that though the books have pleased they have been injurious, that their tendency has been immoral and their teaching vicious; but it is almost needless to say that no such charge has ever been made against Dickens. His teaching has ever been good. From all which, there arises to the critic a question whether, with such evidence against him as to the excellence of this writer, he should not subordinate his own opinion to the collected opinion of the world of readers. To me it almost seems that I must be wrong to place Dickens after Thackeray and George Eliot, knowing as I do that so great a majority put him above those authors.

My own peculiar idiosyncrasy in the matter forbids me to do so. I do acknowledge that Mrs. Gamp, Micawber, Pecksniff, and others have become household words in every house, as though they were human beings; but to my judgement they are not human beings, nor are any of the characters human which Dickens has portrayed. It has been the peculiarity and the marvel of this man's power, that he has invested his puppets with a charm that has enabled him to dispense with human nature. There is a drollery about them, in my estimation, very much below the humour of Thackeray, but which has reached the intellect of all; while Thackeray's humour has escaped the intellect of many. Nor is the pathos of Dickens human. It is stagey and melodramatic. But it is so expressed that it touches every heart a little. There is no real life in Smike. His misery, his idiotcy, his devotion for Nicholas, his love for Kate, are all overdone, and incompatible with each other. But still the reader sheds a tear. Every reader can find a tear for Smike. Dickens's novels are like Boucicault's plays. He has known how to draw his lines broadly, so that all should see the colour.

He, too, in his best days, always lived with his characters;—

and he, too, as he gradually ceased to have the power of doing so, ceased to charm. Though they are not human beings, we all remember Mrs. Gamp and Pickwick. The Boffins and Veneerings do not, I think, dwell in the minds of so many.

Of Dickens's style it is impossible to speak in praise. It is jerky, ungrammatical, and created by himself in defiance of rules—almost as completely as that created by Carlyle. To readers who have taught themselves to regard language, it must therefore be unpleasant. But the critic is driven to feel the weakness of his criticism, when he acknowledges to himself—as he is compelled in all honesty to do—that with the language, such as it is, the writer has satisfied the great mass of the readers of his country. Both these great writers have satisfied the readers of their own pages; but both have done infinite harm by creating a school of imitators. No young novelist should ever dare to imitate the style of Dickens. If such a one wants a model for his language, let him take Thackeray.

GEORGE GISSING: 1898

Dickens's Satiric Portraiture

NOT only does Dickens give poetic shape to the better characteristics of English life; he is also England's satirist. Often directed against abuses in their nature temporary, his satire has in some part lost its edge, and would have only historic interest but for the great preservative, humour, mingled with all his

Charles Dickens (London, 1898), Chapter VI.

books; much of it, however, is of enduring significance, and reminds us that the graver faults of Englishmen are not to be overcome by a few years of popular education, by general increase of comfort and refinement, by the spread of a genuinely democratic spirit. Some of these blemishes, it is true, belong more or less to all mankind; but in Dickens's England they were peculiarly disfiguring, and the worst of them seem inseparable from the national character.

Much as they loved and glorified him, his countrymen did not fail to make protest when wounded by the force of his satiric portraiture. The cry was "exaggeration." As one might surmise, this protest was especially vigorous during the publication of *Martin Chuzzlewit*, in which book the English vice *par excellence* gets its deserts. Dickens used the opportunity of a preface to answer his critics; he remarked that peculiarities of character often escape observation until they are directly pointed out, and asked whether the charge of exaggeration brought against him might not simply mean that he, a professed student of life, saw more than ordinary people. There was undoubted truth in the plea; Browning has put the same thought—as an apology for art—into the mouth of Fra Lippo Lippi. Dickens assuredly saw a great deal more in every day of his life than his average readers in three score years and ten. But it still remained a question whether, in his desire to stigmatize an objectionable peculiarity, the satirist had not erred by making this peculiarity the whole man. Exaggeration there was, beyond dispute, in such a picture as that of Pecksniff; inasmuch as no man can be so consistently illustrative of an evil habit of mind. There was lack of proportion; the figure failed in human symmetry. Just as, in the same book, the pictures of American life erred through one-sidedness. Dickens had written satire, and satire as pointed, as effective, as any in literature. Let the galled jade wince; there was an outcry of many voices, appealing to common judgment. It might be noted that these same sensitive critics had never objected to "exaggeration" when the point at issue was merely one of art; they became aware of their favourite author's defect only when it involved a question of morals or of national character.

Merely as satirist, however, Dickens never for a moment endangered his popularity. The fact, already noticed, that *Martin Chuzzlewit* found fewer admirers than the books preceding it, had nothing to do with its moral theme, but must be traced to causes, generally more or less vague, such as from time to time affect the reception of every author's work; not long after its completion, this book became one of the most widely read. There is the satire which leaves cold, or alienates, the ordinary man, either because it passes above his head, or conflicts with his cherished prejudices; and there is the satire which, by appealing to his better self,—that is, to a standard of morality which he theoretically, or in very deed, accepts,—commands his sympathy as soon as he sees his drift. What is called the "popular conscience" was on Dickens's side; and he had the immense advantage of being able to raise a hearty laugh even whilst pointing his lesson. Among the rarest of things is this thorough understanding between author and public, permitting a man of genius to say aloud with impunity that which all his hearers say within themselves dumbly, inarticulately. Dickens never went too far; never struck at a genuine conviction of the multitude. Let us imagine him, in some moment of aberration, suggesting criticism of the popular idea of sexual morality! Would it have availed him that he had done the state some service? Would argument or authority have helped for one moment to win him a patient hearing? We know that he never desired to provoke such antagonism. Broadly speaking, he was one with his readers, and therein lay his strength for reform.

As for the charge of exaggeration, the truth is that Dickens exaggerated no whit more in his satire than in his sympathetic portraiture. It is an idle objection. Of course he exaggerated, in all but every page. In the last chapter I pointed to exceptional instances of literal or subdued truthfulness; not by these did he achieve his triumphs; they lurk for discovery by the curious. Granting his idealistic method, such censure falls wide of the mark. We are struck more forcibly when a character is exhibited as compact of knavery or grotesque cruelty, than when it presents incarnate goodness; that is all. The one question we are justified in urging is, whether his characterization is consistent with itself. In the great majority of cases, I believe the answer must be affirmative. Were it not so, Dickens's reputation would by this time linger only among the untaught; among those who are content to laugh, no matter how the mirth be raised.

His satire covers a great part of English life, public and private. Education, charity, religion, social morality in its broadest sense, society in its narrowest; legal procedure, the machinery of politics, and the forms of government. Licensed to speak his mind, he aims laughingly or sternly, but always in the same admirable spirit, at every glaring abuse of the day. He devotes a whole book, a prodigy of skilful labour, to that crowning example of the law's delay, which had wrought ruin in innumerable homes; he throws off a brilliant little sketch, in a Christmas number, and makes everybody laugh at the absurd defects of railway refreshment-rooms. We marvel at such breadth of tireless observation in the service of human welfare. Impossible to follow him through all the achievements of his satire; I can but select examples in each field, proceeding in the order just indicated.

It is natural that he should turn, at the beginning of his career, to abuses evident in the parish, the school, the place of worship. These were nearest at hand; they stared at him in his observant childhood, and during his life as a journalist. Consequently we soon meet with Mr. Bumble, with Mr. Squeers, with the Rev. Mr. Stiggins. Of these three figures, the one most open to the charge of exaggeration is the Yorkshire schoolmaster; yet who shall declare with assurance that Squeers's brutality outdoes the probable in his place and generation? There is crude workmanship in the portrait, and still more in the picture of Dotheboys, where overcharging defeats its own end. The extraordinary feature of this bit of work is the inextricable blending of horrors and jocosity. Later, when Dickens had fuller command of his resources, he would have made Dotheboys very much more impressive; it remains an illustration of superabundant spirits in a man of genius. We can hardly help an amiable feeling towards the Squeers family, seeing the hearty gusto with which they pursue their monstrous business. The children who suffer under them are so shadowy that we cannot feel the wrong as we ought; such a spectacle should lay waste the heart, and yet we continue smiling. Dickens, of course, did not intend that this gathering of martyred children should have the effect of reality. Enough if he called attention to the existence of a horror; reflection shall come afterwards; his immediate business is storytelling, that is to say, amusement. Wonderfully did he adapt means to ends; we find, in fact, that nothing could have been practically more effectual than this exhibition of strange gaiety. Mr. Bumble, though he comes earlier, is, in truth, better work than Squeers. Read carefully chapter IV of *Oliver Twist*, and you will discover, probably to your surprise, that the "porochial" functionary is, after all, human: in one line—in a delicate touch—we are shown Bumble softened, to the point of a brief silence, by Oliver's pleading for kind usage. No such moment occurs in the history of Squeers. And we see why not. The master of Dotheboys is not meant for a conscientious study of a human being; he is the representative, pure and simple, of a vile institution. Admit a lurking humanity, and we have suggestion of possible reform. Now the parochial system, bad as it was, seemed a necessity, and only needed a thorough overhauling,—observe the perfectly human behaviour of certain of the guardians before whom Oliver appears; but with the Yorkshire schools, it was root and branch, they must be swept from the earth. I do not think this is refining overmuch. Dickens's genius declared itself so consistently in his adaptation of literary means to ends of various kinds; and, however immature the details of his performance, he shows from the first this marvellous precision in effect.

Dotheboys was of course, even in these bad times, an exceptional method for the rearing of youth. It is not cold-blooded cruelty, but block-headed ignorance, against which Dickens has to fight over the whole ground of education. We have noticed his attitude towards the system of classical training; the genteel private schools of his day invited satire, and supplied him with some of his most entertaining chapters. Dr. Blimber's establishment is a favourable specimen of the kind of thing that satisfied well-to-do parents; genial ridicule suffices for its condemnation. But Dickens went deeper and laid stress upon the initial stages of the absurd system. Mrs. Pipchin, however distinct a personality, was not singular in her mode of dealing with children fresh from the nursery. Always profoundly interested in these little people, Dickens, without reaching any very clear conception of reform, well understood the evil consequences of such gross neglect or mistaken zeal as were common in households of every class. He knew that the vices of society could for the most part be traced to these bad beginnings. A leader in this as in so many other directions, he taught his readers to think much of children just at the time when England had especial need of an educational awakening. Not his satire alone, but his so-called sentimentality, served a great purpose, and the death-bed of Paul Dombey, no less than the sufferings of Mr. Creakle's little victim, helped on the better day.

Though it has been "proved to demonstration"—by persons who care for such proof—that tenderness of heart led him astray in his bitterness against the new Poor Law, we see, of course, that herein he pursued his humane task, seeking in all possible ways to mitigate the harshness of institutions which pressed hardly upon the poor and weak. He could not away with those who held—or spoke as if they held—that a man had no duty to his fellows beyond the strict letter of the law. In this respect that very poor book, *Hard Times*, has noteworthy significance; but the figures of Gradgrind and Bounderby show how completely he could fail when he dispensed (or all but dispensed) with the aid of humour. Oliver Twist's "old gentleman in the white waistcoat" is decidedly better as portraiture, and as satire more effective. Apologists, or rampant glorifiers, of the workhouse, such as appear in the Christmas Books, need not be viewed too seriously; they stood forth at a season of none too refined joviality, and were in keeping with barons of beef, tons of plum-pudding, and other such heavy extravagances. They do not live in one's mind; nor, I think, does any of Dickens's persons meant to satirize poor-law abuses. In this matter, his spirit did its work, his art not greatly assisting.

But when we come to his lashings of religious hypocrisy, the figures castigated are substantial enough. Always delighted to represent a humbug, Dickens can scarce restrain himself when he gets hold of a religious humbug, especially of the coarse type. Brother Stiggins shines immortal in the same pages with Mr. Pickwick and the Wellers. Compare with him the Reverend Mr. Chadband. They are the same men, but one lived in 1837, the other in 1853. Brother Stiggins is, in plain English, a drunkard; Mr. Chadband would think shame of himself to be even once overtaken: he is a consumer of tea and muffins. It suited the author's mood, and the day in which he was writing, to have Mr. Stiggins soundly beaten in a pugilistic encounter with Tony Weller, to say nothing of other undignified positions in which the reverend gentleman finds himself; but Mr. Chadband may discourse upon "Terewth" in Mr. Snagsby's parlour to any length that pleases him with no fear of such outrage. These same discourses are among the most mirth-provoking things in all Dickens: impossible to regard with nothing but contempt or dislike the man who has so shaken our sides. It might be well for the world if the race of Chadband should disappear (a consummation still far out of sight); but the satirist frankly glories in him, and to us he is a joy forever. This is the best of the full-length pictures; but we have many a glimpse of kindred personages, always shown us with infinite gusto. The Rev. Melchisedech Howler, for instance. With what extravagance of humour, with what a rapture of robust mirth, are his characteristics touched off in a short passage of *Dombey and Son*. I must give myself the pleasure of copying it. "The Rev. Melchisedech Howler, who, having been one day discharged from the West India Docks on a false suspicion (got up expressly against him by the general enemy) of screwing gimlets into puncheons, and applying his lips to the orifice, had announced the destruction of the world for that day two years, at ten in the morning, and opened a front parlour for the reception of ladies and gentlemen, of the ranting persuasion, upon whom, on the first occasion of their assemblage, the admonition of the Rev. Melchisedech had produced so powerful an effect, that, in their rapturous performance of a sacred jig, which closed the service, the whole flock broke through into a kitchen below and disabled a mangle belonging to one of the fold" (chap. XV). There is something of sheer boyishness in this irresistible glee; yet the passage was written more than ten years after *Pickwick*. It is the same all but to the end. Dickens treats a thoroughgoing humbug as though he loved him. Reverent of all true religion, and inclined to bitterness against respectable shortcomings in the high places of the church, he goes wild with merriment over back-parlour proselytism and the brayings of Little Bethel. Perhaps in this respect alone did he give grave and lasting offence to numbers of people who would otherwise have been amongst his admirers. At a later time, he could draw, or attempt, a sympathetic portrait of a clergyman of the Established Church, in *Our Mutual Friend,* and, in his last book, could speak respectfully of Canons; but with Dissent he never reconciled himself. To this day, I believe, his books are excluded, on religious grounds, from certain families holding austere views. Remembering the England he sets before us, it is perhaps the highest testimony to his power that such hostility did not make itself more felt when he was mocking so light-heartedly at Stiggins and Chadband and the Rev. Melchisedech.

Connected with hypocrisy in religion, but very skilfully kept apart from it, is his finest satiric portrait, that of Mr. Pecksniff. Think of all that is suggested in this representative of an odious vice, and marvel at the adroitness with which a hundred pitfalls of the incautious satirist are successfully avoided. A moral hypocrite, an incarnation of middle-class respectability in the worst sense of the word, in the sense so loathed by Carlyle, and by every other man of brains then living; yet never a hint at subjects forbidden in the family circle, never a word to which that relative of Mr. Pecksniff, the famous Podsnap, could possibly object. The thing would seem impossible, but that it is done. Let the understanding read between the lines; as in all great art, much is implied that finds no direct expression. Mr. Pecksniff walks and talks before us, a cause of hilarity to old and young, yet the type of as ugly a failing as any class or people can be afflicted withal. The book in which he figures is directed against self-interest in all its forms. We see the sagacious swindler, and the greedy dupe whose unscrupulousness ends in murder. We see the flocking of the Chuzzlewit family, like birds of prey, about the sick-bed of their wealthy relative; and among them the gentlemanly architect of unctuous phrase, who, hearing himself called a hypocrite, signalizes his pre-eminence in an immortal remark. "Charity, my dear, when I take my chamber-candlestick to-night, remind me to be more than usually particular in praying for Mr. Anthony Chuzzlewit, who has done me an injustice." This man is another than Tartuffe; he belongs to a different age, and different country. His religion is not an end in itself; he does not desire to be thought a saint; his prayers are inseparable from the chamber-candlestick, a mere item in the character of British respectability. A like subordination appears in the piety of all Dickens's religious pretenders; their language never becomes offensive to the ordinary reader, simply because it avoids the use of sacred names and phrases, and is seen to have a purely temporal application. Mr. Chadband is a tradesman, dealing in a species of exhortation which his hearers have agreed to call spiritual, and to rate at a certain value in coin of the realm; religion in its true sense never comes into question. Mr. Pecksniff, of course, might have become a shining light in some great conventicle, but destiny has made him a layman; he published his habit of praying, because to pray (over the chamber-candlestick) was incumbent upon an Englishman who had a position to support, who had a stake in the country. A reputation for piety, however, would not suffice to his self-respect, and to the needs of his business; he adds an all-embracing benevolence, his smile falls like the blessed sunshine on all who meet him in his daily walk. This it is which so impresses the simple-minded Tom Pinch. Tom, a thorough Englishman for all his virtues, would not be attracted by a show of merely religious exaltation; faith must be translated into works. Pecksniff must seem to him good, kind, generous, a great man at his profession, sound and trustworthy in all he undertakes. In other words, the Pecksniff whom Tom believes in is the type of English excellence, and evidently no bad type to be set before a nation. Such men existed, and do, and will; we talk little about them, and it is their last desire that we should; they live, mostly in silence, for the honour of their race and of humankind. But, since the Puritan revolution, it has unhappily seemed necessary to our countrymen in general to profess in a peculiar way certain peculiar forms of godliness, and this habit, gradually associated with social prejudices arising from high prosperity, results in the respectable man. Analyzing this person down to his elements, Carlyle found it an essential, if not *the* essential, that he should "keep a gig." If my memory serves me, Mr. Pecksniff did not keep a gig (possibly it is implied in his position), and, after all, the gig is but crudely symbolical. "Let us be moral," says the great man (happening at that moment to be drunk), and here we get to the honest root of the matter. Though the Englishman may dispense with a gig, and remain respectable, he must not be suspected of immorality. "Let us contemplate existence," pursues the inebriate sage. We do so, we English, and find that the term morality (more decidedly than religion) includes all that, in our souls, we rate most highly. According to his proved morality (sexual first and foremost), do we put trust in a man. We are a practical people; we point to our wealth in evidence; and our experience has set it beyond doubt that chastity of thought and act is a nation's prime safeguard.

Could we but be satisfied with the conviction, and simply act upon it! It is not enough. We must hold it as an article of faith that respectability not only does not err, but knows not temptation. A poet who never asked to be thought respectable has put into words we shall not easily forget his thought about immorality:

> "I waive the danger of the sin,
>   The hazard of concealing,
> But oh! it hardens all within,
>   And petrifies the feeling!"

The danger of the sin is so grave, the hazard of concealing so momentous, in English eyes, that we form a national conspiracy to exhibit English nature as distinct, in several points, from the merely human. Hence a characteristic delicacy, a singular refinement, contrasting with the manners, say, of the Latin races, and, at its best, resulting in very sweet and noble lives; hence, also, that counterbalancing vice which would fain atone for vice in the more common sense of the word. Though all within may be hopelessly hardened, the feeling petrified into a little idol of egoism, outwardly there shall be a show of everything we respect. "Homage to virtue," quotha? Well and good, were it nothing more. But Mr. Pecksniff takes up his parable, his innumerable kindred hold forth in the market-place. Respectability cannot hold its tongue, in fact; and the language its affects is wont to be nauseous.

Lower than Pecksniff, but of obvious brotherhood with him, stands Uriah Heep. This example of a low-born man, who, chancing to have brains, deems it most expedient to use them for dishonest purposes, will not yield in the essentials of respectability to the best in the land. He is poor, he is 'umble, but his morals must not for a moment be doubted. The undisguisable fact of poverty is accepted and made the most of; it becomes his tower of strength. Mr. Pecksniff, conscious of a well-filled purse, assumes a certain modesty of demeanour—a foretaste, by the by, of that affectation in rich people which promises such an opportunity for satire in our own day. Uriah Heep wallows in perpetual humility; he grovels before his social superiors, that he may prove to them his equality in soul. With regard to this slimy personage, we note at once that he is a victim of circumstances, the outcome of a bad education and of a society affected with disease. His like abounded at the time; nowadays they will not so easily be discovered. The doctrine that "A man's a man for a' that" has taken solid shape, and our triumphant democracy will soon be ashamed of a motto so disparaging. But Heep saw no prospect when he stood upright; only when he crawled did a chance of issue from that too humble life present itself. "Remember your place!"—from his earliest years this admonition had sounded for him. This prime duty is ever present to his mind; it prompts him to avow, in and out of season, that he belongs to a very 'umble family, that he is himself the 'umblest of mortals. Meanwhile the man's vitals are consumed with envy, hatred, and malice. He cannot respect himself; his training has made the thing impossible; and all men are his enemies. When he is detected in criminal proceedings we are hard upon him, very hard. Dickens cannot relent to this victim of all that is worst in the society he criticises. Had Uriah stopped short of crime, something might have been said for him, but the fellow is fatally logical. Logic of that kind we cannot hear of for a moment; in our own logic of the police-court and the assizes we will take remarkably good care that there is no flaw.

Pecksniff and Uriah have a certain amount of intellect. In his last book Dickens presents us with the monumental humbug who is at the same time an egregious fool. Mr. Sapsea very honestly worships himself; he is respectability weighing a good many stone, with heavy watchguard and expensive tailoring. By incessant lauding of his own virtues to a world always more or less attentive, when such a speaker carries social weight, Sapsea has developed a mania of self-importance. His thickness of hide, his stolidity, are well displayed, but it seems to me that in this case Dickens has been guilty of a piece of exaggeration altogether exceeding the limits of art; perhaps the one instance where his illusion fails to make us accept an extravagance even for a moment. I refer to Sapsea's inscription for his wife's tomb (*Edwin Drood*, chap. IV). Contrasting this with anything to be found in Pecksniff or Uriah Heep, we perceive the limits of his satire, strictly imposed by art, even where he is commonly held to have been most fantastic.

Dickens applied with extraordinary skill the only method which, granted all his genius, could have ensured him so vast a sway over the public of that time. His art, especially as satirist, lies in the judicious use of emphasis and reiteration. Emphasis alone would not have answered his purpose; the striking thing must be said over and over again till the most stupid hearer has it by heart. We of today sometimes congratulate ourselves on an improvement in the public taste and intelligence, and it is true that some popular authors conciliate their admirers by an appeal in a comparatively subdued note. But—who has a popularity like to that of Dickens? Should there again rise an author to be compared with him in sincerity and universality of acceptance, once more will be heard that unmistakable voice of summons to Goodman Dull. We are educated, we are cultured; be it so; but, to say the least, some few millions of us turn with weariness from pages of concentrated art. Fifty years ago the people who did *not* might have been gathered from the English-speaking world into a London hall, without uncomfortable crowding. Dickens well understood that he must cry aloud and spare not; he did it naturally, as a man of his generation; he, and his fellow reformers, educators, popular entertainers, were perforce vociferous to the half-awakened multitudes. Carlyle was even more emphatic, and reiterated throughout a much longer life. Education notwithstanding, these will be the characteristics of any writer for whom fate reserves a gigantic popularity in the century to come.

Yes, it is quite true that Mr. Micawber, Mr. Pecksniff, Uriah Heep, and all Dickens's prominent creations say the same thing in the same way, over and over again. The literary exquisite is disgusted, the man of letters shakes his head with a smile. Remember: for twenty months did these characters of favourite fiction make a periodical appearance, and not the most stupid man in England forgot them between one month and the next. The method is at the disposal of all and sundry; who will use it to this effect?

In his satires on "high life," Dickens was less successful than with the middle class. I have spoken of Sir Leicester Dedlock and Cousin Feenix, both well done, the latter especially, and characterizations worthy of the author, but they hold no place in the general memory. His earliest attempt at this kind of thing was unfortunate; Lord Frederick Verisopht and Sir Mulberry

Hawk are on a par with the literary lady in *Pickwick*, who wrote the ode to an Expiring Frog—an exercise of fancy, which has no relation whatever to the facts of life. Possibly the young author of *Nicholas Nickleby* fancied he had drawn a typical baronet and a lord; more likely he worked with conscious reference to the theatre. In *Little Dorrit* we are introduced to certain high-born or highly-connected people, who make themselves deliberately offensive, but their names cannot be recalled. Much better is the study of an ancient worldling in Edith Dombey's mother, Mrs. Skewton. Her paralytic seizure, her death in life, are fine and grisly realism; but we do not accept Mrs. Skewton as a typical figure. Too obvious is the comparison with Thackeray's work; Dickens is here at a grave disadvantage, and would have done better not to touch that ground at all. Perhaps the same must be said of his incursions into political satire; and yet, one would be loth to lose the Circumlocution Office. Though by the choice of such a name he seems to forbid our expecting any picture of reality, there seems reason to believe that those pages of *Little Dorrit* are not much less true than amusing; at all events they are admirably written. Of the Barnacle family we accept readily enough the one who is described as bright and young; indeed, this youngster is a good deal of a gentleman, and represents the surviving element of that day's civil service; under a competitive system, he alone would have a chance. His relatives have significance enough, but very little life. Dickens wrote of them in anger, which was never the case in his satiric masterpieces. Anger abundantly justified, no doubt; but at the same time another critic of the English government was making heard his wrathful voice (it came from Chelsea), and with more of the true prophetic vehemence. Dickens did not feel at home in this Barnacle atmosphere; something of personal feeling entered into his description of its stifling properties. He could write brilliantly on the subject, but not with the calmness necessary for the creation of lasting characters.

The upstarts of commerce and speculation came more within his scope. Montague Tigg keeps a place in one's recollection, but chiefly, I think, as the impecunious braggart rather than as the successful knave. There is an impressiveness about Mr. Merdle, but perhaps rather in the description of his surroundings than in the figure of the man himself; readers in general know nothing of him, his name never points a paragraph. The Veneerings, in *Our Mutual Friend*, seem better on a rereading than in a memory of the acquaintance with them long ago. This is often the case with Dickens, and speaks strongly in his favour. They smell of furniture polish; their newness in society is a positive distress to the nerves; to read of them is to revive a sensation one has occasionally experienced in fact. Being but sketches, they are of necessity (in Dickens's method) *all* emphasis; we never lose sight of their satiric meaning; their very name (like that of the Circumlocution Office) signals caricature. At this point Dickens connects himself once more with literary traditions; we are reminded of the nomenclature of English drama; of Justice Greedy, of Anthony Absolute, Mrs. Malaprop, and the rest. It is only in his subordinate figures, and rarely then, that he falls into this bad habit, so destructive of illusion. For the most part, his names are aptly selected, or invented with great skill—skill, of course, different from that of Balzac, who aims at another kind of effectiveness. Gamp, Micawber, Bumble, Pipchin—to be sure they are so familiar to us that we associate them inevitably with certain characters, but one recognizes their exquisite rightness. Pecksniff is more daring, and touches the limit of fine discretion. In a very few cases he drew upon that list of grotesque names which anyone can compile from a directory, names which are generally valueless in fiction just because they really exist; Venus, for example.

Anything but a caricature, though as significant a figure as any among these minor groups, is Mr. Casby in *Little Dorrit*, the venerable grandsire, of snowy locks and childlike visage;

the Patriarch, as he is called, who walks in a light of contemplative benevolence. Mr. Casby is a humbug of a peculiarly dangerous kind; under various disguises he is constantly met with in the England of today. This sweetly philosophic being owns houses, and those of the kind which we now call slums. Of course he knows nothing about their evil condition; of course he employs an agent to collect his rents, and is naturally surprised when this agent falls short in the expected receipts. It pains him that human nature should be so dishonest; for the sake of his tenants themselves it behoves him to insist on full and regular payment. When, in the end, Mr. Casby has his impressive locks ruthlessly shorn by the agent risen in revolt against such a mass of lies and cruelty and unclean selfishness, we feel that the punishment is inadequate. This question of landlordism should have been treated by Dickens on a larger scale; it remains one of the curses of English life, and is likely to do so until the victims of house-owners see their way to cut, not the hair, but the throats, of a few selected specimens. Mr. Casby, nowadays, does not take the trouble to assume a sweet or reverend aspect; if he lives in the neighbourhood of his property, he is frankly a brute; if, as is so often the case, he resides in a very different part of the town, his associates are persons who would smile indeed at any affectation of sanctity. In this, and some other directions, hypocrisy has declined among us. Our people of all classes have advanced in the understanding of business, a word which will justify most atrocities, and excuse all but every form of shamelessness.

That rich little book, *Great Expectations*, contains a humbug less offensive than Casby, and on the surface greatly amusing, but illustrative of a contemptible quality closely allied with the commercial spirit. Seen at a distance Mr. Pumblechook is a source of inextinguishable laughter; near at hand he is seen to be a very sordid creature. A time-server to his marrow, he adds the preposterous self-esteem which always gave Dickens so congenial an opportunity. Here we have a form of moral dishonesty peculiar to no one people. Mr. Pumblechook's barefaced pretence that he is the maker of Pip's fortune, his heavy patronage whilst that fortune endures, and his sour desertion of the young man when circumstances alter, is mere overfed humanity discoverable all the world over. He has English traits, and we are constrained to own the man as a relative; we meet him as often as we do the tailor who grovels before the customer unexpectedly become rich. Compare him with the other embodiments of dishonesty, and it is seen, not only what inexhaustible material of this kind lay at Dickens's command, but with what excellent art he differentiates his characters.

Less successful are the last pieces of satire drawing I can find space to mention. In this chapter, rather than in the next, is the place for Mrs. Jellyby, who loses all distinction of sex, and comes near to losing all humanity, in her special craze. Women have gone far towards such a consummation, and one dare not refuse to admit her possibility; but the extravagance of the thing rather repels, and we are never so assured of Mrs. Jellyby as of Mr. Pecksniff. Unacceptable in the same way is that fiercely charitable lady who goes about with her tracts and her insolence among the cottages of the poor. One knows how such persons nowadays demean themselves, and we can readily believe that they behaved more outrageously half a century ago; but being meant as a type, this religious female dragoon misses the mark; we refuse credence and turn away.

Caricature in general is a word of depreciatory meaning. I have already made it clear how far I am from agreeing with the critics who think that to call Dickens a caricaturist, and to praise his humour, is to dismiss him once for all. It seems to me that in all his very best work he pursues an ideal widely apart from that of caricature in any sense; and that in other instances he permits himself an emphasis, like in kind to that of the caricaturist, but by its excellence of art, its fine sincerity of purpose, removed from every inferior association. To call Mrs. Gamp a caricature is an obvious abuse of language; not less so, I think, to apply the word to Mr. Pecksniff or to Uriah Heep. Occasionally, missing the effect he intended, Dickens produced work which invites this definition; at times, again, he deliberately drew a figure with that literary overcharging which corresponds to the exaggeration, small or great, of professed caricaturists with the pencil. His finest humour, his most successful satire, belongs to a different order of art. To be convinced of this one need but think of the multiplicity of detail, all exquisitely finished, which goes to make his best-known portraits. Full justice has never been done to this abounding richness of invention, this untiring felicity of touch in minutiae innumerable. Caricature proceeds by a broad and simple method. It is no more the name for Dickens's full fervour of creation, than for Shakespeare's in his prose comedy. Each is a supreme idealist.

ALICE MEYNELL: 1903

Charles Dickens as
a Man of Letters

THE purely literary character of a greatly popular writer is apt to be neglected; or at least to remain a matter of lax or irresponsible opinion. His admirers have one reason, his detractors another, for leaving it in abeyance; both classes seem to consider it hardly worth attention. In England there has long been a middle public,—a class still sufficiently large,—lettered readers who do not set Dickens aside, and yet who cannot be said to study him; and their tendency is to make light, without much examination, of his specific power as a writer. Men have the habit of saving their reputation as readers by disavowing his literature even while they confess the amplitude of its effects. There is laughter for his humor, tears for his pathos, praise for his spirit, and contempt for his authorship. The least every man holds himself urged to say is that he need not say he prefers Thackeray.

Dickens, however, was very much a craftsman. He had a love of his *métier*, and the genius for words, which the habitual indifference of his time, of his readers, and of his contemporaries in letters could not quench. To read him after a modern man who

Atlantic Monthly, January 1903, pp. 52–59.

had the like preoccupation, displayed it, and was applauded for it phrase by phrase,—Robert Louis Stevenson, for example,—is to undergo a new conviction of his authorship, of the vitality of his diction, of a style that springs, strikes, and makes a way through the burden of custom. Of the great exceptions to that custom—the writers who made a conscious choice of a worthy vocabulary—I need not speak. Few of them were read by Dickens in the years when his own literature was taking shape. He had Fielding and Smollett for his authors as a boy, and nothing read thus by one so ardent is without influence. But his contemporaries—all the journalists, all the novelists of the hour—were not men who cared for the spirit, precision, or nobility of a phrase, or gave much time to any other century than that which was then plodding on a foot neither jocund nor majestic. The daily leading article in the *Times* newspaper (little altered) shows us still what was the best effect looked for in that day from the journeymen of literature. The language had to serve a certain purpose of communication; but as to the nobler, or the fuller, or the more delicate sense of words, it meant as little as was possible to any human tongue.

Refuse words, too emphatic, but with a worn, an abused emphasis; strained rhetoric that had lost its elasticity; grave phrases dimmed and dulled—authors worked with these as with the English of their inheritance, sufficiently well content. The phrase filled the mouth, though there were dregs in the mouthful. In the work of Dickens also there are passages of such English, neither gentle nor simple. He wrote thus as a mere matter of use and custom. But his own lively genius proved itself to be a writer's genius, not only here and there, or suddenly, but often. It had its way of revealing the authentic writer in the springs and sources of his work. For the authentic author is an author throughout. His art is lodged so deeply within as to be beforehand with his emotions and his passions, especially the more vehement. He does not clothe his feeling in poetry or prose, for clothing is assumed. It would be better to say that his thought and feeling are incarnated, not dressed, and that in poetry it wears already the spiritual body. According to this theory of language no man can possibly have a true style who has not something to write, something for the sake of which he writes. This should not need to be said—it is so simple, and seems so plain. Yet authors are found to aspire to style for its own sake, and to miss it as happiness is missed. The writer who has taken captive the fancy and the cheaper emotions—not the imagination and the graver passions—of modern Italy is surely to be very simply and obviously described as an ambitious and a careful author who has little or nothing to say. Against such as he the coming reaction toward blunt and homely writing is as just as a "movement" can ever be. And it is only against such as he that the insults "precious" and "preciosity" are justifiably to be used. The style of Dickens is assuredly not great. It has life enough for movement, but not life enough for peace. That it *has* life, whether restless or at rest, is the fact which proves its title to the name of style. To write much about style is, unfortunately, to tamper somewhat with that rare quality; if only because such writing has suggested to too many the addition of "style" to all their other literary offenses—the last addition, like that of the "architecture" which was to be added to the rich man's new house as soon as he should get it built. Let us, however, leave this mere fashion out of sight; it will soon pass. Already a reaction is beginning, and those who praised what they called style will soon be scorning it, in chorus. Which way such a weak current of criticism may chance to turn between to-day and to-morrow matters nothing. The style that is the life and value of English literature suffers no lasting injury or change; and all who have written well, whether in the greater manner or the lesser which Dickens practiced, have their share in the laws and the constitution of Letters. It cannot be necessary to insist upon Dickens's sense of words. He had his craft at heart, and made instant appropriations of words that describe and define. This felicity is style in a humble form. It even fulfills that ancient demand for frequent "slight surprise," which, so stated, is in itself an example, as well as a precept, of Greek style. See, for an instance of Dickens's felicity, the brief phrase that gives us Mr. Micawber as he sat by to hear Captain Hopkins read the petition in the prison "from His Most Gracious Majesty's unfortunate subjects." Mr. Micawber listened, Dickens tells us, "with a little of an author's vanity, contemplating (not severely) the spikes upon the opposite wall." The happy parenthesis! And here is another masterly phrase: "It went from me with a shock, like a ball from a rifle," says David Copperfield, after the visit of a delirious impulse; and what other writer has named that blow of departure, the volley of passion as it goes?

In comedy again: "Mr. Micawber" (he was making punch) "resumed his peeling with a desperate air." We had read but a moment before that he had made a "random but expressive flourish with the knife" in reference to his own prospects and to those of his disastrous family. Traddles, in the same book, with his hair standing on end, "looked as though he had seen a cheerful ghost." And if the heart-easing humor of this little phrase, which sets laughter free, should be accused of a lower intelligence than that of wit, has Dickens not wit in a phrase, as well as humor? Is it not witty to say of the man who had held a sinecure office against all protest, "He died with his drawn salary in his hand?"

Is it not witty, too, to banter the worst English of his day by an imitation that shows an author's sense of its literary baseness? The mere words, "gratifying emotions of no common description," do this to admiration. It is Mr. Micawber again (excellent figure of comedy—there are no heights of humorous literature whereon Mr. Micawber has not the right to stand with the greatest of companions)—it is he who writes that portly phrase. "Tinged with the prismatic hues of memory" is another sentence in the same paragraph, but this is something more farcical, whereas "gratifying emotions of no common description" hits the whole language as it were with one sure arrow. The thickness of the words, as when Charlotte Brontë, at her primmest, writes of "establishing an eligible connection," and of "an institution on the Continent," has not escaped the ear of Dickens the writer. Try as one may to describe a certain kind of English, one is easily outdone by him with a single phrase, invented for an example, such as this of Mr. Micawber's—"gratifying emotions of no common description."

Comedy in literature is evidently of three kinds, and the kinds are named respectively, humor, wit, and derision. Humor is in the phrase that describes Traddles with his hair—Traddles who looked as though he had seen a cheerful ghost. Wit is in the phrase about the drawn salary. And derision is in that sentence of Mr. Micawber's composition.

In all this—the humor of authorship, its wit and its derision, cited here successively, in representative phrases that had to be chosen among thousands of their kind—the idea is inseparable from the phrase. Nevertheless, perhaps a student might be willing to find so important a thing as style elsewhere, in deliberate description, such as this: The autumn leaves fall thick, "but never fast, for they come circling down with a dead lightness." Here, again, is a noble piece of writing which a classic English name might well have signed: "I held my mother in my embrace, and she held me in hers; and among the still woods in the silence of the summer day there seemed to be nothing but our two troubled minds that was not at peace."

Again, how simple and fine is this: "Now the woods settle into great masses as if they were one profound tree": not only admirably choice in words, but a lesson in vision, a lesson for a painter. It instructs the sense of sight, so that a master of landscape painting could not put a better lesson into words. And this, also simple, also good, seems to instruct the sense of hearing

—the scene is in the Court of Chancery on a London November day: "Leaving this address ringing in the rafters of the roof, the very little counsel drops, and the fog knows him no more." Again: "Mr. Vholes here emerged into the silence he could hardly be said to have broken, so stifled was his tone." Here again are hearing and vision in admirable words: "Within the grill-gate of the chancel, up the steps surmounted loomingly by the fast darkening organ, white robes could be dimly seen, and one feeble voice, rising and falling in a cracked monotonous mutter, could at intervals be faintly heard . . . until the organ and the choir burst forth and drowned it in a sea of music. Then the sea fell, and the dying voice made another feeble effort; and then the sea rose high and beat its life out, and lashed the roof, and surged among the arches, and pierced the heights of the great tower; and then the sea was dry and all was still."

Take another example: This is how a listener overheard men talking in the cathedral hollows: "The word 'confidence,' shattered by the echoes, but still capable of being pieced together, is uttered."

In another passage, moreover, Dickens stops at the mere sense of vision, and confirms that intent impression by instantly using a certain word where a writer of lesser vigilance would have used another; thus: "Mr. Vholes gauntly stalked to the fire, and warmed his funeral gloves." A less simple and less subtle author—a less admirable impressionist—would have surely said "hands" where Dickens, stopping at the sense of vision—as though he did nothing but see—says "gloves." This is the purest and most perfect "impressionism," yet it does not bind Dickens to impressionism as a formula. He uses that manner precisely when he needs it, and only then. There is another similar and excellent passage, where Dickens writes of Mr. Vholes's "sleeve," and writes so with a peculiar appropriateness to the inscrutable person he is describing. " 'I thank you,' said Mr. Vholes, putting out his long black sleeve, to check the ringing of the bell, 'not any.' " And here is the expression of a sense that is hardly either sight or hearing: "Beyond was a burial ground in which the night was very slowly stirring." How subtle a phrase for the earliest dawn!

Then there is the description of the gesture of little David Copperfield at the end of his journey, when he first confronts his aunt: "A movement of my hands, intended to show her my ragged state, and to call it to witness that I had suffered something." If the sense of hearing is opened and urged, and struck to greater life by one phrase; and the sense of vision by another; both are quickened by the storm in *David Copperfield;* and the sense of touch is roused by the touches of that tempest. "I dream of it," says the narrator, "sometimes, though at lengthened and uncertain intervals, to this hour." "There had been a wind all day, and it was rising then, with an extraordinary great sound. . . . We found a cluster of people in the market place." That last phrase, in all its simplicity, marks the strange day. "Long before we saw the sea its spray was on our lips. . . . The water was out, over miles and miles of the flat country; and every sheet and puddle lashed its banks, and had its stress of little breakers setting heavily towards us. When we came within sight of the sea, the waves on the horizon, caught at intervals above the rolling abyss, were like glimpses of another shore, with towers and buildings. When at last we got into the town, the people came out to their doors all aslant, and with streaming hair. I went down to look at the sea, staggering along the street, which was strewn with sand and seaweed, and with flying blotches of sea foam." Here, again, is the storm in the morning light: "The wind by this time might have lulled a little, though not more sensibly than if the cannonading I had dreamed of had been diminished by the silencing of half a dozen guns out of hundreds." Wonderful here, again, is the perception of things silenced within the stress of sound. Then read all that follows, in the unrelaxed urgency of that great chapter, to the end.

Whoever would try to do Dickens this tardy justice (and I have space for no more than an indication of the way of it) must choose passages that have the quality of dignity. They are not so very few. Elegance he has not, but his dignity is clear to readers who prize this quality too much to be hasty to deny it.

In estimating Charles Dickens's capacity for a prose style of dignity we ought to bear in mind his own singular impatience of antiquity of almost all degrees, and also the sense of fresh life he had—his just conviction of his own new leadership. He had read the eighteenth-century novelists in his boyhood, but when he became a man and a master, he broke with the past, and his *renouveau* was somewhat too stimulating to his own genius. It was in spite of this, in spite of his popularity, and in spite of a public that was modern, excitable, boastful of the age, boastful about steam and trade, eager to frolic with a new humorist, and yet more eager to weep with a new sentimentalist, that Dickens possessed himself, in no infrequent passages, of a worthy and difficult dignity.

His people, his populace, and the first critic of his day at the head of all classes, pushed him further and yet further on the way of abandonment—the way of easy extremes; by praise, by popularity, by acclamation they sent their novelist in search of yet more occasion for laughter and tears, for caricature and intemperate pathos.

Moreover, as has just been said, Dickens was urged by his own modern conviction, and excused by his splendid sense of words. He was tempted everywhere. As you read him, you learn to understand how his vitality was at work, how it carried him through his least worthy as well as his most worthy moments, and justified his confidence where a weaker man had confessed unconsciously the ignominies of false art and luxurious senti-ment. Charles Dickens seems to defy us to charge him with these. None the less do we accuse him—at Little Paul's death, for example. Throughout this child's life—admirably told—the art is true, but at the very last few lines the writer seems to yield to applause and to break the strengthening laws of nature down. We may indeed say the strengthening laws; because in what Hamlet calls the modesty of nature there is not only beauty, not only dignity, but an inimitable strength. The limitations of nature, and of natural art, are bracing. A word or two astray in this death scene; a phrase or two put into the mouth of the dying child,—"the light about the head," "shining on me as I go," phrases that no child ever spoke, and that make one shrink as though with pain by their untruthfulness,—and the sincerity of literature is compromised.

But it is not with such things that the work of Dickens is beset; it is rather filled with just felicities—so filled that on our search for passages of composure and dignity we are tempted to linger rather among excellent words that are to be praised merely because they are the words of precision—arms of precision— specific for his purpose. Two proper names are worthy to be placed among these,—that of Vholes, for the predatory yet not fraudulent lawyer in *Bleak House,* and that of Tope, for the cathedral verger in *Edwin Drood:* something dusty and dusky, with wings, is Vholes; something like a church mouse, silent and a little stealthy, is Tope.

Mr. and Mrs. Tope. There is naturally a pair engaged about the cathedral stalls and the hassocks—within the "precincts" generally. It is Christmas; and Mr. and Mrs. Tope, Dickens tells us, "are daintily sticking sprigs of holly into the carvings and sconces of the cathedral stalls, as if they were sticking them into the coat-buttonholes of the Dean and Chapter." From the same book comes this fine description of the young Eurasians: "a certain air upon them of hunter and huntress; yet withal a certain air of being the objects of the chase, rather than the followers." The words may lack elegance, but they are vivid; and these follow: "An indefinable kind of pause coming and going on their whole expression, both of face and form." What enterprising words! How gallantly Dickens sets forward to describe, and how buoyantly!

Fancy, in Charles Dickens, is the most vigilant elf that ever lurked in brilliant human senses. Fancy has her own prose style; doubtless that greater faculty, Imagination, inspires more of the ultimate peace—the continent of peace—that seems to contain the tempests of great tragedies. But if Imagination is capable of peace, Fancy is capable of movement. And amongst the words of Fancy some are vulgarly, and some are finely mobile and alert. Fancy has a vulgar prose and a finer; the finer assuredly is his. Instead of charging him with the vulgar alertness of the street (and this seems to be the accusation used by those who aver that they can no longer read him), we ought to acknowledge the Ariel-delicacy of images and allusions, and the simplicity of his caprice, resembling the simplicity of an unpreoccupied child.

Compare this sense of autumn with that of a writer who has had to pause for secondary words: "There has been rain this afternoon, and a wintry shudder goes among the little pools in the cracked, uneven flagstones. . . . Some of the leaves, in a timid rush, seek sanctuary within the low-arched cathedral door; but two men coming out resist them, and cast them out with their feet."

Less simple and less subtle, but full of the words of perception, is this last description of Volumnia, the elderly, but sprightly Dedlock, in *Bleak House*. The Dedlocks, by the way, are mere convention; but yet Dickens contrives to see even these creatures of tradition with a living eye: "Then, indeed," he says, "does the tuckered sylph . . . proceed to the exhausted old assembly room, fourteen heavy miles off. Then does she twirl and twine, a pastoral nymph of good family, through the mazes of the dance. Then is she kind and cruel, stately and unassuming, various, beautifully willful." "Fourteen heavy miles off." There is the very genius of antithesis in that disheartened phrase, in its exquisite contrast with poor Volumnia's gayeties.

It is appropriately in the passages of childhood—veritable childhood, in which the famous Little Nell seems to me, I must reluctantly confess, to have little or no part—that Dickens writes those words of perception of which literature would do well to be proud. Take the passages of several of the novels in which the heart of a child is uttered by the humorist, in whose heart nothing ceases to live. These passages are too full for citation. But here, in the last word of the phrase, is a most characteristic stroke of literature. Pip, in *Great Expectations*, as every one knows, has taken food to give to his convict; and he goes to church on Christmas morning: Dickens puts these words into his mouth:—

"Under the weight of my wicked secret, I pondered whether the Church would be powerful enough to shield me from the vengeance of the terrible young man, if I divulged to that establishment." The word "establishment" is precisely the one that proves the hopelessness of such a project. A child confessing to an "establishment"! Another word of precision is this: "Trabb's boy, when I had entered, was sweeping the shop; and he had sweetened his labors by sweeping over me." Here is another, and it repeats the effect of Mr. Vholes's sleeve, in a child's apprehension: "Miss Murdstone, who was busy at her writing-desk, gave me her cold finger-nails." Then there is "a sobbing gaslight"; and, again, Mrs. Wilfer's "darkling state," and "lurid indications of the better marriages she might have made" (wherewith she celebrates her silver wedding)—these serve to remind a reader of the thousands of their kind.

I cannot think that the telling of a violent action (most difficult of narrative writing) could be done more dramatically than it is done in the passage that tells the murder in *Martin Chuzzlewit*. So with the half-told murder in *Edwin Drood*. As by strong dramatic drawing in a picture the thing is held. These passages of extreme action are never without dignity. Literary dignity is rarer in the pathetic mood; but it is frequent in landscape. Here is an example: "All beyond his figure was a vast dark curtain, in solemn movement towards one quarter of the heavens."

Nor is dignity absent from this composed thought of Esther Summerson, in that passage of her life where she had resolved to forego an unavowed love: "There was nothing to be undone; no chain for him to drag, or for *me* to break." This has a quality not unworthy of Bolingbroke, and resembling him by nobility. For when Bolingbroke says of the gifts and benefits of Fortune, that she might take, but that she should not snatch, them from him, meaning that his own detaining hold upon them should not be violent, he uses a phrase hardly more majestic than that of Dickens. Thus it is to an eighteenth-century classic, and a master of style; it is to the friend of Pope, and the inspirer of the *Essay on Man*, that we may liken Dickens the man of letters. And this is the author whom so many readers have charged with vulgarity. The vulgarity that is attributable to his early ignorance of social manners is a very unimportant thing in comparison with the high literary distinction of authorship. The pathetic writer, the humorist, the observer, the describer, we all know, but surely the world has not yet done justice to the man of letters and the man of style, who has not only told us stories, but has borne the responsibilities of English authorship.

It is surely worth mentioning that on the point of grammar Dickens is above criticism. Ignorant of those languages which are held to furnish the foundations of grammatical construction he assuredly was. Nevertheless, he knew how to construct. He grasped the language, as it were, from within. I believe that throughout all those volumes of his there is not one example, I will not say of bad grammar, but of weak grammar. Hardly another author is thus infallible. Those critics who think Thackeray to be, in some sort, more literary than Dickens, would be dismayed if they compared the two authors upon this point. No comparison of any kind, perhaps, need be made between them; but it is the Thackeray party that is to blame for first making a kind of rivalry. And I intend no disrespect to that truly great author when I note that Thackeray's grammar is often strangely to seek. Not only so, but he puts, all unconsciously, a solecism into the mouth of Dr. Johnson himself, in the course of the few words which he makes Johnson speak, in his novel, *The Virginians*.

Security of grammar is surely much more than a mere correctness and knowledge of the rules of a language. It is strength, it is logic. It even proves imagination; because loose sentences nearly always imply vagueness of image,—visual and mental uncertainty, something merely rhetorical or ready made. Strong grammar is like strong drawing, and proves a capable grasp of the substance of things. In this matter Dickens is on the heights of authorship. When Dickens was learning to write, English prose, as commonly printed, was in bad condition. There were the great exceptions, as Americans remember, but one does not think of them as coming Dickens's way. The writer at once popular and literary was Macaulay. But in the matter of style Macaulay was little else than an energetic follower of Gibbon; and the following of Gibbon became, through the fine practice of Macaulay, a harmful habit in English prose. Macaulay unfortunately had not the copyright. And as the authors of the articles of the English Church speak, in theology, of a corrupt following of the Apostles, so also was there a corrupt following of Gibbon. The style of Mr. Micawber himself was a corrupt following of Gibbon, and the style of the daily paper and the style of the grocer's circular to-day are also a corrupt following of Gibbon. Gibbon was a master, but it was through a second-hand admiration that Gibbon was placed where he eclipsed the past, so that the early eighteenth-century and the seventeenth-century were neglected for his sake. It was to the broad face of astonishment that Gibbon addressed his phrase. The shortened sentence (for it was he and not Macaulay who introduced the frequent full stop, the pause for historical surprise) was Gibbon's. His was the use, at once weak and rigid, of "the latter and the former," which the corrupt follower at once adopted: "Oh, do not doom me to the latter!" says a lover in one of Mrs. Inchbald's stories after presenting to his mistress the alternative of his hopes and fears. The grocer to-day diffuses (Gibbon himself would write "diffuses") the last ruins of the master's prose by post; and when the author of a work, recently published, on the *Divine Comedy*, says that Paolo and Francesca were to receive from Dante "such alleviation as circumstances would allow," this also is a distant, a shattered Gibbon, a drift of Gibbon.

That last is the innocent burlesque of the far-off corrupt follower. The burlesque so gayly undertaken by Dickens rallies a lofty and a distant Gibbon less innocently, and with an exquisite intelligence. And our admiration of Dickens's warm, living, and unrhetorical writing should surely be increased by our remembrance of the fact that this wreck of a master's style strewed the press in his day. It was everywhere. Dickens not only was clear of the wreckage—he saw it to be the refuse it was; he laughed at it, and even as he laughed he formed a Style.

G. K. CHESTERTON: 1906

The Pickwick Papers

IN *The Pickwick Papers* Dickens sprang suddenly from a comparatively low level to a very high one. To the level of *Sketches by Boz* he never afterwards descended. To the level of *The Pickwick Papers* it is doubtful if he ever afterwards rose. *Pickwick*, indeed, is not a good novel; but it is not a bad novel, for it is not a novel at all. In one sense, indeed, it is something nobler than a novel, for no novel with a plot and a proper termination could emit that sense of everlasting youth—a sense as of the gods gone wandering in England. This is not a novel, for all novels have an end; and *Pickwick*, properly speaking, has no end—he is equal unto the angels. The point at which, as a fact, we find the printed matter terminates is not an end in any artistic sense of the word. Even as a boy I believed that there were some more pages that were torn out of my copy, and I am looking for them still. The book might have been cut short anywhere else. It might have been cut short after Mr. Pickwick was released by Mr. Nupkins, or after Mr. Pickwick was fished out of the water, or at a hundred other places. And we should still have known that this was not really the story's end. We should have known that Mr. Pickwick was still having the same high adventures on the same high roads. As it happens, the book

From *Charles Dickens* (London, 1906).

ends after Mr. Pickwick has taken a house in the neighbourhood of Dulwich. But we know he did not stop there. We know he broke out, that he took again the road of the high adventures; we know that if we take it ourselves in any acre of England, we may come suddenly upon him in a lane.

But this relation of *Pickwick* to the strict form of fiction demands a further word, which should indeed be said in any case before the consideration of any or all of the Dickens tales. Dickens's work is not to be reckoned in novels at all. Dickens's work is to be reckoned always by characters, sometimes by groups, oftener by episodes, but never by novels. You cannot discuss whether *Nicholas Nickleby* is a good novel, or whether *Our Mutual Friend* is a bad novel. Strictly, there is no such novel as *Nicholas Nickleby*. There is no such novel as *Our Mutual Friend*. They are simply lengths cut from the flowing and mixed substance called Dickens—a substance of which any given length will be certain to contain a given proportion of brilliant and of bad stuff. You can say, according to your opinions, "the Crummles part is perfect," or "the Boffins are a mistake," just as a man watching a river go by him could count here a floating flower, and there a streak of scum. But you cannot artistically divide the output into books. The best of his work can be found in the worst of his works. *The Tale of Two Cities* is a good novel; *Little Dorrit* is not a good novel. But the description of "The Circumlocution Office" in *Little Dorrit* is quite as good as the description of "Tellson's Bank" in *The Tale of Two Cities*. *The Old Curiosity Shop* is not so good as *David Copperfield*, but Swiveller is quite as good as Micawber. Nor is there any reason why these superb creatures, as a general rule, should be in one novel any more than another. There is no reason why Sam Weller, in the course of his wanderings, should not wander into *Nicholas Nickleby*. There is no reason why Major Bagstock, in his brisk way, should not walk straight out of *Dombey and Son* and straight into *Martin Chuzzlewit*. To this generalization some modification should be added. *Pickwick* stands by itself, and has even a sort of unity in not pretending to unity. *David Copperfield*, in a less degree, stands by itself, as being the only book in which Dickens wrote of himself; and *The Tale of Two Cities* stands by itself as being the only book in which Dickens slightly altered himself. But as a whole, this should be firmly grasped, that the units of Dickens, the primary elements, are not the stories, but the characters who affect the stories—or, more often still, the characters who do not affect the stories.

This is a plain matter; but, unless it be stated and felt, Dickens may be greatly misunderstood and greatly underrated. For not only is his whole machinery directed to facilitating the self-display of certain characters, but something more deep and more unmodern still is also true of him. It is also true that all the *moving* machinery exists only to display entirely *static* character. Things in the Dickens story shift and change only in order to give us glimpses of great characters that do not change at all. If we had a sequel of Pickwick ten years afterwards, Pickwick would be exactly the same age. We know he would not have fallen into that strange and beautiful second childhood which soothed and simplified the end of Colonel Newcome. Newcome, throughout the book, is in an atmosphere of time: Pickwick, throughout the book, is not. This will probably be taken by most modern people as praise of Thackeray and disparaise of Dickens. But this only shows how few modern people understand Dickens. It also shows how few understand the faiths and fables of mankind. The matter can only be roughly stated in one way. Dickens did not strictly make a literature; he made a mythology.

For a few years our corner of Western Europe has had a fancy for this thing we call fiction; that is, for writing down our own lives or similar lives in order to look at them. But though we call it fiction, it differs from older literatures chiefly in being less fictitious. It imitates not only life, but the limitations of life; it not only reproduces life, it reproduces death. But outside us, in every other country, in every other age, there has been going on from the beginning a more fictitious kind of fiction. I mean the kind now called folklore, the literature of the people. Our modern novels, which deal with men as they are, are chiefly produced by a small and educated section of the society. But this other literature deals with men greater than they are—with demi-gods and heroes; and that is far too important a matter to be trusted to the educated classes. The fashioning of these portents is a popular trade, like ploughing or brick-laying; the men who made hedges, the men who made ditches, were the men who made deities. Men could not elect their kings, but they could elect their gods. So we find ourselves faced with a fundamental contrast between what is called fiction and what is called folklore. The one exhibits an abnormal degree of dexterity operating within our daily limitations; the other exhibits quite normal desires extended beyond those limitations. Fiction means the common things as seen by the uncommon people. Fairy tales mean the uncommon things as seen by the common people.

As our world advances through history towards its present epoch, it becomes more specialist, less democratic, and folklore turns gradually into fiction. But it is only slowly that the old elfin fire fades into the light of common realism. For ages after our characters have dressed up in the clothes of mortals they betray the blood of the gods. Even our phraseology is full of relics of this. When a modern novel is devoted to the bewilderments of a weak young clerk who cannot decide which woman he wants to marry, or which new religion he believes in, we still give this knock-kneed cad the name of "the hero"—the name which is the crown of Achilles. The popular preference for a story with "a happy ending" is not, or at least was not, a mere sweet-stuff optimism; it is the remains of the old idea

of the triumph of the dragon-slayer, the ultimate apotheosis
of the man beloved of heaven.

But there is another and more intangible trace of this fading
supernaturalism—a trace very vivid to the reader, but very
elusive to the critic. It is a certain air of endlessness in the episodes, even in the shortest episodes—a sense that, although we
leave them, they still go on. Our modern attraction to short
stories is not an accident of form; it is the sign of a real sense
of fleetingness and fragility; it means that existence is only an
impression, and, perhaps, only an illusion. A short story of to-
day has the air of a dream; it has the irrevocable beauty of a
falsehood; we get a glimpse of grey streets of London or red
plains of India, as in an opium vision; we see people,—arresting
people, with fiery and appealing faces. But when the story is
ended, the people are ended. We have no instinct of anything
ultimate and enduring behind the episodes. The moderns, in
a word, describe life in short stories because they are possessed
with the sentiment that life itself is an uncommonly short story,
and perhaps not a true one. But in this elder literature, even
in the comic literature (indeed, especially in the comic literature),
the reverse is true. The characters are felt to be fixed things of
which we have fleeting glimpses; that is, they are felt to be divine.
Uncle Toby is talking for ever, as the elves are dancing for
ever. We feel that whenever we hammer on the house of
Falstaff, Falstaff will be at home. We feel it as a Pagan would
feel that, if a cry broke the silence after ages of unbelief, Apollo
would still be listening in his temple. These writers may tell
short stories, but we feel they are only parts of a long story.
And herein lies the peculiar significance, the peculiar sacredness
even, of penny dreadfuls and the common printed matter made
for our errand-boys. Here in dim and desperate forms, under
the ban of our base culture, stormed at by silly magistrates,
sneered at by silly schoolmasters,—here is the old popular litera-

ture still popular; here is the unmistakable voluminousness, the thousand and one tales of Dick Deadshot, like the thousand and one tales of Robin Hood. Here is the splendid and static boy, the boy who remains a boy through a thousand volumes and a thousand years. Here in mean alleys and dim shops, shadowed and shamed by the police, mankind is still driving its dark trade in heroes. And elsewhere, and in all other ages, in braver fashion, under cleaner skies the same eternal tale-telling goes on, and the whole mortal world is a factory of immortals.

Dickens was a mythologist rather than a novelist; he was the last of the mythologists, and perhaps the greatest. He did not always manage to make his characters men, but he always managed, at the least, to make them gods. They are creatures like Punch or Father Christmas. They live statically, in a perpetual summer of being themselves. It was not the aim of Dickens to show the effect of time and circumstance upon a character; it was not even his aim to show the effect of a character on time and circumstance. It is worth remark, in passing, that whenever he tried to describe change in a character, he made a mess of it, as in the repentance of Dombey or the apparent deterioration of Boffin. It was his aim to show character hung in a kind of happy void, in a world apart from time—yes, and essentially apart from circumstance, though the phrase may seem odd in connection with the godlike horse-play of *Pickwick*. But all the Pickwickian events, wild as they often are, were only designed to display the greater wildness of souls, or sometimes merely to bring the reader within touch, so to speak, of that wildness. The author would have fired Mr. Pickwick out of a cannon to get him to Wardle's by Christmas; he would have taken the roof off to drop him into Bob Sawyer's party. But once put Pickwick at Wardle's, with his punch and a group of gorgeous personalities, and nothing will move him from his chair. Once he is at Sawyer's party, he forgets how he got there; he forgets Mrs. Bardell and all his story. For the story was but an incantation to call up a god, and the god (Mr. Jack Hopkins) is present in divine power. Once the great characters are face to face, the ladder by which they climbed is forgotten and falls down, the structure of the story drops to pieces, the plot is abandoned, the other characters deserted at every kind of crisis; the whole crowded thoroughfare of the tale is blocked by two or three talkers, who take their immortal ease as if they were already in Paradise. For they do not exist for the story; the story exists for them; and they know it.

To every man alive, one must hope, it has in some manner happened that he has talked with his more fascinating friends round a table on some night when all the numerous personalities unfolded themselves like great tropical flowers. All fell into their parts as in some delightful impromptu play. Every man was more himself than he had ever been in this vale of tears. Every man was a beautiful caricature of himself. The man who has known such nights will understand the exaggerations of *Pickwick*. The man who has not known such nights will not enjoy *Pickwick* nor (I imagine) heaven. For, as I have said, Dickens is, in this matter, close to popular religion, which is the ultimate and reliable religion. He conceives an endless joy; he conceives creatures as permanent as Puck or Pan—creatures whose will to live aeons upon aeons cannot satisfy. He is not come, as a writer, that his creatures may copy life and copy its narrowness; he is come that they may have life, and that they may have it more abundantly. It is absurd indeed that Christians should be called the enemies of life because they wish life to last for ever; it is more absurd still to call the old comic writers dull because they wished their unchanging characters to last for ever. Both popular religion, with its endless joys, and the old comic story, with its endless jokes, have in our time faded together. We are too weak to desire that undying vigour. We believe that you can have too much of a good thing—a blasphemous belief, which at one blow wrecks all the heavens that men have hoped for. The grand old defiers of God were not afraid of an eternity of torment. We have come to be afraid of an eternity of joy. It is not my business here to take sides in this division between those who like life and long novels and those who like death and short stories; my only business is to point out that those who see in Dickens's unchanging characters and recurring catch-words a mere stiffness and lack of living movement miss the point and nature of his work. His tradition is another tradition altogether; his aim is another aim altogether to those of the modern novelists who trace the alchemy of experience and the autumn tints of character. He is there, like the common people of all ages, to make deities; he is there, as I have said, to exaggerate life in the direction of life. The spirit he at bottom celebrates is that of two friends drinking wine together and talking through the night. But for him they are two deathless friends talking through an endless night and pouring wine from an inexhaustible bottle.

This, then, is the first firm fact to grasp about *Pickwick*—about *Pickwick* more than about any of the other stories. It is, first and foremost, a supernatural story. Mr. Pickwick was a fairy. So was old Mr. Weller. This does not imply that they were suited to swing in a trapeze of gossamer; it merely implies that if they had fallen out of it on their heads they would not have died. But, to speak more strictly, Mr. Samuel Pickwick is not the fairy; he is the fairy prince; that is to say, he is the abstract wanderer and wonderer, the Ulysses of Comedy—the half-human and half-elfin creature—human enough to wander, human enough to wonder, but still sustained with that merry fatalism that is natural to immortal beings—sustained by that hint of divinity which tells him in the darkest hour that he is doomed to live happily ever afterwards. He has set out walking to the end of the world, but he knows he will find an inn there.

And this brings us to the best and boldest element of originality in *Pickwick*. It has not, I think, been observed, and it may be that Dickens did not observe it. Certainly he did not plan it; it grew gradually, perhaps out of the unconscious part of his soul, and warmed the whole story like a slow fire. Of course it transformed the whole story also; transformed it out of all likeness to itself. About this latter point was waged one of the numberless little wars of Dickens. It was a part of his pugnacious vanity that he refused to admit the truth of the mildest criticism. Moreover, he used his inexhaustible ingenuity to find an apologia that was generally an afterthought. Instead of laughingly admitting, in answer to criticism, the glorious improbability of Pecksniff, he retorted with a sneer, clever and very unjust, that he was not surprised that the Pecksniffs should deny the portrait of Pecksniff. When it was objected that the pride of old Paul Dombey breaks as abruptly as a stick, he tried to make out that there had been an absorbing psychological struggle going on in that gentleman all the time, which the reader was too stupid to perceive. Which is, I am afraid, rubbish. And so, in a similar vein, he answered those who pointed out to him the obvious and not very shocking fact that our sentiments about Pickwick are very different in the second part of the book from our sentiments in the first; that we find ourselves at the beginning setting out in the company of a farcical old fool, if not a farcical old humbug, and that we find ourselves at the end saying farewell to a fine old English merchant, a monument of genial sanity. Dickens answered with the same ingenious self-justification as in the other cases—that surely it often happened that a man met us first arrayed in his more grotesque qualities, and that fuller acquaintance unfolded his more serious merits. This, of course, is quite true; but I think any honest admirer of *Pickwick* will feel that it is not an answer. For the fault in *Pickwick* (if it be a fault) is a change, not in the hero but in the whole atmosphere. The point is not that Pickwick turns into a different kind of man; it is that *The Pickwick Papers* turns into a different kind of book. And however artistic both parts may be, this combination must, in strict art, be called inartistic. A man is quite artistically justified in writing a tale in which a man as cowardly as Bob Acres becomes a man as brave as Hector. But a man is not artistically justified in writing a tale which begins in the style of *The Rivals* and ends in the style of the *Iliad*. In other words, we do not mind the hero changing in the course of a book; but we are not prepared for the author changing in the course of the book. And the author did change in the course of this book. He made, in the midst of this book, a great discovery, which was the discovery of his destiny, or, what is more important, of his duty. That discovery turned him from the author of *Sketches by Boz* to the author of *David Copperfield*. And that discovery constituted the thing of which I have spoken —the outstanding and arresting original feature in *The Pickwick Papers*.

Pickwick, I have said, is a romance of adventure, and Samuel Pickwick is the romantic adventurer. So much is indeed obvious. But the strange and stirring discovery which Dickens made was this—that having chosen a fat old man of the middle classes as a good thing of which to make a butt, he found that a fat old man of the middle classes is the very best thing of which to make a romantic adventurer. *Pickwick* is supremely original in that it is the adventures of an old man. It is a fairy tale in which the victor is not the youngest of the three brothers, but one of the oldest of their uncles. The result is both noble and new and true. There is nothing which so much needs simplicity as adventure. And there is no one who so much possesses simplicity as an honest and elderly man of business. For romance he is better than a troop of young troubadours; for the swaggering young fellow anticipates his adventures, just as he anticipates his income. Hence, both the adventures and the income, when he comes up to them, are not there. But a man in late middle-age has grown used to the plain necessities, and his first holiday is a second youth. A good man, as Thackeray said with such thorough and searching truth, grows simpler as he grows older. Samuel Pickwick in his youth was probably an insufferable young coxcomb. He knew then, or thought he knew, all about the confidence tricks of swindlers like Jingle. He knew then, or thought he knew, all about the amatory designs of sly ladies like Mrs. Bardell. But years and real life have relieved him of this idle and evil knowledge. He has had the high good luck in losing the follies of youth, to lose the wisdom of youth also. Dickens has caught, in a manner at once wild and convincing, this queer innocence of the afternoon of life. The round, moon-like face, the round, moon-like spectacles of Samuel Pickwick move through the tale as emblems of a certain spherical simplicity. They are fixed in that grave surprise that may be seen in babies; that grave surprise which is the only real happiness that is possible to man. Pickwick's round face is like a round and honourable mirror, in which are reflected all the fantasies of earthly existence; for surprise is, strictly speaking, the only kind of reflection. All this grew gradually on Dickens. It is odd to recall to our minds the original plan, the plan of the Nimrod Club, and the author who was to be wholly occupied in playing practical jokes on his characters. He had chosen (or somebody else had chosen) that corpulent old simpleton as a person peculiarly fitted to fall down trap-doors, to shoot over butter slides, to struggle with apple-pie beds, to be tipped out of carts and dipped into horse-ponds. But Dickens, and Dickens only, discovered as he went on how fitted the fat old man was to rescue ladies, to defy tyrants, to dance, to leap, to experiment with life, to be a *deus ex machina*, and even a knight-errant. Dickens made this discovery. Dickens went into the Pickwick Club to scoff, and Dickens remained to pray.

Molière and his marquises are very much amused when M. Jourdain, the fat old middle-class fellow, discovers with delight that he has been talking prose all his life. I have often wondered whether Molière saw how in this fact M. Jourdain towers above

them all and touches the stars. He has the freshness to enjoy
a fresh fact, the freshness to enjoy an old one. He can feel that
the common thing prose is an accomplishment like verse; and it
is an accomplishment like verse; it is the miracle of language.
He can feel the subtle taste of water, and roll it on his tongue
like wine. His simple vanity and voracity, his innocent love of
living, his ignorant love of learning, are things far fuller of
romance than the weariness and foppishness of the sniggering
cavaliers. When he consciously speaks prose, he unconsciously
thinks poetry. It would be better for us all if we were as conscious that supper is supper or that life is life, as this true romantic
was that prose is actually prose. M. Jourdain is here the type,
Mr. Pickwick is elsewhere the type, of this true and neglected
thing, the romance of the middle classes. It is the custom in our
little epoch to sneer at the middle classes. Cockney artists profess
to find the bourgeoisie dull; as if artists had any business to find
anything dull. Decadents talk contemptuously of its conventions
and its set tasks; it never occurs to them that conventions and
set tasks are the very way to keep that greenness in the grass
and that redness in the roses—which they had lost for ever.
Stevenson, in his incomparable "Lantern Bearers," describes
the ecstasy of a schoolboy in the mere fact of buttoning a dark
lantern under a dark greatcoat. If you wish for that ecstasy of the
schoolboy, you must have the boy; but you must also have the
school. Strict opportunities and defined hours are the very outline of that enjoyment. A man like Mr. Pickwick has been at
school all his life, and when he comes out he astonishes the
youngsters. His heart, as that acute psychologist, Mr. Weller,
points out, had been born later than his body. It will be remembered that Mr. Pickwick also, when on the escapade of Winkle
and Miss Allen, took immoderate pleasure in the performances
of a dark lantern which was not dark enough, and was nothing
but a nuisance to everybody. His soul also was with Stevenson's
boys on the grey sands of Haddington, talking in the dark by the

sea. He also was of the league of the "Lantern Bearers." Stevenson, I remember, says that in the shops of that town they could purchase "penny Pickwicks (that remarkable cigar)." Let us hope they smoked them, and that the rotund ghost of Pickwick hovered over the rings of smoke.

Pickwick goes through life with that god-like gullibility which is the key to all adventures. The greenhorn is the ultimate victor in everything; it is he that gets the most out of life. Because Pickwick is led away by Jingle, he will be led to the White Hart Inn, and see the only Weller cleaning boots in the courtyard. Because he is bamboozled by Dodson and Fogg, he will enter the prison house like a paladin, and rescue the man and the woman who have wronged him most. His soul will never starve for exploits or excitements who is wise enough to be made a fool of. He will make himself happy in the traps that have been laid for him; he will roll in their nets and sleep. All doors will fly open to him who has a mildness more defiant than mere courage. The whole is unerringly expressed in one fortunate phrase—he will be always "taken in." To be taken in everywhere is to see the inside of everything. It is the hospitality of circumstance. With torches and trumpets, like a guest, the greenhorn is taken in by Life. And the sceptic is cast out by it.

G. K. CHESTERTON: 1906
Dickens and Christmas

THERE is a current prejudice against fogs, and Dickens, perhaps, is their only poet. Considered hygienically no doubt this
may be more or less excusable. But, considered poetically, fog
is not undeserving, it has a real significance. We have in our
great cities abolished the clean and sane darkness of the country.
We have outlawed night and sent her wandering in wild mead-
ows; we have lit eternal watch-fires against her return. We have
made a new cosmos, and as a consequence our own sun and
stars. And, as a consequence also, and most justly, we have made
our own darkness. Just as every lamp is a warm human moon,
so every fog is a rich human nightfall. If it were not for this
mystic accident we should never see darkness, and he who has
never seen darkness has never seen the sun. Fog for us is the
chief form of that outward pressure which compresses mere
luxury into real comfort. It makes the world small, in the same
spirit as in that common and happy cry that the world is small,
meaning that it is full of friends. The first man that emerges
out of the mist with a light, is for us Prometheus, a saviour
bringing fire to men. He is that greatest and best of all men,
greater than the heroes, better than the saints, Man Friday.
Every rumble of a cart, every cry in the distance, marks the

From *Charles Dickens* (London, 1906).

heart of humanity beating undaunted in the darkness. It is wholly human; man toiling in his own cloud. If real darkness is like the embrace of God, this is the dark embrace of man.

In such a sacred cloud the tale called "The Christmas Carol" begins, the first and most typical of all his Christmas tales. It is not irrelevant to dilate upon the geniality of this darkness, because it is characteristic of Dickens that his atmospheres are more important than his stories. The Christmas atmosphere is more important than Scrooge, or the ghosts either; in a sense, the background is more important than the figures. The same thing may be noticed in his dealings with that other atmosphere (besides that of good humour) which he excelled in creating, an atmosphere of mystery and wrong, such as that which gathers round Mrs. Clennam, rigid in her chair, or old Miss Havisham, ironically robed as a bride. Here again the atmosphere altogether eclipses the story, which often seems disappointing in comparison. The secrecy is sensational; the secret is tame. The surface of the thing seems more awful than the core of it. It seems almost as if these grisly figures, Mrs. Chadband and Mrs. Clennam, Miss Havisham and Miss Flite, Nemo and Sally Brass, were keeping something back from the author as well as from the reader. When the book closes we do not know their real secret. They soothed the optimistic Dickens with something less terrible than the truth. The dark house of Arthur Clennam's childhood really depresses us; it is a true glimpse into that quiet street in hell, where live the children of that unique dispensation which theologians call Calvinism and Christians devil-worship. But some stranger crime had really been done there, some more monstrous blasphemy or human sacrifice than the suppression of some silly document advantageous to the silly Dorrits. Something worse than a common tale of jilting lay behind the masquerade and madness of the awful Miss Havisham. Something worse was whispered by the misshapen Quilp to the sinister Sally in that wild, wet summer-house by the river, something worse than the clumsy plot against the clumsy Kit. These dark pictures seem almost as if they were literally visions; things, that is, that Dickens saw but did not understand.

And as with his backgrounds of gloom, so with his backgrounds of good-will, in such tales as "The Christmas Carol." The tone of the tale is kept throughout in a happy monotony, though the tale is everywhere irregular and in some places weak. It has the same kind of artistic unity that belongs to a dream. A dream may begin with the end of the world and end with a tea-party; but either the end of the world will seem as trivial as a tea-party or that tea-party will be as terrible as the day of doom. The incidents change wildly; the story scarcely changes at all. "The Christmas Carol" is a kind of philanthropic dream, an enjoyable nightmare, in which the scenes shift bewilderingly and seem as miscellaneous as the pictures in a scrapbook, but in which there is one constant state of the soul, a state of rowdy benediction and a hunger for human faces. The beginning is about a winter day and a miser; yet the beginning is in no way bleak. The author starts with a kind of happy howl; he bangs on our door like a drunken carol singer; his style is festive and popular; he compares the snow and hail to philanthropists who "come down handsomely"; he compares the fog to unlimited beer. Scrooge is not really inhuman at the beginning any more than he is at the end. There is a heartiness in his inhospitable sentiments that is akin to humour and therefore to humanity; he is only a crusty old bachelor, and had (I strongly suspect) given away turkeys secretly all his life. The beauty and the real blessing of the story do not lie in the mechanical plot of it, the repentance of Scrooge, probable or improbable; they lie in the great furnace of real happiness that glows through Scrooge and everything round him; that great furnace, the heart of Dickens. Whether the Christmas visions would or would not convert Scrooge, they convert us. Whether or no the visions were evoked by real Spirits of the Past, Present, and Future, they were evoked by that truly exalted order of angels who are correctly called High Spirits. They are impelled and sustained by a quality which our contemporary artists ignore or almost deny, but which in a life decently lived is as normal and attainable as sleep, positive, passionate, conscious joy. The story sings from end to end like a happy man going home; and, like a happy and good man, when it cannot sing it yells. It is lyric and exclamatory, from the first exclamatory words of it. It is strictly a Christmas Carol. . . .

GEORGE BERNARD SHAW: 1912
Hard Times

JOHN RUSKIN once declared *Hard Times* Dickens's best novel. It is worth while asking why Ruskin thought this, because he would have been the first to admit that the habit of placing works of art in competition with one another, and wrangling as to which is the best, is the habit of the sportsman, not of the enlightened judge of art. Let us take it that what Ruskin meant was that *Hard Times* was one of his special favorites among Dickens's books. Was this the caprice of fancy? or is there any rational explanation of the preference? I think there is.

Hard Times is the first fruit of that very interesting occurrence which our religious sects call, sometimes conversion, sometimes

Introduction to *Hard Times* (London, 1912).

being saved, sometimes attaining to conviction of sin. Now the great conversions of the XIX century were not convictions of individual, but of social sin. The first half of the XIX century considered itself the greatest of all the centuries. The second discovered that it was the wickedest of all the centuries. The first half despised and pitied the Middle Ages as barbarous, cruel, superstitious, ignorant. The second half saw no hope for mankind except in the recovery of the faith, the art, the humanity of the Middle Ages. In Macaulay's *History of England*, the world is so happy, so progressive, so firmly set in the right path, that the author cannot mention even the National Debt without proclaiming that the deeper the country goes into debt, the more it prospers. In Morris's *News from Nowhere* there is nothing left of all the institutions that Macaulay glorified except an old building, so ugly that it is used only as a manure market, that was once the British House of Parliament. *Hard Times* was written in 1854, just at the turn of the half century; and in it we see Dickens with his eyes newly open and his conscience newly stricken by the discovery of the real state of England. In the book that went immediately before, *Bleak House*, he was still denouncing evils and ridiculing absurdities that were mere symptoms of the anarchy that followed the industrial revolution of the XVIII and XIX centuries, and the conquest of political power by Commercialism in 1832. In *Bleak House* Dickens knows nothing of the industrial revolution: he imagines that what is wrong is that when a dispute arises over the division of the plunder of the nation, the Court of Chancery, instead of settling the dispute cheaply and promptly, beggars the disputants and pockets both their shares. His description of our party system, with its Coodle, Doodle, Foodle, etc., has never been surpassed for accuracy and for penetration of superficial pretence. But he had not dug down to the bed rock of the imposture. His portrait of the ironmaster who visits Sir Leicester Dedlock, and who is so solidly superior to him, might have been drawn by

Macaulay: there is not a touch of Bounderby in it. His horrible and not untruthful portraits of the brickmakers whose abject and battered wives call them "master," and his picture of the now vanished slum between Drury Lane and Catherine Street which he calls Tom All Alone's, suggest (save in the one case of the outcast Jo, who is, like Oliver Twist, a child, and therefore outside the old self-help panacea of Dickens's time) nothing but individual delinquencies, local plague-spots, negligent authorities.

In *Hard Times* you will find all this changed. Coketown, which you can see to-day for yourself in all its grime in the Potteries (the real name of it is Hanley in Staffordshire on the London and North Western Railway), is not, like Tom All Alone's, a patch of slum in a fine city, easily cleared away, as Tom's actually was about fifty years after Dickens called attention to it. Coketown is the whole place; and its rich manufacturers are proud of its dirt, and declare that they like to see the sun blacked out with smoke, because it means that the furnaces are busy and money is being made; whilst its poor factory hands have never known any other sort of town, and are as content with it as a rat is with a hole. Mr. Rouncewell, the pillar of society who snubs Sir Leicester with such dignity, has become Mr. Bounderby, the self-made humbug. The Chancery suitors who are driving themselves mad by hanging about the Courts in the hope of getting a judgment in their favor instead of trying to earn an honest living, are replaced by factory operatives who toil miserably and incessantly only to see the streams of gold they set flowing slip through their fingers into the pockets of men who revile and oppress them.

Clearly this is not the Dickens who burlesqued the old song of the Fine Old English Gentleman, and saw in the evils he attacked only the sins and wickednesses and follies of a great civilization. This is Karl Marx, Carlyle, Ruskin, Morris, Carpenter, rising up against civilization itself as against a disease, and declaring that it is not our disorder but our order that is horrible; that it is not our criminals but our magnates that are robbing and murdering us; and that it is not merely Tom All Alone's that must be demolished and abolished, pulled down, rooted up, and made for ever impossible so that nothing shall remain of it but History's record of its infamy, but our entire social system. For that was how men felt, and how some of them spoke, in the early days of the Great Conversion which produced, first, such books as the *Latter Day Pamphlets* of Carlyle, Dickens's *Hard Times*, and the tracts and sociological novels of the Christian Socialists, and later on the Socialist movement which has now spread all over the world, and which has succeeded in convincing even those who most abhor the name of Socialism that the condition of the civilized world is deplorable, and that the remedy is far beyond the means of individual righteousness. In short, whereas formerly men said to the victim of society who ventured to complain, "Go and reform yourself before you pretend to reform Society," it now has to admit that until Society is reformed, no man can reform himself except in the most insignificantly small ways. He may cease picking your pocket of half crowns; but he cannot cease taking a quarter of a million a year from the community for nothing at one end of the scale, or living under conditions in which health, decency, and gentleness are impossible at the other, if he happens to be born to such a lot.

You must therefore resign yourself, if you are reading Dickens's books in the order in which they were written, to bid adieu now to the light-hearted and only occasionally indignant Dickens of the earlier books, and get such entertainment as you can from him now that the occasional indignation has spread and deepened into a passionate revolt against the whole industrial order of the modern world. Here you will find no more villains and heroes, but only oppressors and victims, oppressing and suffering in spite of themselves, driven by a huge machinery which grinds to pieces the people it should nourish and ennoble, and having for its directors the basest and most foolish of us instead of the noblest and most farsighted.

Many readers find the change disappointing. Others find Dickens worth reading almost for the first time. The increase in strength and intensity is enormous: the power that indicts a nation so terribly is much more impressive than that which ridicules individuals. But it cannot be said that there is an increase of simple pleasure for the reader, though the books are not therefore less attractive. One cannot say that it is pleasanter to look at a battle than at a merry-go-round; but there can be no question which draws the larger crowd.

To describe the change in the readers' feelings more precisely, one may say that it is impossible to enjoy Gradgrind or Bounderby as one enjoys Pecksniff or the Artful Dodger or Mrs. Gamp or Micawber or Dick Swiveller, because these earlier characters have nothing to do with us except to amuse us. We neither hate nor fear them. We do not expect ever to meet them, and should not be in the least afraid of them if we did. England is not full of Micawbers and Swivellers. They are not our fathers, our schoolmasters, our employers, our tyrants. We do not read novels to escape from them and forget them: quite the contrary. But England is full of Bounderbys and Podsnaps and Gradgrinds; and we are all to a quite appalling extent in their power. We either hate and fear them or else we are them, and resent being held up to odium by a novelist. We have only to turn to the article on Dickens in the current edition of the *Encyclopedia Britannica* to find how desperately our able critics still exalt all Dickens's early stories about individuals whilst ignoring or belittling such masterpieces as *Hard Times, Little Dorrit, Our Mutual Friend*, and even *Bleak House* (because of Sir Leicester Dedlock), for their mercilessly faithful and penetrating exposures of English social, industrial, and political life; to see how hard Dickens hits the conscience of the governing class; and how loth we still are to confess, not that we are so wicked (for of that we are rather proud), but so ridiculous, so futile, so incapable of making our country really prosperous. *The Old Curiosity Shop* was written to amuse you, entertain you, touch you; and it succeeded. *Hard Times* was written to make you uncomfortable; and it will make you uncomfortable (and serve you right) though it will perhaps interest you more, and certainly leave a deeper scar on you, than any two of its fore-runners.

At the same time you need not fear to find Dickens losing his good humor and sense of fun and becoming serious in Mr. Gradgrind's way. On the contrary, Dickens in this book casts off, and casts off for ever, all restraint on his wild sense of humor. He had always been inclined to break loose: there are passages in the speeches of Mrs. Nickleby and Pecksniff which are impossible as well as funny. But now it is no longer a question of passages: here he begins at last to exercise quite recklessly his power of presenting a character to you in the most fantastic and outrageous terms, putting into its mouth from one end of the book to the other hardly one word which could conceivably be uttered by any sane human being, and yet leaving you with an unmistakeable and exactly truthful portrait of a character that you recognize at once as not only real but typical. Nobody ever talked, or ever will talk, as Silas Wegg talks to Boffin and Mr. Venus, or as Mr. Venus reports Pleasant Riderhood to have talked, or as Rogue Riderhood talks, or as John Chivery talks. They utter rhapsodies of nonsense conceived in an ecstasy of mirth. And this begins in *Hard Times*. Jack Bunsby in *Dombey and Son* is absurd: the oracles he delivers are very nearly impossible, and yet not quite impossible. But Mrs. Sparsit in this book, though Rembrandt could not have drawn a certain type of real woman more precisely to the life, is grotesque from beginning to end in her way of expressing herself. Her nature, her tricks of manner, her way of taking Mr. Bounderby's marriage, her instinct for hunting down Louisa and Mrs. Pegler, are drawn with an unerring hand; and she says nothing that is out of character. But no clown gone suddenly mad in a very mad harlequinade could express all these truths in more extravagantly ridiculous speeches. Dickens's business in life has become too serious for troubling over the small change of verisimilitude, and denying himself and his readers the indulgence of his humor in inessentials. He even calls the schoolmaster McChoakumchild, which is almost an insult to the serious reader. And it was so afterwards to the end of his life. There are moments when he imperils the whole effect of his character drawing by some overpoweringly comic sally. For instance, happening in *Hard Times* to describe Mr. Bounderby as drumming on his hat as if it were a tambourine, which is quite correct and natural, he presently says that "Mr. Bounderby put his tambourine on his head, like an oriental dancer." Which similitude is so unexpectedly and excruciatingly funny that it is almost impossible to feel duly angry with the odious Bounderby afterwards.

This disregard of naturalness in speech is extraordinarily entertaining in the comic method; but it must be admitted that it is not only not entertaining, but sometimes hardly bearable when it does not make us laugh. There are two persons in *Hard Times*, Louisa Gradgrind and Cissy Jupe, who are serious throughout. Louisa is a figure of poetic tragedy; and there is no question of naturalness in her case: she speaks from beginning to end as an inspired prophetess, conscious of her own doom and finally bearing to her father the judgment of Providence on his blind conceit. If you once consent to overlook her marriage, which is none the less an act of prostitution because she does it to obtain advantages for her brother and not for herself, there is nothing in the solemn poetry of her deadly speech that jars. But Cissy is nothing if not natural; and though Cissy is as true to nature in her character as Mrs. Sparsit, she "speaks like a book" in the most intolerable sense of the words. In her interview with

Mr. James Harthouse, her unconscious courage and simplicity, and his hopeless defeat by them, are quite natural and right; and the contrast between the humble girl of the people and the smart sarcastic man of the world whom she so completely vanquishes is excellently dramatic; but Dickens has allowed himself to be carried away by the scene into a ridiculous substitution of his own most literary and least colloquial style for any language that could conceivably be credited to Cissy.

"Mr. Harthouse: the only reparation that remains with you is to leave her immediately and finally. I am quite sure that you can mitigate in no other way the wrong and harm you have done. I am quite sure that it is the only compensation you have left it in your power to make. I do not say that it is much, or that it is enough; but it is something, and it is necessary. Therefore, though without any other authority than I have given you, and even without the knowledge of any other person than yourself and myself, I ask you to depart from this place to-night, under an obligation never to return to it."

This is the language of a Lord Chief Justice, not of the dunce of an elementary school in the Potteries.

But this is only a surface failure, just as the extravagances of Mrs. Sparsit are only surface extravagances. There is, however, one real failure in the book. Slackbridge, the trade union organizer, is a mere figment of the middle-class imagination. No such man would be listened to by a meeting of English factory hands. Not that such meetings are less susceptible to humbug than meetings of any other class. Not that trade union organizers, worn out by the terribly wearisome and trying work of going from place to place repeating the same commonplaces and trying to "stoke up" meetings to enthusiasm with them, are less apt than other politicians to end as windbags, and sometimes to depend on stimulants to pull them through their work. Not, in short, that the trade union platform is any less humbug-ridden than the platforms of our more highly placed political parties. But even at their worst trade union organizers are not a bit like Slackbridge. Note, too, that Dickens mentions that there was a chairman at the meeting (as if that were rather surprising), and that this chairman makes no attempt to preserve the usual order of public meeting, but allows speakers to address the assembly and interrupt one another in an entirely disorderly way. All this is pure middle-class ignorance. It is much as if a tramp were to write a description of millionaires smoking large cigars in church, with their wives in low-necked dresses and diamonds. We cannot say that Dickens did not know the working classes, because he knew humanity too well to be ignorant of any class. But this sort of knowledge is as compatible with ignorance of class manners and customs as with ignorance of foreign languages. Dickens knew certain classes of working folk very well: domestic servants, village artisans, and employees of petty tradesmen, for example. But of the segregated factory populations of our purely industrial towns he knew no more than an observant professional man can pick up on a flying visit to Manchester.

It is especially important to notice that Dickens expressly says in this book that the workers were wrong to organize themselves in trade unions, thereby endorsing what was perhaps the only practical mistake of the Gradgrind school that really mattered much. And having thus thoughtlessly adopted, or at least repeated, this error, long since exploded, of the philosophic Radical school from which he started, he turns his back frankly on Democracy, and adopts the idealized Toryism of Carlyle and Ruskin, in which the aristocracy are the masters and superiors of the people, and also the servants of the people and of God. Here is a significant passage.

"Now perhaps," said Mr. Bounderby, "you will let the gentleman know how you would set this muddle (as you are so fond of calling it) to rights."

"I donno, sir. I canna be expecten to't. Tis not me as should be looken to for that, sir. Tis they as is put ower me, and ower aw the rest of us. What do they tak upon themseln, sir, if not to do it?"

And to this Dickens sticks for the rest of his life. In *Our Mutual Friend* he appeals again and again to the governing classes, asking them with every device of reproach, invective, sarcasm, and ridicule of which he is master, what they have to say to this or that evil which it is their professed business to amend or avoid. Nowhere does he appeal to the working classes to take their fate into their own hands and try the democratic plan.

Another phrase used by Stephen Blackpool in this remarkable fifth chapter is important. "Nor yet lettin alone will never do it." It is Dickens's express repudiation of *laissez-faire*.

There is nothing more in the book that needs any glossary, except, perhaps, the strange figure of the Victorian "swell," Mr. James Harthouse. His pose has gone out of fashion. Here and there you may still see a man—even a youth—with a single eyeglass, an elaborately bored and weary air, and a little stock of cynicisms and indifferentisms contrasting oddly with a mortal anxiety about his clothes. All he needs is a pair of Dundreary whiskers, like the officers in Desanges' military pictures, to be a fair imitation of Mr. James Harthouse. But he is not in the fashion: he is an eccentric, as Whistler was an eccentric, as Max Beerbohm and the neo-dandies of the *fin de siècle* were eccentrics. It is now the fashion to be strenuous, to be energetic, to hustle as American millionaires are supposed (rather erroneously) to hustle. But the soul of the swell is still unchanged. He has changed his name again and again, become a Masher, a Toff, a Johnny and what not; but fundamentally he remains what he always was, an Idler, and therefore a man bound to find some trick of thought and speech that reduces the world to a thing as empty and purposeless and hopeless as himself. Mr. Harthouse reappears, more seriously and kindly taken, as Eugene

Wrayburn and Mortimer Lightwood in *Our Mutual Friend*. He reappears as a club in The Finches of the Grove of *Great Expectations*. He will reappear in all his essentials in fact and in fiction until he is at last shamed or coerced into honest industry and becomes not only unintelligible but inconceivable.

Note, finally, that in this book Dickens proclaims that marriages are not made in heaven, and that those which are not confirmed there, should be dissolved.

GEORGE SANTAYANA: 1921

Dickens

IF Christendom should lose everything that is now in the melting-pot, human life would still remain amiable and quite adequately human. I draw this comforting assurance from the pages of Dickens. Who could not be happy in his world? Yet there is nothing essential to it which the most destructive revolution would be able to destroy. People would still be as different, as absurd, and as charming as are his characters; the springs of kindness and folly in their lives would not be dried up. Indeed, there is much in Dickens which communism, if it came, would only emphasise and render universal. Those schools, those poorhouses, those prisons, with those surviving shreds of family life in them, show us what in the coming age (with some sanitary

The Dial, LXXI (1921), 537–549; also, *Soliloquies in England* (London, 1922).

improvements) would be the nursery and home of everybody. Everybody would be a waif, like Oliver Twist, like Smike, like Pip, and like David Copperfield; and amongst the agents and underlings of social government, to whom all these waifs would be entrusted, there would surely be a goodly sprinkling of Pecksniffs, Squeers's, and Fangs; whilst the Fagins would be everywhere commissioners of the people. Nor would there fail to be, in high places and in low, the occasional sparkle of some Pickwick or Cheeryble Brothers or Sam Weller or Mark Tapley; and the voluble Flora Finchings would be everywhere in evidence, and the strong-minded Betsey Trotwoods in office. There would also be, among the inefficient, many a Dora and Agnes and Little Emily—with her charm but without her tragedy, since this is one of the things which the promised social reform would happily render impossible; I mean, by removing all the disgrace of it. The only element in the world of Dickens which would become obsolete would be the setting, the atmosphere of material instrumentalities and arrangements, as travelling by coach is obsolete; but travelling by rail, by motor, or by airship will emotionally be much the same thing. It is worth noting how such instrumentalities, which absorb modern life, are admired and enjoyed by Dickens, as they were by Homer. The poets ought not to be afraid of them; they exercise the mind congenially, and can be played with joyfully. Consider the black ships and the chariots of Homer, the coaches and river-boats of Dickens, and the aeroplanes of to-day; to what would an unspoiled young mind turn with more interest? Dickens tells us little of English sports, but he shares the sporting nature of the Englishman, to whom the whole material world is a playing-field, the scene giving ample scope to his love of action, legality, and pleasant achievement. His art is to sport according to the rules of the game, and to do things for the sake of doing them, rather than for any ulterior motive.

It is remarkable, in spite of his ardent simplicity and openness

of heart, how insensible Dickens was to the greater themes of
the human imagination—religion, science, politics, art. He was
a waif himself, and utterly disinherited. For example, the terrible
heritage of contentious religions which fills the world seems
not to exist for him. In this matter he was like a sensitive child,
with a most religious disposition, but no religious ideas. Perhaps,
properly speaking, he had no *ideas* on any subject; what he had
was a vast sympathetic participation in the daily life of mankind;
and what he saw of ancient institutions made him hate them, as
needless sources of oppression, misery, selfishness, and rancour.
His one political passion was philanthropy, genuine but felt
only on its negative, reforming side; of positive utopias, or en-
thusiasms, we hear nothing. The political background of Christendom is only, so to speak, an old faded back-drop for his stage;
a castle, a frigate, a gallows, and a large female angel with white
wings standing above an orphan by an open grave—a decoration
which has to serve for all the melodramas in his theatre, intellect-
ually so provincial and poor. Common life as it is lived was
varied and lovable enough for Dickens, if only the pests and
cruelties could be removed from it. Suffering wounded him, but
not vulgarity; whatever pleased his senses and whatever shocked
them filled his mind alike with romantic wonder, with the endless
delight of observation. Vulgarity—and what can we relish, if
we recoil at vulgarity?—was innocent and amusing; in fact,
for the humourist, it was the spice of life. There was more piety in
being human than in being pious. In reviving Christmas, Dickens
transformed it from the celebration of a metaphysical mystery
into a feast of overflowing simple kindness and good cheer; the
church bells were still there—in the orchestra; and the angels
of Bethlehem were still there—painted on the back-curtain.
Churches, in his novels, are vague, desolate places where one has
ghastly experiences, and where only the pew-opener is human;
and such religious and political conflicts as he depicts in *Barnaby
Rudge* and in *A Tale of Two Cities* are street brawls and prison

scenes and conspiracies in taverns, without any indication of the contrasts in mind or interests between the opposed parties. Nor had Dickens any lively sense for fine art, classical tradition, science, or even the manners and feelings of the upper classes in his own time and country: in his novels we may almost say there is no army, no navy, no church, no sport, no distant travel, no daring adventure, no feelings for the watery wastes and the motley nations of the planet, and—luckily, with his notion of them—no lords and ladies. Even love of the traditional sort is hardly in Dickens's sphere—I mean the soldierly passion in which a rather rakish gallantry was sobered by devotion, and loyalty rested on pride. In Dickens love is sentimental or benevolent or merry or sneaking or canine; in his last book he was going to describe a love that was passionate and criminal; but love for him was never chivalrous, never poetical. What he paints most tragically is a quasi-paternal devotion in the old to the young, the love of Mr. Peggotty for Little Emily, or of Solomon Gills for Walter Gay. A series of shabby little adventures, such as might absorb the interest of an average youth, were romantic enough for Dickens.

I say he was disinherited, but he inherited the most terrible negations. Religion lay on him like the weight of the atmosphere, sixteen pounds to the square inch, yet never noticed nor mentioned. He lived and wrote in the shadow of the most awful prohibitions. Hearts petrified by legality and falsified by worldliness offered, indeed, a good subject for a novelist, and Dickens availed himself of it to the extent of always contrasting natural goodness and happiness with whatever is morose; but his morose people were wicked, not virtuous in their own way; so that the protest of his temperament against his environment never took a radical form nor went back to first principles. He needed to feel, in his writing, that he was carrying the sympathies of every man with him. In him conscience was single, and he could not conceive how it could ever be divided in other men. He denounced scandals without exposing shams, and conformed willingly and scrupulously to the proprieties. Lady Dedlock's secret, for instance, he treats as if it were the sin of Adam, remote, mysterious, inexpiable. Mrs. Dombey is not allowed to deceive her husband except by pretending to deceive him. The seduction of Little Emily is left out altogether, with the whole character of Steerforth, the development of which would have been so important in the moral experience of David Copperfield himself. But it is not public prejudice alone that plays the censor over Dickens's art; his own kindness and even weakness of heart act sometimes as marplots. The character of Miss Mowcher, for example, so brilliantly introduced, was evidently intended to be shady, and to play a very important part in the story; but its original in real life, which was recognised, had to be conciliated, and the sequel was omitted and patched up with an apology—itself admirable—for the poor dwarf. Such a sacrifice does honour to Dickens's heart; but artists should meditate on their works in time, and it is easy to remove any too great likeness in a portrait by a few touches making it more consistent than real people are apt to be; and in this case, if the little creature had been really guilty, how much more subtle and tragic her apology for herself might have been, like that of the bastard Edmund in *King Lear!* So, too, in *Dombey and Son,* Dickens could not bear to let Walter Gay turn out badly, as he had been meant to do, and to break his uncle's heart as well as the heroine's; he was accordingly transformed into a stage hero miraculously saved from shipwreck, and Florence was not allowed to reward the admirable Toots as she should have done, with her trembling hand. But Dickens was no free artist; he had more genius than taste, a warm fancy not aided by a thorough understanding of complex characters. He worked under pressure, for money and applause, and often had to cheapen in execution what his inspiration had so vividly conceived.

What, then, is there left, if Dickens has all these limitations?

In our romantic disgust we might be tempted to say, Nothing. But in fact almost everything is left, almost everything that counts in the daily life of mankind, or that by its presence or absence can determine whether life shall be worth living or not; because a simple good life is worth living, and an elaborate bad life is not. There remain in the first place eating and drinking; relished not bestially, but humanly, jovially, as the sane and exhilarating basis for everything else. This is a sound English beginning; but the immediate sequel, as the England of that day presented it to Dickens, is no less delightful. There is the ruddy glow of the hearth; the sparkle of glasses and brasses and well-scrubbed pewter; the savoury fumes of the hot punch, after the tingle of the wintry air; the coaching-scenes, the motley figures and absurd incidents of travel; the changing sights and joys of the road. And then, to balance this, the traffic of ports and cities, the hubbub of crowded streets, the luxury of shop-windows and of palaces not to be entered; the procession of the passers-by, shabby or ludicrously genteel; the dingy look and musty smell of their lodgings; the labyrinth of back-alleys, courts, and mews, with their crying children, and scolding old women, and listless, half-drunken loiterers. These sights, like fables, have a sort of moral in them to which Dickens was very sensitive; the important airs of nobodies on great occasions, the sadness and preoccupation of the great as they hasten by in their mourning or on their pressing affairs; the sadly comic characters of the tavern; the diligence of shop-keepers, like squirrels turning in their cages; the children peeping out everywhere like grass in an untrodden street; the charm of humble things, the nobleness of humble people, the horror of crime, the ghastliness of vice, the deft hand and shining face of virtue passing through the midst of it all; and finally a fresh wind of indifference and change blowing across our troubles and clearing the most lurid sky.

I do not know whether it was Christian charity or naturalistic insight, or a mixture of both (for they are closely akin) that attracted Dickens particularly to the deformed, the half-witted, the abandoned, or those impeded or misunderstood by virtue of some singular inner consecration. The visible moral of these things, when brutal prejudice does not blind us to it, comes very near to true philosophy; one turn of the screw, one flash of reflection, and we have understood nature and human morality and the relation between them.

In his love of roads and wayfarers, of river-ports and wharves and the idle or sinister figures that lounge about them, Dickens was like Walt Whitman; and I think a second Dickens may any day appear in America, when it is possible in that land of hurry to reach the same degree of saturation, the same unquestioning pleasure in the familiar facts. The spirit of Dickens would be better able to do justice to America than was that of Walt Whitman; because America, although it may seem nothing but a noisy nebula to the impressionist, is not a nebula but a concourse of very distinct individual bodies, natural and social, each with its definite interest and story. Walt Whitman had a sort of transcendental philosophy which swallowed the universe whole, supposing there was a universal spirit in things identical with the absolute spirit that observed them; but Dickens was innocent of any such clap-trap, and remained a true spirit in his own person. Kindly and clear-sighted, but self-identical and unequivocally human, he glided through the slums like one of his own little heroes, uncontaminated by their squalor and confusion, courageous and firm in his clear allegiances amid the flux of things, a pale angel at the Carnival, his heart aflame, his voice always flutelike in its tenderness and warning. This is the true relation of spirit to existence, not the other which confuses them; for this earth (I cannot speak for the universe at large) has no spirit of its own, but brings forth spirits only at certain points, in the hearts and brains of frail living creatures, who like insects flit through it, buzzing and gathering what sweets they can; and it is the spaces they traverse in this career, charged with their own moral burden, that they can report on or describe, not things rolling on to infinity in their vain tides. To be hypnotised by that flood would be a heathen idolatry. Accordingly Walt Whitman, in his comprehensive democratic vistas, could never see the trees for the wood, and remained incapable, for all his diffuse love of the human herd, of ever painting a character or telling a story; the very things in which Dickens was a master. It is this life of the individual, as it may be lived in a given nation, that determines the whole value of that nation to the poet, to the moralist, and to the judicious historian. But for the excellence of the typical single life, no nation deserves to be remembered more than the sands of the sea; and America will not be a success, if every American is a failure.

Dickens entered the theatre of this world by the stage door; the shabby little adventures of the actors in their private capacity replace for him the mock tragedies which they enact before a dreaming public. Mediocrity of circumstances and mediocrity of soul forever return to the centre of his stage; a more wretched or a grander existence is sometimes broached, but the pendulum soon swings back, and we return, with the relief with which we put on our slippers after the most romantic excursion, to a golden mediocrity—to mutton and beer, and to love and babies in a suburban villa with one frowsy maid. Dickens is the poet of those acres of yellow brick streets which the traveller sees from the railway viaducts as he approaches London; they need a poet, and they deserve one, since a complete human life may very well be lived there. Their little excitements and sorrows, their hopes and humours are like those of the Wooden Midshipman in *Dombey and Son;* but the sea is not far off, and sky—Dickens never forgets it—is above all those brief troubles. He had a sentiment in the presence of this vast flatness of human fates, in spite of their individual pungency, which I think might well be the dominant sentiment of mankind in the future; a sense of happy freedom in littleness, an open-eyed reverence and religion without words. This universal human anonymity is like a sea, an infinite democratic desert, chock-full and yet the very image of emptiness, with nothing in it for the mind, except, as the Moslems say, the presence of Allah. Awe is the counterpart of humility—and this is perhaps religion enough. The atom in the universal vortex ought to be humble; he ought to see that, materially, he doesn't much matter, and that morally his loves are merely his own, without authority over the universe. He can admit without obloquy that he is what he is; and he can rejoice in his own being, and in that of all other things in so far as he can share it sympathetically. The apportionment of exist-ence and of fortune is in Other Hands; his own portion is contentment, vision, love, and laughter.

Having humility, that most liberating of sentiments, having a true vision of human existence and joy in that vision, Dickens had in a superlative degree the gift of humour, of mimicry, of unrestrained farce. He was the perfect comedian. When people say Dickens exaggerates, it seems to me they can have no eyes and no ears. They probably have only *notions* of what things and people are; they accept them conventionally, at their diplo-matic value. Their minds run on in the region of discourse, where there are masks only and no faces, ideas and no facts; they have little sense for those living grimaces that play from moment to moment upon the countenance of the world. The world is a perpetual caricature of itself; at every moment it is the mockery and the contradiction of what it is pretending to be. But as it nevertheless intends all the time to be something different and highly dignified, at the next moment it corrects and checks and tries to cover up the absurd thing it was; so that a conventional world, a world of masks, is superimposed on the reality, and passes in every sphere of human interest for the reality itself. Humour is the perception of this illusion, the fact allowed to pierce here and there through the convention, whilst the convention continues to be maintained, as if we had not observed its absurdity. Pure comedy is more radical, cruder, in a certain sense less human; because comedy throws the convention over altogether, revels for a moment in the fact, and brutally says to the notions of mankind, as if it slapped them in the face, There, take that! That's what you really are! At this the polite world pretends to laugh, not tolerantly as it does at humour, but a little angrily. It does not like to see itself by chance in the glass, without having had time to compose its features for demure self-contemplation. "What a bad mirror," it exclaims; "it must be concave or convex; for surely I never looked like that. Mere caricature, farce, and horse play. Dickens exaggerates; *I* never was so sentimental as that; *I* never saw anything so dreadful; *I* don't believe there were ever any people like Quilp, or Squeers, or Serjeant Buzfuz." But the polite world is lying; there *are* such people; we are such people ourselves in our true moments, in our veritable impulses; but we are careful to stifle and to hide those moments from ourselves and from the world; to purse and pucker ourselves into the mask of our conventional personality; and so simpering, we profess that it is very coarse and inartistic of Dickens to undo our life's work for us in an instant, and remind us of what we are. And as to other people, though we may allow that considered superficially they are often absurd, we do not wish to dwell on their eccentricities, nor to mimic them. On the contrary, it is good manners to look away quickly, to suppress a smile, and to say to ourselves that the ludicrous figure in the street is not at all comic, but a dull ordinary Christian, and that it is foolish to give any importance to the fact that its hat has blown off, that it has slipped on an orange-peel and unintentionally sat on the pavement, that it has a pimple on its nose, that its one tooth projects over its lower lip, that it is angry with things in general, and that it is looking everywhere for the penny which it holds tightly in its hand.

That may fairly represent the moral condition of most of us at most times; but we do not want to think of it; we do not want to see; we gloss the fact over; we console ourselves before we are grieved, and reassert our composure before we have laughed. We are afraid, ashamed, anxious to be spared. What displeases us in Dickens is that he does not spare us; he mimics things to the full; he dilates and exhausts and repeats; he wallows. He is too intent on the passing experience to look over his shoulder, and consider whether we have not already understood, and had enough. He is not thinking of us; he is obeying the impulse of the passion, the person, or the story he is enacting. This faculty, which renders him a consummate comedian, is just what alienated from him a later generation in which people of taste were aesthetes and virtuous people were higher snobs; they wanted a mincing art, and he gave them copious improvisation, they wanted analysis and development, and he gave them absolute comedy. I must confess, though the fault is mine and not his, that sometimes his absoluteness is too much for me. When I come to the death of Little Nell, or to What the Waves were always Saying, or even to the incorrigible perversities of the pretty Dora, I skip. I can't take my liquor neat in such draughts, and my inner man says to Dickens, Please don't. But then I am a coward in so many ways! There are so many things in this world that I skip, as I skip the undiluted Dickens! When I reach Dover on a rough day, I wait there until the Channel is smoother; am I not travelling for pleasure? But my prudence does not blind me to the admirable virtue of the sailors that cross in all weathers, nor even to the automatic determination of the seasick ladies, who might so easily have followed my example, if they were not the slaves of their railway tickets and of their labelled luggage. They are loyal to their tour, and I to my philosophy. Yet as wrapped in my great-coat and sure of a good dinner, I pace the windy pier and soliloquise, I feel the superiority of the bluff tar, glad of breeze, stretching a firm arm to the unsteady passenger, and watching with a masterful thrill of emotion the home cliffs receding and the foreign coasts ahead. It is only courage (which Dickens had without knowing it) and universal kindness (which he knew he had) that are requisite to nerve us for a true vision of this world. And as some of us are cowards about crossing the Channel, and others about "crossing the bar," so almost everybody is a coward about his own humanity. We do not consent to be absurd, though absurd we are. We have no fundamental humility. We do not wish the moments of our lives to be caught by a quick eye in their grotesque initiative, and to be pilloried in this way before our own eyes. For that reason we don't like Dickens, and don't like comedy, and don't like the truth. Dickens could don the comic mask with innocent courage; he could wear it with a grace, ease, and irresistible vivacity seldom given to men. We must go back for anything like it to the very greatest comic poets, to Shakespeare or to Aristophanes. Who else, for instance, could have penned this:

"It was all Mrs. Bumble. She *would* do it," urged Mr. Bumble; first looking round to ascertain that his partner had left the room.

"That is no excuse," replied Mr. Brownlow. "You were present on the occasion of the destruction of these trinkets, and indeed are the more guilty of the two, in the eye of the law; for the law supposes that your wife acts under your direction."

"If the law supposes that," said Mr. Bumble, squeezing his hat emphatically in both hands, "The law is a ass, a idiot. If that's the eye of the law, the law is a bachelor; and the worse I wish the law is, that his eye may be opened by experience—by experience."

Laying great stress on the repetition of these two words, Mr. Bumble fixed his hat on very tight, and putting his hands in his pockets, followed his helpmate downstairs.

This is high comedy; the irresistible, absurd, intense dream of the old fool, personifying the law in order to convince and to punish it. I can understand that this sort of thing should not be common in English literature, nor much relished; because pure comedy is scornful, merciless, devastating, holding no door open to anything beyond. Cultivated English feeling winces at this brutality, although the common people love it in clowns and in puppet shows; and I think they are right. Dickens, who surely was tender enough, had so irresistible a comic genius that it carried him beyond the gentle humour which most Englishmen possess to the absolute grotesque reality. Squeers, for instance, when he sips the wretched dilution which he has prepared for his starved and shivering little pupils, smacks his lips and cries: "Here's richness!" It is savage comedy; humour would come in if we understood (what Dickens does not tell us) that the little creatures were duly impressed and thought the thin liquid truly delicious. I suspect that English sensibility prefers the humour and wit of Hamlet to the pure comedy of Falstaff; and that even in Aristophanes it seeks consolation in the lyrical poetry for the flaying of human life in the comedy itself. Tastes are free; but we should not deny that in merciless and rollicking comedy life is caught in the act. The most grotesque creatures of Dickens are not exaggerations or mockeries of something other than themselves; they arise because nature generates them, like toadstools; they exist because they can't help it, as we all do. The fact that these perfectly self-justified beings are absurd appears only by comparison, and from outside; circumstances, or the expectations of other people, make them ridiculous and force them to contradict themselves; but in nature it is no crime to be exceptional. Often, but for the savagery of the average man, it would not even be a misfortune. The sleepy fat boy in *Pickwick* looks foolish; but in himself he is no more foolish, nor less solidly selfjustified, than a pumpkin lying on the ground. Toots seems ridiculous; and we laugh heartily at his incoherence, his beautiful waistcoats, and his extreme modesty; but when did anybody more obviously grow into what he is because he couldn't grow otherwise? So with

Mr. Pickwick, and Sam Weller, and Mrs. Gamp, and Micawber, and all the rest of this wonderful gallery; they are ridiculous only by accident, and in a context in which they never intended to appear. If Oedipus and Lear and Cleopatra do not seem ridiculous, it is only because tragic reflection has taken them out of the context in which, in real life, they would have figured. If we saw them as facts, and not as emanations of a poet's dream, we should laugh at them till doomsday; what grotesque presumption, what silly whims, what mad contradiction of the simplest realities! Yet we should not laugh at them without feeling how real their griefs were; as real and terrible as the griefs of children and of dreams. But facts, however serious inwardly, are always absurd outwardly; and the just critic of life sees both truths at once, as Cervantes did in *Don Quixote*. A pompous idealist who does not see the ridiculous in *all* things is the dupe of his sympathy and abstraction; and a clown, who does not see that these ridiculous creatures are living quite in earnest, is the dupe of his egotism. Dickens saw the absurdity, and understood the life; I think he was a good philosopher.

It is usual to compare Dickens with Thackeray, which is like comparing the grape with the gooseberry; there are obvious points of resemblance, and the gooseberry has some superior qualities of its own; but you can't make red wine of it. The wine of Dickens is of the richest, the purest, the sweetest, the most fortifying to the blood; there is distilled in it, with the perfection of comedy, the perfection of morals. I do not mean, of course, that Dickens appreciated all the values that human life has or might have; that is beyond any man. Even the greatest philosophers, such as Aristotle, have not always much imagination to conceive forms of happiness or folly other than those which their age or their temperament reveals to them; their insight runs only to discovering the *principle* of happiness, that it is spontaneous life of any sort harmonised with circumstances. The sympathies and imagination of Dickens, vivid in their sphere, were no less limited in range; and of course it was not his business to find philosophic formulas; nevertheless I call his the perfection of morals for two reasons: that he put the distinction between good and evil in the right place, and that he felt this distinction intensely. A moralist might have excellent judgment, he might see what sort of life is spontaneous in a given being and how far it may be harmonised with circumstances, yet his heart might remain cold, he might not suffer nor rejoice with the suffering or joy he foresaw. Humanitarians like Bentham and Mill, who talked about the greatest happiness of the greatest number, might conceivably be moral prigs in their own persons, and they might have been chilled to the bone in their theoretic love of mankind, if they had had the wit to imagine in what, as a matter of fact, the majority would place their happiness. Even if their theory had been correct (which I think it was in intention, though not in statement) they would then not have been perfect moralists, because their maxims would not have expressed their hearts. In expressing their hearts, they ought to have embraced one of those forms of "idealism" by which men fortify themselves in their bitter passions or in their helpless commitments; for they do not wish mankind to be happy in its own way, but in theirs. Dickens was not one of those moralists who summon every man to do himself the greatest violence so that he may not offend them, nor defeat their ideals. Love of the good of others is something that shines in every page of Dickens with a truly celestial splendour. How entirely limpid is his sympathy with life—a sympathy uncontaminated by dogma or pedantry or snobbery or bias of any kind! How generous is this keen, light spirit, how pure this open heart! And yet, in spite of this extreme sensibility, not the least wobbling; no deviation from a just severity of judgment, from an uncompromising distinction between white and black. And this happens as it ought to happen; sympathy is not checked by a flatly contrary prejudice or commandment, by some categorical imperative irrelevant to human nature; the check, like the cheer, comes by tracing the course of spontaneous impulse amid circumstances that inexorably lead it to success or to failure. There is a bed to this stream, freely as the water may flow; when it comes to this precipice it must leap, when it runs over these pebbles it must sing, and when it spreads into that marsh it must become livid and malarial. The very sympathy with human impulses quickens in Dickens the sense of danger; his very joy in joy makes him stern to what kills it. How admirably drawn are his surly villains! No rhetorical vilification of them, as in a sermon; no exaggeration of their qualms or fears; rather a sense of how obvious and human all their courses seem from their own point of view; and yet no sentimental apology for them, no romantic worship of rebels in their madness or crime. The pity of it, the waste of it all, are seen not by a second vision but by the same original vision which revealed the lure and the drift of the passion. Vice is a monster here of such sorry mien, that the longer we see it the more we deplore it; that other sort of vice which Pope found so seductive was perhaps only some innocent impulse artificially suppressed, and called a vice because it broke out inconveniently and displeased the company. True vice is human nature strangled by the suicide of attempting the impossible. Those so self-justified villains of Dickens never elude their fates. Bill Sikes is not let off, neither is Nancy; the oddly benevolent Magwitch does not escape from the net, nor does the unfortunate young Richard Carstone, victim of the Court of Chancery. The horror and ugliness of their fall are rendered with the hand of a master; we see here, as in the world, that in spite of the romanticists it is not virtue to rush enthusiastically along any road. I think Dickens is one of the best friends mankind has ever had. He has held the mirror up to nature, and of its reflected fragments has composed a fresh world, where the men and women differ from real people only in that they live in a literary medium, so that all ages and places may

know them. And they are worth knowing, just as one's neighbours are, for their picturesque characters and their pathetic
fates. Their names should be in every child's mouth; they ought
to be adopted members of every household. Their stories cause
the merriest and the sweetest chimes to ring in the fancy, without
confusing our moral judgment or alienating our interest from
the motley commonplaces of daily life. In every English-speaking home, in the four quarters of the globe, parents and children
will do well to read Dickens aloud of a winter's evening; they
will love winter, and one another, and God the better for it.
What a wreath that will be of ever-fresh holly, thick with bright
berries, to hang to this poet's memory—the very crown he would
have chosen.

T. S. ELIOT: 1927

Wilkie Collins and Dickens

DICKENS excelled in character; in the creation of characters of
greater intensity than human beings. Collins was not usually
strong in the creation of character; but he was a master of plot
and situation, of those elements of drama which are most essential to melodrama. *Bleak House* is Dickens's finest piece of
construction; and *The Woman in White* contains Collins's most
real characterization. Every one knows Count Fosco and Marion

From "Wilkie Collins and Dickens," *Times Literary Supplement,* 4
August 1927, pp. 825–826; also, *Selected Essays* (New York, 1932).

Halcombe intimately; only the most perfect Collins reader can remember even half a dozen of his other characters by name.

Count Fosco and Marion are indeed real personages to us; as "real" as much greater characters are, as real as Becky Sharp or Emma Bovary. In comparison with the characters of Dickens they lack only that kind of reality which is almost supernatural, which hardly seems to belong to the character by natural right, but seems rather to descend upon him by a kind of inspiration or grace. Collins's best characters are fabricated, with consummate skill, before our eyes; in Dickens's greatest figures we see no process or calculation. Dickens's figures belong to poetry, like figures of Dante or Shakespeare, in that a single phrase, either by them or about them, may be enough to set them wholly before us. Collins has no phrases. Dickens can with a phrase make a character as real as flesh and blood—"*What a Life Young Bailey's Was!*"—like Farinata

Chi fur gli maggior tui?

or like Cleopatra,

I saw her once
Hop forty paces through the public street.

Dickens's characters are real because there is no one like them; Collins's because they are so painstakingly coherent and lifelike. Whereas Dickens often introduces a great character carelessly, so that we do not realize, until the story is far advanced, with what a powerful personage we have to do, Collins, at least in these two figures in *The Woman in White*, employs every advantage of dramatic effect. . . .

ALDOUS HUXLEY: 1930

The Vulgarity of Little Nell

IT is vulgar, in literature, to make a display of emotions which you do not naturally have, but think you ought to have, because all the best people do have them. It is also vulgar (and this is the more common case) to have emotions, but to express them so badly, with so many too many protestings, that you seem to have no natural feelings, but to be merely fabricating emotions by a process of literary forgery. Sincerity in art, as I have pointed out elsewhere, is mainly a matter of talent. . . .

The case of Dickens is a strange one. The really monstrous emotional vulgarity, of which he is guilty now and then in all his books and almost continuously in *The Old Curiosity Shop*, is not the emotional vulgarity of one who simulates feelings which he does not have. It is evident, on the contrary, that Dickens felt most poignantly for and with his Little Nell; that he wept over her sufferings, piously revered her goodness and exulted in her joys. He had an overflowing heart; but the trouble was that it overflowed with such curious and even rather repellant secretions. The creator of the later Pickwick and the Cheeryble Brothers, of Tim Linkinwater the bachelor and Mr. Garland and so many other gruesome old Peter Pans was obviously a little abnormal in his emotional reactions. There was something

From *Vulgarity in Literature* (London, 1930), pp. 54–59.

Linkinwater chief clerk to Cheeryble Bros.

tearful

rather wrong with a man who could take this lachrymose and
tremulous pleasure in adult infantility. He would doubtless have
justified his rather frightful emotional taste by a reference to
the New Testament. But the child-like qualities of character
commended by Jesus are certainly not the same as those which
distinguish the old infants in Dickens's novels. There is all the
difference in the world between infants and children. Infants
are stupid and unaware and sub-human. Children are remarkable
for their intelligence and ardour, for their curiosity, their intolerance of shams, the clarity and ruthlessness of their vision.
From all accounts Jesus must have been child-like, not at all
infantile. A child-like man is not a man whose development has
been arrested; on the contrary, he is a man who has given himself
a chance of continuing to develop long after most adults have
muffled themselves in the cocoon of middle-aged habit and convention. An infantile man is one who has not developed at all,
or who has regressed towards the womb, into a comfortable
unawareness. So far from being attractive and commendable, an
infantile man is really a most repulsive, because a truly monstrous
and misshapen, being. A writer who can tearfully adore these
stout or cadaverous old babies, snugly ensconced in their mental and economic womb-substitutes and sucking, between false
teeth, their thumbs, must have something seriously amiss with
his emotional constitution.

One of Dickens's most striking peculiarities is that, whenever
in his writing he becomes emotional, he ceases instantly to use his
intelligence. The overflowing of his heart drowns his head and
even dims his eyes; for, whenever he is in the melting mood,
Dickens ceases to be able and probably ceases even to wish to
see reality. His one and only desire on these occasions is just
to overflow, nothing else. Which he does, with a vengeance and
in an atrocious blank verse that is meant to be poetical prose and
succeeds only in being the worst kind of fustian. "When Death
strikes down the innocent and young, from every fragile form

from which he lets the panting spirit free, a hundred virtues rise, in shapes of mercy, charity and love, to walk the world and bless it. Of every tear that sorrowing mortals shed on such green graves, some good is born, some gentler nature comes. In the Destroyer's steps there spring up bright creations that defy his power, and his dark path becomes a way of light to Heaven." And so on, a stanchless flux.

Mentally drowned and blinded by the sticky overflowings of his heart, Dickens was incapable, when moved, of re-creating, in terms of art, the reality which had moved him, was even, it would seem, unable to perceive that reality. Little Nelly's sufferings and death distressed him as, in real life, they would distress any normally constituted man; for the suffering and death of children raise the problem of evil in its most unanswerable form. It was Dickens's business as a writer to re-create in terms of his art this distressing reality. He failed. The history of Little Nell is distressing indeed, but not as Dickens presumably meant it to be distressing; it is distressing in its ineptitude and vulgar sentimentality.

A child, Ilusha, suffers and dies in Dostoevsky's *Brothers Karamazov*. Why is this history so agonizingly moving, when the tale of Little Nell leaves us not merely cold, but derisive? Comparing the two stories, we are instantly struck by the incomparably greater richness in factual detail of Dostoevsky's creation. Feeling did not prevent him from seeing and recording, or rather re-creating. All that happened round Ilusha's deathbed he saw, unerringly. The emotion-blinded Dickens noticed practically nothing of what went on in Little Nelly's neighbourhood during the child's last days. We are almost forced, indeed, to believe that he didn't want to see anything. He wanted to be unaware himself and he wanted his readers to be unaware of everything except Little Nell's sufferings on the one hand and her goodness and innocence on the other. But goodness and innocence and the undeservedness of suffering and even, to some extent, suffering itself are only significant in relation to the actual realities of human life. Isolated, they cease to mean anything, perhaps to exist. Even the classical writers surrounded their abstract and algebraical personages with at least the abstract and algebraical implication of the human realities, in relation to which virtues and vices are significant. Thanks to Dickens's pathologically deliberate unawareness, Nell's virtues are marooned, as it were, in the midst of a boundless waste of unreality; isolated, they fade and die. Even her sufferings and death lack significance because of this isolation. Dickens's unawareness was the death of death itself. Unawareness, according to the ethics of Buddhism, is one of the deadly sins. The stupid are wicked. (Incidentally, the cleverest men can, sometimes and in certain circumstances, reveal themselves as profoundly—criminally—stupid. You can be an acute logician and at the same time an emotional cretin.) Damned in the realm of conduct, the unaware are also damned aesthetically. Their art is bad; instead of creating, they murder.

Art, as I have said, is also philosophy, is also science. Other things being equal, the work of art, which in its own way 'says' more about the universe will be better than the work of art which says less. (The "other things" which have to be equal are the forms of beauty, in terms of which the artist must express his philosophic and scientific truths.) Why is *The Rosary* a less admirable novel than *The Brothers Karamazov?* Because the amount of experience of all kinds understood, "felt into," as the Germans would say, and artistically re-created by Mrs. Barclay is small in comparison with that which Dostoevsky feelingly comprehended and knew so consummately well how to re-create in terms of the novelist's art. Dostoevsky covers all Mrs. Barclay's ground and a vast area beside. The pathetic parts of *The Old Curiosity Shop* are as poor in understood and artistically re-created experience as *The Rosary*—indeed, I think they are even poorer. At the same time they are vulgar (which *The Rosary*, that genuine masterpiece of the servants' hall, is not). They are vulgar, because their poverty is a pretentious poverty, because their disease (for the quality of Dickens's sentimentality is truly pathological) professes to be the most radiant health; because they protest their unintelligence, their lack of understanding with a vehemence of florid utterance that is not only shocking, but ludicrous.

GEORGE ORWELL: 1940

Charles Dickens

BY this time anyone who is a lover of Dickens, and who has read as far as this, will probably be angry with me.

I have been discussing Dickens simply in terms of his "message," and almost ignoring his literary qualities. But every writer, especially every novelist, *has* a "message," whether he admits it or not, and the minutest details of his work are influenced by it. All art is propaganda. Neither Dickens himself nor the majority of Victorian novelists would have thought of denying this. On the other hand, not all propaganda is art. As I said earlier, Dickens is one of those writers who are felt to be worth stealing. He has been stolen by Marxists, by Catholics and, above all, by Conservatives. The question is, What is there to steal? Why does anyone care about Dickens? Why do *I* care about Dickens?

That kind of question is never easy to answer. As a rule, an

From "Charles Dickens," *Inside the Whale* (London, 1940), Parts V and VI.

aesthetic preference is either something inexplicable or it is so corrupted by non-aesthetic motives as to make one wonder whether the whole of literary criticism is not a huge network of humbug. In Dickens's case the complicating factor is his familiarity. He happens to be one of those "great authors" who are ladled down everyone's throat in childhood. At the time this causes rebellion and vomiting, but it may have different after-effects in later life. For instance, nearly everyone feels a sneaking affection for the patriotic poems that he learned by heart as a child, "Ye Mariners of England," the "Charge of the Light Brigade" and so forth. What one enjoys is not so much the poems themselves as the memories they call up. And with Dickens the same forces of association are at work. Probably there are copies of one or two of his books lying about in an actual majority of English homes. Many children begin to know his characters by sight before they can even read, for on the whole Dickens was lucky in his illustrators. A thing that is absorbed as early as that does not come up against any critical judgment. And when one thinks of this, one thinks of all that is bad and silly in Dickens—the cast-iron "plots," the characters who don't come off, the _longueurs_, the paragraphs in blank verse, the awful pages of "pathos." And then the thought arises, when I say I like Dickens, do I simply mean that I like thinking about my childhood? Is Dickens merely an institution?

If so, he is an institution that there is no getting away from. How often one really thinks about any writer, even a writer one cares for, is a difficult thing to decide; but I should doubt whether anyone who has actually read Dickens can go a week without remembering him in one context or another. Whether you approve of him or not, he is _there_, like the Nelson Column. At any moment some scene or character, which may come from some book you cannot even remember the name of, is liable to drop into your mind. Micawber's letters! Winkle in the witness-box! Mrs. Gamp! Mrs. Wititterly and Sir Tumley Snuffim! Todgers's! (George Gissing said that when he passed the Monument it was never of the Fire of London that he thought, always of Todgers's.) Mrs. Leo Hunter! Squeers! Silas Wegg and the Decline and Fall-off of the Russian Empire! Miss Mills and the Desert of Sahara! Wopsle acting Hamlet! Mrs. Jellyby! Mantalini, Jerry Cruncher, Barkis, Pumblechook, Tracy Tupman, Skimpole, Joe Gargery, Pecksniff—and so it goes on and on. It is not so much a series of books, it is more like a world. And not a purely comic world either, for part of what one remembers in Dickens is his Victorian morbidity and necrophilia and the blood-and-thunder scenes—the death of Sikes, Krook's spontaneous combustion, Fagin in the condemned cell, the women knitting round the guillotine. To a surprising extent all this has entered even into the minds of people who do not care about it. A music-hall comedian can (or at any rate could quite recently) go on the stage and impersonate Micawber or Mrs. Gamp with a fair certainty of being understood, although not one in twenty of the audience had ever read a book of Dickens's right through. Even people who affect to despise him quote him unconsciously.

Dickens is a writer who can be imitated, up to a certain point. In genuinely popular literature—for instance, the Elephant and Castle version of *Sweeny Todd*—he has been plagiarised quite shamelessly. What has been imitated, however, is simply a tradition that Dickens himself took from earlier novelists and developed, the cult of "character," *i.e.*, eccentricity. The thing that cannot be imitated is his fertility of invention, which is invention not so much of characters, still less of "situations," as of turns of phrase and concrete details. The outstanding, unmistakable mark of Dickens's writing is the *unnecessary detail*. Here is an example of what I mean. The story given below is not particularly funny, but there is one phrase in it that is as individual as a fingerprint. Mr. Jack Hopkins, at Bob Sawyer's party, is telling the story of the child who swallowed its sister's necklace:

"Next day, child swallowed two beads; the day after that, he treated himself to three, and so on, till in a week's time he had got through the necklace—five-and-twenty beads in all. The sister, who was an industrious girl, and seldom treated herself to a bit of finery, cried her eyes out, at the loss of the necklace; looked high and low for it; but, I needn't say, didn't find it. A few days afterwards, the family were at dinner—baked shoulder of mutton, and potatoes under it—the child, who wasn't hungry, was playing about the room, when suddenly there was heard a devil of a noise, like a small hailstorm. 'Don't do that, my boy,' said the father. 'I aint a-doin' nothing,' said the child. 'Well, don't do it again,' said the father. There was a short silence, and then the noise began again, worse than ever. 'If you don't mind what I say, my boy,' said the father, 'you'll find yourself in bed, in something less than a pig's whisper.' He gave the child a shake to make him obedient, and such a rattling ensued as nobody ever heard before. 'Why, dam' me, it's *in* the child,' said the father, 'he's got the croup in the wrong place!' 'No I haven't father,' said the child, beginning to cry, 'it's the necklace; I swallowed it, father.' —The father caught the child up, and ran with him to the hospital; the beads in the boy's stomach rattling all the way with the jolting; and the people looking up in the air, and down in the cellars, to see where the unusual sound came from. 'He's in the hospital now,' said Jack Hopkins, 'and he makes such a devil of a noise when he walks about, that they're obliged to muffle him in a watchman's coat, for fear he should wake the patients.' "

As a whole, this story might come out of any nineteenth-century comic paper. But the unmistakable Dickens touch, the thing nobody else would have thought of, is the baked shoulder of mutton and potatoes under it. How does this advance the story? The answer is that it doesn't. It is something totally unnecessary, a florid little squiggle on the edge of the page; only, it is by just these squiggles that the special Dickens atmosphere is created. The other thing one would notice here is that Dickens's way of telling a story takes a long time. An interesting example, too long to quote, is Sam Weller's story of the obstinate patient in Chapter XLIV of *The Pickwick Papers*. As it happens, we have a standard of comparison here, because Dickens is plagiarising, consciously or unconsciously. The story is also told by some ancient Greek writer. I cannot now find the passage, but I read it years ago as a boy at school, and it runs more or less like this:

A certain Thracian, renowned for his obstinacy, was warned by his physician that if he drank a flagon of wine it would kill him. The Thracian thereupon drank the flagon of wine and immediately jumped off the house-top and perished. "For," said he, "in this way I shall prove that the wine did not kill me."

As the Greek tells it, that is the whole story—about six lines. As Sam Weller tells it, it takes round about a thousand words. Long before getting to the point we have been told all about the patient's clothes, his meals, his manners, even the newspapers he reads, and about the peculiar construction of the doctor's carriage, which conceals the fact that the coachman's trousers do not match his coat. Then there is the dialogue between the doctor and the patient. " 'Crumpets is wholesome, sir,' said the patient. 'Crumpets is *not* wholesome, sir,' says the doctor, wery fierce," etc. etc. In the end the original story has been buried under the details. And in all of Dickens's most characteristic passages it is the same. His imagination overwhelms everything, like a kind of weed. Squeers stands up to address his boys, and immediately we are hearing about Bolder's father who was two pounds ten short, and Mobbs's stepmother who took to her bed on hearing that Mobbs wouldn't eat fat and hoped Mr. Squeers would flog him into a happier state of mind. Mrs. Leo Hunter writes a poem, "Expiring Frog"; two full stanzas are given. Boffin takes a fancy to pose as a miser, and instantly we are down among the squalid biographies of eighteenth-century misers, with names like Vulture Hopkins and the Rev. Blewberry Jones, and chapter headings like "The Story of the Mutton Pies" and "The Treasures of a Dunghill." Mrs. Harris, who does not even exist, has more detail piled on to her than any three characters in an ordinary novel. Merely in the middle of a sentence we learn, for instance, that her infant nephew has been seen in a bottle at Greenwich Fair, along with the pink-eyed lady, the Prussian dwarf and the living skeleton. Joe Gargery describes how the robbers broke into the house of Pumblechook, the corn and seed merchant— "and they took his till, and they took his cashbox, and they drinked his wine, and they partook of his wittles, and they slapped his face, and they pulled his nose, and they tied him up to his bedpust, and they give him a dozen, and they stuffed his mouth full of flowering annuals to perwent his crying out." Once again the unmistakable Dickens touch, the flowering annuals; but any other novelist would only have mentioned about half of these outrages. Everything is piled up and up, detail on detail, embroidery on embroidery. It is futile to object that this kind of thing is rococo—one might as well make the same objection to a wedding-cake. Either you like it or you do not like it. Other nineteenth-century writers, Surtees, Barham, Thackeray, even Marryat, have something of Dickens's profuse, overflowing quality, but none of them on anything like the same scale. The appeal of all these writers now depends partly on period-flavour and though Marryat is still officially a "boy's writer" and Surtees has a sort of legendary fame among hunting men, it is probable that they are read mostly by bookish people.

Significantly, Dickens's most successful books (not his *best* books) are *The Pickwick Papers,* which is not a novel, and *Hard Times* and *A Tale of Two Cities,* which are not funny. As a novelist his natural fertility greatly hampers him, because the burlesque which he is never able to resist, is constantly breaking into what ought to be serious situations. There is a good example of this in the opening chapter of *Great Expectations.* The escaped convict, Magwitch, has just captured the six-year-old Pip in the churchyard. The scene starts terrifyingly enough, from Pip's point of view. The convict, smothered in mud and with his chain trailing from his leg, suddenly starts up among the tombs, grabs the child, turns him upside down and robs his pockets. Then he begins terrorising him into bringing food and a file:

He held me by the arms in an upright position on the top of the stone, and went on in these fearful terms:

"You bring me, to-morrow morning early, that file and them wittles. You bring the lot to me, at that old Battery over yonder. You do it, and you never dare to say a word or dare to make a sign concerning your having seen such a person as me, or any person sumever, and you shall be let to live. You fail, or you go from my words in any partickler, no matter how small it is, and your heart and your liver shall be tore out, roasted and ate. Now, I ain't alone, as you may think I am. There's a young man hid with me, in comparison with which young man I am an Angel. That young man hears the words I speak. That young man has a secret way pecooliar to himself, of getting at a boy, and at his heart, and at his liver. It is in wain for a boy to attempt to hide himself from that young man. A boy may lock his door, may be warm in bed, may tuck himself up, may draw the clothes over his head, may think himself comfortable and safe, but that young man will softly creep and creep his way to him and tear him open. I am akeeping that young man from harming of you at the present moment, with great difficulty. I find it wery hard to hold that young man off of your inside. Now, what do you say?"

Here Dickens has simply yielded to temptation. To begin with, no starving and hunted man would speak in the least like that. Moreover, although the speech shows a remarkable knowledge of the way in which a child's mind works, its actual words are quite out of tune with what is to follow. It turns Magwitch into a sort of pantomime wicked uncle, or, if one sees him through the child's eyes, into an appalling monster. Later in the book he is to be represented as neither, and his exaggerated gratitude, on which the plot turns, is to be incredible because of just this speech. As usual, Dickens's imagination has overwhelmed him. The picturesque details were too good to be left out. Even with characters who are more of a piece than Magwitch he is liable to be tripped up by some seductive phrase. Mr. Murdstone, for instance, is in the habit of ending David Copperfield's lessons every morning with a dreadful sum in arithmetic. "If I go into a cheesemonger's shop, and buy four thousand double-Gloucester cheeses at fourpence halfpenny each, present payment," it always begins. Once again the typical Dickens detail, the double-Gloucester cheeses. But it is far too human a touch for Murdstone; he would have made it five thousand cashboxes. Every time this note is struck, the unity of the novel suffers. Not that it matters very much, because Dickens is obviously a writer whose parts are greater than his wholes. He is all fragments, all details— rotten architecture, but wonderful gargoyles—and never better than when he is building up some character who will later on be forced to act inconsistently.

Of course it is not usual to urge against Dickens that he makes his characters behave inconsistently. Generally he is accused of doing just the opposite. His characters are supposed to be mere "types," each crudely representing some single trait and fitted with a kind of label by which you recognise him. Dickens is "only a caricaturist"—that is the usual accusation, and it does him both more and less than justice. To begin with, he did not think of himself as a caricaturist, and was constantly setting into action characters who ought to have been purely static. Squeers, Micawber, Miss Mowcher, Wegg, Skimpole, Pecksniff and many others are finally involved in "plots" where they are out of place and where they behave quite incredibly. They start off as magic-lantern slides and they end by getting mixed up in a third-rate movie. Sometimes one can put one's finger on a single sentence in which the original illusion is destroyed. There is such a sentence in *David Copperfield*. After the famous dinner-party (the one where the leg of mutton was underdone), David is showing his guests out. He stops Traddles at the top of the stairs:

"Traddles," said I, "Mr. Micawber don't mean any harm, poor fellow: but if I were you I wouldn't lend him anything."

"My dear Copperfield," returned Traddles smiling, "I haven't got anything to lend."

"You have got a name, you know," I said.

At the place where one reads it this remark jars a little though something of the kind was inevitable sooner or later. The story is a fairly realistic one, and David is growing up; ultimately he is bound to see Mr. Micawber for what he is, a cadging scoundrel. Afterwards, of course, Dickens's sentimentality overcomes him and Micawber is made to turn over a new leaf. But from then on, the original Micawber is never quite recaptured, in spite of desperate efforts. As a rule, the "plot" in which Dickens's characters get entangled is not particularly credible, but at least it makes some pretence at reality, whereas the world to which they belong is a never-never land, a kind of eternity. But just here one sees that "only a caricaturist" is not really a condemnation. The fact that Dickens is always thought of as a caricaturist, although he was constantly trying to be something else, is perhaps the surest mark of his genius. The monstrosities that he created are still remembered as monstrosities, in spite of getting mixed up in would-be probable melodramas. Their first impact is so vivid that nothing that comes afterwards effaces it. As with the people one knew in childhood, one seems always to remember them in one particular attitude, doing one particular thing. Mrs. Squeers is always ladling out brimstone and treacle, Mrs. Gummidge is always weeping, Mrs. Gargery is always banging her husband's head against the wall, Mrs. Jellyby is always scribbling tracts while her children fall into the area—and there they all are, fixed up for ever like little twinkling miniatures painted on snuffbox lids, completely fantastic and incredible, and yet somehow more solid and infinitely more memorable than the efforts of serious novelists. Even by the standards of his time Dickens was an exceptionally artificial writer. As Ruskin said, he "chose to work in a circle of stage fire." His characters are even more distorted and simplified than Smollett's. But there are no rules in novel-writing, and for any work of art there is only one test worth bothering about—survival. By this test Dickens's characters have succeeded, even if the people who remember them hardly think of them as human beings. They are monsters, but at any rate they *exist*.

But all the same there is a disadvantage in writing about monsters. It amounts to this, that it is only certain moods that Dickens can speak to. There are large areas of the human mind that he never touches. There is no poetic feeling anywhere in his books, and no genuine tragedy, and even sexual love is almost outside his scope. Actually his books are not so sexless as they are sometimes declared to be, and considering the time in which he was writing, he is reasonably frank. But there is not a trace in him of the feeling that one finds in *Manon Lescaut, Salammbô, Carmen, Wuthering Heights*. According to Aldous Huxley, D. H. Lawrence once said that Balzac was "a gigantic dwarf," and in a sense the same is true of Dickens. There are whole worlds which he either knows nothing about or does not wish to mention. Except in a rather roundabout way, one cannot *learn* very much from Dickens. And to say this is to think almost immediately of the great Russian novelists of the nineteenth century. Why is it that Tolstoy's grasp seems to be so much larger than Dickens's—why is it that he seems able to tell you so much more *about yourself?* It is not that he is more gifted, or even, in the last analysis, more intelligent. It is because he is writing about people who are growing. His characters are struggling to make their souls, whereas Dickens's are already finished and perfect. In my own mind Dickens's people are present far more often and far more vividly than Tolstoy's, but always in a single unchangeable attitude, like pictures or pieces of furniture. You cannot hold an imaginary conversation with a Dickens character as you can with, say, Peter Bezoukhov. And this is not merely because of Tolstoy's greater seriousness, for there are also comic characters that you can imagine yourself talking to—Bloom, for instance, or Pécuchet, or even Wells's Mr. Polly. It is because Dickens's characters have no mental life. They say perfectly the thing that they have to say, but they cannot be conceived as talking about anything else. They never learn, never speculate. Perhaps the most meditative of his characters is Paul Dombey, and his thoughts are mush. Does this mean that Tolstoy's novels are "better" than Dickens's? The truth is that it is absurd to make such comparisons in terms of "better" and "worse." If I were forced to compare Tolstoy with Dickens, I should say that Tolstoy's appeal will probably be wider in the long run, because Dickens is scarcely intelligible outside the English-speaking culture; on the other hand, Dickens is able to reach simple people, which Tolstoy is not. Tolstoy's characters can cross a frontier, Dickens's can be portrayed on a cigarette-card. But one is no more obliged to choose between them than between a sausage and a rose. Their purposes barely intersect.

If Dickens had been *merely* a comic writer, the chances are that no one would now remember his name. Or at best a few of his books would survive in rather the same way as books like *Frank Fairleigh*, *Mr. Verdant Green* and *Mrs. Caudle's Curtain Lectures*, as a sort of hangover of the Victorian atmosphere, a pleasant little whiff of oysters and brown stout. Who has not felt sometimes that it was "a pity" that Dickens ever deserted the vein of *Pickwick* for things like *Little Dorrit* and *Hard Times?* What people always demand of a popular novelist is that he shall write the same book over and over again, forgetting that a man who would write the same book twice could not even write it once. Any writer who is not utterly lifeless moves upon a kind of parabola, and the downward curve is implied in the upper one. Joyce has to start with the frigid competence of *Dubliners* and end with the dream-language of *Finnegan's Wake*, but *Ulysses* and *Portrait of the Artist* are part of the trajectory. The thing that drove Dickens forward into a form of art for which he was not really suited, and at the same time caused us to remember him, was simply the fact that he was a moralist, the consciousness of "having something to say." He is always preaching a sermon, and that is the final secret of his inventiveness. For you can only create if you can *care*. Types like Squeers and Micawber could not have been produced by a hack writer looking for something to be funny about. A joke worth laughing at always has an idea behind it, and usually a subversive idea. Dickens is able to go on being funny because he is in revolt against authority, and authority is always there to be laughed at. There is always room for one more custard pie.

His radicalism is of the vaguest kind, and yet one always knows that it is there. That is the difference between being a moralist and a politician. He has no constructive suggestions, not even a clear grasp of the nature of the society he is attacking, only an emotional perception that something is wrong. All he can finally say is, "Behave decently," which, as I suggested earlier, is not necessarily so shallow as it sounds. Most revolutionaries are potential Tories, because they imagine that everything can be put right by altering the *shape* of society; once that change is effected, as it sometimes is, they see no need for any other. Dickens has not this kind of mental coarseness. The vagueness of his discontent is the mark of its permanence. What he is out against is not this or that institution, but, as Chesterton put it, "an expression on the human face." Roughly speaking, his morality is the Christian morality, but in spite of his Anglican upbringing he was essentially a Bible-Christian, as he took care to make plain when writing his will. In any case he cannot properly be described as a religious man. He "believed," undoubtedly, but religion in the devotional sense does not seem to have entered much into his thoughts. Where he is Christian is in his quasi-instinctive siding with the oppressed against the oppressors. As a matter of course he is on the side of the underdog, always and everywhere. To carry this to its logical conclusion one has got to change sides when the underdog becomes an upperdog, and in fact Dickens does tend to do so. He loathes the Catholic Church, for instance, but as soon as the Catholics are persecuted (*Barnaby Rudge*) he is on their side. He loathes the aristocratic class even more, but as soon as they are really overthrown (the revolutionary chapters in *A Tale of Two Cities*) his sympathies swing round. Whenever he departs from this emotional attitude he goes astray. A well-known example is at the ending of *David Copperfield*, in which everyone who reads it feels that something has gone wrong. What is wrong is that the closing chapters are pervaded, faintly but not noticeably, by the cult of success. It is the gospel according to Smiles, instead of the gospel according to Dickens. The attractive, out-at-elbow characters are got rid of, Micawber makes a fortune, Heep gets into prison—both of these events are flagrantly impossible—and even Dora is killed off to make way for Agnes. If you like, you can read Dora as Dickens's wife and Agnes as his sister-in-law, but the essential point is that Dickens has "turned respectable" and done violence to his own nature. Perhaps that is why Agnes is the most disagreeable of his heroines, the real legless angel of Victorian romance, almost as bad as Thackeray's Laura.

No grown-up person can read Dickens without feeling his limitations, and yet there does remain his native generosity of mind, which acts as a kind of anchor and nearly always keeps him where he belongs. It is probably the central secret of his popularity. A good-tempered antinomianism rather of Dickens's type is one of the marks of Western popular culture. One sees it in folk-stories and comic songs, in dream-figures like Mickey Mouse and Pop-eye the Sailor (both of them variants of Jack the Giant-killer), in the history of working-class Socialism, in the popular protests (always ineffective but not always a sham) against imperialism, in the impulse that makes a jury award ex-

cessive damages when a rich man's car runs over a poor man; it
is the feeling that one is always on the wrong side of the underdog, on the side of the weak against the strong. In one sense it
is a feeling that is fifty years out of date. The common man is
still living in the mental world of Dickens, but nearly every
modern intellectual has gone over to some or other form of
totalitarianism. From the Marxist or Fascist point of view, nearly
all that Dickens stands for can be written off as "bourgeois
morality." But in moral outlook no one could be more "bourgeois"
than the English working classes. The ordinary people in the
Western countries have never entered, mentally, into the world
of "realism" and power-politics. They may do so before long,
in which case Dickens will be as out of date as the cab-horse. But
in his own age and ours he has been popular chiefly because he
was able to express in a comic, simplified and therefore memorable form the native decency of the common man. And it is
important that from this point of view people of very different
types can be described as "common." In a country like England,
in spite of its class-structure, there does exist a certain cultural
unity. All through the Christian ages, and especially since the
French Revolution, the Western world has been haunted by the
idea of freedom and equality; it is only an *idea*, but it has penetrated to all ranks of society. The most atrocious injustices, cruelties, lies, snobberies exist everywhere, but there are not many
people who can regard these things with the same indifference as,
say, a Roman slave-owner. Even the millionaire suffers from a
vague sense of guilt, like a dog eating a stolen leg of mutton.
Nearly everyone, whatever his actual conduct may be, responds
emotionally to the idea of human brotherhood. Dickens voiced
a code which was and on the whole still is believed in, even by
people who violate it. It is difficult otherwise to explain why he
could be both read by working people (a thing that has happened to no other novelist of his stature) and buried in Westminster Abbey.

When one reads any strongly individual piece of writing, one has the impression of seeing a face somewhere behind the page. It is not necessarily the actual face of the writer. I feel this very strongly with Swift, with Defoe, with Fielding, Stendhal, Thackeray, Flaubert, though in several cases I do not know what these people looked like and do not want to know. What one sees is the face that the writer *ought* to have. Well, in the case of Dickens I see a face that is not quite the face of Dickens's photographs, though it resembles it. It is the face of a man of about forty, with a small beard and a high colour. He is laughing, with a touch of anger in his laughter, but no triumph, no malignity. It is the face of a man who is always fighting against something, but who fights in the open and is not frightened, the face of a man who is *generously angry*—in other words, of a nineteenth-century liberal, a free intelligence, a type hated with equal hatred by all the smelly little orthodoxies which are now contending for our souls.

"ALAIN":   1940

Imagination in the Novel

WHAT is it to imagine? What is the imagination? I want to erase the common assumption we all try to get by on, that the imagination is only a storehouse of memories. I had already seen the inadequacy of this assumption even before I read Malebranche, whose theory of the imagination is admirably sturdy,

Revue de Paris, 1 March 1940, pp. 47–52; also, *En lisant Dickens* (Paris, 1945).

a real step ahead of Descartes'. Fundamentally, the imagination is tied up with the feelings. Imagination is a sort of *a priori* contemplation, which consists in viewing my feeling from a distance, thereby coloring my contemplation and giving it the substance of a world. The best example I know of that sort of enchantment when confronted by a major image is in *David Copperfield*. Every time we draw near to Yarmouth and the drama that takes place there, Dickens evokes the great cloud over the town, as if it had waited for us at every turning of the story. The resulting effect of terror drives us on toward that terrible storm, which thus becomes the central focus of the world of the novel. For the reader to control his thoughts in such a way, by an aroused feeling, is to imagine and not to remember. Memory is simply not enough to explain what happens. For every reader of fiction has sensed that very simple images are often especially insistent, that such images recur and overwhelm us. Similarly, there is the Clennam house in *Little Dorrit*. Every time we confront it, we feel an effect of terror, or mystery, or call it what you will, so violent that it brings the very stones and timbers to life. Why? I suspect it is because Dickens exaggerates. The Clennam house is so somber and tottering that we expect much from it, and even when the action in the novel avoids the house, we can never forget it. This characteristic exaggeration, a bit forced perhaps, gives substance to the parts of that tottering house as well as to Jeremiah Flintwinch (the man already hanged), and even to the visions of his wife. Briefly, then, the imagination may be described as a prelude to feeling, quite simply a foreboding. It is very important to know this, for to the extent that a novelist has not imbued with feeling a certain point of focus, he takes us everywhere in vain; nothing is real. His images are vapid, and we recognize their unreality. They are as unreal as the illustrations sometimes used in novels, whereas the true image, the real image, obliterates all illustrations. Ultimately, we read only for such true images, and only for them do we slow down our pace of reading so as to taste fully this foreboding. The intense feeling stirred by the image arouses and fires the imagination. And often the magic image is contained in a few words and is very simple.

Another example is the valley in Balzac's *Lilies of the Valley*. Each time we see the valley, on arrival either from Pont-de-Ruan or from Sache, it takes possession of us. We never stop re-reading such books, even as far as to repeat to ourselves with joy some simple words, such as "Clochegourde," which, in effect, arouse the tenderest melancholy. These effects depend on what may be called an atmosphere. Thus, the imagination does not consist in producing a certain appearance of things and of people; the memory does that, and the images thus composed have no force. Whereas the atmospheric descriptions within Balzac's novels and those within Stendhal's make you "believe yourself there." Such is the witchcraft. A description can consist of a few words or of pages; it is not the preciseness of details that acts on the reader. Instead, imaginative descriptions act as apparitions. The author brings them back from Hades, and that is perhaps why, like Orpheus, he has not the right to look too much on his Eurydice. He pays for love, he returns the victor, and his description throws inexplicable gleams. For example, there is a small doorway in the story of the misfortunes of Fabrizio that I believe I see and touch; yet it is only named. But it deeply stirs the thoughts; to name it is enough to carry the reader to the highest point of emotion and curiosity.

When the child believes that he sees a ghost, he cannot describe what he sees; nothing replaces the presence, which produces at once its own effect. In just that way, the dreamer Fabrizio experiences the streets and passages which are present to him; because they are in his dream before appearing to his senses. This presentiment is what he describes, for the emotion evokes the objects and makes them present. The description is in reality only a way of drawing on presentiment and expectation, out of which is made an atmosphere which is not at all a complete scene but rather a color and a resonance. At once, I am among the roadways of Fabrizio, and I recognize that melancholy brother, who again seeks me to tell me his melancholy. All the power of the novel comes from that effect and from those roadways that open before the reader.

Thus, those Dickens heroes who take to the road view magically all that happens on their journey. All becomes moving; all takes on grandeur. The narrative of *The Old Curiosity Shop* amounts to a journey from the city to the village; yet Dickens' mystical vision of the old man and the young girl, who go forth alone into the world, is enough to color all they meet. The novelist, at such moments, is inspired. Everything arouses him and gives him eloquence. For another example from *The Old Curiosity Shop*, there is the episode of the school, which stirs us inexplicably by a sort of spontaneous symbolism. In that episode, also, there is implied a destiny which is in turn symbolised by the journey. Hence come these outbursts of happiness, of hope, of tenderness, or melancholy, which are the atmosphere of that mystical journey.

A Dickens novel consists of roadways extended beneath clouds of feelings. In this respect the *Christmas Books* (and *The Old Curiosity Shop* is in effect one of them) are evocations which unfold, as does the journey of Scrooge, out of an atmosphere heaped-up, heavy, smoky, from which the novelist seems to form his figures and make a world where joy, sorrow, friendship, and solitude are multiplied and reflected as by the echoes of a somber substance. The Spirit leads Scrooge forth and makes real to him the world of a Christmas night. This power to call forth is hardly strange to Dickens' nature, and I see him first creating by fiery feeling the Chaos out of which he will in turn create his novel. While reading *Bleak House* I seem to remember having followed through the London streets a certain George, a retired soldier, a creation as fanciful as his shooting-gallery, and his assistant armorer speckled with powder burns. And to the extent that

I had become involved in following that caricature of an old soldier, every thing in the novel was more real, the streets and the people, and even the story of Lady Dedlock—which may be artistically questionable, but is very moving. In other Dickens novels too the least trait, when stressed, gave me at once the expected object, as if the exaggeration underlined the design. I think here of those enormous creations, ridiculous and hardly believable, Micawber, Quilp, Cuttle. What suggestive power in these fantastic faces! The realistic profiles are then conspicuous by contrast. For example, the lobster-like major marvelously sets off Edith's mother and prepares the most tragic scenes of *Dombey*, which grow out of the idea of that ancient fool who is pleased with herself for having sold her daughter at a good price. Thus, the institution of marriage is turned inside out and judged by the effect of these enormous caricatures, in all of which appears Dickens' powerful imagination. I would call it constructive and not at all reproductive. Major Bagstock reproduces nothing, resembles nothing; but, like a master of ceremonies, he announces a carnival hardly ordinary; and the reader is prepared for all, that is to say for the novel of Edith Dombey and of the trusted man with the cat's smile, a novel where there is no love, yet which produces violent drama. That Edith should trick her husband, to punish him, with his close confidant and agent, these feelings must be made ready for. And nothing aids these actions better than Major Bagstock, a lens that enlarges all. The task of the imagination is to construct that sort of lens. That is what sets off the happenings. In reality, nothing is flatter than a household quarrel. But the above take place full-length in the mirror of the world where one sees Bagstock.

Many Englishmen, such as Smith and Hutcheson, have constructed analyses of sympathy, explaining habits by a mechanism of gestures and emotions. Hence I am not surprised to find in an English novel that kind of psychology. For example, what does the actor serve for? He serves to establish certain bonds of sympathy between the character and the spectator. That comes about because all the emotions of the actor, my alter-ego, have an effect on me; if, for example, he is afraid, or if he is too hot. It is an ordinary theory, that is not hard to understand. I cannot but be astonished at finding no trace of it in Dickens. Dickens is absolutely not a psychologist; he does not know how to maneuver the fine points of sympathy and friendship.

What, then, is this man Dickens? How has he penetrated so deeply into the passions, almost always cracking the feeble shell and breaking through corrupt conventionality? I believe that he has proceeded by magnification. He has arrived, like Shakespeare, at the final answer. Thus, Edith replies to Dombey: "I will be exhibited to no one, as the refractory slave you purchased, at such a time. If I kept my marriage-day, I would keep it · as a day of shame." Here the respectable commonplaces are broken up. Here woman appears with her rights and her duties. Here woman exposes systematically her slave's ethic. For it is absurd and injurious to order love like a slave's duty. And by that we can learn to understand the great lady of *Bleak House*. At least, it is according to this principle that the noble lord has understood his wife. Dickens has thus invented a new love; he is as new as was Fielding in *Tom Jones*. Understand that men, and above all women, no longer wish to listen to the insipid speeches by which we reproach them for sometimes doing what pleases them.

From Dickens, we would indeed be able to acquire a profound psychology. But what is it? Two of Dickens' inventions are without match. These are two imaginary characters who exist only to make known the opinions of the persons who invented them. This kind of invention is only the result of a very well-known imaginative process; I imagine very often that I am having a conversation with a friend, who is always supposed to understand me and approve of me. From this, Dickens has invented with pleasure Mrs. Harris, the intimate friend of Mrs. Gamp, the Shakespearean nurse of *Chuzzlewit:* " 'Mrs. Harris,' I says, 'leave the bottle on the chimley-piece, and don't ask me to take none, but let me put my lips to it when I am so dispoged, and then I will do what I'm engaged to do, according to the best of my ability.' " The invention has an admirable scope, for we soon know that there is no Mrs. Harris, and at the same time we reproach ourselves for knowing it; finally we find ourselves in the very house of Mrs. Harris, and then it is too clear that Mrs. Gamp has lost her precious friend.

There is another example, less brilliant, of a character that one makes speak in order to express one's own thoughts. The father of Dora in *David Copperfield,* who is a lawyer at Doctor's Commons, has an associate who, according to him, refuses everything. We perceive finally that the latter is a good man who never has an opinion. This type of humor is moderate; also, it does not flower in adventure novels but in novels of customs and of characters, such as *Copperfield* or *Chuzzlewit;* it is also the type of *Nickleby.* Within these novels we find some psychology properly speaking; for example, the false opinion that we form out of the ordinary thoughts of others. Copperfield believes that he has an enemy, the young butcher, against whom he has fought. After some time, he discovers that the young butcher is very calm and very polite. That happens twice, and it is a lesson for the well-meaning David, who has just barely been responsible for his error.

These are observations that any reader makes quite easily. But still they suffice to put Dickens at the first rank of moralists. Indeed, he is there, and even higher, by a profound and diabolic manner of making our own image grimace in the mirror he holds out to us. For example, the grimace of Quilp in place of a human face. One knows that Dickens paints marvelously the naïve tricks of lovers, but if one wishes something profound on love let him go seek out, in *Dombey,* the exchanges between Dombey and Edith, or, in *Copperfield,* the exchanges between Steerforth and Miss Dartle.

What is astonishing is that Dickens, who knew and loved the theater, had never thought seriously of writing a play; and it seems to me that his best novels are too long to be transposed into the theater. But we know that Dickens declaimed his works in public with an astonishing success, and that act was partly of the theater. He, the author, was a physical support to the characters. It would be necessary, to grasp the idea, to have heard the famous readings of Copeau, who himself read not novels but pieces for the theater. By analysis of these activities, one would know better what the theater is and what the actor serves for. Indeed, the reader of novels has no need at all of either illustrations or actors. But the theater is even more clear than the novel, establishing its character by means of a living man, who moreover can be very mediocre and yet play Augustus. In this there is a certain shift of the imagination which interests me very much. There is a play of sympathy; for that actor who is afraid and who has forgotten his role makes me afraid myself, and, carried away by this effect, I am at once in sympathy with Augustus. "Let us be friends, Cinna." One approaches still more the pleasure of the spectator if one plays a role as an amateur. This sharing among two is very human. "I would say it just as well," says the spectator. The reader is almost the same sort of person. Only, to read aloud is very difficult. Myself, I have always read aloud badly, confusingly, and yet not without effect. This form of representation is very powerful, yet remarkably enough, it loses all force when it arrives at perfection; perhaps we then count too much on the reader, and feel no longer the effect of surprise, so appreciable always in verse.

The novelist does not advise; he orders; he follows his favorites, as if his characters lead him. Also, he is clever enough to maintain that he only observes his characters, with curiosity. Clearly there is something artificial here, a dance before the literary mirror. Yet I believe that the novelist who speaks thus expresses a true bond between himself and his characters. Also,

I will not say that he has imagined it. No. Rather, he rediscovers them; he observes them. The part of the novel thus played by the characters before the author is the *donnée*, the mainstay of the narration. When the narration is inspired, that indicates a powerful feeling by which the author recognizes himself and serves his own happiness. It is in this sense that a very ordinary narration can be as great as an epic. Such are the first pages of the *Charterhouse of Parma*.

What is the tone of a true narration? One would say that the author abstains from showing himself, from whence come words stripped and active, that is to say, words which do not seem contrived for an effect. True narration is a type of singing whose model is: "It is the madness, Goddess, that you are going to sing, the madness of Achilles, son of Peleus." This kind of opening is lively and full of force. There is no true novel without such openings. At such a moment, I say to myself: "There is an author who knows what he means. There he goes, let's follow!" Now, I understand that while he leads me on thus he does not still imagine. The description and the narration are not objects of the imagination, but rather a translation of the winged pace of memory. An author without prudence will believe on the contrary that so much as he can change and choose, at that point he imagines; and thus, judging his narration very exact, and no less interesting than another, he will think that the story of a novel must be invented. But no. It is not at all invented; on the contrary, it is recollected, like a fact of memory, like a thing of nature. For example, the prince of Parma was killed; that may be, but in order for the spirit of the novel to take it to itself, it must become part of the current of affairs. There is a repercussion of this reality on the impact of the story and on the feelings. The reader recognizes a fresh event, which strikes him. In other terms, we find again in that art tangible reality and its satisfactions. People will say that this solidness of fact depends on the force of the imagination. But not at all; the force of imagination consists in endowing a very simple recollection with the force of an hallucination. The imagination, among the great classics, depends not on the imagined object but on the number of active responses aroused and on their shock-power. A clear memory of remorse is quite calm in appearance; but then the flow of such active responses bombards it and makes it terrible. The examples of powerful images that I have taken from Dickens clarify this little-explored process. Dickens, among the novelists, is remarkable by this power of thrusting us at the image which gives his universe a magic resonance.

A Note on Edmund Wilson's "Dickens: The Two Scrooges"

EDMUND WILSON'S long essay on Dickens is undoubtedly the most important critical statement on Dickens of the last twenty-five years. It grew out of a course Wilson gave in the summer school at the University of Chicago in 1939, was first published in part in the *New Republic* in the spring of 1940, and was published in full as the opening essay of *The Wound and the Bow* in 1941. It has directly stimulated much of the best recent criticism of Dickens.

The editors regret that considerations of length and copyright make it impossible to reprint here either the whole essay or a part that would do justice to the whole. Instead they wish, by this note, to remind the reader that Wilson's essay is readily available in *Eight Essays,* an inexpensive reprint, and that the essay belongs in the library of any serious student of Dickens.

In 1948, in the prefatory note to the revised and enlarged edition of *The Triple Thinkers,* Wilson underlined the major scope and intent of his essay on Dickens by stating: "the social and moral criticism embodied in Dickens' later novels have not had justice done to them." Thanks in part to Wilson's own example, this statement is much less true today.

REX WARNER: 1947

On Reading Dickens

CERTAINLY it is a part of Dickens' method to exaggerate rather than to minimise his subjects, and this exaggeration of certain qualities in people leads to sentimentality; but Dickens' view of life is very far from being sentimental. His romantic heroes and heroines, uniformly honourable, reliable and uninteresting, seem to have been designed to cater for the prevailing taste for melodrama and the happy-ever-after conclusion. But these characters are the thinnest and the most quickly forgotten of his creations, and when we consider his development it is important to notice that they hardly appear at all in his later work. One may admit that Dickens could hardly have read Freud; that

From "On Reading Dickens," *The Cult of Power* (New York, 1947).

in so far as his work is concerned with the relations between the sexes he is less revolutionary than are some modern authors; that he held the conventional view of the desirability of a happy marriage. But this is not to say that he was either prudish or un-observant. He criticised remorselessly what he saw around him. The frozen boredom of Sir Leicester and Lady Dedlock, the sacrifice of pride to property that marks the marriage of Edith and Mr. Dombey, the whole world of that great upholder of the sanctity of the home, Podsnap—these are sufficient proofs that Dickens has none of that satisfaction with what is assumed to exist which is the mark of both prudery and sentimentality.

These characters, and many others, are forgotten by those who tax Dickens with being an "optimist." It is a vague enough indictment; for if an optimist means one who believes that every-thing is for the best in the best of all possible worlds, Dickens most obviously was not such a person. If, on the other hand, it means one who can see a real goodness in human nature which can be, in spite of all arguments to the contrary, admired and loved, then nearly all writers have been optimists. In the mouth of our imaginary critic the charge will probably mean simply that Dickens' view of the world was a more encouraging one than that, say, of Thomas Hardy. This criticism will be found to mean little more than that the two writers were looking at the world from quite different angles, Hardy from a philosophical and Dickens from a social point of view.

Here we must return again to the Victorians and notice that, on the whole, they seem to have been the last people in Europe to realise what was going on about them. It was not until the end of their period that it became generally observed that the intellectual, moral and religious principles of their life had been undermined and shaken by the course of events. This was a fact which had been noticed long ago by Tolstoy and Dostoievsky, and the modern development of the novel, by them in Russia, by Hardy in England, was made possible simply because the

authors and a growing element of society had come to doubt the
religious and philosophic assumptions on which their societies
were based and were thus impelled to turn their minds towards
subjects which, before then, had found no place in novels. Dickens
is not a philosopher and in his work he appears no more perplexed
by religious and philosophical theories than had been Fielding
or Smollett, the English picaresque novelists in whose tradition
he wrote, who desired to, and did both instruct and entertain,
but who had no ambition to criticise or even to define the
intellectual foundations of their life. The economic and social
foundations of life were certainly criticised by Dickens, though
from an emotional rather than from a philosophical standpoint.
What he observed with growing clarity as his work developed,
was the glaring inconsistency between the assumptions on which
society was based and society itself. He did not doubt the
assumptions, and so the hypocrisies of actual fact were the more
apparent to him. Writing in the tradition of Fielding, he is both
a satirist and an entertainer, but as his work develops, the element of satire grows more and more in severity and outspoken-
ness. His later books contain no beneficent deities like Pickwick
or the brothers Cheeryble whose part had been to irradiate
jollity and philanthropy over all deserving characters just as
the curtain was going down. In the thirty years from the date
of *The Pickwick Papers* until Dickens' death there is a continual
development that is away from "optimism."

Even in *The Pickwick Papers* Dickens appears not merely as
an entertainer but also as a satirist. His lifelong hatred of the
law is expressed savagely enough in the characters of Dodson
and Fogg, and the description of the debtor's prison in which
Mr. Pickwick is confined is by no means an exercise of wit. Still
it remains true that the book is, as a whole, a comedy in the
English romantic tradition, although Mr. Pickwick, as the book
proceeds, grows into more of a "character" than anything which
has appeared previously in the English novel. From a retired

businessman interested in local antiquities he swells into a kind
of English Dionysus, dispensing good-will and jollity over his
whole environment. Indeed, at one point it almost appears that
Pickwick and Sam are going to turn into something bigger still,
and the book into something which, like *Don Quixote*, is as
close to tragedy as to comedy. But Dickens is not a philosopher,
and Mr. Pickwick emerges from the debtor's prison more or
less as his own rosy, beneficent and amiable self. The book ends
in an atmosphere of handshakes, tenderness and virtue. The good
are all rewarded; the wicked either punished or reformed.

In *Nicholas Nickleby* too there is the conventional happy
ending. This time it is the brothers Cheeryble, to us quite incredibly beneficent employers of labour, who fill the parts of
fairy-godmother and gods from the machine. Dickens tells us
that these characters were drawn from life, and there is no reason
to disbelieve him. But such characters were soon, whether they
liked it or not, overwhelmed by the tide of progress in competition. The scene was becoming grimmer and grimmer, and
Dickens observed it. There are no more Cheerybles after *Nicholas Nickleby*. Indeed in his next book, *The Old Curiosity Shop*,
though there is still one character left to fill the part of a Pickwick by scrupulously correct conduct and considerate treatment
of his employees, his part is a very subordinate one and the
impression he makes is small compared with that of Quilp and
Mr. and Miss Brass. Little Nell, too, for all her virtue, is actually
driven to death. In her story and that of her half-mad grandfather we notice very clearly that allegorical method which
Dickens develops even further in his later work. There is the
old man driven mad by his pursuit of money by gambling, his
belief that his great vice is a means to a good end, namely the
making of his grandchild into a "lady," and the result of all this
is her early death. The fantastic company in which the two find
themselves in their wanderings, even the sentimentality and strain
of some of the scenes between the girl and the old man suggest

that in this part of the book Dickens is describing forces which are bigger than the characters themselves, and is embodying in his people and scenery the cruelties and delusions which he observes in a wider society.

And from now on the novels, though they still show an unwavering faith in human nature, show less and less faith in human society as it was then and is still constituted. *Martin Chuzzlewit* is an important landmark. It contains scenes of extremely bitter satire on American life, and it is important to understand the reason for the bitterness. Dickens, with his faith in human nature once it should become uninhibited by an oppressive social structure, had looked towards America with the kind of hope and enthusiasm which today many socialists have felt for Soviet Russia. His visit to America shocked him profoundly; for, though he noticed and commented upon many admirable features of American life, he observed that in this "land of the free" the tyranny of money was no less powerful, and much more openly admitted, than he knew it to be in England. Slavery was still in existence, and yet the American editors were as ready to glorify falsely the perfection of their constitution as were the English editors and the parliamentarians whom he had left behind. Dickens was not a great political theorist, but he was very much of a radical and held firmly to the radical notion that human nature is essentially good and is, when freed from the obvious encumbrances of stupid and inhuman restraints, capable of betterment. In America he expected to find free men who, because of their freedom, would be good. And when he discovered that in the rising cities of the coast freedom depended on dollars as in England it depended on pounds, he reacted violently. It does him credit that his disappointment did not result in his becoming, like Wordsworth, a "lost leader." Disillusioned about America, he did not react so far as to doubt whether what he had seen in England as evil was in fact what he had thought. His feeling, not for theories, but for human beings, was too warm for that, and even in *Martin Chuzzlewit* the palm of villainy is carried off by Pecksniff, the representative of English middle-class respectability.

And his next novel, *Dombey & Son,* carries his social criticism much further. Here it is not a mean and obscure hypocrite like Pecksniff but the head of a great business house, a pillar of London mercantile society, who is brought to abject ruin by his pride in his possessions and in his name. Here, as in *Bleak House,* and as in all Dickens' later works, we feel the author's outraged sense of the tyranny of the machine, whether social or legal or economic, over the human being of flesh and blood. Nor did Dickens see, as the more facile optimists of his day saw, any great hope of amelioration in the rising industrialism of the time. *Hard Times* shows that the tyranny of modern "efficiency" is just as disgusting to him as are the tyrannies of feudal pride, of inhuman religion, or of stupid parliamentarianism. More and more does he turn his mind to the thought of human suffering that is irremediable. *Great Expectations* is an ironical title, and the book is dominated by the two figures of the escaped convict and the old, mad, deserted bride. The very scenery changes. There are not any more of those sparkling coach rides which the Pickwickians enjoyed. Instead we notice the fog that pervades London and the High Court of Chancery at the beginning of *Bleak House,* or the wilder fog and rain over the marshes in *Great Expectations.*

This development is by no means the record of an incorrigible optimist consistently surveying the world through rose-coloured spectacles. The truth is that, though Dickens' amazing energy and insight are directed towards all parts of his work, he tends, as he grows older, to concentrate them more and more on the less "pleasant" aspects of his environment. He does, it is true, retain to the last a faith, perhaps a somewhat naïve faith, in the essential goodness of human nature, a goodness which is revealed in those characters who are unspoilt by a longing for power, money, prestige, or by the effects of a mechanical social pressure. Such characters are children, one or two retired gentlemen of the old school, and many working-class families which are just above the starvation level. He makes it clear that, in his view, it is intolerable that the human spirit, essentially good, should be warped and twisted by institutions that are heartless or passions which are inhuman. In this sense he is didactic and a preacher; but so are the majority of great writers.

It has often been emphasised that one result of Dickens' work was the abolition of many of the specific wrongs which he attacked. Schools like Dotheboys Hall, for example, no longer exist. This is true, but we should not assume from this that Dickens was merely a social reformer with well-meant but facile remedies for the ills of the world. Actually he was remarkably proof against the illusion of necessary progress, and the great medicines of science and education, unfailing panaceas for later liberals, seem to have afforded Dickens nothing but an unpleasant taste in the mouth. As for amelioration by political methods it is sufficient to quote a sentence from his letters in which he refers to "my hope to have made every man in England feel something of the contempt for the House of Commons that I have. We shall never do anything until the sentiment is universal."

It is this hatred for the insincerity of institutions, this faith in the goodness, if unperverted, of human nature, this English anarchism which, expressed with the exuberance of genius, has made Dickens' characters into household words. But here, finally, our imaginary literary man will interpose and tell us that Dickens, having been born, unluckily for himself, before either Freud or Proust, was of necessity debarred from the creation of anything that can rightly be called a character. He could only manage caricatures; or, to use Mr. E. M. Forster's phrase, he could only produce "flat" as contrasted with "round" characters.

Mr. Forster's distinction between "flat" and "round" is an interesting one. "Dickens' people," he says, "are nearly all 'flat,' " and he seems to imply that this flatness is something rather reprehensible. And yet Dickens is a great author, and the contradiction puzzles Mr. Forster. "Those who dislike Dickens," he says, "have an excellent case. He ought to be bad. He is actually one of our big writers, and his immense success with types suggests that there may be more in flatness than the severer critics admit."

Mr. Forster himself is not among the "severer critics," though he allows them "an excellent case"; his rather wistful surprise that Dickens is as great as he knows him to be is as though Dickens were a cricketer who had hit a six over the bowler's head off a ball which, according to all the text-books should have been dealt with by means of the late cut. And it seems possible that the text-books which Mr. Forster is almost unconsciously applying to the case of Dickens, admirable as they certainly are for Mr. Forster's own uses, do not give good advice to everyone. After all, the six has indubitably been hit, and that is what matters, nor can there be any "case" so "excellent" as to disprove this fact.

These terms "flat" and "round" are misleading if we assume, as Mr. Forster seems to do, that a "round" character is in some way "better" than a "flat" character. It is an odd assumption. No one would maintain that a piece of sculpture is necessarily "better" than a painting. But the modern novel, like everything else, has been profoundly influenced by modern science, and perhaps it is felt to be more scientific to create characters which, because of their psychological complexity and because they can be viewed from many different directions, are assumed to be rounded. This is a fallacy, since it is the effect of the work as a whole that matters, and a thorough-going psycho-analysis may or may not add to this effect. As Mr. Forster admits, Dickens

"achieves effects that are not mechanical and a vision of humanity that is not shallow."

He does this by methods which are very different from those
of Mr. Forster himself, but that is no reason why either of the
two methods should be despised. It may be said that Dickens
is writing in the tradition of Fielding and Smollett, while Mr.
Forster has preferred the more psychological methods of Richardson. Certainly for the Dickens character, who is a "character"
in the colloquial sense of the word, there is a long and distinguished ancestry. Behind Mr. Micawber and Mr. Pickwick
stand great figures of the past—Squire Western, Commodore
Trunion, Thwackum, and the rest—all creations for audiences
who liked to see nature written large rather than meticulously.

And of Dickens one is constantly inclined to use adjectives
which denote size and scope. His whole world is a big one and
he views it rather as a child might view a strange city, but with
the intellect and penetration of an adult. The lights he sees are
more brilliant, the shadows more monstrous than they appear
to habitual inhabitants, at ease in their surroundings. There are
undiscovered meanings and suggestions in every expression of
the face, in the weather, even in the surfaces of articles of
furniture or the angles of roofs. The whole is something to be
viewed with wonder, enthusiasm and trepidation. These too, it
seems, are the emotions which he excites in his readers. We are
amazed at his creative exuberance, at his skill or energy; but
what makes us call him great is, finally, the greatness and extent
of his outlook. It may be true that his characters are types, that
each closely imagined detail is made to serve a dramatic end;
but that is not the whole story. Behind the feeling that "all the
world's a stage" there lies a deeper conviction in which there
is no trace of the cynical or the artificial; for, in the end, Dickens
is more like Prospero than Jacques.

HUMPHRY HOUSE: 1947

The Macabre Dickens

THE present lively interest in Dickens has in it an element never before prominent in all his hundred years of popularity—an interest in his mastery of the macabre and terrible in scene and character. His understanding of and power of describing evil and cruelty, fear and mania and guilt; his overburdening sense, in the crises, of the ultimate loneliness of human life—things like these are now seen to be among the causes of his enigmatic hold on people's hearts. He has worked as much beneath the surface as above it; and he was possibly not himself fully conscious of what he was putting into his books. The floor of consciousness has been lowered. The awful area of human experience in which small cruelty and meanness and stupidity may swell and topple over into murder, insane revenge, sadistic, bloody violence and riot; the area where dream and reality are confused or swiftly alternating—these are now seen to be closer to ourselves and to common life than our grandfathers suspected. They thought that Dickens on his violent and evil side—when he wrote about Sikes and Jonas Chuzzlewit and Bradley Headstone —was writing about a special, separate class called criminals; that Miss Havisham, Mr. Dick and Miss Flite belonged to

All in Due Time (London, 1955); first presented as a broadcast on the B.B.C. Third Programme in 1947.

another separate class called lunatics—at most social problems; at least, wild exaggerated flights of fancy. We now see more plainly that John Jasper may be any one of us; that the murderer is not far beneath the skin; that the thickness of a sheet of paper may divide the proud successful man of the world from the suicide or the lunatic. We have also lived again into what used to be dismissed as melodrama.

Lord Acton once wrote in a letter that Dickens "knows nothing of sin when it is not crime." Within the narrow limits of theological pigeon-holes this is true; the word "sin" hardly occurs in the novels; wickedness is not regarded as an offence against a personal God. But if the judgment is that Dickens knows nothing of evil unless it is recognised and punishable by the law, it is quite false. The great black, ghastly gallows hanging over all, of which Dickens writes in the Preface to *Oliver Twist*, is not just the official retribution of society against those who break its rules; it is a symbol of the internal knowledge of guilt, the knowledge that makes Sikes wander back and forth in the country north of London, dogged not by fear of the police but by the phantom of Nancy, the knowledge that produces the last vision of her eyes which is the immediate cause of his death. Acton, with the logic of Catholicism, thought it a fault in Dickens that he "loved his neighbour for his neighbour's sake"; but, within the range of moral action that this allows, Dickens is continually dealing with the forms of evil which the absence or failure of love may breed, and with the more terrible effects of emotional greed, the exploitation of one person by another, which often overflows into cruelty and violence. His methods of dealing with these moral problems and the conflicts they involve are various, but they are always peculiar and oblique; they are rarely brought out openly on the main surface of the story; they are never analysed as the story goes along. They are sometimes displayed through a grotesque character in such a way that they become so sharp and hideous that it is hard to recognise their seriousness and truth. Such, for example, is Quilp's cruelty towards his wife, which seems a fantastic travesty of human action if one overlooks Mrs. Quilp's one phrase:

Quilp has such a way with him when he likes, that the best-looking woman here couldn't refuse him if I was dead.

That one sentence goes to the core of Quilp: for all his grotesque exterior he has in him a secret and serious human *power:* he is no figure of fun.

Except in such sudden phrases as these, Dickens's imagination usually concentrates through all the greater part of a story now on the black, now on the white, exclusively: the two don't interpenetrate. It is only in the portraits of boyhood and adolescence, such as those of Pip and the early Copperfield, that the medley of moral direction is really convincing. The adult characters for most of their course drive headstrong forward, virtuously or villainously or in some grotesque neutral zone where moral decisions do not have to be made. It is as if Dickens was afraid of attempting to portray the full complexity of an adult. Then, quite suddenly, a portentous thing happens. It is worth noticing first what does *not* happen. I cannot think of a single instance in which one of the good characters suddenly reveals a streak of evil: the Jarndyces and Cheerybles and Brownlows persevere infallible and unsullied to the end. The startling thing that *does* happen is that the villains suddenly reveal, if not a streak of good, a streak of vivid power, and then an immense depth of intricate, confused and pitiable humanity. Suddenly their awakened sense of guilt, their fears, remorse, regrets, and above all their terrible loneliness strike out like lightning from the complex plot. As death comes upon them they are transformed, not by any crude magic of reformation such as works wonders with Scrooge, but by an understanding and sympathy, a knowledge of their fears and weakness, far more heart-rending than the moral judgments which convention and the plot pass against them. Examples of this are Fagin, Sikes, Jonas Chuzzlewit, even Quilp: but for the moment let us look closely at Mr. Carker in *Dombey and Son*.

Carker has most often been regarded as a typical villain out of melodrama. One critic at least has called his drive across France from Dijon to the coast a "masterpiece of melodrama." So persistent has this way of regarding it been that this same critic himself heightens the scene by speaking of Carker's "last journey through the *stormy* night." But Dickens makes no mention of any storm whatever; in fact he writes in quite a different mood of "a sigh of mountain air from the distant Jura, fading along the plain." It is nearer the truth to say that in this scene Carker shakes off the last suggestion of melodrama and becomes a figure of immense significance. I will quote a few paragraphs—not continuous—from the description of the later part of this drive:

Gathered up moodily in a corner of the carriage, and only intent on going fast—except when he stood up, for a mile together, and looked back; which he would do whenever there was a piece of open country—he went on, still postponing thought indefinitely, and still always tormented with thinking to no purpose.

Shame, disappointment, and discomfiture gnawed at his heart; a constant apprehension of being overtaken, or met—for he was groundlessly afraid even of travellers, who came towards him by the way he was going—oppressed him heavily. The same intolerable awe and dread that had come upon him in the night, returned unweakened in the day. The monotonous ringing of the bells and tramping of the horses; the monotony of his anxiety, and useless rage; the monotonous wheel of fear, regret, and passion, he kept turning round and round; made the journey like a vision, in which nothing was quite real but his own torment.

It was a fevered vision of things past and present all confounded together; of his life and journey blended into one. Of being madly hurried somewhere, whither he must go. Of old scenes starting up among the novelties through which he travelled. Of musing and brooding over what was past and distant, and seeming to take no notice of the actual objects he encountered, but with a wearisome exhausting consciousness of being bewildered by them, and having their images all crowded in his hot brain after they were gone.

Whatever language this is, it is not the language of melodrama; it is a tremendous analysis of the psychological effects of guilt, shame and thwarted vanity. It is only in the light of these great final scenes that Carker's character as shown earlier in the book becomes intelligible; it is then seen that he is not the motivelessly malignant villain of melodrama: he is a man of intellect, of great ambition and great sexual vitality; his worse flaws are self-centredness and vanity. It is exactly this sort of man who would be afflicted with a total blindness about what Edith Dombey, in a position, as he thinks, to satisfy both his ambition and his sexual desires, was really thinking and feeling. The final disclosure would have been bitter to Carker for many reasons, but bitterest perhaps because it showed him that he had been abysmally blind and *stupid;* yet he was too self-centred, intricate and cunning to allow reflection on his own stupidity to come uppermost in his tortured thoughts. There is much of Dickens himself in Mr. Carker: and it is startling to see the hopelessness of his wheels within wheels of thought: there is no solution but death.

One of the problems that face the critic of Dickens is to explain how this intimate understanding of morbid and near-morbid psychology links on to his apparent optimism, and above all to his humour. I think we can safely say that the countless scenes of gregarious and hearty happiness, which seem to us so unconvincing, seem so because they represent a revulsion from the abysses of evil, a strenuous and ardent *wish* to achieve happiness, rather than the realisation of it. But what of the great grotesque and humorous characters—Mrs. Gamp, Pecksniff, Mr. Turveydrop and the rest? One very fruitful suggestion was

made by George Henry Lewes, only two years after Dickens's
death:

> In no other perfectly sane mind (Blake I believe was not per-
> fectly sane) have I observed vividness of imagination approaching
> so closely to hallucination. . . . Dickens once declared to me that
> every word said by his characters was distinctly *heard* by him; I
> was at first not a little puzzled to account for the fact that he could
> hear language so utterly unlike the language of real feeling; but the
> surprise vanished when I thought of the phenomena of hallucination.

Lewes applied this idea both to the speaking of certain characters
and also to the visual descriptions of persons and scenes. In
each case it was the definiteness and insistence of the image or
the sound which were abnormal. This idea is, I think, extremely
useful in helping to explain the impression one gets from the
books of isolated spells of intense imagination which then stop;
it also helps to explain the feeling of isolation about the characters: one almost hallucinatory experience succeeded by
another, the two being mutually exclusive. There was no comprehensive, constructive, master imagination which held the
diverse experiences together, except in very rare instances,
mostly to do with memories of childhood. The great grotesque
comic characters—Mrs. Gamp is the purest of the type—are the
best examples of this exclusive, one-track intense development
and could not have their unique stature without it. In other
instances the form of hallucination was not that of something
seen or heard externally, but an internal illusion by which Dickens himself virtually assumed the character of which he was
writing. His daughter Mamie described how she saw him grimac-
ing in a glass, talking aloud the speeches of a character, completely unaware of his actual surroundings, not even noticing
that she was in the room.
   If one starts by thinking of Dickens as a man with an imagination of this quality and intensity and exclusiveness, it helps to

explain not only the recurrent treatment in the novels of various forms of mania and illusion, but also the preoccupation with evil. Similar processes of concentration, exclusion and distortion must have occurred in the mental part of his own life, as distinct from his written work. Edmund Wilson, in his essay *The Two Scrooges*, argued that Dickens was "the victim of a manic-depressive cycle, and a very uncomfortable person." His own life was, in a sense, far beyond what could be said of most men, acting out, or attempting to act out, his own imaginings. His passion for theatricals was only a symptom of the trouble, or an effort to work it off without serious consequences. In real living the concomitant of blindness, especially to the thoughts and feelings of other people, may be resentment and hatred, even to the point of imagining murder, against those who fail to conform to the policy or come up to the idea of themselves that it entails. But there will also be moments of terrible awakening when the illusion and the self-deceit it involved are ended, and there will be a great wave of remorse and guilt and shame for the evils imagined or other evils actually done. There is evidence enough to show that Dickens's personality was strong enough, especially over women, to project his own imagined policies upon others so that in general they conformed; at certain crises the attempt failed and a hideous major conflict came out into the open. Lewes said he saw no traces of insanity in Dickens's life; nor would he; for Dickens normally had a very strong conscious control, and was able to work out many of his conflicts through his novels. But his daughter Kate, Mrs. Perugini, did significantly say to a friend that after his wife left their home Dickens behaved towards the children "like a madman," that all the worst in him came out; and she added that her father was "a very wicked man."

This is a very different matter from saying that he was a commonplace bounder; there is no need for Dickens's descendants to defend him against charges of being a dishonest drunken libertine: neither the charges nor the defence are relevant to a man of his size and complexity and importance. It is clear from the evidence of the novels alone that Dickens's acquaintance with evil was not just acquired *ab extra,* by reading the police-court reports (much as he loved them) and wandering about Seven Dials and the Waterside by night; it was acquired also by introspection. His own temptations and imaginings, isolated and heightened by the peculiar, narrowing, intense quality of his imagination, fed daily by the immense power which he felt himself to possess over others' personalities—these were the authentic sources of his great criminal characters. Their ultimate trembling loneliness, or hunted wanderings, or self-haunted hallucinations, or endless, destroying self-analysis, came also from himself. Our generation has come to recognise this by introspection, too.

ROBERT MORSE: 1949

Our Mutual Friend

"IN these times of ours, though concerning the exact year there is no need to be precise, a boat of dirty and disreputable appearance, with two figures in it, floated on the Thames, between Southwark Bridge which is of iron, and London Bridge which is of stone, as an autumn evening was closing in." The sinister search on the water has begun, and the first chapter of Dickens'

Partisan Review, XVI (1949), 277–289.

sinister masterpiece. We find ourselves on the water, and muddy water is to trickle and seep through all the following pages. The two figures in the boat are Gaffer Hexam and his daughter Lizzie. Lizzie shows a strong dislike for her father's occupation, which is that of robbing the pockets of drowned men. Gaffer remonstrates with her in such terms as these: "How can you be so thankless to your best friend [the river], Lizzie? The very fire that warmed you when you were a baby was picked out of the river alongside the coal barges. The very basket that you slept in, the tide washed ashore. The very rockers that I put it upon to make a cradle of it, I cut out of a piece of wood that drifted from some ship or another." Such rhetoric from the mouth of a man who is pictured as the roughest of waterside scavengers is likely to seem to us, in our day, as Dickens at his most improbable. And when his daughter answers in speech of even greater refinement and purity of grammar, the question arises: How realistic did the works of Dickens seem to his contemporary Londoners?

It is possible that the question of true-to-life did not arise, and that Dickens' contemporaries accepted his dark vision of England and London and London's creatures as readily as we today accept Raymond Chandler's California with its brutal and neurotic crew of killers and private-eyes—or even the sweet mirage of New York presented by our women's magazines. And yet we have been trained in the modern school of realism where naturalness of dialogue and "truth" of psychological reaction are the touchstone, and often the only merit.

With the authority of a teller of folk tales, for whom natural-ness has no purpose, Dickens simply assures his readers: This is what happened. And for the most part we are pleased to believe him, no matter how arbitrary the sequence of events may seem. The disappointing moments in his novels are just those moments when his persuasive genius fails, and disbelief returns us, in spite of ourselves, to the outer world. Such lapses are often quite grave, at least at first view. It is not easy, for example, to believe that the noble old Jew, Riah, could accept his long bondage to an ugly master and an ugly occupation because of gratitude. Nor is it easy to believe that Florence Dombey, in *Dombey and Son*, could have gone on loving her father so faithfully in the face of his harsh treatment. And yet these feeble motivations are essential to much of the action in these novels. Why did Dickens risk weakening his project? On reflection, it will appear that in both cases he has permitted a conception of moral goodness, of moral right, to prevail over human probability.

Riah's gratitude to the monstrous Fascination Fledgeby is seen as a sacred and unalterable obligation, a noble trait in a noble (if far-fetched) character. It is Gratitude itself. Again, in the case of poor Florence Dombey, a good child *ought* to love her parent, and love him she does in spite of all opposition.

But these rare lapses into disbelief, easy as they are to explain away on various grounds, do little damage to our acceptance of Dickens' world. The writer's art confers on his creations an intensity of existence that makes their fantastic proportions seem the true proportions, and, as we read, we believe—just as we do not doubt the distorted forms of Greek sculpture or of Picasso's *baigneuses*, which if translated into flesh would send us screaming in flight.

Why do these monsters of purity and evil, these ridiculous eccentrics and grotesques, hold our attention? What field of experience does Dickens draw on to make us feel their truth? Do they not live under our own skins, waiting to be given the externalized form of myth and art? Dickens has gone underground to that region where the mists of unnameable anxieties and the smoke of infantile terrors prevail. There, at the edge of the sea of sleep, he has built his London. On the opposite shore dwell the Gorgons, Andromeda and Perseus, the Minotaur in the Cretan maze. The Harpies call across the separating waters to Miss Flite's birds—Hope, Joy, Youth, Peace, Rest, Life, Dust, Ashes, Waste, Want, Ruin, Despair, Madness, Death, Cunning, Folly, Words, Wigs, Rags, Sheepskin, Plunder, Precedent, Jargon, Gammon, and Spinach. In this underground metropolis (whose visual aspects have been so wonderfully reported by Phiz) no one need be surprised to see Lady Dedlock emerging from Tom-all-alone's, and Quilp creeping into Little Nell's bed, or eating eggs, shell and all, to terrify his wife.

How does Dickens keep the vaulting of his cave-world secure, and stop each chink against skepticism and outer day, of which the least beam would disintegrate Miss Havisham's wedding cake where generations of rats had failed?

Consider first the variety and energy of invention Dickens infuses into every part of his books, an inventiveness which, like the music of Beethoven, sweeps away any apprehension of fatigue with its great mood of boundless improvisation. Each object, each creature, animal or human, must be given personality and a unique vitality. He will play with the description of a tavern sign with such brilliant fancy, so many allusions to unexpected domains, that one scarcely notices that this painted board occupies two pages of the text. The horse, as in *The Old Curiosity Shop*, is characterized as thoroughly as his drivers. Each waiter, coachman, clerk, although perhaps never to be seen again, during his brief appearance is impaled in the bright center of our attention, and we are obliged to see his qualities and failings ludicrous or sad, before he is released to his invisible life. Dickens is like a medium who bids us look into his crystal ball, and as we see the images form, he keeps a sharp eye on us to see that the spell does not falter, and at the same time urges: Look! Look more closely! Are you sure that you can see it *all*?

In short he can find interest, and the material of art, in almost anything. Often this liveliness is effected by simple but surprising juxtapositions, by odd angles of vision, by ironic reversals of his meaning (as "the *divine* Tippins"), by sheer verbal vivacity, by sonorous rhetorical devices of alliteration and repetition—which sometimes indeed embarrass by their excessiveness. But take this: Mr. Pecksniff is merely warming his hands at the fire, but he warms them "as benevolently as though they were somebody else's, not his." A simple action is made into pure fun, and at the same time the false goodness of Pecksniff is revealed.

The roof of Dickens' cave hangs on a strong ribbing of plot, and here again he shows his invention in a gothic ingenuity. It might be argued that all novels have a plot, but surely *Anna Karenina, For Whom the Bell Tolls, Madame Bovary*, have a kind of narrative structure that differentiates them from *Bleak House, Our Mutual Friend*, or *Great Expectations*. The authors of the first group apply their art to producing an air of naturalness, almost of biography. The "story" of their books given an over-all social and geographical environment, grows out of the nature of their characters. The complexities are those of psychological interrelations; and although there may be a wealth of naturalistic incident, there is a minimum of the old wills, concealed identities, and dramatic coincidence dear to Dickens. Such novels have the cadence of veracity. At their best, they have no more plot than a true account of human lives—which is no plot at all, compared to the abstract pattern of Cinderella, the Oedipus myth, *Bleak House*.

Except for its survival in certain detective novels, the large interwoven design (manipulated, artificial, if you like) has gone out of fashion with its calculated tangles and calculated unravelings. Perhaps, leaving aside the out-and-out folk tale, its inherent drawbacks can be overcome only by such master novelists as Dumas, Balzac, Dickens. But it is comfortable to begin a "plot novel," to feel its bulk in the hand, and to know that all those pages to come will be ordered with a felicity and ingenuity beyond the accidents of actual life, just as it is a satisfaction to hear the opening themes of a Haydn sonata and know in advance that they are going to be worked out according to a beautiful law and will come to an end at the precise moment when the sonata form is satisfied. For a plot does not depend primarily on surprise and suspense; it depends on completeness of resolution. The successful plot novel, like an ingenious fairy tale, can be re-read without loss of interest, and we come again to the ritual triumph of hero and heroine over the opposing (or evil) forces with the same sense of moral order. Indeed we often may guess, before we are halfway through our first reading, the main resolution of the plot, because such and such a denouement is precisely what would please us most. Whereas when we begin a novel by Colette or Dorothy Richardson we have no idea what end we shall arrive at—just as the shape of a Strauss tone poem cannot be guessed from its opening measures.

But whoever has read one Dickens novel takes up a second with the happy confidence that the persons he meets there, however remote from each other they may at first appear, will all interlock in a tightening pattern and each make his influence felt by the others, as in a folk tale the ragged old woman casually befriended by the third son is sure to reappear in his hour of need. And it is not surprising in this mythic England that its inhabitants should be related to each other with a folk-tale coherence.

The major writers of today have been curiously willing to dispense with the advantages of the well-meshed plot. For however mechanical plot may seem, however prefabricated its dovetailing and niceties and knot-tying, it still gives a novelist one of the most obvious means of securing *unity*. Our novelists, like our free-verse poets, have set themselves the appalling task of reaching form by pure intuition—a chancy appeal, at best, to the shifting and unguessable sympathies of their readers.

The author of *Great Expectations* took no such risk. With so much of the eccentric, effervescent, and improbable to impart he could not readily overlook the gross advantages of a unifying plot. But he also used other, more subtle devices to give unity to each novel.

The word "caricature" is often associated with Dickens, perhaps to some extent because of the brilliant Grand Guignol drawings of Cruikshank and Phiz. The term loses much of its force if we view Dickens' world as the imaginative projection of an inner world underlying actuality. A caricaturist and satirist (unless his motives are those of interested propaganda, political or otherwise) stands in a mundane and moral daylight with Voltaire and Aristophanes, directing his missiles cruel or gay at the stupidities, the pretensions, the evil practices of his less enlightened fellows, and thereby wins them to greater sanity. But what are we to think of a writer who pictures virtue as extravagantly as vice? For are not Little Nell and Tom Pinch and Florence Dombey as monstrously overdrawn as Pecksniff and Mrs. Jellyby? Are these caricatures intended as signposts to guide us to more rational and moral behavior, or are they the creations of a sensibility that reveled in the haunts of Dr. Groddeck's "it"? The "caricature" may be simply the intensification or distortion of dream, but from the point of view of *unity*, if Dickens' people are caricatures they are invoked at an almost identical level of caricature, and once slapped on the back by his masterly hand they rise and breathe the same vigorous air.

Although these characters seem so often to emerge from folk tale and dream, they are not all nightmarish. Sleep has its pleasant apparitions. And among the legendary types we fleetingly detect underlying the personages of Dickens there are many Cinderellas, Jack the Giant Killers, Dick Whittingtons, Fairy Godmothers, and Pucks, as well as the Ogres and Robber Bridegrooms. (Who could Mr. and Mrs. Smallweed be, by the way, other than Punch and Judy?) But these lay or archetypal figures do not often oppress us with familiarity; they are so richly clothed in borrowed garments of actuality that the smooth, ancient timbers of their limbs rarely peep through. No, it must not be supposed that Dickens' underground London is cut off entirely from its counterpart. The million sights and sounds of outer life drift downward in a kind of sediment, and, as certain jelly-like organisms gather the debris of the sea bottom about them to form a shell, so Dickens' characters crust themselves in these fragments of actuality.

Dickens notoriously used the names and peculiarities of many persons encountered in his own life, as well as the names and features of buildings and places. He kept the sharpest lookout for traits and manners, for little absurd, grotesque, or pathetic ways. Daily he crammed his memory with this loot, and when the time came for the creation of a new tavern, character, or street, he had only to agitate these thousand bits of observation, and administer, as from a salt shaker, the proper seasoning for person or place. In similar fashion he distributes the deeper traits of pride, hypocrisy, cheerfulness, fidelity, greed, and the like— as well as the general attributes of youth, beauty, intelligence, etc., together with hundreds of occupations such as fishing, body snatching, the law. His salt shaker holds them all. How else, beyond plot and uniformity of caricature, does Dickens integrate his novels?

One soon becomes aware that each book arises from a single theme, although the variations are so brilliant and ingenious it is not always easy to arrive at the most basic statement. However, once the most inclusive statement has been found it will be seen that this main theme is the raison d'être and the explanation of all parts of the book, and the reader may take a special pleasure in tracing much seemingly incongruous material back to its central source. Each novel, then, is *about* something, and furthermore about something serious. *A Tale of Two Cities*, for example, is built on the solemn theme of resurrection.

Usually, to point and illustrate his main theme, Dickens selects some social or moral situation in need of reform, and attacks it with hot indignation. So, in *Bleak House* which has for its theme the dead hand of the past, he attacks the Court of Chancery. In *Nicholas Nickleby*, which is about innocent and generous youth's first acquaintance with "what is called the world—a conventional phrase which, being interpreted, often signifieth all the rascals in it," Dickens attacks the atrocious schools of his day, giving us Dotheboys Hall, a name that even now raises specters of hunger, cold, and injustice. Hypocrisy is the theme of *Martin Chuzzlewit*, and, regrettably, the institution chosen for illustration is the young Republic of the United States. *Our Mutual Friend* deals with Money, and here the Poor Laws are singled out for bitter rhetoric: "It is a remarkable Christian improvement, to have made a pursuing Fury of the Good Samaritan."

Thus it will be seen that these examples of Dickens' zeal for reform arise from the fundamental theme of each novel, and must not be mistaken for the main purpose of his books. They serve merely as illustrations, much as the bas-reliefs Dante introduces in the *Purgatorio* typify the faults to be purged at various levels of the Mount.

But beyond the basic theme, certain unifying sub-themes of another, perhaps more abstract, order can be discovered in these remarkably constructed books. These sub-themes, moving at right angles to the major premise, serve to secure the package already firmly corded lengthwise. Take *Our Mutual Friend* as an example.

Money, to repeat, is the main theme—from the Harmon will, to the ostentation of the Veneerings, the Lammles' cynical marriage, Mr. Boffin's feigned miserliness, the looting of drowned bodies, and so on. It is in these drowned bodies that a counter-theme reveals itself. There are four actual drownings, and three near-drownings, all of them involving important characters. As an embellishment to this subject, Dickens adds an almost gloating description of Gaffer's gruesome wallpaper of police handbills advertising corpses found in the river. ("This is them two young sisters what tied themselves together with a handker-cher.")

Muddy Water might be called a variant of the drowning theme. We are never far from the Thames and its shipping and its dank mysteries—and here again we meet the river as a symbol of Life flowing towards the sea of Death, a symbol constantly recurring in the writings of Dickens. And, as it has been said of Shakespeare that each play follows a consistent imagery, it is easy to point out in *Our Mutual Friend* a poetic revelry in water associations. Here is a description of Rider-hood's headgear: "an old sodden fur cap, formless and mangy, that looked like a furry animal, dog or cat, puppy or kitten, drowned and decaying." (This example is also an instance of Dickens' skill in coloring a character by oblique metaphorical methods. Everything about his personages must reveal and partake of their nature.)

Opposed to Muddy Water is the theme of Dust, with the Harmon dust heaps for starting point: "he grew rich as a Dust Contractor, and lived in a hollow in a hilly country composed of Dust. On his own small estate the growling old vagabond threw up his own mountain range, like an old volcano, and its geological formation was Dust. Coal-dust, vegetable-dust, bone-dust, crockery-dust, rough dust and sifted dust—all manner of dust." Scattered through the other novels there are many refer-ences to dust as the end of all living things, but here it seems more likely that the dust heaps represent the vanity of amassing wealth, or gold-dust—although our author takes care to leave his "good" characters well provided for in the end. (Of course with the felt proviso that these "good" people will use their means nobly towards furthering the great vague cause of Happiness.)

In *Our Mutual Friend* the use of another theme or principle may be observed, a principle which shapes, colors, and binds this novel together no less radically than the theme of money. This may be identified as the principle of *doubleness*. Dickens employs it in much the same way that a composer will unify all the movements of a symphony by repeating the same tone relation, interval, harmonic progression, or family of notes throughout the work. He uses doubleness, although far less simply, as Chopin uses thirds in an étude for thirds, in which the thirds are neither the melody or the musical significance of the piece, but the necessary medium of both.

To begin with, the characters group naturally into pairs—which is, of course, true of many novels. But where were there ever so many pairs, and pairs of pairs, and new pairs formed after a reshuffling of old pairs?

But this is only one aspect of doubleness. Let us consider the many examples of duplicity, disguise, false claims, hourglass reversals, and dual natures. John Harmon appears under two assumed names. We do not even know who he really is for a great part of the book. He exchanges clothes with a physical double, or *Doppelgänger* whose corpse is wrongly identified as Harmon. Harmon also puts on false whiskers and a wig in another disguise. Headstone duplicates Riderhood's clothes in order to make him appear Eugene's murderer. Even Sloppy has *his* disguise.

We find further examples of duplicity in Mr. Boffin's pretense of turning miser; in the Lammles' deception of each other into marriage on the grounds of imaginary wealth; in Fledgeby's concealed traffic in "queer bills"; in Riah's enforced false front, etc.

Doubleness appears again as character duality. Charlie, with his mixture of "uncompleted savagery and uncompleted civilization," provides a good specimen of a divided nature—also Eugene, also Mortimer, among others. Then there is Twemlow who is meek, downtrodden, and vague until at the end he takes his tremendous stand in defense of the principles that make a gentleman.

The most grotesque use of doubleness is found in reversals of the natural role: Bella calls her Pa her younger brother, "with a dear venerable chubbiness on him"—although much of the time she patronizes him in an unpleasantly arch and incestuous way as if he were a faithful but unimportant lover; Lizzie loves her brother as a son; Jenny Wren, the Doll's Dressmaker, treats *her* alcoholic father as if he were a bad little boy— but Jenny is all doubleness, with her double life of visions, her crippled legs and vigorous hair, her precocious insight.

It is easy to cite many simpler instances of two-ness, such as the two wills, the two John Harmons, the Boffins' parlor—half of which, to suit Mrs. Boffin, is carpeted and fashionably furnished, while the other half reflects Mr. Boffin's taste in its resemblance to a tap-room, even to sand and sawdust on the floor.

This unifying sub-theme has been considered in disproportionate detail partly because it is such a curious device in itself, partly because it illumines a little-known aspect of creative writing, and partly because it is the kind of thing that generally goes unnoticed in Dickens' highly artful art.

These then, to summarize, are some of the ways by which Dickens persuades readers to stay in his underground world and to believe, as long as they remain there, that this world is all-inclusive and subject to its own unique law: for the source of emotional vitality he draws on the deepest mythology of mankind, the personages of the myth being presented with a lavishness of minute and general characteristics that rivals the invention of life itself and prevents them from becoming the hollow shapes of folklore, although they embody or demonstrate through their actions the capital letter categories of sin and virtue or the lesser list of foibles and merits; these personages, since they are all lighted by the same searching but subterranean sun, are all evoked on the same level of "caricature" (to borrow a word from the upper world) and thus obey the prime law of their creator's art, which is unity; they obey this law still further in their interrelations, which are as imposed and ordered in pattern as the musical forms of the late eighteenth century—or as the arbitrary sequence of folk tale; unity is again established by the author's choice of a single animating theme for each novel, a theme gravely applicable to the common experience of Western man, and wonderfully reflected and varied in the people and events of the book; the basic theme is usually illustrated by some form of abuse, which Dickens attacks fiercely; lesser themes, more abstract, more "artful," almost *textural*, further the integration of each novel—as the themes of drowning, water-and-dust, and doubleness give coherence to *Our Mutual Friend*, so that wherever the loaf is sliced the same pattern of ingredients is revealed.

If Dickens could read these foregoing sentences, would he be amazed that so much is ascribed to him that he had never intended, and so much that he *had* intended is ignored? An idle question perhaps, but valid enough in an anemic age that squeaks and sips the strong blood of the dead artist. Perhaps our safest answer must be that whoever has made a masterpiece must have known what he was doing, fully as well as his critics. What knowledge we gain of Dickens through his novels reveals a complicated soul, bitterly aware of the causes for despairing, obsessed with death and decay, fascinated by the sordid, the evil, and the grotesque to such an extent that he brings his greatest gusto as a writer to their description. But even to the blackest of these descriptions he gives a tone of wry surface levity, a playfulness of language, that makes the horror of his subject both more ghastly and more supportable. He stands smiling at our elbow and points to the savagery and injustice.

Indeed he is almost too *much* at our elbow, warning us what to feel, addressing us in lachrymose or heated perorations, clucking ruefully over his pathetic contrivances. Often he comes very close to spoiling his effects by this intrusion, but the thing to be felt is there, and even he (unlike Thackeray with his thumb in our buttonhole) cannot take it from us.

But in opposition to the pessimistic darkness, Dickens also exposes an almost childlike faith in Low Church goodness. He sets high value on kindness, patience, the innocence and elation of youth, the power of love to move aside dead mountains, or at least to make their weight bearable. And besides, he is the funniest writer in the world, with more *kinds* of fun than any other, from the broadest burlesque, through all gradations of the comedy of character, situation, manners, speech, parody, cruel and gentle wit, to the final subtlety of the tear-stained smile.

He has many ways of being serious as well, although he never produces in us the exaltation of high tragedy—partly because in these vast, many-peopled entertainments no single character is allowed to reach heroic proportions. The tears are the tears of pathos, and fall for a dying child, for shabby courage and humble fidelity. The tragic issue is simply the general contest of man with his own nature and the nature of things, for Dickens' belief in positive evil is implicit, and all of his characters either struggle against evil, or founder in it, or were born its creatures. But Dickens raises no protagonist of great intellectual, moral, or emotional stature to do battle. Is it because of this that he is usually esteemed in our time as a lesser figure than certain other nineteenth-century novelists? And yet, in its great variety, his work unites almost all of the ingredients to be found in each of these men, so that it is harder to sum up Dickens in a phrase or two than almost any other writer except Shakespeare or Dante. His quality is easily felt, but eludes statement, so that it seems comparatively simple to make some true and basic announcement about Tolstoy, Dostoevsky, or Proust. These three are generally considered "greater writers," but are they better novelists? Do they fuse their meanings, their intentions, their "axe to grind" into a single art form—or do they find the confines of the novel too cramping for the largeness of the thing they have to say, and impatiently brush aside the pretext of fiction in order to communicate directly?

Tolstoy shares Dickens' moral fervor, and his underlying themes are perhaps as serious, but even his supreme *War and Peace* is wanting in a kind of weight because of his optimistic ignorance of evil, and his refusal to use material that might sound "invented." Dostoevsky, of course, knew as much about sin and the irrational and every conceivable blackness as Dickens, and was often the wildest of comedians, but his immense and stormy vision seems to break out of control, and a Western reader, finding himself swept away on the back of the apocalyptic beast into the night, is likely to wish he might be set down on his own feet again, and find his bearings with the help of his own horn-rimmed spectacles. Yet Dickens has far more in common with Dostoevsky than with Proust, who, for all the sharpness of his scalpels, anatomizes a comparatively narrow segment of experience.

And yet Dickens, although he shares the quality of *excessiveness* which marks the Russians and the Frenchmen as great artists, does not produce in the modern mind the same impression of a great immediate experience. Perhaps the secret lies in the word "immediate." We rarely put ourselves in the place of Dickens' characters and feel directly with them. We see them from without, and the romance of Florence Dombey touches us *personally* no more than the lovers in "The Eve of St. Agnes." We become Little Nell, in our own visceral being, no more than we become Rapunzel; and we suffer the pangs of Lady Dedlock with the same remote pain that the torments of Brunetto Latini communicate from the page of Dante. Who weeps for

Peggotty's niece as they weep for Anna Karenina? In short, we are not forced into direct emotional participation, which is the goal of most contemporary writing since Tolstoy and Maupassant. The interest, the meaning, of Dickens' novels lies elsewhere, and if we are moved, we are moved in the serener regions of the spirit where poetry and folk tale make their appeal to understanding. No other major novelist builds his books so frankly by the poet's method.

As a poet he warns of Paul Dombey's death in symbolic terms of the sea's murmurings, for as a poet he deals everywhere in symbols and suggestive images and chanted repetitions and protracted fancies with an abandon denied to the prosier scribes of daily life—and therein lie both the freedom and the *order* of his writing. But as a poet he is far from the sad lyricism of Virginia Woolf or the melomania of D. H. Lawrence, although he touches them both at points; he more nearly resembles Chaucer and the robust poet-dramatists of the Elizabethan age. Yet (since it is hard to say anything "true" of Dickens) this too is a false picture—for whom does he *not* resemble one way or another?

Perhaps it is because of the detachment of the poetic method that Dickens' novels can be read again without loss of pleasure, for, as in a well-loved poem, the sequence is largely independent of the kind of time in which suspense draws us on. Since we have never been invited to identify ourselves passionately with the fate of the characters, and have not lived through their story as if it were our own, we do not return to Dickens as we are likely to return even to Tolstoy, with a sense of chill, of lost magic and shrunken dimension. For there are certain books as difficult to recapture in their essence as an old love, as difficult to relive as a passage in our past, simply because they *were* our love and our past, and their truth for us has been assimilated and has actually modified our present. Dickens' books are not of

this kind; like a sonnet, or Jack and the Beanstalk, their rewards
belong to a perpetual present.

DOROTHY VAN GHENT: 1950

The Dickens World:
A View from Todgers's

THE course of things demonically possessed is to imitate the
human, while the course of human possession is to imitate the
inhuman. This transposition of attributes, producing a world
like that of ballet, is the principle of relationship between things
and people in the novels of Dickens. The masks, the stances,
and the shock-tempo are comic. The style which they have for
their perspective is the style of a world undergoing a gruesome
spiritual transformation.

Things, like animal pets, have adopted the disposition and
expression of their masters. The "tight-clenched" old bureau
of a miser has a "bad and secret forehead." But this argues a
demonic life in things; and as it takes a demon to know a demon,
they have maliciously felt out and imitated, in their relationships
with each other and even with people, the secret of the human arrangement. A four-poster bed in an inn is a despotic monster
that straddles over the whole room, "putting one of his arbitrary

Sewanee Review, LVIII (1950), 419–438.

legs into the fireplace, and another into the doorway, and squeezing the wretched little washing-stand in quite a Divinely Righteous manner." The animation of inanimate objects suggests both the quaint gaiety of a forbidden life and an aggressiveness that has got out of control. Even a meek little muffin has to be "confined with the utmost precaution under a strong iron cover," and a hat, set on a mantelpiece, demands constant attention and the greatest quickness of eye and hand to catch it neatly as it tumbles off, but it is an ingenious demon and finally manages to fall into the slop-basin.

These continual broadsides of the pathetic fallacy might be considered as incidental embellishment if the description of people did not everywhere show a reciprocal metaphor. The animate is treated as if it were a thing. It is as if the life absorbed by things had been drained out of people who have become incapable of their humanity. Grandfather Smallweed, in *Bleak House*, has to be beaten up periodically like a cushion in order to be restored to the shape of a man. The ignominy is horrifying, suggesting unspeakable deterioration. Those who have engaged, as Grandfather Smallweed has, in the manipulation of their fellows as if they were things, themselves develop thing-attributes, like Podsnap, the capitalist, who has hair-brushes on his head instead of hair; while those who suffer the aggressiveness which is the dynamics of this economy are similarly transformed, like the convict Magwitch, mechanized by oppression and fear, who has a clockwork apparatus in his throat that clicks as if it were going to strike, or poor little Twemlow, whose hosts put leaves in him like a dining-table, extending or depressing him according to the size of the party.

The progressive keys of the transformation may be illustrated by those people who have wooden parts, Silas Wegg and Sarah Gamp's famous husband offering the examples. The wooden leg of Mr. Gamp, "which in its constancy of walkin' into wine vaults, and never comin' out again 'till fetched by force, was quite as weak as flesh, if not weaker," has taken over the man. More ominous is the deliberate choice of a lower order of being, when the man takes over or becomes his member. (Lady Scadgers, in *Hard Times*, is "an immensely fat old woman, with an inordinate appetite for butcher's meat, and a mysterious leg which had now refused to get out of bed for fourteen years." The lady is "thinged" into her own leg, which is clearly the repository of all that butcher's meat.) In Silas Wegg, the humanity of the man with the wooden leg is so reduced to the quality of his appendage that he is expected to develop another leg of the same kind in about six months, if his development receive no untimely check. The inanimate member of the organism signifies spiritual necrosis, and Silas does in fact identify himself with his deceased member, which has been disposed of by the hospital porter to an articulator of bones. "Now, look here, what did you give for me?" he demands, and he bargains for his leg in a grotesque parody of the Resurrection of the Body. The man with the wooden leg, however harmless in appearance, is ominous of something out of nature; he is death-in-life. The comedy of this is comedy with immense stylistic tension.

Dickens told Forster that he was always losing sight of a man in his diversion by the mechanical play of some part of the man's face, which "would acquire a sudden ludicrous life of its own." His habit of seeing the parts of the body as separable and manipulable makes in his first writings for funny foolishness, as in the case of the tall lady, eating sandwiches, in *Pickwick*, who "forgot the arch—crash—knock—children look around—mother's head off—sandwich in her hand—no mouth to put it in." Where it is put to use most seriously and spectacularly, it is a technique of surgical division serving to characterize personality that has given itself over to deceit, thus dividing itself unnaturally into a manipulating and a manipulated part, a me-half and an it-half. General Scadder, the agent of the land-swindle in *Martin Chuzzlewit,* has one sightless eye that stands stock still: "With that side of his face he seemed to listen to what the other side was doing. Thus each profile had a distinct expression; and when the movable side was most in action, the rigid one was in its coldest state of watchfulness." Pecksniff, warming his hands before the fire "as benevolently as if they were somebody else's, not his," has divided himself from his imagination of himself, and the image is one of mayhem and of a surgical graft. In Mr. Vholes, the lawyer in *Bleak House,* deceit is not even a personal matter, as it is with Pecksniff. Mr. Vholes is only a cog in the mechanics of Chancery, which has institutionalized the manipulation of living creatures as if they were not human but things. The norms of this hell enable Mr. Vholes to do more violent physical damage on himself than Pecksniff, a kind of damage of which only the mediaeval and twentieth-century imaginations have been thought capable. He "takes off his close black gloves as if he were skinning his hands, lifts off his tight hat as if he were scalping himself, and sits down at his desk."

The more rugged criminals, among those who still move in respectable society, are radically cloven into two people, and it is but a question of point of view from the eccentric *appearance* of Mr. Flintwinch, in *Little Dorrit,* whose neck is so twisted that he looks as if he had hanged himself at one time, to the schizophrenia of the murderer Jonas Chuzzlewit, who, after his crime, is "not only fearful *for* himself but *of* himself," and half expects when he returns home to find himself asleep in bed. The ultimate development of this imagery of division is total transformation of the me-half into the it-half, as in the spontaneous combustion of Krook. Krook, not even a hanger-on of the colossal deceit of Chancery, has established himself in a business which is a parody of Chancery; he lives off the refuse paper of the court, and at the time of his decease has just found a promising speculation in blackmail. Here personality has so developed its thing-constitution that it has become a purely chemical phenomenon, and the moment of Krook's death is the moment when his chemicals (largely gin) have finally consummated their possession of him. The nastiness of the image is proportional to the horror of the idea. A defiling yellow liquor is the last of Krook, slowly dripping and creeping down the bricks.

Krook's mortification is the savagely simple working out of the law of conversion of spirit into matter that operates in the Dickens world. In the case of Miss Havisham, in *Great Expectations*, the decayed wedding cake offers a supplementary image of the necrosis that is taking place in the human agent. Miss Havisham is guilty of aggression against life in using the two children, Pip and Estella, as inanimate instruments of revenge for her broken heart, and she has been changed retributively into a fungus. The cake on the banquet table acts by homeopathic magic, like a burning effigy or a doll stuck with pins: "when the ruin is complete," she says, pointing to the cake but referring to herself, she will be laid out on the same table and her relatives will be invited to "feast on" her corpse. But this is not the only conversion. The "little quickened hearts" of the mice behind the panels have been quickened by what was Miss Havisham, carried off crumb by crumb. The principle of reciprocal changes bears on the characteristic lack of complex inner life on the part of Dickens's people; it is inconceivable that the fungoid Miss Havisham or the spirituous Krook should have complex inner lives, in the moral sense. In the *art* of Dickens (distinguishing that moral dialectic that arises not solely from character but from total aesthetic occasion) there is a great deal of "inner life," transposed to other forms than that of character; partially transposed in this scene, for instance, to the symbolic activity of the speckled-legged spiders with blotchy bodies and to the gropings and pausings of the black beetles on Miss Havisham's hearth.

In Balzac, environment is literally natural; in Dickens, environment is literally *un*natural. Mme. Vauquer's pension or Old

Grandet's house in Saumur, as physical constructions, partake eminently of the harshness and constriction of the forms of life which they help to render intelligible, but there is never any doubt as tó their natural limitations; formally they correspond to the human nature for which they provide the scene, and they set physical and in time spiritual bonds to the human development within them; but in no sense do they actively intrude upon the human. Their symbolic value lies in their natural rigidity. They are that beyond which the soul cannot go. In Dickens, environment constantly exceeds its material limitations. Its mode of existence is altered by the human purposes and deeds it circumscribes, and its animation is antagonistic; it fearfully intrudes upon the soul.

The room occupied by Jonas Chuzzlewit at the time of the murder is charged with the tensions of a straining life—but not Jonas's life.

The room in which he had shut himself up was on the ground-floor, at the back of the house. It was lighted by a dirty skylight, and had a door in the wall, opening into a narrow, covered passage or blind alley. . . . It was a blotched, stained, mouldering room, like a vault; and there were water-pipes running through it, which, at unexpected times in the night, when other things were quiet, clicked and gurgled suddenly, as if they were choking.

It is not only that the water-pipes serve to interpret Jonas's fears —as if they had tattle-tale tongues—but they appear to have been released, by the act which dehumanizes Jonas, into a busy life of their own. What is shocking is not their relevance to the murder but their irrelevance to it. On a larger scale, the same transposition of attributes has taken place in Coketown, in *Hard Times*, whose fortifications are more alive than the race they shelter. The Coketown "hands" have been approximately reduced to those members for which they are named,—or, Dickens says, they are "like the lower creatures of the seashore, only hands and stomachs,"—while the two-way law has also had the effect of converting their material environment into passion, complicated, lunatic, and uncontrollable: Coketown is a labyrinth of "narrow courts upon courts and close streets upon streets, which had come into existence piecemeal, every piece in a violent hurry for some one man's purpose, and the whole an unnatural family, shouldering, and trampling, and pressing one another to death."

The description of Coketown is strongly felt because it represents an objective evil favored by industrialism; the image of a deformed, totem-like life in its chimneys and chimney-pots —"which, for want of air to make a draught, were built in an immense variety of stunted and crooked shapes, as though every house put out a sign of the kind of people who might be expected to be born in it"—has an hallucinatory vividness; but more hallucinatory is the relatively innocent prospect from the roof of Todgers's boarding-house, in *Martin Chuzzlewit*, a description which bears a curious resemblance to passages in M. Sartre's *La Nausée* and other writings, where non-human existences rage with an indiscriminate life of their own.

The revolving chimney-pots on one great stack of buildings seemed to be turning gravely to each other every now and then, and whispering the result of their separate observation of what was going on below. Others, of a crook-backed shape, appeared to be maliciously holding themselves askew, that they might shut the prospect out and baffle Todgers's. The man who was mending a pen at an upper window over the way, became of paramount importance in the scene, and made a blank in it, ridiculously disproportionate in its extent, when he retired. The gambols of a piece of cloth upon the dyer's pole had far more interest for the moment than all the changing motion of the crowd. Yet even while the looker-on felt angry with himself for this, and wondered how it was, the tumult swelled into a roar; the hosts of objects seemed to thicken and expand a hundredfold; and after gazing round him, quite scared, he turned into Todgers's

again, much more rapidly than he came out; and ten to one he told
M. Todgers afterwards that if he hadn't done so, he would certainly
have come into the street by the shortest cut; that is to say, head-
foremost.

Much of the description is turned upon the conservative "seemed
to be" and "as if," and the pathetic fallacy provides a familiar
bourgeois security, but the technique changes in the middle,
betrayed by a discomfort which the "as if's" are no longer
able to conceal. The prospect from Todgers's is one in which
categorical determinations of the relative significance of objects—as of the chimney-pots, the blank upper window, or
the dyer's cloth—have broken down, and the observer on
Todgers's roof is seized with suicidal nausea at the momentary
vision of a world in which significance has been replaced by
naked and aggressive existence.

It has so often been said that Dickens's point of view is that
of the undernourished child roving London streets at night,
that one hesitates to say it again, although with no reference
to biography. The point of view is hallucinated and often fearful, as the insecure and ill-fed child's might be. It is not childish.
The grotesque transpositions are a coherent imagination of a
reality that has lost coherence, comic because they form a pattern integrating the disintegrated and lying athwart the reality
that has not got itself imagined. Everything has to be mentioned
—like the "strange solitary pumps" found near Todgers's, "hiding themselves in blind alleys, and keeping company with fire
ladders"—for, assuming that there is coherence in a world
visibly disintegrated into things, one way to find it is to mention everything. Hence the indefatigable attention to detail. No
thing must be lost, as it is doubtless essential to the mysterious
organization of the system. The system itself is assumed to be
a nervous one, and for this reason Dickens's language has its
almost inexhaustible vitality and vivacity, inasmuch as its predica-

tions about persons or objects tend to be statements of metabolic conversion of one into the other.

II

The changes are still wrought out of the broad common intuition of the connections between moral and physical phenomena, often using the ancient image of the bacillus-like physical reality of the evil spirit. The moral atmosphere of the Merdle swindle, in *Little Dorrit*, is treated in terms of a malignant physical infection, that, disseminated in the air they breathe, lays hold on people in the soundest health. On the other hand, the physical plague that arises out of the slum district of Tom All Alone's, in *Bleak House*, and that creeps to the houses of the great, is itself a moral plague, the conditions for it having been created by moral acquiescence. Its ambiguity is enforced by the conversion of the slum-dwellers into vermin parasites— "a crowd of foul existence that crawls in and out of gaps in walls and boards; and coils itself to sleep, in maggot numbers, where the rain drips in; and comes and goes, fetching and carrying fever, and sowing . . . evil in its every footprint." The Transformation of spiritual into physical being is reversed by an imagery of inferno, which translates the physical fact as a spiritual one: "the crowd . . . hovers round the three visitors, like a dream of horrible faces, and fades away up alleys and into ruins, and behind walls; and with occasional cries and shrill whistles of warning, thenceforth flits about them until they leave the place." This is Hell, and however verifiable on earth, is "unnatural" in nature. It is representative of Dickens's method, which is a scrupulous rendering of nature gone wrong in all its parts.

Imperceptibly, by changes that are themselves psychologically valid, the atoms of the physical world have been impregnated with moral aptitude, so that it is not inconsistent that at the crisis of plot, a giant beam should loosen itself and fall on the head of the villain. Stephen Blackpool, returning home and thinking of the drunken wife whom he will find there in her filth and madness, has "an unwholesome sense of growing larger, of being placed in some new and diseased relation towards the objects among which he passed, of seeing the iris round every misty light turn red. . . ." Gaffer Hexam, coming from the river where he has been at his usual business of trolling for corpses, is shunned by the other river-men when they suspect him of improving his occupation by manufacture of the commodity on which he lives, and he says fiercely as he looks around, now over this shoulder, now over that, "Have we got a pest in the house? Is there summ'at deadly sticking to my clothes? What's let loose upon us? Who loosed it?" Pip, standing waiting for Estella in the neighborhood of Newgate, and beginning dimly to be aware of his implication in the guilt for which that establishment stands, has the same sensation of a deadly dust clinging to him and tries to beat it out of his clothes. Still not without psychological validity is the minute change from the subjective atmosphere of guilt, or the apprehension of evil, which *seems* to be reflected in the physical world, to its actualization in the behavior of physical things, as in those mysterious rustlings and tremblings which frighten Affery in *Little Dorrit*, "as if a step had shaken the floor, or even as if she had been touched by some awful hand," which are the real warnings of dissolution in the worm-eaten old house and of its final providential collapse on Blandois, when he is alone in it in the purity of his evil. Considered in this way, Dickens's use of physical coincidence in his plots is consistent with his imagination of a thoroughly nervous universe, whose ganglia spread through things and people alike, so that moral contagion, from its breeding center in the human, transforms also the non-human and gives it the aptitude of the diabolic.

Coincidence is the violent connection of the unconnected; but there is no discontinuity in the Dickens world, either between persons and things, or between the private and the public act. What connection can there be, Dickens asks, between proud Lady Dedlock and Jo the outlaw with the broom: "What connection can there have been between many people in the innumerable histories of this world, who, from opposite sides of great gulfs, have, nevertheless, been very curiously brought together!" What brings Lady Dedlock and Jo together, from opposite sides of great gulfs, is the bond between the public guilt for Jo and the private guilt of Lady Dedlock for her daughter, these two offering to each other—as usual in Dickens —the model of parental irresponsibility, and the models coalescing when the woman who has denied her child, and the diseased boy to whom society has been an unnatural father, are laid side by side in the same churchyard to be consumed by the same worms, physical nature asserting the organicity which moral nature had revoked. What brings the convict Magwitch across "great gulfs" to the boy Pip is again a profoundly implicit compact of guilt, as binding as the convict's leg-iron which is its recurrent symbol, and again the model is that of parental irresponsibility—although the terms shift subtly here, and it is sometimes Magwitch, the criminal foster-father, who is the abused child, and Pip, the corrupted child, who bears the social guilt for Magwitch. The multiplying likenesses in the street as Magwitch draws nearer, coming over the sea, the mysterious warnings of his approach on the night of his reappearance, are moral projections as real as the storm outside the windows and as the crouched form of the vicious Orlick on the dark stairs. The conception of what brings people together—the total change in the texture of experience that follows upon the private or the public act, the concreteness of its effect on the very atoms of external matter, as upon the heart, so that physical nature itself collaborates in the drama of reprisal—is deep and valid in this book. It is, however, the same conception of linked changes in the universe that, clumsily in *David Copperfield*, allows Steerforth's body to be washed up on the sands of Yarmouth just at David's feet. The sea itself has not remained neutral.

It is for this reason that the river is so effective a symbol in these novels, appearing in almost every story in closely observed, vivid, and obsessive detail. It is the common passage and the actual flowing element that unites individuals and classes, and it has a malignant potentiality that impregnates everything upon it—discolored copper, rotten wood, honeycombed stone, green dank deposit. The corpse is shunted there secretly at night; but the river has a terrible capacity to act, and it will turn suddenly upon the ghoul, reach up, crush him, suck him under, converting him into the commodity he has been engaged in producing; and at obscure intervals along the banks are those night-stations of the law, with nets and pumps, and with bookkeepers employed to docket the ordinary apparition—"a face, rising out of the dreaded water." Lizzie Hexam, waiting at the riverside for her father's return, feels in the tidal swell breaking at her feet, without her seeing how it had gathered, the rush of *her own thoughts*, dim before her like the great black river.

In *Great Expectations*, in a finely lucid atmosphere of fairy-tale, Dickens uses a kind of montage to represent an organization of reality crossing spatial and temporal determinations, super-imposing them in a moral present; as in the scene in which Estella walks the casks in the old brewery. Estella's walking the casks is an enchanting ritual dance of childhood (like walking fence-rails or railroad-ties), but inexplicably present in the tableau is the suicidal figure of Miss Havisham hanging by the neck from a brewery beam. Accompanying each appearance of Estella—who is the star and jewel of Pip's great expectations, wearing jewels in her hair and on her breast ("I and the jewels," she says)—is a disturbing ghostly suggestion of the same kind, an unformed dread; the star shudders in the wind from over the marshes; Pip tries to strike the dust of Newgate from his clothes as he sees her face in a coach-window; her slender knitting fingers are suddenly horribly displaced by the marred wrists of a murderess. This duality of vision is paralleled by a psychological duplicity. In the sense that one implies the other, the glittering frosty girl and the decayed and false old woman, Miss Havisham, are not two characters but a single one, a continuum (representing the tainted wish, the unpurchased good); as the boy Pip and the criminal Magwitch form another continuum. This bears on the commonplace of criticism that Dickens was usually unable, as Edmund Wilson puts it, "to get the good and bad together in one character," a criticism which holds in a world of neutral and simple matter, with its qualitative and quantitative disjunctions, and where character alone feels the stress of spirit; but in Dickens's nervous world, one simplex is superimposed upon or is continuous with another, and together they form the complex of good-in-evil or of evil-in-good. Pip carries Magwitch (his "father") within him, and the apparition of the criminal is the apparition of Pip's own guilt. Similarly Joe Gargery, saintly simpleton of the folk, and the journeyman Orlick, dark beast of the Teutonic marshes (who comes "from the ooze"), as the opposed extremes of spiritual possibility, form a spiritual continuum that frames and gives meaning to the others.

Two kinds of crime form Dickens's two chief themes, the crime against the child, and the calculated social crime. They are formally analogous, their form being the treatment of persons as things; but, on the usual principle of inherence that obtains here, they are also inherent in each other, whether the private will is to be considered as depraved by the operation of a public institution, or the institution as a bold concert of private depravities. The correspondence of the two is constantly suggested. In *Little Dorrit*, for example, where old Dorrit's exploitation of his daughter supplies the main substance of the story, the crime against the child is a private type of the public morality represented by the Merdle swindle and by the ineffably criminal business of the Circumlocution Office. (The name Merdle may be a play on both *merde* and murder. Having murdered public welfare on a grand scale, then murdered himself with a pen-knife, Mr. Merdle is discovered as "certain carrion at the bottom of a bath.") In the same book, Arthur Clennam lives under an oppressive conviction that his father has committed a crime; without knowing what it is, he feels that the expiation of it is part of his inheritance: "there was some one with an unsatisfied claim upon his justice." The suggestion is strong here that the public and the private guilt spring from each other, or from the same root: that the "father" is the social mechanism, informed by the corrupt individual will. In *Bleak House,* the public crime is the operation of Chancery, and clearly Chancery is the "father" of Richard Carstone, as the slum of Tom All Alone's is the "father" of the pariah Jo.

Generally, in the Dickens novels, the public and private crimes are infinitely serial (a fact which gives the later plots their elaborately epicyclic character), in a series that can never be really closed, but only cut off, for which reason the plot resolutions are as nominal as the resolution of *Tartufe* or *l'Avare;* for, seen thus serially, the crimes are actually bottomless. The bottomless permutation of the crimes of the fathers and institutionalized crime is felt in the passage describing the neighborhood of Arthur Clennam's grim home. Somewhere, hidden in the corner of a desk-drawer, or behind the frame of a portrait, is the secret of his own father's crime, and the whole neighborhood is tainted by it.

The dim streets by which he went, seemed all depositories of oppressive secrets. The deserted counting-houses, with their secrets of books and papers locked up in chests and safes; the banking-houses, with their secrets of strong rooms and wells, the keys of which were in a very few secret pockets and a very few secret breasts; the secrets of all the dispersed grinders in the vast mill, among whom there were doubtless plunderers, forgers, and trust-betrayers of many sorts, whom the light of any day that dawned might reveal; he could have fancied that these things, in hiding, imparted a heaviness to the air.

Though the plot may discover the secret of the portrait-frame or of the desk-drawer, that is, though it may particularize this or that crime, there is left over a pervasive anxiety about things in hiding, indefinitely and obscurely webbed, as if the permutation of public and private crimes constantly created a new and autonomous mystery, like the secret transforming principle of the concentration camp. The prison-symbol in *Little Dorrit* is a deliberate attempt to organize these perceptions; and when old Dorrit, in his mad speech of welcome at the Roman reception, says, "Welcome to the Marshalsea! The space is—ha—limited—limited—the parade might be wider; but you will find it apparently grow larger after a time—a time, ladies and gentlemen . . ." the words carry an equivocal sense which refers them beyond certain evident particular meanings (as that, among the elegant guests, there are cheats and forgers; or that the economy of the great world demands a prison-like suppression of the human quality) to another that is less tangible, a mysterious impotence in the face of that inevitable adjustment to the narrowness of the parade, a distracted hoplessness that will seize on the specific reference (industrialism in Coketown, big business in the city) but that is not exhausted by the specific. Little Dorrit, it is said, "began with sorrowful unwillingness to acknowledge to herself, that . . . no space in the life of man could overcome that quarter of a century behind the prison bars." There is, one feels, a crime behind a crime, created by or creating the other, and making of the earth a foul and pestilent congregation of vapors, without revealing what it is.

It is somewhere behind, overlooking but not to be looked at, like the Chief Butler, who undoubtedly is in the secret. One is seated at the table in the act of drinking, and one sees him through the wine-glass, the glazed fixedness of his cold and ghostly eye. One tries to recall having met him in prison, for his distant attention argues previous acquaintance, but his face is unfamiliar. His relationship with the Law is identified in the person of Jaggers, the criminal lawyer in *Great Expectations*, chief butler of Newgate, whose office is wholly pertinent to one's own case (for he is the Father's lieutenant) but also wholly ambiguous, and whose manner is "expressive of knowing something secret about every one of us that would effectually do for each individual if he chose to disclose it."

The prevailing anxiety, still exceeding its occasions, is felt in the "maze," the "labyrinth," and the "wilderness" of Dickens's streets. To find Todgers's

you groped your way for an hour through lanes and bye-ways, and court-yards, and passages; and you never once emerged upon anything that might be reasonably called a street. A kind of resigned distraction came over the stranger as he trod these devious mazes, and, giving himself up for lost, went in and out and round about and quietly turned back again when he came to a dead wall or was stopped by an iron railing, and felt that the means of escape might possibly present themselves in their own good time, but that to anticipate them was hopeless.

Todgers's is, in a sense, all of London, as London is the whole world; for it is impossible for the reader to dissociate these mazes of a squalid metropolitan district from the Coketown "labyrinth of narrow courts upon courts, and close streets upon streets"; or from the "wildernesses" of semi-fashionable Park Lane, with their be-crutched and scrofulous tenements "that looked like the last result of the great mansions' breeding in-and-in," where Arthur Clennam goes looking for Miss Wade; or from the maggoty honeycomb of Tom All Alone's; or, for that matter, from the corridors of the Circumlocution Office, which is a purely moral phenomenon. The anxiety is felt also in the immense number of claustral interiors—the chamber offered to the Misses Pecksniff at Todgers's, commanding "at a perspective of two feet, a brown wall with a black cistern on the top" ("Not the damp side," said Mrs. Todgers. "*That* is Mr. Jinkins's."); Jonas Chuzzlewit's "blotched, stained, mouldering room, like a vault"; Gaffer Hexam's hovel, "smeared with red-lead and damp, with a look of decomposition"; Grandfather Smallweed's "dark little parlour, certain feet below the level of the street"—interiors suggesting, in one detail or another of underground darkness and damp, the grave.

Dickens's plots seldom serve to canalize this submerged hysteria, to resolve it with the resolution of the particular set of plotted circumstances. The Todgers world requires an act of redemption. A symbolic act of this kind is again and again indicated, in the charity of the uncherished and sinned-against child for the inadequate or criminal father—what might be called the theme of the Prodigal Father, Dickens's usual modification of the Prodigal Son theme. But the act should be such that it would redeem not only the individual fathers, but society at large; one might almost say—thinking of those grave-like rooms where this vast population burrows, and of the monstrous caricature of death which the living themselves offer—that it should be such as to redeem the dead. *Great Expectations* is an exception in that, in this novel, the redemptive act is adequate to and structural for both bodies of thematic material—the sins of the individual and the sins of society.

III

Pip first becomes aware of the "identity of things" as he is held suspended heels over head by the convict; that is, in a world literally turned upside down. Thenceforth Pip's interior landscape is inverted by his guilty knowledge of this man "who had been soaked in water, and smothered in mud, and lamed by stones, and cut by flints, and stung by nettles, and torn by briars," and it is as much as to say that the inversion of natural order begins with self-consciousness, that self-consciousness co-incides with guilt. The "crime" that is always at the center of the Dickens universe is thus identified in a new way—not primarily as that of the father, nor as that of some public institution, but as that of the child. It is for this reason that the child is able to redeem his world.

The guilt of the child is realized on several levels. Pip experiences the psychological form of guilt before he is capable of voluntary evil; he is treated by adults—Mrs. Joe, and Pumble-chook, and Wopsle—as if he were a felon, a young George Barnwell wanting only to murder his nearest relative. This is the usual nightmare of the child in Dickens, a vision of imminent incarceration, fetters like sausages, lurid accusatory texts. He is treated, that is, as if he were a thing, manipulable by adults for the extraction of certain sensations; by making him feel guilty and diminished, they are able to feel virtuous and great. But the psychological form of guilt acquires spiritual content when he formulates the tainted wish (the wish to be as the most powerful adult) and begins to treat others as things: at the literal level, Pip's guilt is that of snobbery toward Joe Gargery. Symbolically, however, it is that of murder: for he steals the file with which the convict rids himself of his leg-iron, and it is this leg-iron, picked up on the marshes, with which Orlick attacks Mrs. Joe; so that the child does inevitably overtake his destiny, which was, like George Barnwell, to murder his relative. But the "relative" whom the young George Barnwell, adopting the venerable criminality of society, is destined, in the widest scope of intention, to murder is not Mrs. Joe but his "father," Magwitch—to murder in the socially chronic fashion of the Dickens world, which consists in the dehumanization of the weak, or in moral acquiescence to such murder. These are the possibilities that are projected in the opening scene of the book, when the young child, left with a burden on his soul, watches the convict limping off under an angry red sky, toward the black marshes, the gibbet, and the savage lair of the sea, in a still rotating landscape.

In Dickens's modification of the folk-pattern of the fairy-wishing, Magwitch is Pip's "fairy god-father," and like all the fathers, he uses the child as a thing, in order to obtain through him sensations of grandeur. In relation to society, however, Magwitch is the child, and society the prodigal father; from the time he was first taken for stealing turnips, the convict's career has duplicated brutally and in public the pathos of the ordinary child. Again, in relation to Pip, Magwitch is still the child; for, having been dedicated from the first to criminality, Pip has carried his criminal father within him, and is projectively responsible for Magwitch's existence and for his brutalization; so that Pip is the father of his father. Thus the ambiguities of each term of the relationship between Pip and Magwitch are such that each is both child and father; and the act of love which is redemptive is reinforced four-fold, and the redemption is a four-fold redemption—that is to say, infinite, as it serves for all the meanings Dickens finds it possible to attach to the child-father relationship, and this is the only relationship that obtains among men.

As the child's original alienation is essentially mysterious—a guilty inheritance from the fathers which invades first aware-ness—the redemptive act is also a mysterious one. The mysterious nature of the act is first indicated, in the manner of a motif, when Mrs. Joe, in imbecile pantomime, tries to propitiate her attacker, the bestial Orlick. In Orlick is concretized all the undefined evil of the Dickens world, that has nourished itself underground and crept along walls, like the ancient stains on the house of Atreus; he is the lawlessness implied in the unnatural conversions of the human into the non-human, the retributive death that invades those who have grown lean in life and who have exercised the powers of death over others; he is the instinct of aggression and destruction, and Dickens does not try to "psy-chologize" him through plotted cause and effect. His modality is that character of the visitations of evil which Kierkegaard called "suddenness," and he emerges without warning "from the ooze" where he has been unconsciously cultivated. As Orlick is one form of spiritual excess, Joe Gargery is the opposed form, unqualified love. Given these terms of the spiritual framework, the redemptive act itself could scarcely be anything but gro-tesque, and it is by a grotesque gesture—one of the most pro-foundly intuitive things in Dickens—that Mrs. Joe is redeemed. What is implied by her humble bowing down to the beast is a recognition of the essentiality of evil, and of its dialectical relationship with love. The motif reappears in the moment of major illumination in the book. Pip "bows down," not to Joe Gargery, toward whom he has been privately and literally guilty, but to the wounded, hunted, shackled man, Magwitch. It is in this way that the manifold organic relationships among men are revealed, and that the Todgers world, with its baffling labyrinths, its animated chimneys, its illicit bacillary invasions, its hints and signals of a cancerous organization, is healed.

JACK LINDSAY: 1950

Final Judgment

HOW may we best sum up Dickens's achievement? In a career
which takes in such a huge span of human change and manages
to give artistic expression to that change, there are endless points
of interest, which demand explication. Many of these points
have been touched on in the narrative. Here we must concentrate
on certain essentials.

First, there is the aspect already mentioned: the huge span
which Dickens covers. Very few writers on his work seem to
be even vaguely aware of the remarkable inner development
which it reveals. If dimly conscious of a deepening gloom in the
later works, they put it down to irritability or unhappiness in
the domestic sphere. Criticism of Dickens has so far been very
largely at the level which Shakespearean criticism clung to before 1800. Dickens is not of Shakespeare's stature; but the comparison is not altogether inept. For Dickens is the first writer
in England after Shakespeare (except Blake) who is centrally
and continuously aware of the problem of dissociation.

He begins in a pre-industrialist world, partly borrowed from
childhood fantasy and partly borrowed from eighteenth-century
novelists like Smollett. He moves step by step into the hell of
the actual world, always consolidating his position by the build-

From *Charles Dickens* (New York, 1950).

ing-up of significant symbols that grasp the basic plight of men.
The fusion of these symbols and the realistic depiction of the
world goes on all the while, till it reaches the major definitions
of *Bleak House, Little Dorrit,* and *Our Mutual Friend*—with
Great Expectations as the more personal commentary on the
situation, and *Edwin Drood* as a masterly epilogue which sets
out the tensions of the next phase of life and art.

Even Balzac, Dostoevsky, or Tolstoy cannot show such an
orderly progression of penetrating definitions illuminating the
fate of man under capitalism in all its aspects. This progression
it is that makes the comparison with Shakespeare necessary and
relevant.

We can put the claim in another way. Dickens defines in his
work all the pangs of national growth from the first stages of
an emerging petty-bourgeois (still implicating many pre-
industrialist elements of festival fellowship and hospitality)
right on up to the point of conflict beyond which lies the full
egalitarian harmony that transcends all existing relationships.
Thus his work spans the whole process of nationhood, and defines the various conflicts and tensions of that process, the
discovery of dissociation and the alienation of man from his
fellows and his own essence, the stages of struggle against the
dissociative forces, and the intuition (uttered in symbolic forms)
of the resolving unity. He and Blake are still the prophets of
our epoch.

What I am discussing is not any explicit statement of ends,
but the total direction of a definition: the artistic integration.
For in such an integration the term *artistic* is always to be
equated with the term *human*. Dickens (with Blake) is the
writer who gives full expression to the human forces caught
up in the throes of national development, moving powerfully
from folk-levels to the resolving and unifying levels of socialism,
and, in between, defining all the complex conflicts of love
and fear, dissociation and integration. Blake, in the primary

period of uprooting, gave deep poetic expression to the whole arc of transformation; Dickens, coming in the secondary phase, gave an extended novel-expression to the same arc. Now, as we reach the end of the arc, we can pick up their struggle anew, understand it at last, and find the forms that carry it forward through the decisive final phase.

Yet this steady unfolding of the fate of dissociated man in terms of dynamic imagery which looked forward beyond the dissociation, was made by a writer who managed to keep a general popularity in the Victorian world. How can we speak of the revolutionary virtue and integrity of a man who remained a best seller to Victorian audiences?

That question goes to the heart of the terrible strain that tugged at Dickens all his life after the first simple burst of creative energy. He gained his popularity, his union with the Victorian audience, at a moment of general upheaval and transition. He drew on popular sources and on the eighteenth-century novelists, and built up a world of bonhomie and hospitable happiness, a nostalgic picture which consoled and heartened in a callous society. Almost at once (even before he had finished *Pickwick*) he had discovered the other side of the picture and begun introducing it into his passionate imagery. His readers felt in his work, not only the consolations of a lost Eden (ultimately the family bosom), but also the pang of loss, the imagery of all the fears they felt in a world not understood, a world busily bent on excluding them from all satisfactions of love and peace.

Here lay the function of Dickens's sentimentality—an expression of the overwrought emotions of men at this difficult moment of loss and thwarted development. I have explored the psychological mechanism of this sentimentality in Dickens, its relation to his childhood, to Fanny and his mother, to Mary Hogarth and Mary Weller. But what gave that mechanism its social and artistic import was the way in which it set him in immediate union with the vast homeless pang of the people in the convulsions of change. Without it he would never have laid the basis for his unity with the mass audience and his capacity to grasp the inner structure of historical crisis. Its weakness lay in the tendency to smudge out conflict in the fathomless pang of the tear, the intolerable sense of a shared loss. But it was humanly sound while the astringent gusto of his delight in life and his savage hatred of greed and oppression accompanied it.

Thus in the earlier stages of his work he built that strong basis of union with his public that was able to weather the difficult strains of the later years.

If we can imagine him somehow having written *Little Dorrit* in the 'fifties without the preceding works, we can see that he would never have managed to get the work across to the general public as he did. If he had managed to get it published, it would have been furiously rejected on all sides.

The story I have told makes clear how bitterly hard he found it to keep on writing almost from the very start. All the themes which stirred his creative faculty had at their core a deep-going antagonism to the major trends of respectable society. Being built as he was, having reached expression by the road he had, he could neither set himself simply into opposition with the trends about him, nor accept them in any terms used by their exponents. He remained a lone fighter—and in that there may be detected his petty-bourgeois origins. But if we see only that, we see little. His lone fighting derived in the long run from his need to fight for a concept of unity that lay far ahead and had no hope of actualization in his world. On the one hand, he stands for all the constructive and brotherly elements going to build up the nation; on the other hand, he is too aware of the actual contradictions and distortions everywhere in the contemporary situation to take any obviously partisan position. He speaks for the soul of the struggle, and therefore for a future in which the existing contradictions will be humanly resolved. For this fully human resolution he is an uncompromising fighter, a consistent partisan.

Hence the enormous strain he felt from the moment he introduced the prison episode into *Pickwick*. (Personally, much of the strain expressed itself as a fear of exposure as a jail-bird's son, who had worked in a blacking factory; but this fear was only a rationalization of a much deeper conflict between himself and society.) He had to keep his union with the struggling, broken, aspiring human being of his world, and yet he had to speak in terms of a resolving unity which did not yet possess the means of actualizing itself. If he failed on either count, he failed as an artist—and also went bankrupt. Hence the important part that financial responsibilities play in his life (with far-reaching effects on his work, its themes and its characters). He had to go on making money, but he could not write powerfully unless he remained true to himself, and if he remained true to himself he threatened to lose his public by too explicit attack on the ruling values of society.

Therein lies the tug-of-war that made him so restless, so hectically happy or unhappy, so unable to find any secure personal relationships, boisterously expansive and yet always aware of a cold reservation.

When, however, the utmost has been said about his compromises, confusions, and obliquities, there remains as the central dynamic of his work a critical vision which we can only call revolutionary, since it draws its creative virtues from a fundamental rejection of existing values. Bernard Shaw has well brought out this point. "Dickens never regarded himself as a revolutionist, though he certainly was one. His implacable contempt for the House of Commons . . . never wavered." He points out that Thackeray could write as fiercely about the ruling classes, and yet Thackeray remained a bourgeois; for he had a basic agreement on social doctrine with the persons he reviled. Dickens had a basic disagreement. "*Little Dorrit* is a more seditious book than *Das Kapital*." A pardonable exaggeration.

I have already sketched the way in which Dickens's work grew up out of ferment of popular forms and forces. *The key nature of such popular elements is to be found in the emphasis on the notion of transformation and on all images or characters that seem to embody the transformative processes.* Dickens found his deepest contact with these elements through his subtle and pervasive use of the day-dream, the childhood fantasy. It is because he always fuses the fantasy with realism that he redeems realism from its bourgeois distortion (naturalism) and shows himself an outstanding upholder of the great creative tradition which the triumph of the bourgeoisie threatened. The mass tradition is one of fantasy, moving between dream-image and poetic symbol; naturalism (i.e. realism minus fantasy) is historically the bourgeois form of expression. Dickens captures this form and re-fuses it with fantasy, orientates it towards the concept of transformation.

It is precisely the great creative power in Dickens which has been belittled by those who, one way or another, employ a naturalistic critique—Taine or G. H. Lewes in Dickens's own day, or E. M. Forster in ours. Taine thought Dickens's image-making power to be monomaniacal; Lewes called it hallucinative. ("Dickens once declared to me that every word said by one of his characters was distinctly *heard* by him; I was at first not a little puzzled to account for the fact that he could hear language so utterly unlike the language of real feeling, and not be aware of its preposterousness; but the surprise vanished when I thought of the phenomena of hallucination.") Forster finds Dickens's world flat and [two]-dimensional—i.e. is perfectly blind to the spiritual depths from which Dickens's characters emerge with their dynamic energies. Such an attitude is quite logical if one has no sense whatever of the creative unity of a Dickens novel. Then what could one see but a crowd of gal-

vanic marionettes, strange figures of theatric violence wandering
in a mad and yet prearranged void? Forster by his comment
gives away that he himself lives in an utterly unreal world, in
which the knowledge of the key factor in experience, without
which all experience is essentially unmeaning and pettily personal, is totally missing. Dickens is the poet who knows simultaneously what alienation and union mean in capitalist society.

Barker Fairley says of Goethe's *Faust*, in reply to Santayana's
complaint that Faust does not develop: "The development is
in the poem as a whole, not in its supposed hero." The point
is equally true of Dickens's important novels. The comment
that his characters are marionettes, bright, exciting, over life-
size, has its slight measure of truth, in so far as it points to the
folk-elements of humour and symbolism in his work; but in
the form in which it is usually made (with the implication that
the people lack Soul or Inwardness), it shows a sad lack of response to Dickens's creative method and its importance for the
post-1830 world. Like Goethe, he makes a fundamentally lyrical
approach, and this means that his figures are not Shakespearean
persons realized individually but fitting into a single symbolic
conception, or Ibsen characters in whom the pattern of unconscious memory is psychologically united with naturalism as
both fate and revelatory liberation. His people are lyrical images
which gain profundity and symbolic significance through their
relation to a total concept, a total movement, born out of a
personal tension. The Shakespearean and Goethean methods
are equally valid; the virtue of either depends on the extent to
which the personal tension is realized in unity with the envi-
roning pressures of history. Dickens, from this angle, shows up
as a creator of the highest order; and to call his people flatly
[two]-dimensional is to miss the terrific inwardness of the whole
concept which reacts on each single figure, giving it a depth
of emotional overtones.

The best statement of his method is perhaps that made by himself in later years:

It does not seem to me to be enough to say of any description that it is the exact truth. The exact truth must be there; but the merit or art in the narrator, is the manner of stating the truth. As to which thing in literature, it always seemed to me that there is a world to be done. And in these times, when the tendency is to be frightfully literal and catalogue-like—to make the thing, in short, a sort of sum in reduction that any miserable creature can do in that way—I have an idea (really founded on love of what I profess), that the very holding of popular literature through a kind of popular dark age, may depend on such fanciful treatment.

That goes to the very heart of the problem. In a "popular dark age"—an age when the mass audience reasserts itself but in situations of the direst self-alienation—the carrying on of the vital popular elements, fantasy and imagery of dream-transformation, is the only way in which to keep alive the great tradition of art and to defeat the bourgeois dissociation of naturalism.

Here Dickens turns out, in his own way, to be making exactly the same kind of protest as the great Romantic and Symbolist poets—though he was inevitably unaware of the relation. Those poets proclaimed the need for a new organic integration in art and life, and, in a society falling away into worse dissociations, they fought to act as pathfinders towards the harmonies that men would need in completing their revolt against the dehumanizing pressures. By his fantasy-method Dickens picks up all that has been most poetically vigorous in our tradition, re-creates it on a new level, and sets his dynamite inside the bourgeois form, the novel. Into the novel he blasts the poetic tradition (which includes Shakespeare and folk-tale, transformative images on the high tragic level or at the folk-level of marvel, burlesque, dream-tale). He thus completes on a grand scale the work which the Gothic novel, the novel of fantasy and sensibility, the *roman noir*, had begun.

Bulwer Lytton, in 1845, in his preface to *Night and Morning*, had given the best contemporary statement of what was at issue. "The vast and dark Poetry around us—the Poetry of Modern Civilization and Daily Existence, is shut out from us in much, by the shadowy giants of Prejudice and Fear. He who would arrive at the Fairy Land must face the Phantoms." *The vast and dark Poetry around us, the Poetry of modern civilization and daily existence:* those words go to the very heart of the artistic problem, and they reveal the link between the work of Bulwer and Dickens and that of the French symbolists. But though Bulwer had done his best, the proud claim with which he continues can only be truly taken into the mouth of Dickens: "Betimes, I set myself to the task of investigating the motley world to which our progress in humanity has attained, caring little about misrepresentation. I incurred what hostility I provoked, in searching through a devious labyrinth for the footprints of Truth."

Now, if what I have said is true, what becomes of his influence? If his attitudes are fundamentally revolutionary, do they peter out in misconceptions, falsifications—till Chesterton can get away with a picture of him as a roaring loon of gusto, or Forster can seem to sniff validly at his tremendous universe of creation as at a flat shadow-show? Or does his work find devious ways, in the rapidly extending and complicated situation of world capitalism, to reassert its basic energy and stir further artistic developments along the same lines?

If one looks at England, it seems at first glance as if Dickens's influence does indeed peter out. Clearly, he has a strong effect, directly or indirectly, on the post-1848 novelists of Victorian England, the Brontës, Trollope, Collins, Reade, George Eliot; but they move, on the whole, steadily towards naturalism.

Enough of the grand tradition remains in their work to give it breadth, dignity, fullness; but the weakening side of their definition shows up in the epigones who succeed them. Dickens's influence seems fairly well quenched.

True, he entered powerfully into the lives of writers like Swinburne and William Morris, though he did not directly affect their styles. More importantly, he had a strong effect on Ruskin, helping to bring about the redirection of his energies from art criticism to a method which embraced both art and social problems in a single concept of integration. *Unto This Last*, the decisive work of revolt by Ruskin, reveals this effect of his. But still we are far from finding any successor in the realm of fiction who carries on his work.

The successor is, however, there: George Bernard Shaw, who has abundantly paid tribute to the decisive impact on his life of works like *Little Dorrit* and *Our Mutual Friend*. I do not wish here to enter into any examination of the strengths and weaknesses of Shaw; but even a cursory glance shows that his great virtue has been the fact that throughout his work he is aware of people as living in a capitalist society. This it is which marks him out from all the other writers of his period in England. And this virtue he owed first to Dickens, and then to Marx. Dickens gave him the vision of what the alienating pressures meant, and Marx gave him intellectual confidence.

Other writers, from Gissing to Wells, owed much to Dickens; but they did not share the fully penetrative sense that Shaw had of Dickens's essential meaning.

Dickens's influence has then been by no means negligible in Britain; but it is to the European novel in general that we must look for the full fertilizing results of his work. In France and even more in Germany he helped to broaden the sphere of the novel; but it was in Russia and Scandinavia that he found his natural kinsmen. For there it was that a number of factors made possible the rebirth of the novel as a great tragic medium. Through

Dostoevsky and Strindberg, on whom he had a profound effect at key moments of their development, his influence broadly enters the whole European stream.

Here were writers who were able to carry on in terms of the post-1860 situation his awareness of what self-alienation meant, and to apply in various ways his method of fantasy-projection and dream-process. (Strindberg's novels, in which Dickens's influence is paramount, must be recalled here.)

To examine the new forms, the new tensions, which his ideas and methods assume in Dostoevsky and Strindberg, would require another book; but I must emphasize the kinship to bring out the part which he played in the European developments since 1850. They lacked his broad resolutions, but they carried on his definition of the *alienation of man from man, man from himself*, in a capitalist society.

It is because I believe that the revaluation of Dickens's work and influence can yet play a very important part in the cultural struggle of to-day, that I have written this study. The "dark popular age" is still with us, is with us, indeed, to an extent that Dickens could not have guessed at. Mass-media like radio and cinema make incomparably more pressing the problem of transmuting naturalistic and decadent forms with a new life, a poetic life which will utter the truth of the human condition and recapture tradition. Dickens is the master who has shown how this can be done; his method is more relevant to-day than ever.

I do not mean that we should start trying to write novels like Dickens's or ape his tricks of style. I mean that we should realize his fundamental method of fusing dream-process and realism in terms of essential human conflict, and find our own ways of relating this method to contemporary issues.

Dickens is still ahead of us.

GRAHAM GREENE: 1950
The Young Dickens

A CRITIC must try to avoid being a prisoner of his time, and
if we are to appreciate *Oliver Twist* at its full value we must forget that long shelf-load of books, all the stifling importance of
a great author, the scandals and the controversies of the private
life; it would be well too if we could forget the Phiz and the
Cruikshank illustrations that have frozen the excited, excitable
world of Dickens into a hall of waxworks, where Mr. Mantalini's
whiskers have always the same trim, where Mr. Pickwick perpetually turns up the tails of his coat, and in the Chamber of
Horrors Fagin crouches over an undying fire. His illustrators,
brilliant craftsmen though they were, did Dickens a disservice,
for no character any more will walk for the first time into our
memory as we ourselves imagine him, and *our* imagination after
all has just as much claim to truth as Cruikshank's.

Nevertheless the effort to go back is well worth while. The
journey is only a little more than a hundred years long, and at
the other end of the road is a young author whose sole claim
to renown in 1837 had been the publication of some journalistic
sketches and a number of comic operas: *The Strange Gentleman,
The Village Coquette, Is She His Wife?* I doubt whether any

Introduction to *Oliver Twist* (London, 1950); also, *The Lost Childhood and Other Essays* (London, 1951).

literary Cortez at that date would have yet stood them upon his shelves. Then suddenly with *The Pickwick Papers* came popularity and fame. Fame falls like a dead hand on an author's shoulder, and it is well for him when it falls only in later life. How many in Dickens's place would have withstood what James called "the great corrupting contact of the public," the popularity founded, as it almost always is, on the weakness and not the strength of an author?

The young Dickens, at the age of twenty-five, had hit on a mine that paid him a tremendous dividend. Fielding and Smollett, tidied and refined for the new industrial bourgeoisie, had both salted it; Goldsmith had contributed sentimentality and Monk Lewis horror. The book was enormous, shapeless, familiar (that important recipe for popularity). What Henry James wrote of a long-forgotten French critic applies well to the young Dickens: "He is homely, familiar and colloquial; he leans his elbows on his desk and does up his weekly budget into a parcel the reverse of compact. You can fancy him a grocer retailing tapioca and hominy full weight for the price; his style seems a sort of integument of brown paper."

This is, of course, unfair to *The Pickwick Papers*. The driest critic could not have quite blinkered his eyes to those sudden wide illuminations of comic genius that flap across the waste of words like sheet lightning, but could he have foreseen the second novel, not a repetition of this great loose popular hold-all, but a short melodrama, tight in construction, almost entirely lacking in broad comedy, and possessing only the sad twisted humour of the orphans' asylum?

"You'll make your fortune, Mr. Sowerberry," said the beadle, as he thrust his thumb and forefinger into the proffered snuff-box of the undertaker: which was an ingenious little model of a patent coffin.

Such a development was as inconceivable as the gradual transformation of that thick boggy prose into the delicate and exact poetic cadences, the music of memory, that so influenced Proust.

We are too inclined to take Dickens as a whole and to treat his juvenilia with the same kindness or harshness as his later work. *Oliver Twist* is still juvenilia—magnificent juvenilia: it is the first step on the road that led from *Pickwick* to *Great Expectations*, and we can condone the faults of taste in the early book the more readily if we recognize the distance Dickens had to travel. These two typical didactic passages can act as the first two milestones at the opening of the journey, the first from *Pickwick*, the second from *Oliver Twist*.

And numerous indeed are the hearts to which Christmas brings a brief season of happiness and enjoyment. How many families, whose members have been dispersed and scattered far and wide, in the restless struggles of life, are then reunited, and meet once again in that happy state of companionship and mutual goodwill, which is a source of such pure and unalloyed delight, and one so incompatible with the cares and sorrows of the world, that the religious belief of the most civilised nations, and the rude traditions of the roughest savages, alike number it among the first joys of a future condition of existence, provided for the blest and happy!

The boy stirred, and smiled in his sleep, as though these marks of pity and compassion had awakened some pleasant dream of a love and affection he had never known. Thus, a strain of gentle music, or the rippling of water in a silent place, or the odour of a flower, or the mention of a familiar word, will sometimes call up sudden dim remembrances of scenes that never were, in this life; which vanish like a breath; which some brief memory of a happier existence, long gone by, would seem to have awakened; which no voluntary exertion of the mind can ever recall.

The first is certainly brown paper: what it wraps has been chosen by the grocer to suit his clients' tastes, but cannot we detect already in the second passage the tone of Dickens's secret prose, that sense of a mind speaking to itself with no one there to listen, as we find it in *Great Expectations?*

It was fine summer weather again, and, as I walked along, the times when I was a little helpless creature, and my sister did not spare me, vividly returned. But they returned with a gentle tone upon them, that softened even the edge of Tickler. For now, the very breath of the beans and clover whispered to my heart that the day must come when it would be well for my memory that others walking in the sunshine should be softened as they thought of me.

It is a mistake to think of *Oliver Twist* as a realistic story: only late in his career did Dickens learn to write realistically of human beings; at the beginning he invented life and we no more believe in the temporal existence of Fagin or Bill Sikes than we believe in the existence of that Giant whom Jack slew as he bellowed his Fee Fi Fo Fum. There were real Fagins and Bill Sikes's and real Bumbles in the England of his day, but he had not drawn them, as he was later to draw the convict Magwitch; these characters in *Oliver Twist* are simply parts of one huge invented scene, what Dickens in his own preface called "the cold wet shelterless midnight streets of London." How the phrase goes echoing on through the books of Dickens until we meet it again so many years later in "the weary western streets of London on a cold dusty spring night" which were so melancholy to Pip. But Pip was to be as real as the weary streets, while Oliver was as unrealistic as the cold wet midnight of which he formed a part.

This is not to criticize the book so much as to describe it. For what an imagination this youth of twenty-six had that he could invent so monstrous and complete a legend! We are not lost with Oliver Twist round Saffron Hill: we are lost in the interstices of one young, angry, gloomy brain, and the oppressive images stand out along the track like the lit figures in a Ghost Train tunnel.

Against the wall were ranged, in regular array, a long row of elm boards cut into the same shape: looking in the dim light, like high-shouldered ghosts with their hands in their breeches-pockets.

We have most of us seen those nineteenth-century prints where the bodies of naked women form the face of a character, the Diplomat, the Miser and the like. So the crouching figure of Fagin seems to form the mouth, Sikes with his bludgeon the jutting features and the sad lost Oliver the eyes of one man, as lost as Oliver.

Chesterton, in a fine imaginative passage, has described the mystery behind Dickens's plots, the sense that even the author was unaware of what was really going on, so that when the explanations come and we reach, huddled into the last pages of *Oliver Twist*, a naked complex narrative of illegitimacy and burnt wills and destroyed evidence, we simply do not believe. "The secrecy is sensational; the secret is tame. The surface of the thing seems more awful than the core of it. It seems almost as if these grisly figures, Mrs. Chadband and Mrs. Clennam, Miss Havisham and Miss Flite, Nemo and Sally Brass, were keeping something back from the author as well as from the reader. When the book closes we do not know their real secret. They soothed the optimistic Dickens with something less terrible than the truth."

What strikes the attention most in this closed Fagin universe are the different levels of unreality. If, as one is inclined to believe, the creative writer perceives his world once and for all in childhood and adolescence, and his whole career is an effort to illustrate his private world in terms of the great public world we all share, we can understand why Fagin and Sikes in their most extreme exaggerations move us more than the benevolence of Mr. Brownlow or the sweetness of Mrs. Maylie—they touch with fear as the others never really touch with love. It was not that the unhappy child, with his hurt pride and his sense of hopeless insecurity, had not encountered human goodness—he had simply failed to recognize it in those streets between Gadshill and Hungerford Market which had been as narrowly enclosed as Oliver Twist's. When Dickens at this early period tried to describe goodness he seems to have remembered the small stationers' shops on the way to the blacking factory with their coloured paper scraps of angels and virgins, or perhaps the face of some old gentleman who had spoken kindly to him outside Warren's factory. He has swum up towards goodness from the deepest world of his experience, and on this shallow level the conscious brain has taken a hand, trying to construct characters to represent virtue and, because his age demanded it, triumphant virtue, but all he can produce are powdered wigs and gleaming spectacles and a lot of bustle with bowls of broth and a pale angelic face. Compare the way in which we first meet evil with his introduction of goodness.

The walls and ceiling of the room were perfectly black with age and dirt. There was a deal table before the fire: upon which were a candle, stuck in a ginger-beer bottle, two or three pewter pots, a loaf and butter, and a plate. In a frying-pan, which was on the fire, and which was secured to the mantelshelf by a string, some sausages were cooking; and standing over them, with a toasting-fork in his hand, was a very old shrivelled Jew, whose villainous-looking and repulsive face was obscured by a quantity of matted red hair. He was dressed in a greasy flannel gown, with his throat bare. . . . "This is him, Fagin," said Jack Dawkins: "my friend Oliver Twist." The Jew grinned; and, making a low obeisance to Oliver, took him by the hand, and hoped he should have the honour of his intimate acquaintance.

Fagin has always about him this quality of darkness and nightmare. He never appears on the daylight streets. Even when we see him last in the condemned cell, it is in the hours before the dawn. In the Fagin darkness Dickens's hand seldom fumbles. Hear him turning the screw of horror when Nancy speaks of the thoughts of death that have haunted her:

"Imagination," said the gentleman, soothing her.

"No imagination," replied the girl in a hoarse voice. "I'll swear I saw 'coffin' written in every page of the book in large black letters, —aye, and they carried one close to me, in the streets tonight."

"There is nothing unusual in that," said the gentleman. "They have passed me often."

"*Real* ones," rejoined the girl. "This was not."

Now turn to the daylight world and our first sight of Rose:

The younger lady was in the lovely bloom and springtime of womanhood; at that age, when, if ever angels be for God's good purposes enthroned in mortal forms, they may be, without impiety, supposed to abide in such as hers.

She was not past seventeen. Cast in so slight and exquisite a mould; so mild and gentle; so pure and beautiful; that earth seemed not her element, nor its rough creatures her fit companions.

Or Mr. Brownlow as he first appeared to Oliver:

Now, the old gentleman came in as brisk as need be; but he had no sooner raised his spectacles on his forehead, and thrust his hands behind the skirts of his dressing-gown to take a good long look at Oliver, than his countenance underwent a very great variety of odd contortions. . . . The fact is, if the truth must be told, that Mr. Brownlow's heart, being large enough for any six ordinary old gentlemen of humane disposition, forced a supply of tears into his eyes, by some hydraulic process which we are not sufficiently philosophical to be in a condition to explain.

How can we really believe that these inadequate ghosts of goodness can triumph over Fagin, Monks and Sikes? And the answer, of course, is that they never could have triumphed without the elaborate machinery of the plot disclosed in the last pages. This world of Dickens is a world without God; and as a substitute for the power and the glory of the omnipotent and omniscient are a few sentimental references to heaven, angels, the sweet faces of the dead, and Oliver saying, "Heaven is a long way off, and they are too happy there to come down to the bedside of a poor boy." In this Manichean world we can believe in evil-doing, but goodness wilts into philanthropy, kindness, and those strange vague sicknesses into which Dickens's young women so frequently fall and which seem in his eyes a kind of badge of virtue, as though there were a merit in death.

But how instinctively Dickens's genius recognized the flaw and made a virtue out of it. We cannot believe in the power of Mr. Brownlow, but nor did Dickens, and from his inability to believe in his own good characters springs the real tension of his novel. The boy Oliver may not lodge in our brain like David Copperfield, and though many of Mr. Bumble's phrases have become and deserve to have become familiar quotations we can feel he was manufactured: he never breathes like Mr. Dorrit; yet Oliver's predicament, the nightmare fight between the darkness where the demons walk and the sunlight where ineffective goodness makes its last stand in a condemned world, will remain part of our imaginations forever. We read of the defeat of Monks, and of Fagin screaming in the condemned cell, and of Sikes dangling from his self-made noose, but we don't believe. We have witnessed Oliver's temporary escapes too often and his inevitable recapture: *there* is the truth and the creative experience. We know that when Oliver leaves Mr. Brownlow's house to walk a few hundred yards to the bookseller, his friends will wait in vain for his return. All London outside the quiet, shady street in Pentonville belongs to his pursuers; and when he escapes again into the house of Mrs. Maylie in the fields beyond Shepperton, we know his security is false. The seasons may pass, but safety depends not on time but on daylight. As children we all knew that: how all day we could forget the dark and the journey to bed. It is with a sense of relief that at last in twilight we see the faces of the Jew and Monks peer into the cottage window between the sprays of jessamine. At that moment we realize how the whole world, and not London only, belongs to these two after dark. Dickens, dealing out his happy endings and his unreal retributions, can never ruin the validity and dignity of that moment. "They had recognized him, and he them; and their look was as firmly impressed upon his memory, as if it had been deeply carved in stone, and set before him from his birth."

"From his birth"—Dickens may have intended that phrase to refer to the complicated imbroglios of the plot that lie outside the novel, "something less terrible than the truth." As for the truth, is it too fantastic to imagine that in this novel, as in many of his later books, creeps in, unrecognized by the author, the eternal and alluring taint of the Manichee, with its simple and terrible explanation of our plight, how the world was made by Satan and not by God, lulling us with the music of despair?

ARNOLD KETTLE: 1951

Dickens: *Oliver Twist*

IN the twelfth chapter of *Oliver Twist*, Oliver, carried insensible by Mr. Brownlow from the magistrate's court, wakes up to find himself in a comfortable bed:

Weak, and thin, and pallid, he awoke at last from what seemed to have been a long and troubled dream. Feebly raising himself in the bed, with his head resting on his trembling arm, he looked anxiously around.

"What room is this? Where have I been brought to?" said Oliver. "This is not the place I went to sleep in."

From *An Introduction to the English Novel* (London, 1951), Volume I.

He uttered these words in a feeble voice, being very faint and weak, but they were overheard at once; for the curtain at the bed's head was hastily drawn back, and a motherly old lady, very neatly and precisely dressed, rose as she withdrew it, from an armchair close by, in which she had been sitting at needlework.

"Hush, my dear," said the old lady softly. "You must be very quiet, or you will be ill again; and you have been very bad—as bad as bad could be, pretty nigh. Lie down again; there's a dear!" With these words, the old lady very gently placed Oliver's head upon the pillow, and, smoothing back his hair from his forehead, looked so kindly and lovingly in his face, that he could not help placing his little withered hand in hers, and drawing it round his neck.

"Save us!" said the old lady, with tears in her eyes, "what a grateful little dear it is! Pretty creature! What would his mother feel if she had sat by him as I have, and could see him now?"

It is a central situation in the book—this emergence out of squalor into comfort and kindliness—and it is repeated later in the story when once again Oliver, after the robbery in which he has been wounded, wakes to find himself cared for and defended by the Maylies. There is more than mere chance in the repetition and we meet here, indeed, a pattern recurring throughout Dickens's novels. It is worth while examining it more closely.

The first eleven chapters of *Oliver Twist* are an evocation of misery and horror. We have been drawn straight with the first sentence (of which workhouse is the key word) into a world of the most appalling poverty and ugliness, a world of brutality and violence in which life is cheap, suffering general and death welcome. That the evocation is crude, that it is marred by moments of false feeling and by a heavy-handed irony which weakens all it comments on, is not for the moment the consideration. By and large, the effect is of extraordinary power. No such effect (for good or ill) has emerged from any novel we have previously discussed. It is an effect which is, in the precise sense of a hackneyed word, unforgettable. The workhouse, the parochial baby-farm, Mr. Sowerberry's shop, the funeral, the Artful Dodger, Fagin's lair: they have the haunting quality, but nothing of the unreality, of a nightmare. It is a curious comment on Victorian civilization that this was considered suitable reading for children.

What is the secret of the power? Is it merely the objective existence of the horrors, the fact that such things were, that strikes at our minds? Fairly obviously not or we should be moved in just the same way by a social history. There is a particularity about this world which is not the effect of even a well-documented history. It is not just any evocation of the life of the poor after the Industrial Revolution; when we read the Hammonds' *Town Labourer* or Engels's *Condition of the Working Class in England in 1844* our reaction may not be less profound than our reaction to *Oliver Twist*, but it is different, more generalized, less vivid, less intense.

The most obvious difference between *Oliver Twist* and a social history is, of course, that it deals with actual characters whose personalities we envisage, whose careers we follow, and whose feelings we share. But this difference is not, I think, quite so important as we might assume. For in fact we do not become involved in the world of *Oliver Twist* in the way we become involved in the world of *Emma*. We do not really know very much about any of these characters, even Oliver himself, or participate very closely in their motives and reactions. We are sorry for Oliver; we are on his side; but our feeling for him is not very different from our feeling for any child we see ill-treated in the street. We are outraged and our sense of outrage no doubt comes, ultimately, from a feeling of common humanity, a kind of identification of ourselves with the child in his misery and struggles; but our entanglement in his situation is not really very deep.

In the famous scene when Oliver asks for more it is not the precise sense of Oliver's feelings and reactions that grips us; we do not feel what he is feeling in the way we share Miss Bates's emotion on Box Hill, and in this sense Oliver is less close to us and matters to us less than Miss Bates and Emma. But in another way Oliver matters to us a great deal more. For when he walks up to the master of the workhouse and asks for more gruel, issues are at stake which make the whole world of Jane Austen tremble. We care, we are involved, not because it is Oliver and we are close to Oliver (though that of course enters into it), but because every starved orphan in the world, and indeed everyone who is poor and oppressed and hungry is involved, and the master of the workhouse (his name has not been revealed) is not anyone in particular but every agent of an oppressive system everywhere. And that, incidentally, is why millions of people all over the world (including many who have never read a page of Dickens) can tell you what happened in Oliver Twist's workhouse, while comparatively few can tell you what happened on Box Hill.

That this episode from *Oliver Twist* should have become a myth, a part of the cultural consciousness of the people, is due not merely to its subject-matter but to the kind of novel Dickens wrote. He is dealing not, like Jane Austen, with personal relationships, not with the quality of feeling involved in detailed living, but with something which can without fatuity be called Life. What we get from *Oliver Twist* is not a greater precision of sensitiveness about the day-to-day problems of human behaviour but a sharpened sense of the large movement of life within which particular problems arise. It is pointless to argue whether the way Dickens tackles life is better or worse than the way Jane Austen tackles it. One might just as well argue whether it is better to earn one's living or to get married. Not merely are the two issues not exclusive, they are indissolubly bound up. In a sense they are the same problem—how best to live in society— but, for all their interdependence, one does not tackle them in precisely the same way.

What distinguishes the opening chapters of *Oliver Twist*

from, on the one side, a social history and, on the other side, *Emma*, is that they are symbolic. It is not a sense of participation in the personal emotions of any of the characters that engages our imagination but a sense of participation in a world that is strikingly, appallingly relevant to our world.

The *Oliver Twist* world is a world of poverty, oppression and death. The poverty is complete, utterly degrading and utterly realistic.

The houses on either side were high and large, but very old and tenanted by people of the poorest class: as their neglected appearance would have sufficiently denoted, without the concurrent testimony afforded by the squalid looks of the few men and women who, with folded arms and bodies half-doubled, occasionally skulked along. A great many of the tenements had shop fronts; but these were fast closed, and mouldering away, only the upper rooms being inhabited. Some houses which had become insecure from age and decay were prevented from falling into the street, by huge beams of wood reared against the walls, and firmly planted in the road; but even these crazy dens seemed to have been selected as the nightly haunts of some houseless wretches, for many of the rough boards, which supplied the place of door and window, were wrenched from their positions, to afford an aperture wide enough for the passage of a human body. The kennel was stagnant and filthy. The very rats, which here and there lay putrefying in its rottenness, were hideous with famine.

The oppression stems from the "board"—eight or ten fat gentlemen sitting round a table—and particularly (the image is repeated) from a fat gentleman in a white waistcoat; but its agents are the (under) paid officers of the state, beadle, matron, etc., corrupt, pompous, cruel. The methods of oppression are simple: violence and starvation. The workhouse is a symbol of the oppression but by no means its limit. Outside, the world is a vast workhouse with the "parish" run by the same gentleman in a white waistcoat, assisted by magistrates fatuous or inhuman, by clergymen who can scarcely be bothered to bury the dead, by

Mr. Bumble. London is no different from the parish, only bigger.

The oppressed are degraded and corrupted by their life (plus a little gin) and either become themselves oppressors or else criminals or corpses. Of all the recurring themes and images of these opening chapters that of death is the most insistent. Oliver's mother dies. " 'It's all over, Mrs. Thingummy' said the surgeon. . . ." The note of impersonal and irresponsible horror is immediately struck. It is not fortuitous that Mr. Sowerberry should be an undertaker, presiding over an unending funeral. Oliver and Dick long for death. Fagin gives a twist of new and dreadful cynicism to the theme: " 'What a fine thing capital punishment is! Dead men never repent; dead men never bring awkward stories to light.' " The ultimate sanction of the oppressive state becomes the ultimate weapon of its degraded creatures in their struggles against one another.

The strength of these opening chapters lies in the power and justice of the symbols, through which is achieved an objective picture arousing our compassion not through any extraneous comment but through its own validity. The weakness lies in Dickens's conscious attitudes, his attempts to comment on the situation. These attempts are at best (the ironical) inadequate, at worst (the sentimental) nauseating.

Although I am not disposed to maintain that the being born in a workhouse is in itself the most fortunate and enviable circumstance that can possibly befall a human being.

The heaviness of the prose reflects the stodginess and unsubtlety of the thought. So does the reiteration of the "kind old gentleman" as a description of Fagin. (The less satisfactory side of Dickens's treatment of the thieves obviously comes direct from *Jonathan Wild;* the same irony—even to the very words—is used, but because it is not based on Fielding's secure moral preoccupation it becomes tedious far more quickly.) The incursions of "sentiment" (i.e. every reference to motherhood, the little scene between Oliver and Dick) are even more unsatisfactory. After Dickens has tried to wring an easy tear by playing on responses which he has done nothing to satisfy, we begin to be suspicious of the moments when we really *are* moved, fearing a facile trick.

But the weaknesses—which may be summed up as the inadequacy of Dickens's conscious view of life—are in the first eleven chapters of *Oliver Twist* almost obliterated by the strength. The subjective inadequacy is obscured by the objective profundity. Again and again Dickens leaves behind his heavy humour, forgets that he ought to be trying to copy Fielding or vindicating our faith in the beauty of motherhood, and achieves a moment of drama or insight which burns into the imagination by its truth and vividness. We have already noticed the surgeon's comment on Oliver's mother's death. Most of the Mr. Bumble–Mrs. Mann conversations, the whole of the undertaker section, the meeting with the Artful Dodger, the first description of the thieves' kitchen are on the same level of achievement. So is the moment when Oliver asks for more and the passage when Oliver and Sowerberry go to visit the corpse of a dead woman.

The terrified children cried bitterly; but the old woman, who had hitherto remained as quiet as if she had been wholly deaf to all that passed, menaced them into silence. Having unloosed the cravat of the man, who still remained extended on the ground, she tottered towards the undertaker.

"She was my daughter," said the old woman, nodding her head in the direction of the corpse; and speaking with an idiotic leer, more ghastly than even the presence of death in such a place. "Lord, Lord! Well, it *is* strange that I who gave birth to her, and was a woman then, should be alive and merry now, and she lying there, so cold and stiff! Lord, Lord!—to think of it; it's as good as a play—as good as a play!"

As the wretched creature mumbled and chuckled in her hideous merriment, the undertaker turned to go away.

"Stop, stop!" said the old woman in a loud whisper. "Will she be buried to-morrow, or next day, or to-night? I laid her out and I must walk, you know. Send me a large cloak—a good warm one, for it is bitter cold. We should have cake and wine, too, before we go! Never mind; send some bread—only a loaf of bread and a cup of water. Shall we have some bread, dear?" she said eagerly, catching at the undertaker's coat, as he once more moved towards the door.

"Yes, yes," said the undertaker, "of course. Anything, everything." He disengaged himself from the old woman's grasp, and, drawing Oliver after him, hurried away.

There is no sentimentality here, only horror, and with something of the quality which one associates particularly with Dostoievsky, the strengthening of realism by the moment of fantasy, the blurring of the line between reality and nightmare, a stretching to the ultimate of the capacity of the mind to deal with the world it has inherited.

And then from the desperate horror of the nightmare world Oliver awakes, lying in a comfortable bed, surrounded by kindly middle-class people. He has become all of a sudden a pretty creature, a grateful little dear. And from that moment the plot of the novel becomes important.

It is generally agreed that the plots of Dickens's novels are their weakest feature but it is not always understood why this should be so. The plot of *Oliver Twist* is very complicated and very unsatisfactory. It is a conventional plot about a wronged woman, an illegitimate baby, a destroyed will, a death-bed secret, a locket thrown into the river, a wicked elder brother and the restoration to the hero of name and property. That it should depend on a number of extraordinary coincidences (the only two robberies in which Oliver is called upon to participate are perpetrated, fortuitously, on his father's best friend and his mother's sister's guardian!) is the least of its shortcomings. Literal probability is not an essential quality of an adequate plot. Nor is it a damning criticism that Dickens should have used his plot for the purposes of serial-publication, i.e., to provide a climax at the end of each instalment and the necessary twists and manoeuvres which popular serialization invited. (It is not a fault in a dramatist that he should provide a climax to each act of his play, and the serial instalment is no more or less artificial a convention than the act of a play.) What we may legitimately object to in the plot of *Oliver Twist* is the very substance of that plot in its relation to the essential pattern of the novel.

The conflict in the plot is the struggle between the innocent Oliver, aided by his friends at Pentonville and Chertsey, against the machinations of those who are conspiring from self-interest to do him out of his fortune. These latter stem from and centre in his half-brother Monks. It is not, even by its own standards, a good plot. Oliver is too passive a hero to win our very lively sympathy and Monks is a rather unconvincing villain who is, anyway, outshone in interest by his agents. The good characters are, by and large, too good and the bad too bad. If the centre of interest of the novel were indeed the plot then the conventional assessment of a Dickens novel—a poor story enlivened by magnificent though irrelevant "characters"—would be fair enough. But in fact the centre of interest, the essential pattern of the novel, is not its plot, and it is the major fault of the plot that it does not correspond with this central interest.

The core of the novel, and what gives it value, is its consideration of the plight of the poor. Its pattern is the contrasted relation of two worlds—the underworld of the workhouse, the funeral, the thieves' kitchen, and the comfortable world of the Brownlows and Maylies. It is this pattern that stamps the novel on our minds. We do not remember, when we think back on it, the intricacies of the plot; we are not interested in the affairs of Rose and Harry Maylie; we do not care who Oliver's father was and, though we sympathize with Oliver's struggles, we do not mind whether or not he gets his fortune. What we do remember is that vision of the underworld of the first eleven chapters, the horror of Fagin, the fate of Mr. Bumble, the trial of the Artful Dodger, the murder of Nancy, the end of Sikes. What engages our sympathy is not Oliver's feeling for the mother he never saw, but his struggle against his oppressors of which the famous gruel scene is indeed a central and adequate symbol.

The contrast of the two worlds is at the very heart of the book, so that we see a total picture of contrasted darkness and light. Often the two are explicitly contrasted in divided chapters. The two worlds are so utterly separated that Oliver's two metamorphoses from one to the other must inevitably take the form of an awakening to a new existence and the root of the weakness as "characters" of both Oliver and Monks is that they are not fully absorbed in either world. Oliver is rather a thin hero because, though he is called upon to play a hero's part, he never becomes identified with the heroic forces of the book; while Monks's stature as the fountain-head of evil is wrecked by his parentage; how can he compete with Sikes and Fagin when he is to be allowed, because he is a gentleman, to escape his just deserts?

The power of the book, then, proceeds from the wonderful evocation of the underworld and the engagement of our sympathy on behalf of the inhabitants of that world. Its weakness lies in Dickens's failure to develop and carry through the pattern so powerfully presented in the first quarter of the novel. It is by no means a complete failure; on the contrary, there are passages in the latter part of the book quite as successful as the early scenes: and in the final impression of the novel the sense of the two worlds is, as has been suggested, the dominant factor. But the failure is, nevertheless, sufficiently striking to be worth consideration.

It is not by chance that the plot and Mr. Brownlow emerge in the novel at the same moment, for their purpose is identical. It is they who are to rescue Oliver from the underworld and establish him as a respectable member of society. It is not through his own efforts that the metamorphosis takes place and indeed

it cannot be. For if the whole first section of the novel has convinced us of anything at all it is that against the whole apparatus
set in motion by the gentleman in the white waistcoat the Oliver
Twists of that world could stand no possible chance.

The introduction of the plot, then, savours from the very first
of a trick. It is only by reducing the whole of Oliver's experiences up till now to the status of "a long and troubled dream"
that he can be saved for the plot. But we know perfectly well
that these experiences are not a dream; they have a reality for
us which the nice houses in Pentonville and Chertsey never
achieve. Indeed, as far as the imaginative impact of the novel
is concerned, it is the Brownlow-Maylie world that is a dream,
a dream-world into which Oliver is lucky enough to be trans-
ported by the plot but which all the real and vital people of the
book never even glimpse. The Brownlow-Maylie world is indeed no world at all; it is merely the romantic escape-world of
the lost wills and dispossessed foundlings and idiotic coincidences
which make up the paraphernalia of the conventional romantic
plot.

The plot makes impossible the realization of the living pattern
and conflict of the book. This conflict—symbolized, as we have
seen, by the gruel scene—is the struggle of the poor against the
bourgeois state, the whole army of greater and lesser Bumbles
whom the gentleman in the white waistcoat employs to maintain
morality (all the members of the board are "philosophers") and
the *status quo*. The appalling difficulties of this struggle are impressed on our minds and it is because Oliver, however unwill-
ingly, becomes an actor in it that he takes on a certain symbolic
significance and wins more than our casual pity.

It is notable that Dickens makes no serious effort to present
Oliver with any psychological realism: his reactions are not,
for the most part, the reactions of any child of nine or ten years
old; he is not surprised by what would surprise a child and his
moral attitudes are those of an adult. And yet something of the

quality of precocious suffering, of childish terror, is somehow achieved, partly by the means by which other characters are presented, with a kind of exaggerated, almost grotesque simplicity, and partly through the very fact that Oliver is—we are persuaded—a figure of symbolic significance. Because he is *all* workhouse orphans the lack of a convincing individual psychology does not matter; it is Oliver's situation rather than himself that moves us and the situation is presented with all of Dickens's dramatic symbolic power.

Once he becomes involved in the plot the entire symbolic significance of Oliver changes. Until he wakes up in Mr. Brownlow's house he is a poor boy struggling against the inhumanity of the state. After he has slept himself into the Brownlow world he is a young bourgeois who has been done out of his property. A complete transformation has taken place in the organization of the novel. The state, which in the pattern of the book, is the organ of oppression of the poor and therefore of Oliver, now becomes the servant of Oliver. The oppressed are now divided (through the working of the plot) into the good and deserving poor who help Oliver win his rights and the bad and criminal poor who help Monks and must be eliminated. It is a conception which makes a mockery of the opening chapters of the book, where poverty has been revealed to us in a light which makes the facile terms of good and bad irrelevant.

By the end of the book Nancy can be pigeon-holed as good, Sikes as bad. But who can say whether the starving creatures of the opening chapters are good or bad? It is for this kind of reason that the plot of *Oliver Twist* has so disastrous an effect on the novel. Not merely is it silly and mechanical and troublesome, but it expresses an interpretation of life infinitely less profound and honest than the novel itself reveals.

The disaster, happily, is not complete. For one thing, the plot does not immediately, with the entrance of Mr. Brownlow, gain entire ascendancy. The kidnapping of Oliver by Nancy and

Sikes and his return to the thieves gives the novel a reprieve. The robbery episode is excellently done. But in this section (Chaps. XII to XXIX) the plot is beginning to seep into the underworld. Monks appears. And the reintroduction of the workhouse (the death of old Sally, the marriage of Mr. Bumble), despite some delicious moments ("It's all U.P. here, Mrs. Corney"; Noah and Charlotte eating oysters; "Won't you tell your own B?"), too obviously serves the contrivances of the plot.

Once, however, the robbery is done with and Oliver awakes for a second time in the respectable world, the plot completely reasserts itself. The third quarter of the book (Chaps. XXIX to XXXIX) is its weakest section. Oliver is here entirely at the mercy of the Maylies and the plot. Monks bobs up all over the place. And our interest is held (if at all) only by the Bumble passages, now completely involved in the plot, and the incidental "characters," Giles and Brittles, Blathers and Duff. And because these characters have no part in the underlying pattern of the book and are therefore, unlike Bumble and Fagin and the Artful Dodger and Noah Claypole, without symbolic significance, they are merely eccentrics, comic relief, with all the limitations the phrase implies.

The basic conflict of the novel is brought, in this quarter, almost to a standstill; the people who have captured our imagination scarcely appear at all. The world of the opening chapters has been replaced by another world in which kindly old doctors like Losberne and crusty but amiable eccentrics like Grimwig are in control of the situation. But after what we have already experienced, we simply cannot believe in this world in the way we believed in the other.

In the final quarter of the book (Chap. XXXIX onwards) plot and pattern, artifice and truth, struggle in a last, violent encounter. The plot wins the first round by extracting Nancy from the clutches of the pattern. The girl's genuine humanity, revealed earlier in the novel by the simple moving language of her moment of compassion for the suffering wretches within the walls of the jail, is debased by the plot into the conventional clichés of cheap melodrama. But Nancy's abduction is countered almost at once by one of the great episodes of the novel, the trial of the Artful Dodger. This scene is irrelevant to the plot except in so far as the Dodger has to be got out of the way before the final dispensing of reward and punishment. It is an interesting instance of the power of Dickens's genius that he should have realized that in the Dodger he had created a figure which the plot was quite incapable either of absorbing or obliterating. And so he is obliged to give the irrepressible boy his final fling, a fling which again raises the book into serious art and plays an essential part in its (by this time) almost forgotten pattern.

The trial of the Artful Dodger (it is a greater because emotionally and morally a profounder scene than Jonathan Wild's dance without music) re-states in an astonishing form the central theme of *Oliver Twist:* what are the poor to do against the oppressive state? The Dodger throughout the book is magnificently done: his precosity, the laboured irony of his conversation (which becomes involuntarily a comment on the quality of Dickens's own irony), his shrewdness, his grotesque urbanity, his resourcefulness (gloriously at variance with his appearance), his tremendous vitality, all are revealed without false pathos but with an effect of great profundity.

For what is so important about the Artful Dodger is not his oddity but his normality, not his inability to cope with the world but his very ability to cope with it on its own terms. Oliver is afraid of the world, the Dodger defies it; it has made him what he is and he will give back as good as he got. His trial contrasts in the novel with all the other trials. He turns up with all his guns loaded and fires broadside after broadside which for all their fantastic unexpectedness and apparent inappropriateness have an irony beyond any other statements in the novel.

It was indeed Mr. Dawkins, who, shuffling into the office with the big coat-sleeves tucked up as usual, his left hand in his pocket, and his hat in his right hand, preceded the jailer, with a rolling gait altogether indescribable, and, taking his place in the dock, requested in an audible voice to know what he was placed in that 'ere disgraceful sitivation for.

"Hold your tongue, will you?" said the jailer.

"I'm an Englishman, ain't I?" rejoined the Dodger: "where are my priwileges?"

"You'll get your privileges soon enough," retorted the jailer, "and pepper with 'em."

"We'll see wot the Secretary of State for the Home Affairs has got to say to the beaks, if I don't," replied Mr. Dawkins. "Now then! Wot is this here business? I shall thank the madg'strates to dispose of this here little affair, and not to keep me while they read the paper for I've got an appointment with a genelman in the city, and as I'm a man of my word and wery punctual in business matters, he'll go away if I ain't there to my time, and then pr'aps there won't be an action for damage against them as kept me away. Oh, no, certainly not!"

At this point the Dodger, with a show of being very particular with a view to proceedings to be had thereafter, desired the jailer to communicate "the names of them two files as was on the bench," which so tickled the spectators, that they laughed almost as heartily as Master Bates could have done if he had heard the request.

"Silence there!" cried the jailer.

"What is this?" inquired one of the magistrates.

"A pick-pocketing case, your worship."

"Has the boy ever been here before?"

"He ought to have been, a many times," replied the jailer. "He has been pretty well everywhere else. *I* know him well, your worship."

"Oh! you know me, do you?" cried the Artful, making a note of the statement. "Wery good. That's a case of deformation of character anyway."

Here there was another laugh, and another cry of silence.

"Now then, where are the witnesses?" said the clerk.

"Ah! that's right," added the Dodger. "Where are they? I should like to see 'em."

This wish was immediately gratified, for a policeman stepped forward who had seen the prisoner attempt the pocket of an unknown gentleman in a crowd, and indeed take a handkerchief therefrom, which, being a very old one, he deliberately put back again, after trying it on his own countenance. For this reason, he took the Dodger into custody as soon as he could get near him, and the said Dodger being searched, had upon his person a silver snuff-box, with the owner's name engraved upon the lid. This gentleman had been discovered on reference to the Court Guide, and being then and there present, swore that the snuff-box was his, and that he had missed it on the previous day, the moment he had disengaged himself from the crowd before referred to. He had also remarked a young gentleman in the throng particularly active in making his way about, and that young gentleman was the prisoner before him.

"Have you anything to ask this witness, boy?" said the magistrate.

"I wouldn't abase myself by descending to hold no conversation with him," replied the Dodger.

"Have you anything to say at all?"

"Do you hear his worship ask if you have anything to say?" inquired the jailer, nudging the silent Dodger with his elbow.

"I beg your pardon," said the Dodger, looking up with an air of abstraction. "Did you redress yourself to me, my man?"

"I never see such an out-and-out young wagabond, your worship," observed the officer with a grin. "Do you mean to say anything, you young shaver?"

"No," replied the Dodger, "not here, for this ain't the shop for justice; besides which, my attorney is a-breakfasting this morning with the Wice-President of the House of Commons; but I shall have something to say elsewhere, and so will he, and so will a wery numerous and 'spectable circle of acquaintance, as'll make them beaks wish they'd never been born, or that they'd got their footmen to hang 'em up to their own hat-pegs afore they let 'em come out this morning to try it on upon me. I'll—"

"There! He's fully committed!" interposed the clerk. "Take him away."

"Come on," said the jailer.

"Oh, ah! I'll come on," replied the Dodger, brushing his hat with the palm of his hand. "Ah! (to the Bench), it's no use your looking frightened; I won't show you no mercy, not a ha'porth of it. *You'll* pay for this, my fine fellers. I wouldn't be you for something! I wouldn't go free, now, if you was to fall down on your knees and ask me. Here, carry me off to prison! Take me away!"

Now the point about the Dodger's defiance which is apt to escape our notice, so fantastic and uproarious is the scene and so used are we to regarding a Dickens novel simply in terms of a display of eccentric "character," is the actual substance of his comments. Yet in fact, if we recall the court in which Mr. Fang had heard Oliver's case, we must realize the justice of the Dodger's complaints, which strike at the very heart of the judicial system that is doing its worst on him. Where *are* the Englishman's privileges? Where *is* the law that allows the jailer to say what he does? What, in sober fact, *are* these magistrates? What comment could be more relevant than the contemptuous "this ain't the shop for justice"? The importance of the Artful Dodger in the pattern of the novel is that he, almost alone of the characters of the underworld, does stick up for himself, does continue and develop the conflict that Oliver had begun when he asked for more.

The final section of the book (the murder of Nancy, the flight and end of Sikes, the death of Fagin and the tying-up of the plot) is an extraordinary mixture of the genuine and the bogus. The violence which has run right through the novel reaches its climax with the murder of Nancy; and the sense of terror is remarkably well sustained right up to the death of Sikes.

Here again Dickens's instinct for the symbolic background is what grips our imagination. The atmosphere of squalid London, powerfully present in so much of the novel, is here immensely effective, especially the description of Folly Ditch and Jacob's Island, sombre and decayed, "crazy wooden galleries common to the backs of half a dozen houses, with holes from which to look upon the slime beneath; windows broken and patched, with poles thrust out on which to dry the linen that is never there . . . chimneys half crushed, half hesitating to fall. . . ." The scene itself ceases to be a mere backcloth and becomes a sculptured mass making an integral part of the novel's pattern. So that in the end it is not Sikes's conscience that we remember but a black picture of human squalor and desolation. Sikes is gathered into the world that has begotten him and the image of that world makes us understand him and even pity him, not with an easy sentimentality, but through a sense of all the hideous forces that have made him what he is.

The end of Fagin is a different matter. It is sensational in the worst sense, with a *News of the World* interest which touches nothing adequately and is worse than inadequate because it actually coarsens our perceptions. It is conceived entirely within the terms of the plot (Oliver is taken—in the name of morality—to the condemned cell to find out where the missing papers are hidden) and the whole debasing effect of the plot on the novel is immediately illustrated; for it is because he is working within the moral framework of the plot—in which the only standards are those of the sanctity of property and complacent respectability—that Dickens *cannot* offer us any valuable human insights, *cannot* give his characters freedom to live as human beings.

That is why the struggle throughout *Oliver Twist* between the plot and the pattern is indeed a life and death struggle, a struggle as to whether the novel shall live or not. And in so far as the plot succeeds in twisting and negating the pattern the value of the novel is in fact weakened. To a considerable degree the novel *is* thus ruined; the loss of tension in the third quarter and the dubious close are the testimony. But the total effect is not one of disaster. The truth and depth of the central vision are such that a vitality is generated which struggles against and survives the plot. Oliver himself does not survive; but the force he has set in motion does. This force—let us call it the sense of the doom and aspirations of the oppressed—is too strong to be satisfied with the dream-solution of Oliver's metamorphosis, too enduring to let us forget the fat gentleman in the white waistcoat who has so conveniently faded from the picture till he is recalled by the Artful Dodger. Confused, uneven, topsy-turvy as the effect of the novel is we would yet be doing it great injustice to discuss it, as it is often discussed, simply in terms of random moments and exuberant caricature. There is pattern behind that power, art behind the vitality, and if we recognize this in *Oliver Twist* we shall not come unarmed to Dickens's later, more mature and greater books: *Bleak House, Little Dorrit, Great Expectations, Our Mutual Friend.*

EDGAR JOHNSON:

1952

The Christmas Carol and the Economic Man

EVERYONE knows Dickens's *Christmas Carol* for its colorful painting of a rosy fireside good cheer and warmth of feeling, made all the more vivid by the contrasting chill wintry darkness in which its radiant scenes are framed. Most readers realize too how characteristic of all Dickens's sentiments about the Christmas season are the laughter and tenderness and jollity he poured into the *Carol*. What is not so widely understood is that it was also consistently and deliberately created as a critical blast against

American Scholar, XXI (1952), 91–98; also, *Charles Dickens: His Tragedy and Triumph* (New York, 1952).

the very rationale of industrialism and its assumptions about the organizing principles of society. It is an attack upon both the economic behavior of the nineteenth century business man and the supporting theory of doctrinaire utilitarianism. As such it is a good deal more significant than the mere outburst of warm-hearted sentimentality it is often taken to be.

Its sharper intent is, indeed, ingeniously disguised. Not even the festivities at Dingley Dell, in *Pickwick Papers,* seem to have a more genial innocence than the scenes of the *Christmas Carol.* It is full of the tang of snow and cold air and crisp green holly-leaves, and warm with the glow of crimson holly-berries, blazing hearths, and human hearts. Deeper than this, however, Dickens makes of the Christmas spirit a symbolic criticism of the relations that throughout almost all the rest of the year subsist among men. It is a touchstone, revealing and drawing forth the gold of generosity ordinarily crusted over with selfish habit, an earnest of the truth that our natures are not entirely or even essentially devoted to competitive struggle.

Dickens is certain that the enjoyment most men are able to feel in the happiness of others can play a larger part than it does in the tenor of their lives. The sense of brotherhood, he feels, can be broadened to a deeper and more active concern for the welfare of all mankind. It is in this light that Dickens sees the Spirit of Christmas. So understood, as the distinguished scholar Professor Louis Cazamian rightly points out, his "philosophie de Noël" becomes the very core of his social thinking.

Not that Christmas has for Dickens more than the very smallest connection with Christian dogma or theology. It involves no conception of the virgin birth or transubstantiation or sacrificial atonement or redemption by faith. For Dickens Christmas is primarily a human, not a supernatural, feast, with glowing emphasis on goose and gravy, plum-pudding and punch, mistletoe, and kissing-games, dancing and frolic, as well as open-handedness, sympathy, and warmth of heart. Dickens does not believe that love of others demands utter abnegation or mortification of the flesh; it is not sadness but joyful fellowship. The triumphal meaning of Christmas peals in the angel voices ringing through the sky: "On earth peace, good will to men." It is a sign that men do not live by bread alone, that they do not live for barter and sale alone. No way of life is either true or rewarding that leaves out men's need of loving and of being loved.

The theme of the *Christmas Carol* is thus closely linked with the theme of *Martin Chuzzlewit*, which was being written and published as a serial during the very time in which the shorter story appeared. The selfishness so variously manifested in the one is limited in the other to the selfishness of financial gain. For in an acquisitive society the form that selfishness predominantly takes is monetary greed. The purpose of such a society is the protection of property rights. Its rules are created by those who have money and power, and are designed, to the extent that they are consistent, for the perpetuation of money and power. With the growing importance of commerce in the eighteenth century, and of industry in the nineteenth, political economists—the "philosophers" Dickens detested—rationalized the spirit of ruthless greed into a system claiming authority throughout society.

Services as well as goods, they said, were subject only to the laws of profitable trade. There was no just price. One bought in the cheapest market and sold in the dearest. There was no just wage. The mill owner paid the mill hand what competition decreed under the determination of the "iron law of wage." If the poor, the insufficiently aggressive, and the mediocre in ability were unable to live on what they could get, they must starve—or put up with the treadmill and the workhouse—and even these institutions represented concessions to mere humanity that must be made as forbidding as possible. Ideally, no sentimental conceptions must be allowed to obstruct the workings of the law of supply and demand. "Cash-nexus" was the sole bond between man and man. The supreme embodiment of this social theory was the notion of the "economic man," that curiously fragmentary picture of human nature, who never performed any action except at the dictates of monetary gain. And Scrooge, in the *Christmas Carol,* is nothing other than a personification of economic man.

Scrooge's entire life is limited to cash-boxes, ledgers, and bills of sale. He underpays and bullies and terrifies his clerk, and grudges him even enough coal in his office fire to keep warm. All sentiment, kindness, generosity, tenderness, he dismisses as humbug. All imagination he regards as a species of mental indigestion. He feels that he has discharged his full duty to society in contributing his share of the taxes that pay for the prison, the workhouse, the operation of the treadmill and the poor law, and he bitterly resents having his pocket picked to keep even them going. The out-of-work and the indigent sick are to him merely idle and useless; they had better die and decrease the surplus population. So entirely does Scrooge exemplify the economic man that, like that abstraction, his grasping rapacity has ceased to have any purpose beyond itself: when he closes up his office for the night he takes his pinched heart off to a solitary dinner at a tavern and then to his bleak chambers where he sits alone over his gruel.

Now from one angle, of course, *A Christmas Carol* indicts the economic philosophy represented by Scrooge for its unhappy influence on society. England's prosperity was not so uncertain —if, indeed, any nation's ever is—that she needed to be parsimonious and cruel to her waifs and strays, or even to the incompetents and casualties of life. To neglect the poor, to deny them education, to give them no protection from covetous employers, to let them be thrown out of work and fall ill and die in filthy surroundings that then engender spreading pestilence, to allow them to be harried by misery into crime—all these turn out in the long run to be the most disastrous shortsightedness.

That is what the Ghost of Christmas Present means in showing Scrooge the two ragged and wolfish children glaring from beneath its robes. "They are Man's," says the Spirit. "And they cling to me, appealing from their fathers. This boy is Ignorance. This girl is Want. Beware them both, and all of their degree, but most of all beware this boy, for on his brow I see that written which is Doom, unless the writing be erased." And when Scrooge asks if they have no refuge, the Spirit ironically echoes his own words: "Are there no prisons? Are there no workhouses?"

Scrooge's relation with his clerk Bob Cratchit is another illustration of the same point. To say, as some commentators have done, that Scrooge is paying Cratchit all he is worth on the open market (or he would get another job) is to assume the very conditions Dickens is attacking. It is not only that timid, uncompetitive people like Bob Cratchit may lack the courage to bargain for their rights. But, as Dickens knows well, there are many things other than the usefulness of a man's work that determine his wage—the existence, for example, of a large body of other men able to do the same job. And if Cratchit is getting the established remuneration for his work, that makes the situation worse, not better; for instead of an isolated one, his is a general case. What Dickens has at heart is not any economic conception like Marx's labor theory of value, but a feeling of the human value of human beings. Unless a man is a noxious danger to society, Dickens feels, a beast of prey to be segregated or destroyed, if he is able and willing to work, whatever the work may be—he is entitled at least to enough for him to live on, by the mere virtue of his humanity alone.

But the actual organization that Dickens saw in society callously disregarded all such humane principles. The hardened criminal was maintained in jail with more care than the helpless debtor who had broken no law. The pauper who owed nobody, but whom age, illness, or industrial change might have thrown out of work, was treated more severely than many a debtor and jailbird. And the poor clerk or laborer, rendered powerless by his need or the number of others like him, could be held to a pittance barely sufficient to keep him and his family from starvation.

Against such inequities Dickens maintains that any work worth doing should be paid enough to maintain a man and his family without grinding worry. How are the Bob Cratchits and their helpless children to live? Or are we to let the crippled Tiny Tims die and decrease the surplus population? "Man," says the Ghost, "if man you be in heart, not adamant, forbear that wicked cant until you have discovered What the surplus is and Where it is. . . . It may be, that in the sight of Heaven, you are more worthless and less fit to live than millions like this poor man's child. Oh God! to hear the Insect on the leaf pronouncing on the too much life among his hungry brothers in the dust!"

Coldhearted arrogance and injustice storing up a dangerous heritage of poverty and ignorance—such is Dickens's judgment of the economic system that Scrooge exemplifies. But its consequences do not end with the cruelties it inflicts upon the masses of the people or the evils it works in society. It injures Scrooge as well. All the more generous impulses of humanity he has stifled and mutilated in himself. All natural affection he has crushed. The lonely boy he used to be, weeping in school, the tender brother, the eager youth, the young man who once fell disinterestedly in love with a dowerless girl—what has he done to them in making himself into a money-making machine, as hard and sharp as flint, and frozen with the internal ice that clutches his shriveled heart? That dismal cell, his office, and his gloomy rooms, are only a prison within which he dwells self-confined, barred and close-locked as he drags a chain of his own cash-boxes and dusty ledgers. Acting on a distortedly inadequate conception of self-interest, Scrooge has deformed and crippled himself to bitter sterility.

And Scrooge's fallacy is the fallacy of organized society. Like his house, which Dickens fancifully imagines playing hide-and-seek with other houses when it was a young house, and losing its way in a blind alley it has forgotten how to get out of, Scrooge has lost his way between youth and maturity. Society too in the course of its development has gone astray and then hardened itself in obdurate error with a heartless economic theory. Scrooge's conversion is more than the transformation of a single human being. It is a plea for society itself to undergo a change of heart.

Dickens does not, it should be noticed, take the uncompromising position that the self-regarding emotions are to be eradicated altogether. He is not one of those austere theorists who hold that the individual must be subordinated to the state or immolate himself to the service of an abstract humanity. Concern for one's self and one's own welfare is necessary and right, but true self-love cannot be severed from love of others without growing barren and diseased. Only in the communion of brotherhood is it healthy and fruitful. When Scrooge has truly changed, and has dispatched the anonymous gift of the turkey to Bob Cratchit as an earnest of repentance, his next move is to go to his nephew's house and ask wistfully, "Will you let me in, Fred?" With love reanimated in his heart, he may hope for love.

There have been readers who objected to Scrooge's conversion as too sudden and radical to be psychologically convincing. But this is to mistake a semi-serious fantasy for a piece of prosaic realism. Even so, the emotions in Scrooge to which the Ghosts appeal are no unsound means to the intended end: the awakened memories of a past when he had known warmer and gentler ties than in any of his later years, the realization of his exclusion from all kindness and affection in others now, the fears of a future when he may be lonelier and more unloved still. And William James in *The Varieties of Religious Experience* provides scores of case-histories that parallel both the suddenness of

Scrooge's conversion and the sense of radiant joy he feels in the world around him after it has taken place. It may be that what really gives the skeptics pause is that Scrooge is converted to a gospel of good cheer. They could probably believe easily enough if he espoused some gloomy doctrine of intolerance.

But it is doubtful whether such questions ever arise when one is actually reading the *Christmas Carol*. From the very beginning Dickens strikes a tone of playful exaggeration that warns us this is no exercise in naturalism. Scrooge carries "his own low temperature always about with him; he iced his office in the dog-days." Blind men's dogs, when they see him coming, tug their masters into doorways to avoid him. The entire world of the story is an animistic one: houses play hide-and-seek, door-knockers come to life as human heads, the tuning of a fiddle is "like fifty stomach aches," old Fezziwig's legs wink as he dances, potatoes bubbling in a saucepan knock loudly at the lid "to be let out and peeled." Scrooge's own language has a jocose hyperbole, even when he is supposed to be most ferocious or most terrified, that makes his very utterance seem half a masquerade. "If I could work my will," he snarls, "every idiot who goes about with 'Merry Christmas' on his lips should be boiled with his own pudding, and buried with a stake of holly through his heart. He should!" Is that the accent of a genuine curmudgeon or of a man trying to sound more violent than he feels? And to Marley's Ghost, despite his disquiet, he remarks, "You may be an undigested bit of beef, a blob of mustard, a crumb of cheese, a fragment of an underdone potato. There's more of gravy than of grave about you, whatever you are!"

All these things make it clear that Dickens—as always when he is most deeply moved and most profound—is speaking in terms of unavowed allegory. But the allegory of Dickens is in one way subtler than the allegory of writers like Kafka or Melville. Kafka is always hinting the existence of hidden meanings by making the experience of his characters so baffling and irrational on a merely realistic level that we are obliged to search for symbolic significances. And Melville, too, by a score of devices, from those rolling, darkly magnificent, and extraordinary soliloquies to the mystery of Ahab's intense and impassioned pursuit of the White Whale, forces us to realize that this is a more metaphysical duel than one with a mere deep-sea beast.

Dickens, however, leaves his surface action so entirely clear and the behavior of his characters so plain that they do not puzzle us into groping for gnomic meanings. Scrooge is a miser, his nephew a warmhearted fellow, Bob Cratchit a poor clerk—what could be simpler? If there is a touch of oddity in the details, that is merely Dickens's well-known comic grotesquerie; if Scrooge's change of heart is sharp and antithetical, that is only Dickens's melodramatic sentimentality. Surely all the world knows that Dickens is never profound?

But the truth is that Dickens has so fused his abstract thought and its imaginative forming that one melts almost entirely into the other. Though our emotional perception of Dickens's meaning is immediate and spontaneous, nothing in his handling thrusts upon us an intellectual statement of that meaning. But more than a warmhearted outpouring of holiday sentiment, the *Christmas Carol* is in essence a serio-comic parable of social redemption. Marley's Ghost is the symbol of divine grace, and the three Christmas Spirits are the working of that grace through the agencies of memory, example and fear. And Scrooge, although of course he is himself too, is not himself alone: he is the embodiment of all that concentration upon material power and callous indifference to the welfare of human beings that the economists had erected into a system, businessmen and industrialists pursued relentlessly, and society taken for granted as inevitable and proper. The conversion of Scrooge is an image of the conversion for which Dickens hopes among mankind.

LIONEL TRILLING: 1953

Little Dorrit

LITTLE DORRIT is one of the three great novels of Dickens' great last period, but of the three it is perhaps the least established with modern readers. When it first appeared—in monthly parts from December 1855 to June 1857—its success was even more decisive than that of *Bleak House,* but the suffrage of later audiences has gone the other way, and of all Dickens' later works it is *Bleak House* that has come to be the best known. As for *Our Mutual Friend,* after having for some time met with adverse critical opinion among the enlightened—one recalls that the youthful Henry James attacked it for standing in the way of art and truth—it has of recent years been regarded with ever-growing admiration. But *Little Dorrit* seems to have retired to the background and shadow of our consciousness of Dickens.

This does not make an occasion for concern or indignation. With a body of works as large and as enduring as that of Dickens, taste and opinion will never be done. They will shift and veer as they have shifted and veered with the canon of Shakespeare, and each generation will have its special favorites and make its surprised discoveries. *Little Dorrit,* one of the most profound of Dickens' novels and one of the most significant

Introduction to *Little Dorrit* (London, 1953); also, *The Opposing Self* (New York, 1955).

works of the nineteenth century, will not fail to be thought of as speaking with a peculiar and passionate intimacy to our own time.

Little Dorrit is about society, which certainly does not distinguish it from the rest of Dickens' novels unless we go on to say, as we must, that it is *more* about society than any other of the novels, that it is about society in its very essence. This essential quality of the book has become apparent as many of the particular social conditions to which it refers have passed into history. Some of these conditions were already of the past when Dickens wrote, for although imprisonment for debt was indeed not wholly given up until 1869, yet imprisonment for small debts had been done away with in 1844, the prison of the Marshalsea had been abolished in 1842 and the Court of the Marshalsea in 1849. Bernard Shaw said of *Little Dorrit* that it converted him to socialism; it is not likely that any contemporary English reader would feel it appropriate to respond to its social message in the same way. The dead hand of outworn tradition no longer supports special privilege in England. For good or bad, in scarcely any country in the world can the whole art of government be said to be How Not To Do It. Mrs. General cannot impose the genteel discipline of Prunes and Prisms, and no prestige whatever attaches to "the truly refined mind" of her definition—"one that will seem to be ignorant of the existence of anything that is not perfectly proper, placid, and pleasant." At no point, perhaps, do the particular abuses and absurdities upon which Dickens directed his terrible cold anger represent the problems of social life as we now conceive them.

Yet this makes *Little Dorrit* not less but more relevant to our sense of things. As the particulars seem less immediate to our case, the general force of the novel becomes greater, and *Little Dorrit* is seen to be about a problem which does not yield easily to time. It is about society in relation to the individual human will. This is certainly a matter general enough—general to the point of tautology, were it not for the bitterness with which the tautology is articulated, were it not for the specificity and the subtlety and the boldness with which the human will is anatomized.

The subject of *Little Dorrit* is borne in upon us by the symbol, or emblem, of the book, which is the prison. The story opens in a prison in Marseilles. It goes on to the Marshalsea, which in effect it never leaves. The second of the two parts of the novel begins in what we are urged to think of as a sort of prison, the monastery of the Great St. Bernard. The Circumlocution Office is the prison of the creative mind of England. Mr. Merdle is shown habitually holding himself by the wrist, taking himself into custody, and in a score of ways the theme of incarceration is carried out, persons and classes being imprisoned by their notions of their predestined fate or their religious duty, or by their occupations, their life schemes, their ideas of themselves, their very habits of language.

Symbolic or emblematic devices are used by Dickens to one degree or another in several of the novels of his late period, but nowhere to such good effects as in *Little Dorrit*. The fog of *Bleak House*, the dust heap and the river of *Our Mutual Friend* are very striking, but they scarcely equal in force the prison image which dominates *Little Dorrit*. This is because the prison is an actuality before it is ever a symbol;[1] its connection with

---

[1] Since writing this, I have had to revise my idea of the actuality of the symbols of *Our Mutual Friend*. Professor Johnson's biography of Dickens has taught me much about the nature of dust heaps, including their monetary value, which was very large, quite large enough to represent a considerable fortune: I had never quite believed that Dickens was telling the literal truth about this. From Professor Dodd's *The Age of Paradox* I have learned to what an extent the Thames was visibly the sewer of London, of how pressing was the problem of the sewage in the city as Dickens knew it, of how present to the mind was the sensible and even the tangible evidence that the problem was not being solved. The moral *disgust* of the book is thus seen to be quite adequately comprehended by the symbols which are used to represent it.

the will is real, it is the practical instrument for the negation of man's will which the will of society has contrived. As such, the prison haunted the mind of the nineteenth century, which may be said to have had its birth at the fall of the Bastille. The genius of the age, conceiving itself as creative will, naturally thought of the prisons from which it must be freed, and the trumpet call of the "Leonore" overture sounds through the century, the signal for the opening of the gates, for a general deliverance, although it grows fainter as men come to think of the prison not as a political instrument merely but as the ineluctable condition of life in society. "Most men in a brazen prison live"—the line in which Matthew Arnold echoes Wordsworth's "shades of the prison-house begin to close / Upon the growing boy," might have served as the epigraph of *Little Dorrit*. In the mind of Dickens himself the idea of the prison was obsessive, not merely because of his own boyhood experience of prison life through his father's three months in the Marshalsea (although this must be given great weight in our understanding of his intense preoccupation with the theme), but because of his own consciousness of the force and scope of his will.

If we speak of the place which the image of the prison occupied in the mind of the nineteenth century, we ought to recollect a certain German picture of the time, inconsiderable in itself but made significant by its use in a famous work of the early twentieth century. It represents a man lying in a medieval dungeon; he is asleep, his head pillowed on straw, and we know that he dreams of freedom because the bars on his window are shown being sawed by gnomes. This picture serves as the frontispiece of Freud's *Introductory Lectures on Psychoanalysis*—Freud uses it to make plain one of the more elementary ideas of his psychology, the idea of the fulfillment in dream or fantasy of impulses of the will that cannot be fulfilled in actuality. His choice of this particular picture is not fortuitous; other graphic representations of wish-fulfillment exist which might have served equally well his immediate didactic purpose, but Freud's general conception of the mind does indeed make the prison image peculiarly appropriate. And Freud is in point here because in a passage of *Little Dorrit* Dickens anticipates one of Freud's ideas, and not one of the simplest but nothing less bold and inclusive than the essential theory of the neurosis.

The brief passage to which I make reference occurs in the course of Arthur Clennam's pursuit of the obsessive notion that his family is in some way guilty, that its fortune, although now greatly diminished, has been built on injury done to someone. And he conjectures that the injured person is William Dorrit, who has been confined for debt in the Marshalsea for twenty years. Clennam is not wholly wrong in his supposition—there is indeed guilt in the family, incurred by Arthur's mother, and it consists in part of an injury done to a member of the Dorrit family. But he is not wholly right, for Mr. Dorrit has not been imprisoned through the wish or agency of Mrs. Clennam. The reasoning by which Arthur reaches his partly mistaken conclusion is of the greatest interest. It is based upon the fact that his mother, although mentally very vigorous, has lived as an invalid for many years. She has been imprisoned in a single room of her house, confined to her chair, which she leaves only for her bed. And her son conjectures that her imprisoning illness is the price she pays for the guilty gratification of keeping William Dorrit in *his* prison—that is, in order to have the right to injure another, she must unconsciously injure herself in an equivalent way: "A swift thought shot into [Arthur Clennam's] mind. In that long imprisonment here [i.e., Mr. Dorrit's] and in her long confinement to her room, did his mother find a balance to be struck? I admit that I was accessory to that man's captivity. I have suffered it in kind. He has decayed in his prison; I in mine. I have paid the penalty."

I have dwelt on this detail because it suggests, even more than the naked fact of the prison itself, the nature of the vision of society of *Little Dorrit*. One way of describing Freud's conception of the mind is to say that it is based upon the primacy of the will, and that the organization of the internal life is in the form, often fantastically parodic, of a criminal process in which the mind is at once the criminal, the victim, the police, the judge, and the executioner. And this is a fair description of Dickens' own view of the mind, as, having received the social impress, it becomes in turn the matrix of society.

In emphasizing the psychological aspects of the representation of society of *Little Dorrit* I do not wish to slight those more immediate institutional aspects of which earlier readers of the novel were chiefly aware. These are of as great importance now as they ever were in Dickens' career. Dickens is far from having lost his sense of the cruelty and stupidity of institutions and functionaries, his sense of the general rightness of the people as a whole and of the general wrongness of those who are put in authority over them. He certainly has not moved to that specious position in which all injustice is laid at the door of the original Old Adam in each of us, not to be done away with until we shall all, at the same moment, become the new Adam. The Circumlocution Office is a constraint upon the life of England which nothing can justify. Mr. Dorrit's sufferings and the injustice done to him are not denied or mitigated by his passionate commitment to some of the worst aspects of the society which deals with him so badly.

Yet the emphasis on the internal life and on personal responsibility is very strong in *Little Dorrit*. Thus, to take but one example, in the matter of the Circumlocution Office Dickens is at pains to remind us that the responsibility for its existence lies even with so good a man as Mr. Meagles. In the alliance against the torpor of the Office which he has made with Daniel Doyce, the engineer and inventor, Mr. Meagles has been undeviatingly faithful. Yet Clennam finds occasion to wonder whether there might not be "in the breast of this honest, affectionate, and cordial Mr. Meagles, any microscopic portion of the mustard-seed that had sprung up into the great tree of the Circumlocution Office." He is led to this speculation by his awareness that Mr. Meagles feels "a general superiority to Daniel Doyce, which seemed to be founded, not so much on anything in Doyce's personal character, as on the mere fact of [Doyce's] being an originator and a man out of the beaten track of other men."

Perhaps the single best index of the degree of complexity with which Dickens views society in *Little Dorrit* is afforded by the character of Blandois and his place in the novel. Blandois is wholly wicked, the embodiment of evil; he is, indeed, a devil. One of the effects of his presence in *Little Dorrit* is to complicate our response to the theme of the prison, to deprive us of the comfortable, philanthropic thought that prisons are nothing but instruments of injustice. Because Blandois exists, prisons are necessary. The generation of readers that preceded our own was inclined, I think, to withhold credence from Blandois—they did not believe in his aesthetic actuality because they did not believe in his moral actuality, the less so because they could not account for his existence in specific terms of social causation. But events have required us to believe that there really are people who seem entirely wicked, and almost unaccountably so; the social causes of their badness lie so far back that they can scarcely be reached, and in any case causation pales into irrelevance before the effects of their actions; our effort to "understand" them becomes a mere form of thought.

In this novel about the will and society, the devilish nature of Blandois is confirmed by his maniac insistence upon his gentility, his mad reiteration that it is the right and necessity of his existence to be served by others. He is the exemplification of the line in *Lear:* "The prince of darkness is a gentleman." The influence of Dickens upon Dostoevski is perhaps nowhere exhibited in a more detailed way than in the similarities between

Blandois and the shabby-genteel devil of *The Brothers Kara-mazov*, and also between him and Smerdyakov of the same novel. It is of consequence to Dickens as to Dostoevski that the evil of the unmitigated social will should own no country, yet that the flavor of its cosmopolitanism should be "French"—that is, rationalistic and subversive of the very assumption of society. Blandois enfolds himself in the soiled tatters of the revolutionary pathos. So long as he can play the game in his chosen style, he is nature's gentleman dispossessed of his rightful place, he is the natural genius against whom the philistine world closes its dull ranks. And when the disguise, which deceives no one, is off, he makes use of the classic social rationalization: Society has made him what he is; he does in his own person only what society does in its corporate form and with its corporate self-justification. "Society sells itself and sells me: and I sell society." [2]

Around Blandois are grouped certain characters of the novel of whose manner of life he is the pure principle. In these people the social will, the will to status, is the ruling faculty. To be recognized, deferred to, and served—this is their master passion. Money is of course of great consequence in the exercise of this passion, yet in *Little Dorrit* the desire for money is subordinated to the desire for deference. The Midas figure of Mr. Merdle must not mislead us on this point—should, indeed, guide us aright, for Mr. Merdle, despite his destructive power, is an innocent and passive man among those who live by the social will. It is to be noted of all these people that they justify their

---

[2] This is in effect the doctrine of Balzac's philosophical-anarchist criminal, Vautrin. But in all other respects the difference between Blandois and Vautrin is extreme. Vautrin is a "noble" and justified character; for all his cynicism, he is on the side of virtue and innocence. He is not corrupted by the social injustices he has suffered and perceived, by the self-pity to which they might have given rise; his wholesomeness may be said to be the result of his preference for power as against the status which Blandois desires. The development of Blandois from Vautrin—I do not know whether Dickens's creation was actually influenced by Balzac's—is a literary fact which has considerable social import.

insensate demand for status by some version of Blandois's pathos; they are confirmed in their lives by self-pity, they rely on the great modern strategy of being the insulted and injured. Mr. Dorrit is too soft a man for his gentility mania ever to be quite diabolical, but his younger daughter Fanny sells herself to the devil, damns herself entirely, in order to torture the woman who once questioned her social position. Henry Gowan, the cynical, incompetent gentleman-artist who associates himself with Blandois in order to *épater* society, is very nearly as diabolical as his companion. From his mother—who must dismiss once and for all any lingering doubt of Dickens' ability to portray what Chesterton calls the delicate or deadly in human character —he has learned to base his attack on society upon the unquestionable rightness of wronged gentility. Miss Wade lives a life of tortured self-commiseration which gives her license to turn her hatred and her hand against everyone, and she imposes her principle of judgment and conduct upon Tattycoram.

In short, it is part of the complexity of this novel which deals so bitterly with society that those of its characters who share its social bitterness are by that very fact condemned. And yet— so much further does the complexity extend—the subversive pathos of self-pity is by no means wholly dismissed, the devil has not wholly lied. No reader of *Little Dorrit* can possibly conclude that the rage of envy which Tattycoram feels is not justified in some degree, or that Miss Wade is wholly wrong in pointing out to her the insupportable ambiguity of her position as the daughter-servant of Mr. and Mrs. Meagles and the sister-servant of Pet Meagles. Nor is it possible to read Miss Wade's account of her life, "The History of a Self Tormentor," without an understanding that amounts to sympathy. We feel this the more—Dickens meant us to feel it the more—because the two young women have been orphaned from infancy, and are illegitimate. Their bitterness is seen to be the perversion of the desire for love. The self-torture of Miss Wade—who becomes

the more interesting if we think of her as the exact inversion of
Esther Summerson of *Bleak House*—is the classic maneuver of
the child who is unloved, or believes herself to be unloved; she
refuses to be lovable, she elects to be hateful. In all of us the
sense of injustice precedes the sense of justice by many years.
It haunts our infancy, and even the most dearly loved of children
may conceive themselves to be oppressed. Such is the nature of
the human will, so perplexed is it by the disparity between what
it desires and what it is allowed to have. With Dickens as with
Blake, the perfect image of injustice is the unhappy child, and,
like the historian Burckhardt, he connects the fate of nations
with the treatment of children. It is a commonplace of the biography and criticism of Dickens that this reflects his own sense
of having been unjustly treated by his parents, specifically in
ways which injured his own sense of social status, his own
gentility; the general force of Dickens' social feelings derives
from their being rooted in childhood experience, and something
of the special force of *Little Dorrit* derives from Dickens' having
discovered its matter in the depths of his own social will.

At this point we become aware of the remarkable number of
false and inadequate parents in *Little Dorrit*. To what pains
Dickens goes to represent delinquent parenthood, with what an
elaboration of irony he sets it forth! "The Father of the Marshalsea"—this is the title borne by Mr. Dorrit, who, preoccupied
by the gratification of being the First Gentleman of a prison,
is unable to exercise the simplest paternal function; who corrupts
two of his children by his dream of gentility; who will accept
any sacrifice from his saintly daughter Amy, Little Dorrit, to
whom he is the beloved child to be cherished and forgiven. "The
Patriarch"—this is the name bestowed upon Mr. Casby, who
stands as a parody of all Dickens' benevolent old gentlemen
from Mr. Pickwick through the Cheerybles to John Jarndyce,
an astounding unreality of a man who, living only to grip and
grind, has convinced the world by the iconography of his dress

and mein that he is the repository of all benevolence. The primitive appropriateness of the strange—the un-English!—punishment which Mr. Pancks metes out to this hollow paternity, the cutting off of his long hair and the broad brim of his hat, will be understood by any reader with the least tincture of psychoanalytical knowledge. Then the Meagles, however solicitous of their own daughter, are, as we have seen, but indifferent parents to Tattycoram. Mrs. Gowan's rearing of her son is the root of his corruption. It is Fanny Dorrit's complaint of her enemy, Mrs. Merdle, that she refuses to surrender the appearance of youth, as a mother should. And at the very center of the novel is Mrs. Clennam, a false mother in more ways than one; she does not deny love but she perverts and prevents it by denying all that love feeds on—liberty, demonstrative tenderness, joy, and, what for Dickens is the guardian of love in society, art. It is her harsh rearing of her son that has given him cause to say in his fortieth year, "I have no will."

Some grace—it is, of course, the secret of his birth, of his being really a child of love and art—has kept Arthur Clennam from responding to the will of his mother with a bitter, clenched will of his own. The alternative he has chosen has not, contrary to his declaration, left him no will at all. He has by no means been robbed of his ethical will, he can exert energy to help others, and for the sake of Mr. Dorrit or Daniel Doyce's invention he can haunt the Circumlocution Office with his mild, stubborn, "I want to know. . . ." But the very accent of that phrase seems to forecast the terrible "I prefer not to" of Bartleby the Scrivener in Melville's great story of the will in its ultimate fatigue.

It is impossible, I think, not to find in Arthur Clennam the evidence of Dickens' deep personal involvement in *Little Dorrit*. If we ask what Charles Dickens has to do with poor Clennam, what The Inimitable has to do with this sad depleted failure, the answer must be: nothing, save what is implied by Clennam's consciousness that he has passed the summit of life and that the path from now on leads downward, by his belief that the pleasures of love are not for him, by his "I want to know . . . ," by his wish to negate the will in death. Arthur Clennam is that mode of Dickens' existence at the time of *Little Dorrit* which makes it possible for him to write to his friend Macready, "However strange it is never to be at rest, and never satisfied, and ever trying after something that is never reached, and to be always laden with plot and plan and care and worry, how clear it is that it must be, and that one is driven by an irresistible might until the journey is worked out." And somewhat earlier and with a yet more poignant relevance: "Why is it, that as with poor David, a sense always comes crushing upon me now, when I fall into low spirits, as of one happiness I have missed in life, and one friend and companion I have never made?"

If we become aware of an autobiographical element in *Little Dorrit*, we must of course take notice of the fact that the novel was conceived after the famous incident of Maria Beadnell, who, poor woman, was the original of Arthur Clennam's Flora Finching. She was the first love of Dickens' proud, unfledged youth; she had married what Dickens has taught us to call Another, and now, after twenty years, she had chosen to come back into his life. Familiarity with the story cannot diminish our amazement at it—Dickens was a subtle and worldly man, but his sophistication was not proof against his passionate sentimentality, and he fully expected the past to come back to him, borne in the little hands of the adorable Maria. The actuality had a quite extreme effect upon him, and Flora, fat and foolish, is his monument to the discovered discontinuity between youth and middle age; she is the nonsensical spirit of the anticlimax of the years. And if she is in some degree forgiven, being represented as the kindest of foolish women, yet it is not without meaning that she is everywhere attended by Mr. F's Aunt, one of Dickens' most astonishing ideas, the embodiment of senile rage and spite, flinging to the world the crusts of her buttered toast. "He has a proud stomach, this chap," she cries when poor Arthur hesitates over her dreadful gift. "Give him a meal of chaff!" It is the voice of one of the Parcae.

It did not, of course, need the sad comedy of Maria Beadnell for Dickens to conceive that something in his life had come to an end. It did not even need his growing certainty that, after so many years and so many children, his relations with his wife were insupportable—this realization was as much a consequence as it was a cause of the sense of termination. He was forty-three years old and at the pinnacle of a success unique in the history of letters. The wildest ambitions of his youth could not have comprehended the actuality of his fame. But the last infirmity of noble mind may lead to the first infirmity of noble will. Dickens, to be sure, never lost his love of fame, or of whatever of life's goods his miraculous powers might bring him, but there came a moment when the old primitive motive could no longer serve, when the joy of impressing his powers on the world no longer seemed delightful in itself, and when the first, simple, honest, vulgar energy of desire no longer seemed appropriate to his idea of himself.

We may say of Dickens that at the time of *Little Dorrit* he was at a crisis of the will which is expressed in the characters and forces of the novel, in the extremity of its bitterness against the social will, in its vision of peace and selflessness. This moral crisis is most immediately represented by the condition of Arthur Clennam's will, by his sense of guilt, by his belief that he is unloved and unlovable, by his retirement to the Marshalsea as by an act of choice, by his sickness unto death. We have here the analogy to the familiar elements of a religious crisis. This is not the place to raise the question of Dickens' relation to the Christian religion, which was a complicated one. But we cannot speak of *Little Dorrit* without taking notice of its reference to Christian feeling, if only because this is of considerable importance in its effect upon the aesthetic of the novel.

It has been observed of *Little Dorrit* that certain of Dickens' characteristic delights are not present in their usual force. Something of his gusto is diminished in at least one of its aspects. We do not have the amazing thickness of fact and incident that marks, say, *Bleak House* or *Our Mutual Friend*—not that we do not have sufficient thickness, but we do not have what Dickens usually gives us. We do not have the great population of characters from whom shines the freshness of their autonomous life. Mr. Pancks and Mrs. Plornish and Flora Finching and Flintwinch are interesting and amusing, but they seem to be the fruit of conscious intention rather than of free creation. This is sometimes explained by saying that Dickens was fatigued. Perhaps so, but if we are aware that Dickens is here expending less of one kind of creative energy, we must at the same time be aware that he is expending more than ever before of another kind. The imagination of *Little Dorrit* is marked not so much by its powers of particularization as by its powers of generalization and abstraction. It is an imagination under the dominion of a great articulated idea, a moral idea which tends to find its full development in a religious experience. It is an imagination akin to that which created *Piers Plowman* and *Pilgrim's Progress*. And, indeed, it is akin to the imagination of *The Divine Comedy*. Never before has Dickens made so full, so Dantean, a claim for the virtue of the artist, and there is a Dantean pride and a Dantean reason in what he says of Daniel Doyce, who, although an engineer, stands for the creative mind in general and for its appropriate virtue: "His dismissal of himself [was] remarkable. He never said, I discovered this adaptation or invented that combination; but showed the whole thing as if the Divine Artificer had made it, and he had happened to find it. So modest was he about it, such a pleasant touch of respect was mingled with his quiet admiration of it, and so calmly convinced was he that it was established on irrefragable laws." Like much else that might be pointed to, this confirms us in the sense that the whole energy of the imagination of *Little Dorrit* is directed to the transcending of the personal will, to the search for the Will in which shall be our peace.

We must accept—and we easily do accept, if we do not permit critical cliché to interfere—the aesthetic of such an imagination, which will inevitably tend toward a certain formality of pattern and toward the generalization and the abstraction we have re-marked. In a novel in which a house falls physically to ruins from the moral collapse of its inhabitants, in which the heavens open over London to show a crown of thorns, in which the devil has something like an actual existence, we quite easily accept characters named nothing else than Bar, Bishop, Physician. And we do not reject, despite our inevitable first impulse to do so, the character of Little Dorrit herself. Her untinctured goodness does not appall us or make us misdoubt her, as we expected it to do. This novel at its best is only incidentally realistic; its finest power of imagination appears in the great general images whose abstractness is their actuality, like Mr. Merdle's dinner parties, or the Circumlocution Office itself, and in such a con-text we understand Little Dorrit to be the Beatrice of the *Com-edy*, the Paraclete in female form. Even the physical littleness of this grown woman, an attribute which is insisted on and which seems likely to repel us, does not do so, for we perceive it to be the sign that she is not only the Child of the Marshalsea, as she is called, but also the Child of the Parable, the negation of the social will.

G. ROBERT STANGE: 1954

Expectations Well Lost:
Dickens' Fable for His Time

GREAT EXPECTATIONS is a peculiarly satisfying and impressive novel. It is unusual to find in Dickens' work so rigorous a control of detail, so simple and organic a pattern. In this very late novel the usual features of his art—proliferating sub-plots, legions of minor grotesques—are almost entirely absent. The simplicity is that of an art form that belongs to an ancient type and concentrates on permanently significant issues. *Great Expectations* is conceived as a moral fable; it is the story of a young man's development from the moment of his first self-awareness, to that of his mature acceptance of the human condition.

So natural a theme imposes an elemental form on the novel: the over-all pattern is defined by the process of growth, and Dickens employs many of the motifs of folklore. The story of Pip falls into three phases which clearly display a dialectic progression. We see the boy first in his natural condition in the country, responding and acting instinctively and therefore virtuously. The second stage of his career involves a negation of child-like simplicity; Pip acquires his "expectations," renounces his origins, and moves to the city. He rises in society, but since he acts

College English, XVI (1954–1955), 9–17.

through calculation rather than through instinctive charity, his moral values deteriorate as his social graces improve. This middle phase of his career culminates in a sudden fall, the beginning of a redemptive suffering which is dramatically concluded by an attack of brain fever leading to a long coma. It is not too fanciful to regard this illness as a symbolic death; Pip rises from it regenerate and percipient. In the final stage of growth he returns to his birthplace, abandons his false expectations, accepts the limitations of his condition, and achieves a partial synthesis of the virtue of his innocent youth and the melancholy insight of his later experience.

Variants of such a narrative are found in the myths of many heroes. In Dickens' novel the legend has the advantage of providing an action which appeals to the great primary human affections and serves as unifying center for the richly conceived minor themes and images which form the body of the novel. It is a signal virtue of this simple structure that it saves *Great Expectations* from some of the startling weaknesses of such excellent but inconsistently developed novels as *Martin Chuzzlewit* or *Our Mutual Friend*.

The particular fable that Dickens elaborates is as interesting for its historical as for its timeless aspects. In its particulars the story of Pip is the classic legend of the nineteenth century: *Great Expectations* belongs to that class of education or development-novels which describe the young man of talents who progresses from the country to the city, ascends in the social hierarchy, and moves from innocence to experience. Stendhal in *Le Rouge et le Noir*, Balzac in *Le Père Goriot* and *Les Illusions perdues*, use the plot as a means of dissecting the post-Napoleonic world and exposing its moral poverty. This novelistic form reflects the lives of the successful children of the century, and usually expresses the mixed attitudes of its artists. Dickens, Stendhal, Balzac communicate their horror of a materialist society, but they are not without admiration for the possibilities of the new social mobility; *la carrière ouverte aux talents* had a personal meaning for all three of these energetic men.

Pip, then, must be considered in the highly competitive company of Julien Sorel, Rubempré, and Eugène de Rastignac. Dickens' tale of lost illusions, however, is very different from the French novelists'; *Great Expectations* is not more profound than other development-novels, but it is more mysterious. The recurrent themes of the genre are all there: city is posed against country, experience against innocence; there is a search for the true father; there is the exposure to crime and the acceptance of guilt and expiation. What Dickens' novel lacks is the clarity and, one is tempted to say, the essential tolerance of the French. He could not command either the saving ironic vision of Stendhal or the disenchanted practicality and secure Catholicism of Balzac. For Dickens, always the Victorian protestant, the issues of a young man's rise or fall are conceived as a drama of the individual conscience; enlightenment (partial at best) is to be found only in the agony of personal guilt.

With these considerations and possible comparisons in mind I should like to comment on some of the conspicuous features of *Great Expectations*. The novel is interesting for many reasons: it demonstrates the subtlety of Dickens' art; it displays a consistent control of narrative, imagery, and theme which gives meaning to the stark outline of the fable, and symbolic weight to every character and detail. It proves Dickens' ability (which has frequently been denied) to combine his genius for comedy with his fictional presentation of some of the most serious and permanently interesting of human concerns.

The principal themes are announced and the mood of the whole novel established in the opening pages of *Great Expectations*. The first scene with the boy Pip in the graveyard is one of the best of the superbly energetic beginnings found in almost all Dickens' mature novels. In less than a page we are given a character, his background, and his setting; within a few paragraphs more we are immersed in a decisive action. Young Pip is first seen against the background of his parents' gravestones—monuments which communicate to him no clear knowledge either of his parentage or of his position in the world. He is an orphan who must search for a father and define his own condition. The moment of this opening scene, we learn, is that at which the hero has first realized his individuality and gained his "first most vivid and broad impression of the identity of things." This information given the reader, the violent meeting between Pip and the escaped convict abruptly takes place.

The impression of the identity of things that Pip is supposed to have received is highly equivocal. The convict rises up like a ghost from among the graves, seizes the boy suddenly, threatens to kill him, holds him upside down through most of their conversation, and ends by forcing the boy to steal food for him. The children of Dickens' novels always receive rather strange impressions of things, but Pip's epiphany is the oddest of all, and in some ways the most ingenious. This encounter in the graveyard is the germinal scene of the novel. While he is held by the convict, Pip sees his world upside down; in the course of Dickens' fable the reader is invited to try the same view. This particular change of viewpoint is an ancient device of irony, but an excellent one: Dickens' satire asks us to try reversing the accepted senses of innocence and guilt, success and failure, to think of the world's goods as the world's evils.

A number of ironic reversals and ambiguous situations develop out of the first scene. The convict, Magwitch, is permanently grateful to Pip for having brought him food and a file with which to take off his leg-iron. Years later he expresses his gratitude by assuming in secrecy an economic parenthood; with the money he has made in Australia he will, unbeknownst to Pip, make "his boy" a gentleman. But the money the convict furnishes him makes

Pip not a true gentleman, but a cad. He lives as a flâneur in London, and when he later discovers the disreputable source of his income is snobbishly horrified.

Pip's career is a parable which illustrates several religious paradoxes: he can gain only by losing all he has; only by being defiled can he be cleansed. Magwitch returns to claim his gentleman, and finally the convict's devotion and suffering arouse Pip's charity; by the time Magwitch has been captured and is dying Pip has accepted him and come to love him as a true father. The relationship is the most important one in the novel: in sympathizing with Magwitch Pip assumes the criminal's guilt; in suffering with and finally loving the despised and rejected man he finds his own real self.

Magwitch did not have to learn to love Pip. He was naturally devoted to "the small bundle of shivers," the outcast boy who brought him the stolen food and the file in the misty graveyard. There is a natural bond, Dickens suggests, between the child and the criminal; they are alike in their helplessness; both are repressed and tortured by established society, and both rebel against its incomprehensible authority. In the first scene Magwitch forces Pip to commit his first "criminal" act, to steal the file and food from his sister's house. Though this theft produces agonies of guilt in Pip, we are led to see it not as a sin but as an instinctive act of mercy. Magwitch, much later, tells Pip: "I first become aware of myself, down in Essex, a thieving turnips for my living." Dickens would have us, in some obscure way, conceive the illicit act as the means of self-realization.

In the opening section of the novel the view moves back and forth between the escaped criminal on the marshes and the harsh life in the house of Pip's sister, Mrs. Joe Gargery. The "criminality" of Pip and the convict is contrasted with the socially approved cruelty and injustice of Mrs. Joe and her respectable friends. The elders who come to the Christmas feast at the Gargerys' are pleased to describe Pip as a criminal: the young are, according to Mr. Hubble, "naterally wicious." During this most bleak of Christmas dinners the child is treated not only as outlaw, but as animal. In Mrs. Joe's first speech Pip is called a "young monkey"; then, as the spirits of the revellers rise, more and more comparisons are made between boys and animals. Uncle Pumblechook, devouring his pork, toys with the notion of Pip's having been born a "Squeaker":

"If you had been born such, would you have been here now? Not you. . . ."

"Unless in that form," said Mr. Wopsle, nodding towards the dish.

"But I don't mean in that form, sir," returned Mr. Pumblechook, who had an objection to being interrupted; "I mean, enjoying himself with his elders and betters, and improving himself with their conversation, and rolling in the lap of luxury. Would he have been doing that? No, he wouldn't. And what would have been your destination?" turning on me again. "You would have been disposed of for so many shillings according to the market price of the article, and Dunstable the butcher would have come up to you as you lay in your straw, and he would have whipped you under his left arm, and with his right he would have tucked up his frock to get a penknife from out of his waistcoat-pocket, and he would have shed your blood and had your life. No bringing up by hand then. Not a bit of it!"

This identification of animal and human is continually repeated in the opening chapters of the novel, and we catch its resonance throughout the book. When the two convicts—Pip's "friend" and the other fugitive, Magwitch's ancient enemy—are captured, we experience the horror of official justice, which treats the prisoners as if they were less than human: "No one seemed surprised to see him, or interested in seeing him, or glad to see him, or sorry to see him, or spoke a word, except that somebody in the boat growled as if to dogs, 'Give way, you!'" And the prison ship, lying beyond the mud of the shore, looked to Pip "like a wicked Noah's ark."

The theme of this first section of the novel—which concludes with the capture of Magwitch and his return to the prison ship —might be called "the several meanings of humanity." Only the three characters who are in some way social outcasts—Pip, Magwitch, and Joe Gargery the child-like blacksmith—act in charity and respect the humanity of others. To Magwitch Pip is distinctly not an animal, and not capable of adult wickedness: "You'd be but a fierce young hound indeed, if at your time of life you could help to hunt a wretched warmint." And when, after he is taken, the convict shields Pip by confessing to have stolen the Gargerys' pork pie, Joe's absolution affirms the dignity of man:

"God knows you're welcome to it—so far as it was ever mine," returned Joe, with a saving remembrance of Mrs. Joe. "We don't know what you have done, but we wouldn't have you starved to death for it, poor miserable fellow-creatur.—Would us, Pip?"

The next section of the narrative is less tightly conceived than the introductory action. Time is handled loosely; Pip goes to school, and becomes acquainted with Miss Havisham of Satis House and the beautiful Estella. The section concludes when Pip has reached early manhood, been told of his expectations, and has prepared to leave for London. These episodes develop, with variations, the theme of childhood betrayed. Pip himself renounces his childhood by coming to accept the false social values of middle-class society. His perverse development is expressed by persistent images of the opposition between the human and the non-human, the living and the dead.

On his way to visit Miss Havisham for the first time, Pip spends the night with Mr. Pumblechook, the corn-chandler, in his lodgings behind his shop. The contrast between the aridity of this old hypocrite's spirit and the viability of his wares is a type of the conflict between natural growth and social form. Pip looks at all the shop-keeper's little drawers filled with bulbs and seed packets and wonders "whether the flower-seeds and bulbs ever wanted of a fine day to break out of those jails and bloom." The imagery of life repressed is developed further in the descriptions of Miss Havisham and Satis House. The first detail Pip notices is the abandoned brewery where the once active ferment has ceased; no germ of life is to be found in Satis House or in its occupants:

. . . there were no pigeons in the dove-cot, no horses in the stable, no pigs in the sty, no malt in the storehouse, no smells of grains and beer in the copper or the vat. All the uses and scents of the brewery might have evaporated with its last reek of smoke. In a by-yard, there was a wilderness of empty casks. . . .

On top of these casks Estella dances with solitary concentration, and behind her, in a dark corner of the building, Pip fancies that he sees a figure hanging by the neck from a wooden beam, "a figure all in yellow white, with but one shoe to the feet; and it hung so, that I could see that the faded trimmings of the dress were like earthy paper, and that the face was Miss Havisham's."

Miss Havisham *is* death. From his visits to Satis House Pip acquires his false admiration for the genteel; he falls in love with Estella and fails to see that she is the cold instrument of Miss Havisham's revenge on human passion and on life itself. When Pip learns he may expect a large inheritance from an unknown source he immediately assumes (incorrectly) that Miss Havisham is his benefactor; she does not undeceive him. Money, which is also death, is appropriately connected with the old lady rotting away in her darkened room.

Conflicting values in Pip's life are also expressed by the opposed imagery of stars and fire. Estella is by name a star, and throughout the novel stars are conceived as pitiless: "And then I looked at the stars, and considered how awful it would be for a man to turn his face up to them as he froze to death, and see no help or pity in all the glittering multitude." Estella and her light are described as coming down the dark passage of Satis

House "like a star," and when she has become a woman she is constantly surrounded by the bright glitter of jewelry.

Joe Gargery, on the other hand, is associated with the warm fire of the hearth or forge. It was his habit to sit and rake the fire between the lower bars of the kitchen grate, and his workday was spent at the forge. The extent to which Dickens intended the contrast between the warm and the cold lights—the vitality of Joe and the frigid glitter of Estella—is indicated in a passage that describes the beginnings of Pip's disillusionment with his expectations:

When I woke up in the night . . . I used to think, with a weariness on my spirits, that I should have been happier and better if I had never seen Miss Havisham's face, and had risen to manhood content to be partners with Joe in the honest old forge. Many a time of an evening, when I sat alone looking at the fire, I thought, after all, there was no fire like the forge fire and the kitchen fire at home.

Yet Estella was so inseparable from all my restlessness and disquiet of mind, that I really fell into confusion as to the limits of my own part in its production.

At the end of the novel Pip finds the true light on the homely hearth, and in a last twist of the father-son theme, Joe emerges as a true parent—the only kind of parent that Dickens could ever fully approve, one that remains a child. The moral of this return to Joe sharply contradicts the accepted picture of Dickens as a radical critic of society: Joe is a humble countryman who is content with the place in the social order he has been appointed to fulfill. He fills it "well and with respect"; Pip learns that he can do no better than to emulate him.

The second stage of Pip's three-phased story is set in London, and the moral issues of the fiction are modulated accordingly. Instead of the opposition between custom and the instinctive life, the novelist treats the conflict between man and his social institutions. The topics and themes are specific, and the satire, some of it wonderfully deft, is more social than moral. Not all Dickens' social message is presented by means that seem adequate. By satirizing Pip and his leisure class friends (The Finches of the Grove, they call themselves) the novelist would have us realize that idle young men will come to a bad end. Dickens is here expressing the Victorian Doctrine of Work—a pervasive notion that both inspired and reassured his industrious contemporaries.

The difficulty for the modern reader, who is unmoved by the objects of Victorian piety, is that the doctrine appears to be the result, not of moral insight, but of didactic intent; it is presented as statement, rather than as experience or dramatized perception, and consequently it never modifies the course of fictional action or the formation of character. The distinction is crucial: it is between the Dickens who *sees* and the Dickens who *professes;* often between the good and the bad sides of his art.

The novelist is on surer ground when he comes to define the nature of wealth in a mercantile society. Instead of moralistic condemnation we have a technique that resembles parable. Pip eventually learns that his ornamental life is supported, not by Miss Havisham, but by the labor and suffering of the convict Magwitch:

"I swore arterwards, sure as ever I spec'lated and got rich, you should get rich. I lived rough, that you should live smooth; I worked hard that you should be above work. What odds, dear boy? Do I tell it fur you to feel a obligation? Not a bit. I tell it, fur you to know as that there dunghill dog wot you kep life in, got his head so high that he could make a gentleman—and, Pip, you're him!"

The convict would not only make a gentleman but own him. The blood horses of the colonists might fling up the dust over him as he was walking but, "I says to myself, 'If I ain't a gentleman, nor yet ain't got no learning, I'm the owner of such. All on you owns stock and land; which on you owns a brought-up London gentleman?' "

In this action Dickens has subtly led us to speculate on the connections between a gentleman and his money, on the dark origins of even the most respectable fortunes. We find Magwitch guilty of trying to own another human being, but we ask whether his actions are any more sinful than those of the wealthy *bourgeois*. There is a deeper moral in the fact that Magwitch's fortune at first destroyed the natural gentleman in Pip, but that after it was lost (it had to be forfeited to the state when Magwitch was finally captured) the "dung-hill dog" did actually make Pip a gentleman by evoking his finer feelings. This ironic distinction between "gentility" and what the father of English poetry meant by "gentilesse" is traditional in our literature and our mythology. In *Great Expectations* it arises out of the action and language of the fiction; consequently it moves and persuades us as literal statement never can.

The middle sections of the novel are dominated by the solid yet mysterious figure of Mr. Jaggers, Pip's legal guardian. Though Jaggers is not one of Dickens' greatest characters he is heavy with implication; he is so much at the center of this fable that we are challenged to interpret him—only to find that his meaning is ambiguous. On his first appearance Jaggers strikes a characteristic note of sinister authority:

He was a burly man of an exceedingly dark complexion, with an exceedingly large head and a correspondingly large hand. He took my chin in his large hand and turned up my face to have a look at me by the light of the candle. . . . His eyes were set very deep in his head, and were disagreeably sharp and suspicious. . . .
"How do you come here?"
"Miss Havisham sent for me, sir," I explained.
"Well! Behave yourself. I have a pretty large experience of boys, and you're a bad set of fellows. Now mind!" said he, biting the side of his great forefinger, as he frowned at me, "you behave yourself."

Pip wonders at first if Jaggers is a doctor. It is soon explained that he is a lawyer—what we now ambiguously call a *criminal* lawyer—but he is like a physician who treats moral malignancy, with the doctor's necessary detachment from individual suffering. Jaggers is interested not in the social operations of the law, but in the varieties of criminality. He exudes an antiseptic smell of soap and is described as washing his clients off as if he were a surgeon or a dentist.

Pip finds that Jaggers has "an air of authority not to be disputed . . . with a manner expressive of knowing something secret about every one of us that would effectually do for each individual if he chose to disclose it." When Pip and his friends go to dinner at Jaggers' house Pip observes that he "wrenched the weakest parts of our dispositions out of us." After the party his guardian tells Pip that he particularly liked the sullen young man they called Spider: " 'Keep as clear of him as you can. But I like the fellow, Pip; he is one of the true sort. Why if I was a fortune-teller. . . . But I am not a fortune-teller,' he said. . . . 'You know what I am don't you?' " This question is repeated when Pip is being shown through Newgate Prison by Jaggers' assistant, Wemmick. The turnkey says of Pip: "Why then . . . he knows what Mr. Jaggers is."

But neither Pip nor the reader ever fully knows what Mr. Jaggers is. We learn, along with Pip, that Jaggers has manipulated the events which have shaped the lives of most of the characters in the novel; he has, in the case of Estella and her mother, dispensed a merciful but entirely personal justice; he is the only character who knows the web of secret relationships that are finally revealed to Pip. He dominates by the strength of his knowledge the world of guilt and sin—called *Little Britain*—of which his office is the center. He has, in brief, the powers that an artist exerts over the creatures of his fictional world, and that a god exerts over his creation.

As surrogate of the artist, Jaggers displays qualities of mind—complete impassibility, all-seeing unfeelingness—which are the opposite of Dickens', but of a sort that Dickens may at times have desired. Jaggers can be considered a fantasy figure created by a novelist who is forced by his intense sensibility to re-live the sufferings of his fellow men and who feels their agonies too deeply.

In both the poetry and fiction of the nineteenth century there are examples of a persistent desire of the artist *not to care*. The mood, which is perhaps an inevitable concomitant of Romanticism, is expressed in Balzac's ambivalence toward his great character Vautrin. As arch-criminal and Rousseauistic man, Vautrin represents all the attitudes that Balzac the churchman and monarchist ostensibly rejects, yet is presented as a kind of artist-hero, above the law, who sees through the social system with an almost noble cynicism.

Related attitudes are expressed in the theories of art developed by such different writers as Flaubert and Yeats. While—perhaps because—Flaubert himself suffered from hyperaesthesia, he conceived the ideal novelist as coldly detached, performing his examination with the deft impassivity of the surgeon. Yeats, the "last Romantic," found the construction of a mask or anti-self necessary to poetic creation, and insisted that the anti-self be cold and hard—all that he as poet and feeling man was not.

Dickens' evocation of this complex of attitudes is less political than Balzac's, less philosophical than Flaubert's or Yeats'. Jaggers has a complete understanding of human evil but, unlike the living artist, can wash his hands of it. He is above ordinary institutions; like a god he dispenses justice, and like a god displays infinite mercy through unrelenting severity:

"Mind you, Mr. Pip," said Wemmick, gravely in my ear, as he took my arm to be more confidential; "I don't know that Mr. Jaggers does a better thing than the way in which he keeps himself so high. He's always so high. His constant height is of a piece with his immense abilities. That Colonel durst no more take leave of *him*, than that turnkey durst ask him his intentions respecting a case. Then between his height and them, he slips in his subordinate—don't you see? —and so he has 'em soul and body."

Pip merely wishes that he had "some other guardian of minor abilities."

The final moral vision of *Great Expectations* has to do with the nature of sin and guilt. After visiting Newgate Pip, still complacent and self-deceived, thinks how strange it was that he should be encompassed by the taint of prison and crime. He tries to beat the prison dust off his feet and to exhale its air from his lungs; he is going to meet Estella, who must not be contaminated by the smell of crime. Later it is revealed that Estella, the pure, is the bastard child of Magwitch and a murderess. Newgate is figuratively described as a greenhouse, and the prisoners as plants carefully tended by Wemmick, assistant to Mr. Jaggers. These disturbing metaphors suggest that criminality is the condition of life. Dickens would distinguish between the native, inherent sinfulness from which men can be redeemed, and that evil which destroys life: the sin of the hypocrite or oppressor, the smothering wickedness of corrupt institutions. The last stage of Pip's progression is reached when he learns to love the criminal and to accept his own implication in the common guilt.

Though Dickens' interpretation is theologically heterodox, he deals conventionally with the ancient question of free will and predestination. In one dramatic paragraph Pip's "fall" is compared with the descent of the rock slab on the sleeping victim in the Arabian Nights tale: Slowly, slowly, "all the work, near and afar, that tended to the end, had been accomplished; and in an instant the blow was struck, and the roof of my stronghold dropped upon me." Pip's fall was the result of a chain of predetermined events but he was, nevertheless, responsible for his own actions; toward the end of the novel Miss Havisham gravely informs him: "You have made your own snares. *I* never made them."

The patterns of culpability in *Great Expectations* are so intricate that the whole world of the novel is eventually caught in a single web of awful responsibility. The leg-iron, for example, which the convict removed with the file Pip stole for him is found by Orlick and used as a weapon to brain Mrs. Joe. By this fearsome chain of circumstance Pip shares the guilt for his sister's death.

Profound and suggestive as is Dickens' treatment of guilt and expiation in this novel, to trace its remoter implications is to find something excessive and idiosyncratic. A few years after he wrote *Great Expectations* Dickens remarked to a friend that he felt always as if he were wanted by the police—"irretrievably tainted." Compared to most of the writers of his time the Dickens of the later novels seems to be obsessed with guilt. The way in which his development-novel differs from those of his French compeers emphasizes an important quality of Dickens' art. The young heroes of *Le Rouge et le Noir* and *Le Père Goriot* proceed from innocence, through suffering to learning. They are surrounded by evil, and they can be destroyed by it. But Stendhal, writing in a rationalist tradition, and Balzac displaying the worldliness that only a Catholic novelist can command, seem astonishingly cool, even callous, beside Dickens. *Great Expectations* is outside either Cartesian or Catholic rationalism; profound as only an elementally simple book can be, it finds its analogues not in the novels of Dickens' English or French contemporaries, but in the writings of that other irretrievably tainted artist, Fyodor Dostoevski.

V. S. PRITCHETT: 1954

The Comic World of Dickens

THOSE who have written the best criticism of Dickens in the last twenty years are united in their belief that the serious and later Dickens is more important and has more meaning for the modern reader, than the comic Dickens; or, that, in any case, the comic Dickens has been overdone. I do not share this opinion, nor do I think that those intelligent readers who read for pleasure hold the opinion either. Dickens' reputation and achievement rests on his comic writing and above all on his comic sense of life. The comic world is a complete world in itself. It is, as Mr. Middleton Murry has said in a recent book on Swift, an orgiastic world, with only a dubious relation with the moral hierarchy. It is, in short, an alternative world to that of ordinary experience and as valid as the poetic which it often criticizes or inverts. It is true that, in the narrow sense of being humorous, Dickens is not continually comic; one can, more accurately, call him pictur-esque, theatrical, Gothic; even so, it is impossible to divide a writer into sections which have no relationship with each other. We cannot separate the comic from the indignant, sermonizing, melodramatic, revolutionary or murderous Dickens, for the comic, in him, was not mere comic relief. The Wilfers are an-

The Listener, 3 June 1954, pp. 970–973; also, *The Avon Book of Modern Writing* (New York, 1955).

other way of laughing at the Veneerings, just as the Veneerings are a way of laughing at the obsession with money in Victorian society; and that laughter is joined to the hatred and despair Dickens felt about it. It is above all in the comic Dickens that we find the artist who has resolved, for a moment, the violent conflicts in his disorderly genius and who has found, what all the greatest artists have sought, the means of forgiving life. In these comic passages we find his poetry and a quality we can only call radiant. It is important to remember that, with the exception of *Edwin Drood*, where there is a change in prose style, the serious Dickens is *not* a realist. There are brilliantly funny things in *Edwin Drood*, but we notice how detachable they are from the realism of the background and the main story. The contrast between realism and fantasy becomes awkward in this book.

The early Dickens is, of course, soaked in Fielding, and Smollett. He can, at any period of his life, make use of their tradition when he wants to do so. The general, discursive, ironical tone of *Oliver Twist* is Fielding; the picaresque incident of *Pickwick* comes from him also. Sterne and the romantic movement have taught him the value of pathos, tears, changeableness, and the gestures against an unjust world. When I say that Fielding has had his effect, I refer to Fielding's Victorian novel *Amelia* rather than to the other novels. A very important difference is that Dickens is more violent than Fielding, yet far softer hearted— I mean violent in emotional temperament. Fielding's violence in *Jonathan Wild* is purely intellectual. We can explain this by saying that the sedate and abstract preconceptions of the eighteenth century have gone and that Man and Nature have been replaced by talkative men and women. There is also a class difference: the eighteenth-century writers were gentlemen or aspired to be men of the world of fashion. Dickens is plainly lower middle class—the most energetic, intelligent and insecure class of that society. Always on the defensive, they are the richest in fantasy life. They cannot afford the great passions, but demand to be judged by their dreams and sentiments. Oddity, being "characters," is their great solace.

If a debtor is thrown into prison in the eighteenth century, we know he is a rash *rentier:* he has simply behaved thoughtlessly as gentlemen and men of honor do. In Dickens, debt is an undeserved human misfortune which comes unreasonably to people who are trapped by character or circumstance despite all their conscientious efforts. Mild cadging and borrowing have entered the purview of satire, of sentiment and of the genteel world of euphemism. Skimpole, Micawber, the Marshalsea figures, are all debtors. Debts become tragic and comic at once. They lead to delicate moral casuistries, amusing hypocrisies and the evasions of middle-class life. Dickens, of course, got all this from his father who was a part source of the immense comedy of money and rhetoric which is basic in the novelist. Money and humbug—they are the new subjects of a commercial age. The father of the Marshalsea, that old professional borrower, says to his son who is angry because he is refused a loan:

And is it Christian, let me ask you, to stigmatise and denounce an individual for begging to be excused this time when the same individual may—ha—respond with the required accommodation next time? Is it part of a Christian not to—hum—not to try again?

The old man (Dickens says) had worked himself into a religious fervor when he said this. Not (we notice) into the disdain of a gentleman.

We have moved from the eighteenth century's grandiloquent sense of Fortune, to the nineteenth century's sense of cash. Another change, is that Dickens depends far more on *character* than on events, except perhaps in *Pickwick*. The horseplay is far less, the misadventures and knockabout have declined. The situations have become more subtle and depend on the characters themselves. Dickens' comedy is the comedy of people who *are* something, rather than the comedy of people who *do* something which leads to new plot, farces or messes. In the plot sense, Dickens stands still.

But the most important change is the dropping of sexual love. The ribald or sensual humor of the English tradition which puritanism did not really destroy, goes down before another enemy; the immense effort toward material progress which we call the industrial revolution or that great assertion of will which we call the Victorian age. Already in the eighteenth century there were many signs of a dichotomy: Hogarth contrasted *The Rake's Progress* with the story of *The Industrious Apprentice.* I need not go into the whole question of Victorianism and sex for it has often been done, except to say that the Victorian attitude is an aspect of the *violence* of Victorian society and Dickens was both a tender and a violent writer. Huge changes in the traditions of society produce their self-mutilations. It may well be that the violence, the rebellion, the histrionics, the egotism and fantasy of Dickens, all of which are manifest in his comedy just as they are in his social indignation, were deeply affected by a willful impatience with love. Of course, love has always been a stock comic subject: its illusions are irresistibly funny. Some have traced the hardening of Dickens' heart to the humiliation of his failure with Maria Beadnell. They have said this was the point at which the poet was injured and turned into the comedian. It seems to me more likely that his incredible and very Victorian will to success had already done that much earlier in childhood. Against sex are built up the steadfast yet gentle defense of the sentiments, the drama of a black and white morality, and Dickens' personal feeling for power.

For the comic Dickens women are mainly of the insecure middle class, soured by marriage, capricious sluts, and termagants, a terrible sisterhood of scolds or frantic spinsters. This is essentially a boy's view derived from a nagging home, or from a boy's vanity. He was pretty enough and clever enough to want all attention for himself. Women are also fools, in his comedy, pettish in love, tiresome in childbirth, perpetually snuffling, continuously breeding. The hatred of children is another fundamental Victorian theme. Dickens is full of it and its natural daydream: the child-wife and the idealized child. What replaced the sane eighteenth-century attitude to sex in the comic writings of Dickens? I think probably the stress was put on another hunger —the hunger for food, drink and security, the jollity and good cheer. Domestic life means meals. Good food makes people good. To our taste now this doesn't seem very amusing. Half of Victorian England was disgustedly overfed, and since Dickens was an extremist he pushed the note of jollity much too far. The jolly Dickens is the one part of him that has become unreadable.

A more important change is in the *ground* or point of view of comedy. In the eighteenth century, this ground is the experience of the grown man. Even Sterne is a grown man. These writers are secure. In Dickens, the ground is the high visual sense and sharp ear of the experienced child who is insecure. The children of the Victorian age are precisely in the situation of the poor, and get much the same treatment: a huge, inevitable, sharp-witted and accusing class. Dickens' grotesque sense of physical appearance is the kind of sense the child has, and in the graver, later books, the sense that the writer is on his *own* and *alone* is very strong. He has grown up from the child *alone* into the man *alone*. Dickens is not following the Way of the World, but, in his satire, he is a rebel attacking the Way from outside. In personal life, he was quite incapable of keeping up with worldly characters like Wilkie Collins.

The gallery of Dickens' comic characters is so huge that it is hard to know where to begin. Dickens was a city. He was chiefly London, just as Joyce was Dublin. We can call Dickens' comedy gothic, a thing of saints, gargoyles, fantastic disorderly carvings. We can call it *mad*. A large number of his comic characters can be called *mad* because they live or speak as if they were *the only self in the world*. They live alone by some private idea. Mrs.

Gamp lives by the fiction of the approval of her imaginary friend Mrs. Harris. Augustus Moddle lives by the fixed idea of a demon and by the profound psychological, even metaphysical truth that, in this life, everyone seems to belong to a person whom he calls "another." In our time Moddle would be reading Kierkegaard. Mr. Gradgrind lives by the passionate superstition that only "Facts" exist, Mr. Dick by his obsession with King Charles's head. Mr. Micawber lives by the surveying of dreams. Mr. Pecksniff lives by metaphors; Mr. Sapsea thinks he is something called Mind and, in one special flight of fancy, gets himself described as "Oh thou" by his dead betrothed. These people are known to us because they are turned inside out: we know at once their inner life and the illusions they live by. An illusionist and a solitary himself, Dickens understands this immediately.

In Dickens, the comic characters who belong to what I call the *sane* tradition are comparatively few and they come notably early in his work. Mr. Pickwick, for example, is the standard unworldly, benevolent man of the eighteenth century. His chief troubles—the bedroom scene at Ipswich and the breach of promise case—seem to spring from being in an eighteenth-century situation with a nineteenth-century mind. If anyone gets into the wrong bedroom in the eighteenth century they either intend to do so or are prepared to fight their way out. Mr. Pickwick would never think of fighting and is genuinely shocked, as no eighteenth-century man could be, when his motives are impugned. Sam Weller is a sane character. But Tony Weller has the madness creeping on: the obsession with widows.

I shall have more to say about the madness of Dickens' characters later on. What I want to do first of all is to look at his method. The sketches by Boz start by being character sketches of types. We see for example a beadle. We see the election of a beadle. Here the characteristic thing happens. Dickens notes the fact that the job is apt to be given to the most deserving candidate and the deserts are reckoned by the number of children a man has. Dickens at once turns this idea into fantasy. Bung with five children is only thirty years old, therefore likely to surpass Mr. Spruggins in philoprogenitiveness, because Spruggins has the advantage of eleven children but the disadvantage of being fifty years old. Once more, the Victorian joke about the wretched children, the swarm, the basis of Dickens' idea that childbirth is funny; it is thought to be funny because the idea of pain and poverty—more mouths to feed—is intolerable. A comic protest, not altogether indignant, against the horrors of the Victorian swarm. (Dickens couldn't stand the sight of his own children after the age of two or three.) Dickens' comic method is to take a real situation and to add an idea to it. There are four spinsters, for example. Add the *idea* that a man is known to be paying court to one of them but none of the neighbors knows which. Add to this the *idea* that for all the neighbors know he *may* have married the whole four of them. This *"adding of an idea"* is the basis of the simplest kind of humor and especially of farce. The interesting thing is that Dickens started on the lowest rung of the comic ladder. He is a comic who comes up from the vulgar or facetious level.

The next fundamental element is that Dickens began his long observation of human mannerisms in speech, as a parliamentary reporter. He noticed, as he listened to the awful speeches of politicians, that they are punctuated by mechanical emphasis and repetition. The following passage could very well be literal observation:

Then would he be there to tell that honorable gentleman that the Circumlocution Office not only was blameless in this matter but was commendable in this matter, was extollable to the skies in this matter. Then would he be there to tell that honorable gentleman that although the Circumlocution Office was invariably right and wholly right it never was so right as in this matter.

To this Dickens added the fantastic idea that people speak in a public manner in private life.

Jinkins is a man of superior talents. I have conceived a great respect for Jinkins. I take Jinkins' desire to pay polite attention to my daughters as an *additional* proof of the friendly feelings of Jinkins.

That is Mr. Pecksniff speaking, but in fact many of Dickens' characters of the pompous kind talk like that. Is it real observation or comic trick? We can only judge each case on its merits. In Mr. Pecksniff's case it *is* his character to be a phrase-maker, a lover of platitudes; but it is also in his character to be arch, affected and cold. Mr. Pecksniff is funny when he says that about Jinkins because we do not really believe anyone would talk privately in a parliamentary fashion; but there is reason to suspect that while we are laughing at Pecksniff, Pecksniff himself has invented this absurd way of speaking in order to mock at Jinkins in a cold, ironical, artificial way. For Pecksniff is not a simple black and white hypocrite, he has a very mannered detachment. His speech is that of a man amusing himself at someone else's expense.

There is also a double laughter, a laugh within a laugh, when for example Mr. Pecksniff says: "To draw a lamp post has a tendency to refine the mind and give it *a classical turn*."

When he was charged with exaggeration Dickens replied that he simply saw and heard far more than most people. But it is also true that he added to the material given to him by one or two overwhelming characters and transformed people by presenting not only their characters, but their persona and their self-made myth. Dickens was a myth-maker when he said that "even Mr. Pecksniff's throat was moral."

Dickens certainly caught the comedy of English self-consequence but, in many cases, he *also* caught the fact that these people knew exactly what they were up to. Biographers tell us that he learned this, as I have said, from studying the large, oratorical manner of his father. His father's manner was like a farcical parliamentary manner transposed to private life. One can distinguish in Dickens I think between those repetitions of words which tend to caricature *from the outside* and those which fix a character by taking us into his *inner* fantasy world. The repetition of the word "fact" in the portrait of the Fact-Hound, Mr. Gradgrind, is a device of caricature, something discharged from a hostile position outside the character. It's the old, distorting formula of the dominant passion. But take another instance. The repetition of "the silent tomb" motif in the character of Mr. Pecksniff is more complex. Look at the passage at the end of *Martin Chuzzlewit* where Pecksniff takes his leave, shamed and exposed but not silenced:

"If you ever contemplate the silent tomb, Sir, which you will excuse me for entertaining some *doubt* of your doing, after the conduct into which you have allowed yourself to be betrayed this day; if you ever contemplate the silent tomb, Sir, think of me. If you find yourself *approaching* the silent tomb, Sir, think of *me*. If you should wish to have anything *inscribed* upon your silent tomb, Sir, let it be that I—ah, my remorseful Sir, that I—the humble individual who has now the honor of *reproaching* you *forgave* you."

The repetition is done in different tones of voice and insinuation. And this is a traditional device of comedy. Dickens was a considerable actor himself and he caught the actor in others and also the highly emotional temper of Victorian society; he liked writing actable lines; but Pecksniff is not only giving a polished performance, now sarcastic, now threatening, now ironical and mocking his tormentors. He is making himself ridiculous but he *thinks he is making fools of his listeners*. He is also using an image—"silent tomb"—which may be ludicrous but which also exactly corresponds to the condition of the hypocritical mind. A life of hypocrisy can succeed on the condition that it reduces moral standards, moral words, and life itself to meaninglessness. The hypocrite is indeed an empty tomb for he has killed life with words. He is also called traditionally a "whited sepulchre." It must have terrified the interminably talkative Pecksniff that the chief condition of tombs is their silence.

I know it is very dangerous to pay too close attention to a writer's images and phrases. The fact is that to Dickens, as to all primitive natures, there was something comic in death. Especially there was something funny in dead wives. Mr. Sapsea's betrothed is idiotic in the grave. Mr. Pecksniff drags the dead into his comedy. The height of Dickens' comedy of birth and death is reached by Mrs. Gamp.

"Which Mr. Chuzzlewit" said Mrs. Gamp "is well-known to Mrs. Harris as has one sweet infant (tho she do not wish it known) in her own family by the mother's side, kep in spirits in a bottle; and that sweet babe she see at Greenwich Fair, a travelling in company with the pink eyed lady Prooshan dwarf, and livin skelinton, which judge her feeling when the barrel organ played and she was showed her own dear sister's child, the same not being expected from the outside picter, where it was painted quite contrairy in a living state, many sizes larger, and performing beautiful on the arp, which never did that dear child know or do; since breathe it never did, to speak on, in this wale."

The foetus in the bottle, the child with the harp. That is going pretty far, but it is the fundamental, almost stock stuff of macabre comedy.

Pecksniff, Mrs. Gamp and Micawber belong to what we call, in a cliché, "the great comic characters"; that is to say they are part human beings and part myth or projection of the character's own imaginative conception of themselves. Mrs. Gamp belongs to the same order of character as the Wife of Bath, Juliet's nurse and Mrs. Bloom. It is commonly said of Pecksniff that he is too hateful. The same criticism is made of that great Russian hypocrite Iudushka in *The Golovlyov Family*. Pecksniff is certainly superficially hateful. The paradox of literature is that if a writer hates his hateful character too much he kills him; indeed it is the necessity of art that a writer must delight imaginatively even in his hateful characters. The art of the comic is to correct vice by laughter, because laughter is living. Or it is an orgiastic alternative to living. And in the laughter, the character was, as it were, reborn in a more tolerable dimension. Pecksniff will never be lovable but that does not mean that his author has not delighted in him. Dickens sees into the peculiarity of Pecksniff's mind and it is in the comic movements of the mind and inner life rather than in the comic events and plot—as I have said—that Dickens reaches his heights. Of course there *are* comic incidents in Pecksniff's career, the finest one being his drunkenness and his love-making to Mrs. Todgers. He makes a speech with a muffin stuck, butter side down, to the knee of his trousers. Dickens is capable of the most delicate ironical comedy too—for example, the scene in the Marshalsea in *Little Dorrit* where the penniless bankrupt, the father of the Marshalsea, makes a point of entertaining, with aristocratic condescension, one of his even less fortunate friends. This has an irony as fully drawn as anything in Cervantes. But Dickens mainly goes *first* for mannerism; at the next stage, for mannerism that reveals the conflict between the inner and outer man; at the *next* stage for that poetic clown —the inner consciousness itself. The clown may be innocent as Mr. Dick is, or Betsy Trotwood or Moddle, but he may be corrupt like Mr. Pecksniff and Mrs. Gamp. If he is corrupt his inner life becomes grotesque.

"My feelings, Mrs. Todgers, will not consent to be entirely smothered like the young children in the tower. They are grown up and the more I press the bolster on them, the more they look round the corner of it."

It has been said that if the comic characters of Dickens are not exaggerations and caricatures, then at any rate, they are flat and static. They circle round in the strange dog basket of their minds, and never escape from their compulsions. But I cannot really agree that the compulsive pattern in these characters makes *all* of them static and flat. There is a considerable growth in Pecksniff. It is true that he certainly does not move forward and develop very far as a character in action in the manner of Iudushka or in the manner of Oblomov; unless we say that Pecksniff begins by being a humbug and ends by becoming a villain. And we must admit that the comic or rather the fantastic characters are awkward when they have to act within the terms of a realistic, dramatic plot. They are essentially sedentary soliloquists, not people made for action.

The fact is that Dickens had a merely theatrical notion of evil. He thought bad men became evil men merely by becoming theatrical and non-comic; there is no need for Pecksniff to be a swindler; he is evil enough in rendering life meaningless. Yet there is a moment when Pecksniff does become permissibly evil and when his character shows a terrifying side. I am thinking of the scene when he proposes marriage of Mary Graham: a comic character dealing with a straight character. No metaphors now, no clowning, but smooth, persistent, planned and skillful tactics. Mr. Pecksniff is a cold hard libertine. He is capable of lust and violence and actually has courage in this scene. His courage makes him frightening and certainly shows a development in his character. When Miss Graham turns Mr. Pecksniff down Dickens writes in a different tone:

He seemed to be shrunk and reduced, to be trying to hide himself within himself; and to be wretched at not having the power to do it. His shoes looked too large; his sleeves looked too long; his hair looked too limp; his features looked too mean; and his exposed throat looked as if a halter would have done it good. For a minute or two, he was hot and pale, mean and shy and slinking and consequently, not at all Pecksniffian.

You can see now why Dickens was so keen on Pecksniff's moral throat. That phrase, "not at all Pecksniffian," is a serious development in depth. Yet it is out of key. The great characters of Dickens grow inwardly, if they do happen to grow. If it is true that they move very little forward they grow larger on the spot where they stand, because they are worked over in detail. This detail is not analytical but is a further encrustation of foolery. We recognize the imaginative truth of Dickens' fantasies because, at their heart, lies the comic fact that men behave as if they were solitary animals. A large number of the comic characters of Dickens think they are totally alone.

How does Pecksniff compare with figures like Tartuffe or Iudushka? There can hardly be a correct analogy with Tartuffe simply because the theater has to simplify and intensify. Molière is more imaginative than Dickens in showing that Tartuffe not only gains his ends by pretending virtue, but gets out of the attacks made on him, by grandiloquently confessing, knowing no one will believe him. Tartuffe, in other words, exploits vice as well as virtue. Since Tartuffe embodies the idea of hypocrisy he cannot be loved. Iudushka also surpasses Pecksniff because he is grimmer. He is comical because he is a bore. And he is also shown as self-corrupting. He bores himself. Dickens is certainly not as perceptive as the Russian writer, nor does Dickens rise to the heights that the Russian reaches in the scenes describing Iudushka's old age. Dickens had no real sense of the mind diseased. Closer to reality, facing the dreadful *fact* not the poetic fantasy of human solitude, the Russian sees the pathos indeed the tragedy of the egotist. Pecksniff goes out of his comedy with a speech and a gesture; Iudushka goes out of the squalid comedy with a scream of loss, pain, terror.

There is of course a movement, in Dickens' work, away from the fantasy and the gothic to the realistic form of humor. The figure of Mr. Bounderby is an example from *Hard Times*. Mr. Bounderby has the absurd pride of the self-made man. He is proud of his own hard times and he is well worked out. That is to say "hard times" is an idea added to all the characters and seen, in his case, on the comic level. He is a figure out of social satire who is not visited by the grace of the comic forgiveness. The more blasting kind of comic realism is to be found in certain minor characters, and especially among the aggressive poor. Here

Dickens reaches very fine points of social irony, for the poor
are capable of looking after themselves. They are not solitaries.
They are not clowns. They speak out with the skill of rival
comic authors. There is that famous visit of Mrs. Pardiggle to
the poor man. There is nothing eccentric about him.

"Is my daughter a-washing? Yes she is a-washing. Look at the
water. Smell it. That's wot we drinks. How d'you like it and what
d'you think of gin instead. Ain't my place dirty? Yes it is dirty; it's
naturally dirty and it's naturally unwholesome and we've had five
dirty and unwholesome children, as is all dead infants, and so much
the better for them and for us besides. And how did my wife get
that black eye? Why, I give it to her: an if she says I didn't she's a
liar."

Let us turn from the individual comic characters to the mass
comic effects of Dickens, to that mode of comedy which generalizes and which is commonly employed in satire. This satire
becomes harsher and I think cruder as Dickens grows older, as
his nerves became exacerbated by domestic unhappiness, by over-
work, by straining after money, and as Victorianism became more
vulgar and more blatant. There is an increase in hatred and violence as the years go by. These are dulling to the poetic genius
and the comic portrait of Mr. Gradgrind, for example, is actually
dull. There is a point in Dickens where one catches the note
of untransmuted hysteria and megalomania. In this sense one can
understand the resentment of conservative critics like Walter
Bagehot who thought, with some justice, that the picture of the
Circumlocution Office was a libel. But of course Bagehot was
wrong if he expected comic writers to bow to a moral hierarchy.
The essence of satire is its anger, fantasy and untruth, and when
Dickens describes a bureaucracy he was creating a mythical in-
stitution. All bureaucracies are tyrannies of the individual.
Dickens' ridicule is the soliloquist's protest against institutions.

The tradition of comic generalization is one of the strongholds of English comedy. These generalizations are social rather than intellectual. The comic generalizations in the eighteenth century are concerned with man and human nature, vice and virtue and so on; these ideas are indeed intellectual but realism pulls the idea down into the roaring gutters and vulnerable bedrooms of everyday life, so that "man in society," "man in the way of the world" are the tests. From Scott and Jane Austen the elaborate English class system replaces man, vice, virtue, etc., and quickly absorbs the comic genius. In Thackeray, in Trollope, in Meredith, in the very Dickensian Wells of *Tono-Bungay*, these festive social generalizations, stuffed with comical allusions to class, define our comic tradition.

But there is of course an anarchic and rebellious process continually going on against the pressure of society and the generalizations of Dickens are meant to reduce institutions to idiocy. He proceeds, in his usual way, to lift them off the ground, make them float absurdly in mid-air. The famous analysis of parliamentary government in *Bleak House* (which can be checked up in the acquiescent political comedies of Trollope) is an indignant lark. Dickens understood the art of calling people funny names and his ear for funny sounds is always splendid. The farce of the Circumlocution Office is not only funny itself, but, with deadly eye, Dickens sees that the place is not only a bureaucracy but is also a family stronghold. His comic genealogy of the Chuzzlewit family is not all of a piece. It satirizes many kinds of believers in genealogy. Beginning in the spacious manner of Fielding, in order to set a grave tone, it proceeds to irony about William the Conqueror; and at this point, by a stroke of genius, he has his brilliant idea that the Chuzzlewits must be descended from Guy Fawkes because there was a lady in the family known as "the matchmaker." Having run through the gamut of family snobbery he ends up with the superb statement of the outrageously common member of the family, that his grandfather was a nobleman called The Lord No Zoo. The generalizations about the Veneering Family have the same quality of irresponsible comic investigations, in depth.

When one reads the critics and hears this or that writer described as Dickensian, one very soon finds that this deeply important capacity for comic social generalization is missing. I rather think Wells was the last to have it—in the first part of *Tono-Bungay*. It has gone because the sense of the whole of a society has gone. The novel has become departmentalized. We now talk of novels of private life, and novels of public life. In Dickens, on the contrary, the private imagination, comic, poetical and fantastic, was inseparable from the public imagination and the operation of conscience and rebellion. This amalgamation was possible, I think, because he felt from childhood the sense of being outside society, because he was a sort of showman, not because he was a social or political thinker with a program.

MORTON DAUWEN ZABEL: 1956

Bleak House: The Undivided Imagination

THE first chapter of *Bleak House* is consciously an overture. It sets the theme, strikes the chords, establishes the ground and motif, of the drama that follows. London—but more than London, England herself: "the Essex marshes," "the Kentish heights," river, ports, and countryside—steam, drip, choke, and stifle in the all-enveloping fog that becomes the dominating symbol of the tale and one of Dickens' greatest strokes of atmospheric evocation. The fog is immediately established as the cognate of the High Court of Chancery itself and of the "foggy glory" of its Lord High Chancellor where he sits in state in Lincoln's Inn Hall, dispensing the suffocating tedium and procrastinations of obsolete law. It also equates with the eternally unresolved litigation of the Jarndyce estate case, dragging its course through

This essay comprises parts III and IV of the Introduction to *Bleak House* as written originally for the Riverside Edition of the novel (Boston: Houghton Mifflin Company, 1956), and as included in *Craft and Character in Modern Fiction* by Morton Dauwen Zabel (New York: The Viking Press, 1957). The latter version of the essay is reproduced here, with the omission of parts I and II, which deal with Dickens' situation in his age and the thematic development of his work as a whole. [AUTHOR'S NOTE] the courts decade after decade, blighting the hopes and desperate expectations of countless litigants. When, moreover, we hear in the first paragraph that "it would not be wonderful," in this world of mud, slime, smoke, and sooty drizzle, "to meet a Megalosaurus, forty feet long or so, waddling like an elephantine lizard up Holborn Hill," we know that Chancery and Jarndyce embody frustrations that cast humanity back into the darkest abyss of ancient blindness and primitive futility—into a dead past whose hand will blight or deform every life, high or low, that it touches.

"How many people out of the suit, Jarndyce and Jarndyce has stretched forth its unwholesome hand to spoil and corrupt, would be a very wide question": it is the great question the novel sets out to investigate. Scarcely a noun or adjective in this opening chapter leaves the nature of that doom unsuggested. We are in a world of the "dim," the "sallow," the "murky," the "hopeless," the "pestilent"; of the "haggard and unwilling," the "dense" and the "muddy," the "sepulchral" and the "dusty," the "ill-fated" and the "grimly writhed"; a world, in a word, of a kind of "death." "This"—to make the matter unmistakable—"is the Court of Chancery; which has its decaying houses and its blighted lands in every shire; which has its worn-out lunatic in every madhouse, and its dead in every church-yard; which has its ruined suitor, with his slipshod heels and threadbare dress, borrowing and begging through the round of every man's acquaintance; which gives to monied might, the means abundantly of wearying out the right; which so exhausts finances, patience, courage, hope; so overthrows the brain and breaks the heart; that there is not an honorable man among its practitioners who would not give—who does not often give—the warning, 'Suffer any wrong that can be done you, rather than come here!' "

Dickens always handled his London geography with sure skill and specificity. Each of his London novels has its particular setting or group of related settings. *Bleak House* centers in legal London, "the very heart of the fog": in Temple Bar, Chancery

Lane, Lincoln's Inn, and their satellite streets and quarters—Lincoln's Inn Fields where Mr. Tulkinghorn's gloomy house stands; Thavies Inn where the Jellybys live; Cook's Court off Cursitor Street where the Snagsbys have their law-stationer's shop and house, where old Krook reigns in his rag-and-bone shop like another Lord Chancellor over his accumulated trash, where Miss Flite lives in her eyrie of captive birds and Nemo dies in his pauper's bed, and where the rapacious Smallweeds nest like goblins nearby; and, not far off, the slum of Tom-all-Alone's stinks and rots, a disease-ridden outpost of the pervading stagnation.

All this forms the heart of the corruption, the central ganglion of the deadly contagion which the novel will trace. That contagion will extend its pestilence into the English world far and wide—to Chesney Wold in Lincolnshire and the great house in London where the Dedlocks hold their state; to Mr. Jarndyce's home near St. Albans where Ada, Richard, and Esther find a haven from the doom that threatens them; to the byways of Leicester Square where Mr. George has his shooting gallery; to the Kentish suburb where the Bagnets make their home; and even more tenuously to the house of Mr. Boythorn in the north, to Gridley's origins in Shropshire, to the kiln-workers' hovels in Hertfordshire, and even beyond England to the Africa of Borrioboola-Gha where Mrs. Jellyby dreams of civilizing the savages while her own home and family sink into chaos and bankruptcy, or the America of the Tockahoopo Indians whom Mrs. Pardiggle is determined to redeem with her smug philanthropic gospel.

For we soon discover that Chancery and Jarndyce present only one face of the blight. Moral presumption and tyranny are not prerogatives of the past alone. They are equally active in the present. Social arrogance and parasitism can operate not only in impersonal institutions and stultified traditions. They appear with equal deadliness in modern creeds and living indi-

viduals. Fanaticism in the modern world is only a logical extension of the torpid oppressions of the dead. The sublime complacency of Sir Leicester Dedlock, with his retinue of fawning
relations and political yea-sayers, instruments of a moribund
parliamentary system and pride-blinded aristocracy, may join
in fatuity with Chancery itself, but they have formidable rivals
in another order of arrogance which Dickens viewed with equal
detestation—the rapacity of moral self-importance and self-deluded idealism which preys on its victims as ruthlessly as the
dead past does. Parasitism, arrogance, and moral presumption
ramify the world of *Bleak House*. Chancery, Sir Leicester, and
the tribes they seal—Lord Chancellor, Tulkinghorns, Vholeses,
lawyers and time-servers, Coodles, Doodles, Foodles, and the rest
—have their cognates in the whole gallery of tyrants and blood-
suckers that populates the novel—not only Mrs. Jellyby with
her idiotic dreams for Africa and Mrs. Pardiggle with her Puseyite
religious dictates but also Harold Skimpole, sponging his way
through life on the pretenses of an artistic temperament, old
Turveydrop, draining the life-blood from his children on the
claims of his Regency "Deportment," the Chadbands with their
fatuous moral pomposity, the Smallweeds with their vulturous
usury, Miss Barbary with her guilt-ridden religiosity. They are
all a part of a conspiracy of pretension and tyranny which in-
filtrates the body of life and society. But the center of that conspiracy and of the drama that *Bleak House* unfolds will remain
Chancery and Lincoln's Inn. What they represent remains from
first to last the focus of the novel, and it will be to that center
that all the destinies of the drama will eventually return—as Lady
Dedlock herself will be drawn, when disgrace overtakes her, to
the slum graveyard where her dead lover lies and at whose gate
she dies.

"Ganglion: a sort of swelling or excrescence; a mass of nerve
tissue containing nerve cells; a tumor caused by inflammation."
The dictionary's definition is convenient, for Dickens conceived

his novel in terms of morbid growth and infection, and of their pervasion throughout the body of society. As various critics have observed, he was acting in the office of an anatomist or pathologist.[1] He brought all the powers of his mature invention to tracing an infection to its farthest workings, and to devising a plot which should embody his diagnosis with scientific thoroughness—a plot which became, in the process, one of his major feats of dramatic complexity and ingenious knot-tying. Though he had little contact with Victorian science, he felt some of Balzac's fascination by scientific method and theory. When he brought about the death of old Krook by spontaneous combustion, and tried to defend the phenomenon as a scientific possibility,[2] he was perhaps doing something more than exercising his dramatic ingenuity or proposing a symbol for the cataclysmic force required to blow Chancery and all its corruptions to perdition. He may also have been making a furtive appeal to the laws of science in the desperation he felt before the insoluble corruptions which had come to curse and sicken the life of humanity like an incurable disease.

That appeal, and the outlandish symbol of Krook's combustion which he planted squarely in the middle of his story, did not however exempt him from the prodigious complexities to which his social and moral analysis had committed him. He taxed his dramatic skill to the utmost in the plot he devised for *Bleak House*. In sheer invention it surpasses even the lavish actions of *Dombey*, *Little Dorrit*, and *Our Mutual Friend*. Such invention had been part of his equipment from the time of *Oliver Twist*.

---

[1] Edgar Johnson, for one, calls his chapter on *Bleak House* in his *Charles Dickens* (1952), Vol. II, pp. 762–82, "The Anatomy of Society."

[2] The controversy aroused by Krook's combustion, George Henry Lewes's attack on Dickens' scientific claims in the London *Leader* (December 11, 1852, January 15, 1853, February 5 and 12, 1853) and Dickens' letters of defense, have been summarized by Gordon Haight in his article "Dickens and Lewes on Spontaneous Combustion" in *Nineteenth-Century Fiction*, Vol. X (June 1955), pp. 53–63.

Dickens' plots belong to a fictional convention which it became one of the special objects of the art of the modern novel to reject. That art, with its standards of aesthetic consistency, psychological truth, and moral integration, had already before Dickens' death in 1870 taken his work as an object of attack and resistance. *Bleak House* represents the convention in which he worked at its most lavish development. The book is a feat of complex calculation, a supreme tour de force of dramatic artifice and contrivance. Unlikely chance, accident, coincidence, and melodrama operate throughout the proliferations of the plot. The test of such a novel must be the degree to which its contrivance is sustained and justified by symbolic force and logic—the power by which its moral argument vindicates the fable which it employs for its use and demonstration. The claims of *Bleak House* to a rank among the great modern novels hang on that test.

"In all Mr. Dickens's works the fantastic has been his great resource," said Henry James in his youthful criticism of *Our Mutual Friend* in 1865, "and while his fancy was lively and vigorous it accomplished great things." "But," he further announced, "the fantastic, when the fancy is dead, is a very poor business," and so was led to assert that *"Bleak House* was forced, *Little Dorrit* was laboured; [*Our Mutual Friend*] is dug out as with a spade and pickaxe." [3] James wrote this in the first severity of his reaction to the Dickens convention; he was one of the first to announce the modern resistance to it. Later he moderated his judgment. He admitted how Dickens had "laid his hand on us in a way to undermine as in no other case the power of detached appraisement"; how he had "entered so early into the blood and bone of our intelligence that it always remained better than the taste of overhauling him"; "how tremendously it had been laid

---

[3] Henry James, "The Limitations of Dickens," in *The Nation*, December 21, 1865; reprinted in *Views and Reviews* by Henry James, edited by LeRoy Phillips (1908), pp. 153–61, and in *The Portable Henry James*, edited by Morton Dauwen Zabel (1951), pp. 433–40.

upon young persons of our generation to feel Dickens, down to the soles of our shoes"; and how "no other debt in our time had been piled so high." [4]

The modern critical reader of a novel like *Bleak House* still faces the necessity of harmonizing these two reactions as James himself felt them. The book is, on the one hand, a prodigious case, a preeminent Victorian instance, of what James called "the manufacture of fiction." On the other it offers, particularly to our more eclectic and experimental view, an equally prodigious example of social vision operating on a heroic scale and with a force of criticism that counterbalances the sentimentality and artifice that are integral to its conception and treatment.

Artifice of a theatrical kind is certainly integral to the tale. We feel its workings from the moment, in Chapter II, when Lady Dedlock, "bored to death" in her London house as she had already been bored to death in Lincolnshire, rests her languid glance on the Jarndyce documents Mr. Tulkinghorn has brought to show her, vaguely recognizes the script in which they have been written, suddenly rouses herself and "asks impulsively," "Who copied that?" Coincidence has shown its hand at the outset of the novel, and it will not work itself out until, fifty-eight chapters and many hundreds of pages later, Lady Dedlock dies by her lover's grave in the slum graveyard. Before that long thread is traced to its end, countless others will cross and entangle it—Esther's life as a lost daughter and child of mischance; Trooper George's life as another lost child, involved equally in the doom of his old hero Captain Hawdon, in the machinations of Mr. Tulkinghorn, and in the usuries of the Smallweeds; the street-waif Jo's martyrdom as an outcast of the London streets, victim alike of Lady Dedlock's secret guilt, of Tulkinghorn's vengeance,

[4] See James's *A Small Boy and Others* (1913), pp. 117–18, and *Notes of a Son and Brother* (1914), pp. 253–56. The passages are quoted by Leon Edel in his *Henry James: The Untried Years* (1953), pp. 98–99, 277–78.

and of the pollution of the slum; old Krook's sinister fanaticism and spectacular death; Ada's and Richard's ruin in the snare of the "great expectations" Chancery and Jarndyce had promised them; the resistance of Mr. Rouncewell, the iron-master, exponent of the new self-made industrial power, to the hereditary social and political assumptions of the Dedlocks; the detective work of Inspector Bucket and those two other ferreters of hidden secrets, Tulkinghorn and Guppy; and then, crossing and accompanying these intermeshing lines of action, the peripheral fates of the many other characters who become involved in the action—Caddy Jellyby and her husband and their wizened child, victims of old Turveydrop's pretenses; Miss Flite and Gridley, victims of Chancery; Lawrence Boythorn and his maniacal litigations; Harold Skimpole and his parasitic cadgings; the Smallweeds with their plots and schemes; the Snagsbys with their inadvertent part in the mystery; the perverse philanthropies and sorry defeats of Mrs. Jellyby and Mrs. Pardiggle; the hard fates of the brick-makers and their wives. Merely to itemize the ramifications of the plot is to be astonished at Dickens' feat in threading the maze of complications he has devised and in keeping his reader in suspense until the center of the labyrinth has been reached. Or, to change the figure and adopt Edgar Johnson's: *Bleak House* shows a movement that "becomes a centripetal one like a whirlpool, at first slow and almost imperceptible, but fatefully drawing in successive groups of characters, circling faster and faster, and ultimately sucking them into the dark funnel whence none will escape uninjured and where many will be crushed and destroyed."

To control so vast an action, so complex a design, demands ingenuity and invention in maximum degrees, though to make a valid and impressive novel of them requires something more. No reader of *Bleak House* can close the book without an impression of inventive prodigality and dramatic manipulation perhaps unsurpassed in fiction. What is necessary to note is that these appear in a form quite different from the comprehensive amplitude and scale of Tolstoy in *War and Peace*, of Zola in the Rougon-Macquart epic, of Proust in *A la Recherche du Temps perdu*, or of Faulkner in his Yoknapatawpha saga. Those fictions, in differing degrees, work on wholly different principles of dramatic creation. Their impulse is the impulse of a purer historical logic, a natural and organic energy in their materials, a more realistic necessity in social and psychological analysis. Even Balzac yielded more instinctively to the social and moral situations in which he dealt; he is less the manipulator of events than Dickens is and less explicitly the manipulator of his moral arguments. In books like *Bleak House, Little Dorrit,* and *Our Mutual Friend* Dickens did—the verdict seems unavoidable—"manufacture fiction." To ask what redeems these books from the artifice and contrivance of the genre to which they belong; why they have survived when countless of their Victorian rivals bred of the same method and conditions have fallen into neglect and oblivion; or what makes *Bleak House* the powerful book it remains after a hundred years, as much an artistic as a moral landmark in English fiction, is to suggest the essential test and question of Dickens' genius.

To answer it involves us in the practical problems of his craft as well as in its larger moral vision. From the first he had shown himself a born conjuror of spells. The appeal of story purely as such, basic and primitive in all fiction, was the magic that sped *Pickwick* and *Oliver Twist* to their triumphs, and it never wholly deserted Dickens, even when his purpose became more complex and his powers more strained. Yet this appeal, in spite of its supreme advantages, involves the novelist in a risk. Once his critical intelligence matures, once his sense of realism sharpens, his craft as a conjuror may become as much a liability as an asset. Dickens, whatever his skill in humor, melodrama, and artifice, was saved by an acute instinct of realism from the fate that eventually overtook most of the facile inventors of his time, but he had never been bred in the stricter authority of fact which, after 1850, asserted itself as a discipline in fiction and drama. What a recent critic, Philip Rahv, has said of Tolstoy, could never be said of Dickens: that in his work "the cleavage between art and life is of a minimal nature"; that "in a sense there are no plots in Tolstoy but simply the unquestioned and unalterable process of life itself; such is the astonishing immediacy with which he possesses his characters that he can dispense with manipulative techniques, as he dispenses with the belletristic devices of exaggeration, distortion, and dissimulation."

When Percy Lubbock dealt with Dickens in *The Craft of Fiction*, he was obliged to admit his "incurable love of labyrinthine mystification," a tendency which, "when it really ran away with him, certainly defeated all precautions." But by taking a clue from an observation made by Stevenson, Lubbock was also able to define Dickens' skill in mastering that tendency when his genius worked at its strongest. Then his way "of dealing with his romantic intrigues was to lead gradually into them, through well-populated scenes of character and humor; so that his world is actual, its air familiar, by the time that his plot begins to thicken. He gives himself an ample margin in which to make the impression of the kind of truth he needs, before beginning to concentrate upon the fabulous action of the climax." In *Bleak House* notably, "a broad stream of diversified life moves slowly in a certain direction, so deliberately at first that its scope, its spread, is much more evident than its movement," until "presently we are in the thick of the story, hurrying to the catastrophe, without having noticed at all, it may be, that our novel of manners has turned into a romantic drama, with a mysterious crime to crown it." [5]

Lubbock took as the "chief characteristic" of Dickens' method "this careful introduction of violent drama into a scene already prepared to vouch for it," and he believed that Dickens managed

[5] Percy Lubbock, *The Craft of Fiction* (1921), pp. 212–17.

it more artfully than Balzac did "because his imagination is not, like Balzac's, divided against itself." What he says emphasizes what is perhaps the major fact about Dickens' imagination: that whatever its distractions, strains, exacerbations, and whatever its struggle toward increasingly greater moral and historical capacities, it remained basically instinctive and primitive. It succeeded, where so many other novelists have failed, in reconciling fancy with realism, fact with parable, history with fable. It may be, as George Orwell has said, that we must read Dickens at two ages of our lives: in youth, when we can take his plots and fables uncritically, and in maturity, when we can relegate his devices and dramatic apparatus to the status of a convention and devote our attention to his human and moral values.

But a novel remains finally a unity, a total organism, at whatever age we read it. Its final truth or validity must rest as much on its means as on its content, on its form as much as on its moral or social vision. If in Dickens these never arrived at the wholeness or coincidence they achieve in Tolstoy or Proust, they nevertheless come to us joined and equal in appeal. *Bleak House* is massively and extravagantly plotted, and the plotting is inseparable from the social analysis which is the major concern and *raison d'être* of the book—indeed, it was conceived as a means toward such analysis. The fog, Chancery, and Jarndyce establish the continuum of theme and atmosphere that supports the fable, and they sustain it in all its ramifications. It was Dickens' greatest sign of imaginative energy that he should, in his most ambitious novels, have come into powers of symbolic control and authority which were scarcely evident in his work before 1846, or, if evident there, were chiefly based on the cruder moralistic sentiments and dramatic conventions of a now decadent romantic tradition. The fog of *Bleak House*, the prisons of *Little Dorrit*, the resurrection theme of *A Tale of Two Cities*, the river and dust-heap of *Our Mutual Friend*, dominate and sustain these novels from end to end, reinforce their plots even when the plots verge on the incredible, and so give moral strength to the drama even when the drama resorts to devices of melodrama, contrivance, coincidence, and, even in his mature work, to the old vein of willful fantasy that he was never to exorcise from his work or character. But the symbolic without a basis in truth, moral passion without a basis in character, parable without the reinforcement of conflict and solid plot structure, deprive a novelist of the substance of his art—the fact, action, and actuality which remain the stuff and basis of his craft.

By 1851 Dickens was at a stage of his career when he felt acutely the dangers of overworking his material, of repeating and exhausting his resources. His public must be kept avid at all costs. His monthly numbers must continue to sell and to increase in sales. His prodigious powers of invention were under the constant strain of renewing and alerting themselves. The old plots and spells must extend and refresh their appeal. The mounting expenses of his home, children, public undertakings and hospitality, and an increasing number of dependent relatives, his wife's as well as his own ("I never had anything left to me but relations," he once wrote with some bitterness), meant chronic anxiety that his sway over his readers must not only not diminish but increase. *Bleak House*, more than any previous novel, shows Dickens experimenting with his form and material.

It is, to begin with, a double novel, composed of two alternating narratives, the novelist's own and Esther Summerson's. Dickens' chapters (as we may call them) are written in the third person and in the present tense. Esther's are told in the first person and in the past tense. Here, at the outset, is an arbitrary scheme. What are its purpose and results? How does the incongruity of method justify itself? That it put Dickens to unprecedented effort and to a certain strain on credulity is apparent. Esther's story, Dickens' next attempt after *Copperfield* at an autobiographical novel—Pip's in *Great Expectations* was still nine years in the future—must not only tell what Esther sees and hears from the point of view of a simple, virtuous and naïve intelligence; it must also cover a great deal of ground to which she has access by fairly factitious means, and it is bound to include many passages, observations, and insights of a sophisticated kind which can be credited less to her than to the novelist who looks over her shoulder. She must not only sustain a tone of reticence and modesty but register all the affection and tribute to which her friends treat her as the Dame Durden, Dame Trot, or Little Old Woman who discreetly ministers her love and benevolence to them. Her mock-modesty, in fact, can become one of the tiresome features of her tale, as her expeditious canvassing of events and subplots can become at times too efficient to believe.

Dickens' chapters, meanwhile, are written in deliberate contrast to hers. They sustain from the first the tone of high-stilted irony which had already appeared in large parts of *Chuzzlewit* and *Dombey*. The present tense supports this effect. Retrospective sentiment, the moderating distance of things remembered, the softening haze of historic pathos, are supplanted by the voice of acerbity, harsh immediacy, and a scathing contempt. This voice can rise to the heat of passion, exhortation, even to a sermonizing denunciation when it comes to dealing with Krook's combustion, Jo's death, or Lady Dedlock's flight; it can evoke a spectral atmosphere for Chesney Wold or a doom-struck suspense for Mr. Tulkinghorn's chambers; but it will remain from first to last a voice of ironic severity and implicit moral judgment—the sustaining critical basis of the book.

Yet it is by the alternation of his two narratives that Dickens achieves something new in his art in this book: a depth of focus, a third dimension in his perspective, a moral resonance, and an implicit ambiguity of sympathy and insight. The actual substance of the novel, moral as well as dramatic, becomes enriched in a way he had not yet defined so realistically; indeed, the complication of his form supports the complication and depth of his drama and intelligence. It gave his emotions, sympathies, and critical powers a new lease on life, a tougher energy and resilience of insight. Increasingly he had, especially after *The Old Curiosity Shop* in 1840, written in terms of a double attitude toward his material: he had come to stand both inside his story and outside of it. Sentiment and criticism, pathos and irony, had slowly achieved a high-strung balance in tales like *Barnaby Rudge, Chuzzlewit,* and *Dombey and Son*—a token, no doubt, of his own increasing ambiguity of mind and feeling, the sentimentalist at grips with the radical in his nature, the conformist at odds with the critic and social rebel. *Bleak House* certified and demonstrated the conflict in its very method, and so exercised in Dickens a complexity of moral sympathy and dramatic ambiguity which were to serve him powerfully in the books he was to write in the future—in *Little Dorrit, A Tale of Two Cities, Great Expectations,* and *Our Mutual Friend,* in all of which the significant figure of the man divided against himself —Arthur Clennam, Sydney Carton, Pip, Bradley Headstone— was to appear, until finally, in John Jasper of *Edwin Drood,* that divided self and *âme damnée* becomes the clue and center of Dickens' essential drama in a way that brings that novel into the company of a whole line of Nineteenth Century parables —Poe's *William Wilson,* Balzac's *Illusions Perdues,* Dostoevsky's *Crime and Punishment,* Wilde's *Dorian Gray,* and Stevenson's *Dr. Jekyll and Mr. Hyde.*[6]

Something more, however, was needed than a double novel to sustain Dickens' plot in the proliferations of its central mystery and the solution of it. As alert as Balzac to the social and scientific phenomena which the age was offering its novelists, Dickens was almost as quick as Balzac to seize upon one of the chief of these, the police detective. *Le Père Goriot* in 1834 had transformed into the sinister police agent Vautrin the career of that

---

[6] Edmund Wilson, in *The Wound and the Bow* (1941), makes the figure of the divided man the central argument in his study of Dickens.

phenomenal character of Napoleonic France, Eugène François Vidocq, the adventurer, forger, criminal and *galérien* who, by a feat of transformation that symbolizes the duplicity and opportunism of a new bourgeois age, became chief of the Paris *Sûreté*, dread nemesis of criminals, and publisher in 1829 of his semi-apochryphal *Mémoires* which bared the whole corrupt under-life of the uneasy century. In 1829 Sir Robert Peel, then Home Secretary, had by act of Parliament established the metropolitan Police Force in London. Law officers of an earlier time had been used by Dickens in *Pickwick*, *Barnaby Rudge*, *The Old Curiosity Shop*, and *Martin Chuzzlewit*. Now he was ready to make effective use of Peel's detective constable, who becomes the Inspector Bucket of *Bleak House*. The "sensation novel" whose great mid-Victorian vogue was already afoot was to make special use of the apparatus of modern law and police detection. Wilkie Collins, Dickens' favorite protégé and disciple, was to carry it to its highest triumphs in *The Woman in White*, *No Name*, *Armadale*, and *The Moonstone* in the sixties. Bulwer-Lytton, Charles Reade, Mrs. Henry Wood, and a host of their imitators were to capitalize on its attractions. Dickens pioneered for all of them. *Bleak House* antedates by eight years *The Woman in White* (1860) and by sixteen *The Moonstone*, which T. S. Eliot has rated "the first and greatest of English detective novels." [7] *Bleak House* is, in fact, a novel of multiple detectives. Bucket is reinforced by both Tulkinghorn and Guppy. They are all in search of secrets; they all, for purposes unofficial as well as official, thread the maze of the mystery. And they all cut ruthlessly across the class distinctions, protective barriers, and social ranks that foster mystery or breed crime, alienate souls and corrupt human instincts. No device could have served

---

[7] T. S. Eliot, "Wilkie Collins and Dickens," in *Selected Essays, 1917–1932* (1932), pp. 373–82; here p. 377. The whole essay traces Dickens' advances in plot construction and motivation and the connection of these with Collins' methods.

Dickens better than the impersonal critical agency of Inspector
Bucket in carrying out what Eliot has noted in John Forster's
Life as a lifelong preoccupation:

On the coincidences, resemblances, and surprises of life [said
Forster] Dickens liked especially to dwell, and few things moved
his fancy so pleasantly. The world, he would say, was so much smaller
than we thought it; we were all so connected by fate without knowing it; people supposed to be far apart were so constantly elbowing
each other; and tomorrow bore so close a resemblance to nothing half
so much as to yesterday.

It is with these links of fate, crossed lines of destiny, secret
moral alliances, this community in error, guilt, and responsibility,
that *Bleak House*, indeed that all of Dickens' novels, are finally
concerned. When he came to write *Little Dorrit*, he first intended to name it *Nobody's Fault*. The phrase was intended in
its fullest irony. The guilt and error in society are "nobody's"
because the whole ethic of evasion, casuistry, and moral shirking
in modern society refuses to accept it. But what Dickens meant
was that the fault is everybody's. All society is implicated in the
responsibility. If crime, subterfuge, and suffering infect and
stultify life, their consequences can be escaped by no one. "Dead,
your Majesty," cries Dickens in the most passionate outburst
in *Bleak House*, when little Jo dies, martyr of society and
pathetic sacrifice both to the remorseless heart of Chancery and
Jarndyce and to the fetid evil of Tom-all-Alone's: "Dead, my
lords and gentlemen. Dead, Right Reverends and Wrong Reverends of every order. Dead, men and women, born with Heav-
enly compassion in your hearts. And dying thus around us every
day."

II

It required something more than the conventions of moral
justice and his long-tested practice in the arts of sentiment and

nemesis—something more even than his massive skill in plot invention and dramatic manipulation—to bring Dickens to the feat of sustained suspense and penetrating social inquisition he achieved in *Bleak House*. The novel does more than collapse society to its essential unity and singleness in moral destiny, its community in error and common participation in evil. The book is a "dark novel" in more than its atmosphere of murk, fog, rain, and suffocation; it is dark in its instinct of tragedy and, whatever its final rewards for the virtuous, in its view of the social and human future. In it, for the first time, Dickens allowed himself to do what he had shrunk from doing in Walter Gay's case in *Dombey and Son:* he shows his romantic hero, Richard Carstone, degenerate into weakness, apathy, and the demoralization that ensues from those "great expectations" which had become the *ignis fatuus* of a century deluded by false prosperity and deceiving appearance; Richard indeed shifts the whole ground of the Dickens hero, and so prepares the fates of Arthur Clennam, Sydney Carton, Pip, and Bradley Headstone that lie ahead. The title of the novel itself is a portent. "Bleak House" is more than the name of Mr. Jarndyce's home. Like the cherry orchard of Chekhov's title it names a phase of modern history; and like Shaw's *Heartbreak House*, which obviously echoes Dickens' title—possibly in tribute to the profound debt Shaw felt he owed the author of *Bleak House* (whose political criticism alone, he said, "has never been surpassed for accuracy and for penetration of superficial pretense") and of *Little Dorrit* ("a more seditious book than *Das Kapital*. All over Europe men and women are in prison for pamphlets and speeches which are to *Little Dorrit* as red pepper to dynamite")—*Bleak House* stands for the England and the Europe which, to Dickens' appalled dismay, had taken shape and form around him. When Shaw coupled *Heartbreak House* with the plays of Chekhov and Ibsen as a treatise on the "cultured, leisured Europe" of the Nineteenth Century, he may have had the equally close case of Dickens as much in his mind:

The same nice people, the same utter futility. The nice people could read; some of them could write; and they were the sole repositories of culture who had social opportunities of contact with our politicians, administrators, and newspaper proprietors, or any chance of sharing or influencing their activities. But they shrank from that contact. . . . They did not wish to realize Utopia for the common people: they wished to realize their favorite fictions and poems in their own lives; and, when they could, they lived without scruple on incomes which they did nothing to earn. . . . They took the only part of our society in which there was leisure for high culture, and made it an economic, political, and, as far as practicable, a moral vacuum.[8]

These angry sentences echo Dickens' own. *Bleak House* is an angry novel, eloquent of the resentment, cold fury, and passionate impatience its author came to feel as he saw the generous hopes, romantic ardor, and high promise of the world of his young manhood driven headlong against the implacable materialism and hypocrisy of a new age. The anger had its source in personal conflict as much as in public conflict. Dickens was now advancing into those riddled, passionate years of his middle life when his secret desires and ambitions were to come to grief, distress, and bitter disappointment. His marriage was foundering; in 1858 it was wrecked and his wife banished from his home. His children were becoming a new source of anxiety and worry. The "old unhappy feeling" David Copperfield had felt had become chronic in Dickens himself: "a vague unhappy loss or want of something," something "incapable of realization," some "dream of youthful fancy," some desire for "renewal in another world," that could "never never more be reanimated here." None of the "dreadful insatiability" with which he threw himself into his work, his public life, his theatricals, charities, and projects,

[8] Bernard Shaw, Preface to *Heartbreak House, &c.* (1919), pp. x–xi and *passim*. The quotations from Shaw above are from his Introduction to the Limited Editions Club edition of *Great Expectations* (1937).

seemed able to dispel the dread of a spiritual death. To become somehow "recalled to life" fixed itself on him like an obsession: was written as such into his future tales of prisons, deathtraps, entombments of the living, losses of identity, imprisoning morbid states. But the England Dickens saw around him in 1851, when *Bleak House* began shaping itself in his mind, gave him practical reasons for the venting of his exasperation and undoubtedly precipitated the mood of anger in which the book was written.

Though 1851 marked a turning of the tide of depression, self-criticism, and humiliation through which England had passed during the years of Chartism, labor strife, and the "hungry Forties," Dickens viewed the return to nationalistic solidarity and public complacency with uneasiness and distaste.[9] The Great Exhibition, creation of the Prince Consort and fulsome token of England's industrial genius and imperialistic prowess, he saw chiefly as an encouragement to self-satisfaction and public self-flattery. The revival of religious enthusiasm in the wake of the Oxford reformers went hand in hand with this general taste for self-deception: the Puseyism he was to ridicule in Mrs. Pardiggle had only succeeded in "putting back the hands upon the Clock of Time, and cancelling a few hundred years of history," and helped bring about the "intolerable enormity," as he called it, of a re-established Roman hierarchy in 1850. Parliament and Government were rife with ineptitude. The session of Parliament had hardly opened in February 1851 when Lord John Russell was defeated and the country left without a government for two weeks, one leader after another trying to form a new cabinet and finally forming one too weak to last—"Boodle and his retinue, and Buffy and *his* retinue" seeming to be the incompetents "for whom the stage is reserved."

Meanwhile the condition of the English and London poor was

9 "*Bleak House* in the Context of 1851" is discussed and documented by John Butt in *Nineteenth-Century Fiction*, Vol. X (June 1955), pp. 1–21.

as wretched as ever. Dickens had become almost professionally aware of it in the help he gave the heiress Angela Burdett Coutts in negotiating her projects for slum clearance and workmen's houses. The cause of sanitary reform had called public attention to the horrors of London's inadequate sewage system and the diseases it bred throughout the city. When Dr. Simon wrote his report on the Sanitary Condition of the City for the Commissioners of Sewers late in 1850, the *Times*, discussing it on December 31, 1850, and on January 2, 1851, called attention to the "definite, palpable, removable evils" that caused the "unhealthiness of towns"—the "dense overcrowding of a population," the "defective drainage," the "intricate ramifications of courts and alleys, excluding light and air," the "organic decomposition," "contaminated water," and "stinking atmosphere," all of them "distinct causes of disease and death." Twice Dickens had been chosen as speaker at the dinners of the Metropolitan Sanitary Association, in February 1850, and in May 1851; and when, shortly thereafter, he published a new edition of *Oliver Twist*, he took occasion to say that the reform of slums and sanitation "must precede all other Social Reforms," must "prepare the way for Education, even for Religion," and that "without it, those classes of the people which increase the fastest, must become so desperate, and be made so miserable, as to bear within themselves the certain seeds of ruin to the whole community." He had supported Mrs. Caroline Chisholm's Family Colonization Loan Society when it was set up in May 1850, but he remembered Mrs. Chisholm's slovenly housekeeping and dirty children as a nightmare symptom of what Carlyle had also despised: Utopia abroad and chaos at home. All these conditions and the vexation they caused him were to find place in *Bleak House;* but what found chief place there was the age-old and colossal ineptitude of Chancery.

In the first year of *Household Words* he had written two papers for its pages on "The Martyrs of Chancery." Its malpractices had been notorious for decades. The Day estate case, begun in 1834, had involved dozens of lawyers, and by 1851 had already incurred costs of seventy thousand pounds. The Jennings case, begun in 1798, and involving the disputed fortune (some one and a half million pounds) of an Acton eccentric who had died intestate, had already wasted the costs and hopes of its litigants for five decades (by 1915, when the case was still unsettled, its costs had amounted to two hundred fifty thousand pounds), and became the immediate model of Jarndyce and Jarndyce.[10] When Queen Victoria opened Parliament in February 1851, she presumed that the reform of various departments of law and equity would "doubtless receive serious attention," a suggestion which led the *Times,* which had long agitated against "the inertia of an antiquated jurisprudence," to say that "the state of the Court of Chancery is . . . an evil of extreme magnitude," and that "a suit in that court is endless, bottomless, and insatiable": "There is no word so terrible to an Englishman as this. An honest, industrious man . . . will turn pale and sick at heart at the bare mention of Chancery." "Success and defeat are alike fatal to litigants," the *Times* had said on December 24, 1850; "The lingering and expectant suitors waste their lives as well as their substance in vain hopes, and death robs them of their wished-for triumph, if ruin have not already rendered it impossible."

Here Dickens found his clue, his device for attacking the entire apparatus of inertia, casuistry, opportunism, shirking hypocrisy, and do-nothingism which he had always felt to be the curse of English tradition. The law had already been scathed in Dodson, Fogg, and Buzfuz in *Pickwick;* the poor laws in *Oliver Twist;* the predatory aristocracy in *Nicholas Nickleby;* greed, misers, and money-lust in *Chuzzlewit;* money power in *Dombey.* The turn of utilitarian economy and self-seeking trade unionism

[10] Edgar Johnson, *op. cit.,* II, p. 771, quoting from *The Dickensian* (London), Vol. XI, p. 2.

was to come in *Hard Times;* of the "Circumlocution Office" of Government in *Little Dorrit;* of corrupt wealth in *Our Mutual Friend;* of smug philanthropy, his ancient detestation, again in *Edwin Drood.* Chancery gave him an organism of irresponsibility more comprehensive than any of these. It permitted him to organize a novel in which the ramifications of legalized incompetence and the dead past reach to every stratum of English life. It became his task in *Bleak House* to treat the whole body of society as the organism of the blight and desiccation to which these evils led, and to make of the novel an epic warning on the fate of England if the evil were to persist.

Thus the novel became, and remains, a fable of modern society at a point of crisis. That sense of crisis was powerful in Dickens' work throughout the two decades (1846–1865) of his major novels. They all rest on a basis of the critical and the didactic; form a sequence of exempla of social and moral wrong; are impelled by a reformer's zeal and a crusader's purpose. All of them turn on a conviction that had become for Dickens an informing passion: namely, that there is in mankind an instinct for life, self-realization, hope, liberty, and love, and that this instinct is forever preyed upon by forces of selfishness, timidity, fear, irresponsibility, and possessive greed. His books are part of a standard Victorian commodity: they are "tracts for the times." But though Dickens was always bound and tethered to his age, he had in himself a force of larger vision and humanity that overleaped his age and enabled him to produce fables that define deep-seated and permanent elements in the condition and ordeal of mankind.

That condition is defined in his books as primarily social, yet had it remained social and nothing more, they would have long since receded to the status of merely historical documents. What has saved them from that diminution was what finally saved Dickens as an artist. He saw superficial evil as rooted in what he himself knew so intimately in his personal life and character:

in the moral ambiguity and confusion of the human personality and in the psychic conflict that impels it to its crimes, if also to its ultimate heroism. He may not give us the purest drama, the truest plots, and the greatest characters the modern novel has produced. For these we must look elsewhere. An essential criticism of Dickens was suggested in what is perhaps the most acute passage of George Orwell's essay: "Why," he asks, "is it that Tolstoy's grasp seems to be so much larger than Dickens' —why is it that he seems able to tell you so much more *about yourself?*" "It is not," he believes, that Tolstoy "is more gifted, or even, in the last analysis, more intelligent," but because "he is writing about people who are growing," who "are struggling to make their souls," whereas "Dickens' are already finished and perfect." They "have no mental life. They say perfectly the thing that they have to say, but they cannot be conceived as talking about anything else. They never learn, never speculate." "In my own mind," he continues, "Dickens' people are present far more often and far more vividly than Tolstoy's, but always in a single unchangeable attitude, like pictures or pieces of furniture. You cannot hold an imaginary conversation with a Dickens character as you can with, say, Pierre Bezoukhov." [11] Or, one might add, with Flaubert's Frédéric Moreau and Marie Arnoux, with Dostoevsky's Kirilov and Prince Myshkin, with Turgenev's Bazarov and Lavretsky, with Isabel Archer, Ransom, Strether, Kate Croy, and a large number of other characters in Henry James, with the Swann, Odette, Mme. Verdurin, Saint-Loup, and Mme. de Guermantes of Proust.

But if the power of creating characters that become an intimate and self-perpetuating part of our experience was not the essential of Dickens' genius, he owned another power necessary to the novelist of moral and historical capacity. He fixed the elements

[11] George Orwell, "Charles Dickens," first published in his *Inside the Whale* (1940); later in *Dickens, Dali, and Others* (1946), pp. 1–75; here pp. 68–69.

of virtue and evil in human nature in essential and definitive forms; infused in his plots and fables a vision of justice that disengages itself from their artifice and applies itself to historic situations and recurring crises in society which his moral passion and instinct of conflict could prophesy as vital and constitutional. If, as Humphry House has said, "he made out of Victorian England a complete world, with a life and vigour and idiom of its own, quite unlike any other world there has ever been," the energy of his human and social insight made of that world an imaginative organism which becomes more than Victorian. It generalizes itself as an image of experience and history, and so becomes what epic and fable are by definition—modes of radical truth, and of its workings in men and society. Much as he contributed to the resources and animus of the modern novel by his invention and fantasy, it was the primitive instinct in Dickens' nature that finally made him a symbolist and prophet of human ordeal. Few novelists have worked under severer conditions of public pressure, moral vexation, and agitated conscience. But distracted as he was by the social unrest and moral duplicity of his age, confused by the impulses at conflict in his own temperament, divided in his sentimental and critical values, there worked in him a force that persisted to the end as single and integral—an imagination that remained undivided and so enabled him to combine judgment with compassion, his critical insight with his moral sympathy, in a vision that holds its authority because it is at once real and just. Of this order of genius Dickens stands a classic type, as *Bleak House,* in which his powers worked at their most ambitious, remains a fable classic not only in its own century and society, but beyond them in ours.

GEORGE H. FORD:　　　1958

David Copperfield

DAVID COPPERFIELD suffers, like *Hamlet*, from being the most popular of its author's writings. The word *suffers* is appropriate not only for the jaded palate of the sophisticate but also for any of us who assume, as we are all inclined to do, that by reading it once in early childhood we have squeezed from this orange all the juices it contains.

The fondness most children have for *David Copperfield* is readily understandable. George Orwell reports that when he first began reading it, at the age of nine, its mental atmosphere was "so immediately intelligible" that he thought it must have been written "by a child." This is because Dickens contrives to place us so that we see through the boy's eyes: we look *up* at those towering monsters, more than life-size: Miss Murdstone with her jail of a bag, or Mr. Creakle with his fiery red face and his whisper. When we come back to the book later, the same nightmare-like vividness remains, and so does the humor. Uriah Heep is, among other things, a great humorous creation; the peculiar laughter he provokes can be shared by child and adult alike. The fun to be enjoyed in *David Copperfield* could be overlooked only by a studied variety of solemnity or dullness, yet a rereading of it after childhood has passed may make us aware

Introduction to *David Copperfield* (Boston, 1958).

that this is a sadder book than we had remembered it to be. Dickens himself recognized its predominant tone when in later years he was looking back over his own life from the lonely pinnacle of the monumentally successful man, and asked: "Why is it, that as with poor David, a sense comes always crushing on me now, when I fall into low spirits, as of one happiness that I have missed in life, and one friend and companion I have never made?" All the steam that rises from Mr. Micawber's delectable hot rum punch cannot obscure the nostalgic impression, in almost every chapter, of roads not taken and of doors that never opened.

To reread *David Copperfield* may also make us more painfully aware of gaucheries we had forgotten: the high-pitched theatricality of some of the renunciation scenes, the contrived circumlocutions in the representation of Martha, and the excessive coziness that cloys the style when the domestic affections are being celebrated. If a fresh reading increases our awareness of these lapses, perhaps this is because it likewise increases our awareness not only of the extraordinary creative power displayed in the novel—that we expected—but also of the subtlety of its art and the challenge it makes to the critical intelligence of the adult reader.

II

One adult reader who admired *David Copperfield* was Sigmund Freud, whose methods of analysis provide an interesting but limited way of approaching an autobiographical novel such as this. If our primary concern is to treat the book as if it had been recited upon a psychoanalyst's couch we may consult Leonard Manheim's revealing and professionally expert essay, which appeared in *American Imago* in 1952. Much less satisfactory is Somerset Maugham's amateurish attempt to use a Freudian approach. Maugham never explains why he ranks *David Copperfield* as one of the ten greatest novels in the world; instead he devotes almost all of his introduction to some weary speculations about Dickens' relations with women. The controversial story of Dickens' affair with a young actress is fascinating in its own right, but inasmuch as he did not meet her until several years after *Copperfield* was published it is hardly relevant to a discussion of this novel. In general, to minimize the benefits of approaching the book as if it were merely the case-history of its author is not a matter of squeamishness but of more significant considerations. Out of the depths of his imagination as well as from the experiences of his life, Dickens constructed a coherent fiction with a life of its own. Only as such has it survived or can it survive.

Sigmund Freud's admiration for *Copperfield* can nevertheless raise questions that lead into the novel itself. For the opening chapter Freud may have had a singular kind of admiration because he, like Dickens' hero, was born with a caul. To the whole novel he was drawn, one suspects, by its brilliant symbolic expression of situations and themes which he himself was to explore in his own special fashion. In particular he would be drawn by its preoccupation with children in relation to fathers and mothers.

To say that *David Copperfield* is primarily concerned with the bond between children and parents may seem absurd. One of the principal differences between the life of Charles Dickens and the life of David Copperfield is in this very area. Dickens himself was a member of a large family and, at the time he wrote the novel, both of his parents were living. David, on the other hand, is portrayed as an only child, born after his father's death, whose mother dies when the boy is nine. It would seem that such modifications demonstrate that Dickens wanted to play down the importance of familial relationships, and that *David Copperfield* would have little in common with such novels as *Fathers and Sons* by Turgenev, *Sons and Lovers* by Lawrence, or *Absalom, Absalom!* by Faulkner—the very titles of which forewarn us of the central preoccupation in each work. The conventional presentation of this topic (a favorite topic in prose fiction) is to portray the tensions within a family, especially one in which the son is reacting against his father. Wolfe in *Look Homeward, Angel,* Joyce in the fragmentary *Stephen Hero,* or Butler in *The Way of All Flesh* characteristically employ this frontal attack. Dickens is less direct, more subtle in fact. Just as Mr. Dick instead of referring directly to what obsesses him (the misfortunes of his sister) speaks of King Charles' head, so Dickens, instead of presenting normal family relationships writes of children without parents. It is, says Aunt Betsey, Mr. Dick's "allegorical way of expressing it . . . the figure, or the simile, or whatever it's called, which he chooses to use."

We become aware of this preoccupation if we compile a list of the orphans in Dickens' book. The collection is an extraordinary one, for almost all the important characters are included in it. Those who in childhood have lost both parents include David himself who becomes "an orphan in the wide world" at an early age, as well as Emily, Traddles, the Orfling who is attached to the Micawbers, Mrs. Copperfield, Martha Endell ("early left fatherless and motherless"), and Rosa Dartle. Those who in childhood have lost one parent, the half-orphans as they might be called, include Steerforth, Uriah Heep, Annie Strong (whose husband she admires as a "father" for herself), Agnes, and Dora. The last named, having lost her remaining parent during the course of the story, is referred to thereafter by Agnes as "the orphan child."

By representing the world as a place where normal family relationships are abnormal or non-existent, by giving us a sense that we are all, in effect, orphaned, Dickens achieves a consistent perspective from which to view the drives and desires of the child and the man. What, in particular, does the orphaned person want? In a world where unpredictability seems to reign, he needs warm love and affection to compensate for the mother he has lost; security and wisdom to compensate for the father he has lost.

When Steerforth is pictured reflecting gloomily upon the consequences of his plan to seduce Emily, he is overcome with a fit of
remorse and blurts out: "David, I wish to God I had had a judicious father these last twenty years! . . . I wish with all my
soul I had been better guided!" It is strange that Steerforth should
choose as his confidant here an orphan who, some years before,
had watched the boys in villages he traveled through and "wondered whether their fathers were alive, and whether they were
happy at home." It is also strange that the man whose home is to
be devastated by Steerforth's actions, Mr. Peggotty, is the most
ideally paternal figure in the book, whose kindly strength and
reliability embody what has been missing in Steerforth's own
family life. The paternal role of Mr. Peggotty is specified by
Ham, who sends him "the lovingest duty and thanks of the
orphan, as he was ever more than a father to."

David Copperfield himself does not have quite such good
fortune. No man is ever really a substitute for this boy's dead
father. Micawber, who makes David a member of his own family
for a period, does provide some warmth and charm, but he is
the reverse of a good provider; there is no security under his
roof. Murdstone, of course, makes a travesty of the paternal role;
he is both tyrant and hated rival for the love of the boy's mother.
There are, however, other substitutes. When David is seventeen,
a visit to the graves of his parents leads him to reflect "with
a grateful heart how blest I was in having such a friend as Steerforth, such a friend as Peggotty, and such a substitute for what
I had lost as my excellent and generous aunt." At a later point,
David addresses his aunt as "my second mother." It is true that
Aunt Betsey's affections enable her to fulfil such a role, but she
is really more of a father to David than a mother. Her cottage
at Dover is the haven and fortress where the despairing orphan at
last finds security after his terrifying and lonely pilgrimage; she
provides for his education and advises him wisely about how to

get along in the world, and she has the strength of mind, if not of body, to cut his enemies down to size. "Don't be galvanic, sir!" she says to Uriah Heep.

David does not really find his "second mother" until he meets Dora. His aunt recognizes clearly enough that the young man has fallen in love with a doll-like girl who has all the same attractions and limitations of the child-wife whose son he was. Dickens himself does not explain why the hero makes such a choice; he simply presents it. The orphan's need to replace what he has lost by an identical substitute makes him, as his aunt says, "blind." In the final part of the novel, as the experiences of friendship and love become more complicated, David is groping his way toward what he calls a "disciplined" attitude which involves attention to suitability of "mind and purpose" in personal relations. Throughout most of the narrative, however, he is impelled by the needs of the orphan's "undisciplined heart."

In many novels and plays, an orphan's search for the affection and authority of which he has been deprived can readily take on religious significance. Dickens' friend Carlyle represented the hero of *Sartor Resartus* as an orphan stripped not only of parents but of religious faith. At the climax of the book, the Devil addresses him: "Behold, thou art fatherless, outcast, and the Universe is mine." Although Carlyle, for once, does not capitalize the word in this passage, the implication is clear. His hero's search for a father is ultimately a search for the Father. Dickens, it will be noted, does not emphasize the possible religious significance of David's plight. As is fitting for a novelist in the proper sense, he finds the field of personal and social relations more than vast enough for his kind of myth. Nevertheless, to view the world as if it were peopled with orphans is itself a comment upon the condition of man in a universal context as well as in a social one.

One effect of thus viewing the world is apparent in the dialogue. There are times when Dickens' characters do not seem to be talking to each other but *at* each other, like people at parties in

America, especially at crowded cocktail parties, where conversation is made up of a cacophony of non-intersecting soliloquies, each speaker isolated and alone. Mrs. Gummidge is, until she is reformed, a capital example, and so are the Micawbers. The effect of such isolated oratory can be extremely funny, but there are also occasions when we sense instead the loneliness of mankind. There is a striking passage when David returns for his mother's funeral. Absorbed in his own private grief, he is startled to observe that singing and love-making go on in Mr. Omer's establishment within sound of the coffin-maker's hammer. Afterwards as he is traveling in the hearse with Minnie and Joram and Mr. Omer, and noting that they are enjoying the ride, he remarks: "I was not angry with them; I was more afraid of them, as if I were cast among creatures with whom I had no community of nature. They were very cheerful." This incident is really more disquieting than the one in which the boy is whipped by his stepfather. Its theme is identical with Auden's *Musée des Beaux Arts*, a poem often admired for its astringent modernity.

It is in the scenes at Murdstone and Grinby's warehouse, however, that we encounter the most vivid account of human isolation. "I know enough of the world now, to have almost lost the capacity of being surprised by anything," says David, as he begins this part of his story; yet he is still more than surprised as he looks back upon his own ordeal, that "a child of excellent abilities . . . soon hurt bodily or mentally" should have been thus abandoned, and "that nobody should have made any sign in my behalf. But none was made." In Hardy's *Jude the Obscure*, there is a similar scene. On one of the many occasions when the orphaned Jude is cast down with despair and frustration, Hardy steps in to comment: "Somebody might have come along that way who would have asked him his trouble, and might have cheered him. . . . But nobody did come, *because nobody does*."

The bitter comment, which I have italicized, at once distinguishes Hardy's world from that of Dickens, for Dickens shows that someone does come, eventually. There are Peggotty, the Micawbers, Aunt Betsey, Traddles—the colorful alliance of the good-hearted who will pit themselves against the powerful forces of darkness and who will provide here, as always in Dickens' books, his fundamental drama. Moreover, with their aid, and with the strength and will of his own character, David can fight to win, whereas "the predestinate Jude," as Hardy calls him, is doomed to lose. This difference is fundamental, and yet the revelation of the orphan's lonely role still remains at the heart of Dickens' book.

III

We may wonder why Dickens was preoccupied with the orphan's view of the world at the time of his writing *Copperfield*. The surface of his life gives no clue whatever. At thirty-seven, an age at which many novelists have written nothing of consequence, he had already published seven novels and was at the height of his power and fame. He seemed to be happily married; he had a large family, and he had troops of friends among whom his gaiety and high spirits were taken for granted. Yet like the Victorian age itself, with its surface of exuberant confidence (unmatched since Elizabethan days) and its undersurface of uncertainty, the appearance of Dickens' happy position was a deceptive and incomplete indication of his state of mind.

A few years before starting *David Copperfield* he had been led to reflect back upon his own career and to write an autobiography which he planned to leave among papers to be found after his death. This intimate document was to include an airing of the two most painful experiences of his life, experiences which he himself believed were crucial in forming his own character, and which certainly affected the kind of novels he was to write. The first occurred when he was twelve years of age. After having been taken away from school and a comfortable home, he had been put to work for a few months in a London blacking-warehouse until rescued by his father against the wishes of his mother, who wanted him to be kept at work. The second experience, which began when he was seventeen, was his unhappy and unsuccessful pursuit of a banker's daughter, Maria Beadnell. The frustrations of youthful love he found too painful to confront in autobiographical form, but the warehouse experiences he did succeed in getting down on paper in the version later published by John Forster, after the novelist's death.

In America, where the school-of-hard-knocks is often made glamorous at the expense of the ordinary school, Dickens' intensity of feelings about his warehouse experiences (as expressed in both the autobiography and the novel) may seem especially strange.

I never had the courage to go back to the place where my servitude began. I never saw it. I could not endure to go near it. For many years, when I came near to Robert Warren's in the Strand, I crossed over to the opposite side of the way, to avoid a certain smell of the cement they put upon the blacking-corks, which reminded me of what I was once. . . . My old way home by the borough made me cry, after my eldest child could speak.

What the school-of-hard-knocks critic may overlook is that the boy saw no possible terminus to his span of employment. Temporarily "roughing it" in a factory to get a taste of working-class experience (like the novelist Henry Green, in his father's factory) is a different matter altogether. At the most crucial stage of a child's development, the twelve-year-old Dickens believed that he had been wilfully abandoned by his parents and sentenced to remain in the house of rats for life.

From this well-known incident, then, the specter of insecurity became lodged in Dickens' mind and would never disappear. The pattern was evident: the Lord gave, and the Lord taketh away.

In 1847, when John Forster, Dickens' closest friend, had the privileged opportunity of reading the autobiographical sketch, he recognized that the warehouse incident might be effectively used as part of a novel. For almost two years Dickens thought over Forster's suggestion. His first visit to the fishing-town of Yarmouth, in January, 1849, may have served as a final stimulus, and early in the spring *David Copperfield* was begun. Once the opening chapters were completed, the writing came easily. Unlike his two previous novels, *Martin Chuzzlewit* (1844) and *Dombey and Son* (1848), the new work gave him almost constant pleasure during the eighteen months he was writing it, and among all his works it remained his favorite.

IV

Because of Dickens' having incorporated fragments of his autobiography into *David Copperfield* (especially in Chapter 11), and because David is represented as having become, like his creator, a successful writer, we may be inclined to read the whole novel as autobiography. We may also enjoy speculating how the novelist's unconscious wishes affected his narrative. An amusing example, in view of Dickens' difficulties with Mrs. Hogarth, is the scene exposing the busybody mother-in-law in Chapter 45; and the idealization of Agnes as a sister and wife has suggested to some readers that Dickens was betraying a preference for his sister-in-law over his wife (although contrary evidence is provided by Hans Christian Andersen, who found Catherine, not Georgina, to be the model for Agnes). In any event, it is more interesting to notice how Dickens contrives to modify his own intimate experiences and to transform them into new wholes, as has already been suggested concerning his picture of the relations of children and parents. Viewed from one angle, his own parents might provide models for the Micawbers, but viewed from another angle, for the Murdstones. The transformation is thus extraordinarily complex. Even when the story of Charles Dickens and the story of David Copperfield seem most alike, the novelist usually introduces significant changes. One example, among many, is his account of David's schooling. Dickens himself attended a good school before his experience in the warehouse and an inferior school afterwards. In the novel, the sequence is artfully reversed; a clear narrative-line tracing a descent into the pit and an ascent out of it is thus imposed upon the raw materials. The differences between Dickens' own character and that of his hero are also marked. Combined with his evident tenderness there was a hard, almost ruthless streak in Dickens' character (he himself attributed it to the traumatic experience of his childhood) which is omitted entirely from the character of his consistently gentle hero. In effect, Dickens demonstrates in *David Copperfield* and in *Great Expectations* that autobiographical materials can be effectively used by a novelist provided that they are controlled and shaped. Thomas Wolfe and some other exponents of autobiography in fiction might have profited from his example.

V

Shortly before he began to write *David Copperfield*, Dickens decided to name his latest born son after Henry Fielding. This tribute he made in the belief that *Tom Jones*, which records the development of a hero from birth to maturity, might provide him with a model for the book which was taking shape in his own mind. Because we have no satisfactory term in English for this kind of novel, the German term *Bildungsroman* is usually called into service. As the novice writer of fiction learns, a *Bildungsroman* seems the easiest kind of novel to write and is actually the most difficult kind of novel to write well. The difficulty is its looseness. Which experiences out of the thousands occurring during the hero's development are to be selected as illustrative?

When such a novel is presented in the first person, some restrictions at least are imposed. The hero must himself see or hear almost everything that happens, a restriction that raises special problems of its own, as is evident in the scene when David overhears the sadistic Rosa Dartle's tirade against Emily. This clumsy scene which, as the manuscript shows, gave Dickens an unusual amount of trouble to write, is exceptional, but it does show up a disadvantage of narratives told in the first person. As Joyce Cary (a modern master of this form) admits, those scenes in which the narrator is not himself fully involved are "further removed from actuality than a story told in the third person." One solution is rigorously to exclude anything that does not obviously happen *to* the narrator, as Defoe easily manages to do in *Robinson Crusoe*. Dickens attempts the more challenging task of presenting not only David's development but the subplots of Steerforth and Emily, Dr. Strong and his wife, Uriah Heep and Micawber, Traddles and the daughters from Devonshire, Aunt Betsey and her beggarly husband. The difficulties of this thickening of the mixture are evident, and yet the skill with which each of these subplots is blended into the development of David's own point of view is equally evident. Indeed Dickens himself was later to discover how artfully the book is integrated when he tried to make selections from it for his public readings. As he said: "There is still the huge difficulty that I constructed the whole with immense pains, and have so woven it up and blended it together, that I cannot yet so separate the parts as to tell the story of David's married life with Dora." He finally contrived to patch together a series of extracts in which he concentrated upon the flight and return of Little Emily. His choice is significant. For public readings he needed stage-effects, and it is in the clashing action of the subplots that we find the most stagey parts of *David Copperfield*. Excellent theater is often achieved, as in the exposure of the Murdstones by Aunt Betsey, or the more elaborate scene of the exposure of Uriah Heep, but in the long set speeches of such overwrought scenes as Annie Strong's confession to her husband there is mere theatricality.

With reference to the element of drama, an interesting theory was developed by Edwin Muir in his *Structure of the Novel*. Muir argues that Dickens' books belong to a class he calls "novels of character." As such, they are closer in form to a ballet than to a drama, for in a drama the characters change and develop; in a dance they merely move in space. Muir's theory is helpful, for *David Copperfield* can certainly be viewed as a dance-sequence. One group of characters is associated with Blunderstone, another with Yarmouth, another with Salem House, another with Dover and Canterbury. As the hero moves from place to place, each group performs its dance. By the end of the novel, we know each of these brilliantly-executed routines intimately. We see Barkis go through his delightful number about half a dozen times. It is always the same, and the repetitions make the whole an unforgettable performance. New combinations may be introduced, but the "flatness" of such characters (to use a term of E. M. Forster's that is often misused) is a constant. There seem to be hundreds of such static creations in the densely populated world of Dickens' novels.

Yet this choreographical analogy, however helpful, is really not adequate. *David Copperfield* involves movement in time as well as in space. Such characters as Steerforth and David himself do develop and change. Dramatist and choreographer are thus combined. The developments in time are indicated not only by David's having "growed out of knowledge," but by the unified tone in which the narrator recollects these changes—a nostalgia most evident in the Canterbury scenes but everywhere coloring the presentation. It is dependent upon what Graham Greene calls Dickens' "secret prose" with its "delicate and exact poetic cadences, the music of memory, that so influenced Proust." In the following passage, for example, the picture itself is static, but the distance from which it is viewed suggests the changes that have intervened:

I never hear the name, or read the name, of Yarmouth, but I am reminded of a certain Sunday morning on the beach, the bells ringing for church, little Em'ly leaning on my shoulder, Ham lazily dropping stones into the water, and the sun, away at sea, just breaking through the heavy mist, and showing us the ships, like their own shadows.

The passage of time is rarely specified; it is felt.

A different kind of structural analogy is suggested by the likeness of *Copperfield* to a Gothic cathedral. Our critical emphasis today upon over-all structural unity need not obscure the enjoyments to be derived from a close view of the intricate workmanship that distinguishes every niche of the vast building. The Gothic faces carved on the beam-ends at Canterbury remind David of Uriah Heep, but it is not only in such gargoyles as Uriah that the Gothic quality is evident; it is in the lavishness of detail to which George Orwell has paid tribute. "If I go into a cheesemonger's shop," says Mr. Murdstone, "and buy five thousand double-Gloucester cheeses at fourpence-halfpenny each, present payment." The unmistakable touch is here. As David's wife is dying, and as he thinks back over their short life together, he reflects that "trifles make the sum of life." The novel fairly bulges with trifles: the feel of a finger-tip, the smell of cake at a funeral-party, the feeling of drowsiness on a warm afternoon in a schoolroom, the sound of rats' feet in a cellar. A more ambitious kind of observation is at work in the scene of the storm at Yarmouth, which Tolstoy considered one of the most memorable scenes in all fiction, but it is on the smaller scale of trifles, affectionately created, that the book conveys its sense of richness and life.

This power of observation is not confined to sensory perceptions. After the expectedly tender scenes between David and his mother, it is startling to learn that during the two weeks he spent in Yarmouth he virtually forgot about her until he started on his journey back to Blunderstone. And when he learns of her death while he is at school, he is overcome with grief, of course, yet at the same time he enjoys the attention he receives from his schoolfellows. "I felt distinguished," he reports. Exactly the same realistic comment was later used by Somerset Maugham in *Of Human Bondage* after the death of the hero's mother. For his Dickens-like observation Maugham was attacked by some critics as a sour twentieth-century cynic.

VI

As a final example of the appropriateness of the details, we may consider the episode of David's prolonged attempt to sell his coat to a second-hand clothes dealer who cries "Goroo!" The Goroo man is certainly a vivid gargoyle; readers remember him long after they have closed the book. But does the episode serve any larger function? Its context, we should note, is a sequence which represents the whole novel in miniature. David's flight from London to Dover is the play within the play. The flight begins with the boy's having his box and money stolen by a London donkey-driver, an incident which Kafka admired and deliberately imitated in his novel *Amerika*. David's experience does have qualities similar to one of Kafka's nightmare scenes in which the deprivations suffered by the hero are doubly alarming because behind each of the incidents of cruelty or unkindness there seems to be a logic which the boy senses but cannot understand. The Goroo man, like the donkey-driver and the brutal tinker, remains in David's consciousness (and in the reader's) as representative of a baffling and predatory world out of which he is to climb, but which is still there beneath him, and into which he may again fall. The goblins, as E. M. Forster says in *Howards End*, are still there. Seven years after the Goroo man incident, David is traveling back to London by coach. He is now, as he says, "well educated, well dressed, and with plenty of money in my pocket." His exultancy is disturbed, however, as the coach clatters through Chatham and he catches a glimpse "of the lane where the old monster lived who had bought my jacket."

The flight from London ends, like the novel itself, happily enough, in the bedroom of the Dover cottage with its "white-curtained bed" and its "snow-white sheets." Yet even while nestling into its warmth, the boy is reminded of a world outside his windows. "I prayed that I might never be houseless any more, and never might forget the houseless."

The vow of never forgetting the houseless is fulfilled in many of Dickens' novels such as *Oliver Twist* or *Bleak House* and especially in his Christmas stories such as *The Chimes*. Oddly enough, in *David Copperfield*, much less attention is given to the plight of the poor than in these other works. Also absent is the savage invective which Dickens customarily employs in attacking social abuses. A little crusading does appear during David's visit to the so-called model prison or in his accounts of the muddledom of Parliament and the law-courts, but the satire is subdued because David Copperfield rather than Charles Dickens reports to us his impressions in a manner sometimes gently ironic but never quiveringly indignant. The use of the first-person narrative explains why John Forster could praise *David Copperfield* for its "uniform pleasantness of tone." It also explains why readers who prefer the adrenal excitements of such novels as *Little Dorrit*, with its bitter frontal attacks on society, are sometimes dissatisfied with Dickens' own favorite among his works of fiction.

Fervent expression of moral indignation is said to be a popular indulgence of the middle classes (as Letters to the Editor, in any newspaper, will illustrate). If Dickens has denied his readers much of this indulgence in *David Copperfield*, he provides compensations. The circumference may have decreased a little, but the circle is still a mighty one. Instead of exposing the plight of the houseless as a class, Dickens concentrates upon the story of an individual's struggle to remedy his own houseless condition by his search for love, friendship, security, and wisdom. On this score of what makes an appropriate "message," Lawrence Durrell, the contemporary poet, has remarked: "If art has any message it must be this: to remind us that we are dying without having properly lived."

When *David Copperfield* was first published in parts, the cover for each number featured a crowded design by Hâblot K. Browne. The illustration itself emphasizes the traditional cycle of life and death—an Echoing Green—that characterizes Dickens' story of an orphan's search. Whether or not Browne's illustrations—delightful in their own right—give a distorted notion of Dickens' scenes and characters has often been debated. In this particular design for a title page, however, where he is seeking to anticipate the dominant impression of the whole novel, the illustrator has come close to imitating the Inimitable.

J. HILLIS MILLER: 1958
Dombey and Son

IN *Dombey and Son*, as Kathleen Tillotson has shown,[1] Dickens
consciously attempted to curb his exuberant proliferation of characters and scenes, and to concentrate his novel around a single
unifying theme. And, indeed, though it is no more the whole
truth to say that the theme of *Dombey and Son* is pride than it
is to say that the theme of *Martin Chuzzlewit* is selfishness, the
reader is conscious in the former of a single steady current of
duration which follows with a slow and stately curve the relations
of a proud father and his daughter from their beginning to their
end. *Dombey and Son* has a temporal coherence which was entirely lacking in *Pickwick Papers*, though not altogether in *Oliver
Twist* or in *The Old Curiosity Shop*. But perhaps for that very
reason we are all the more conscious of the temporal and spatial
gaps between chapters. Each scene is represented in such elaborate
detail and completeness as a self-enclosed place and time that we
become intensely aware of what has been left out between chapters and not represented at all. The novel is really not so much
a continuous curve as a series of short, nearly straight lines, each
of which advances the action a little way. Seen from a distance
as we view the totality of the novel these lines organize themselves

From *Charles Dickens: The World of His Novels* (Cambridge, Mass.,
1958).
[1] See *Novels of the Eighteen-Forties* (Oxford, 1954), pp. 157–201.

into a single curve. As always in Dickens there is a conflict between the comic or pathetic moment, presented with intense immediacy, for its own sake, and the organization of these moments into a whole.

In the same way, Dickens' deliberate effort to achieve unity of action and theme makes us more aware of the mutual exclusion of diverse milieus in *Dombey and Son*, the milieu of Mr. Dombey's somber mansion and the milieu of Sol Gills' shop at the sign of the wooden midshipman. A character like Florence Dombey who moves between them becomes in a way a different person as she moves from one milieu to another. At least she moves in each case within the circuit of different radiations and influences which make it seem as if the other ambience could hardly exist. Each milieu represents a different social class, and one of the central purposes of *Dombey and Son* is to confront the pride, falsity, and isolation of the upper class, immured in its riches, living in a perpetual masquerade of pretense, and the lower class, with its warmth of generosity and sentiment, breaking down all barriers between person and person.

But another theme of *Dombey and Son* is the exact opposite of this: it asserts that though upper and lower classes are indeed mutually exclusive circles, they nonetheless repeat one another without knowing it, as the "sale" of Edith Dombey is repeated in the lower class by the sale of Alice, her cousin: "Were this miserable mother, and this miserable daughter, only the reduction to their lowest grade, of certain social vices sometimes prevailing higher up? In this round world of many circles within circles, do we make a weary journey from the high grade to the low, to find at last that they lie close together, that the two extremes touch, and that our journey's end is but our starting-place? Allowing for great difference of stuff and texture, was the pattern of this woof repeated among gentle blood at all?" Yes, upper class repeats lower, and the same moral and psychological laws prevail throughout the human world.

One of the most striking proofs of this is our recognition that both upper- and lower-class people, both the "serious" characters and the comic grotesques, live in the same isolation. For the incompatible milieus are made, here as in other Dickens novels, by the lives that are lived within them, and the exclusiveness of scene is determined by the exclusiveness of each person. Of all the characters it would be true to say, as Dickens says of Carker: "with the daily breath of that original and master of all here [in his house], there issues forth some subtle portion of himself, which gives a vague expression of himself to everything about him." Dickens here finds a term to define the enclosure of personality within itself and within the things it has transformed into a mirror of itself: *habit*, the unconscious repetition of the same narrow judgments, feelings, and view of things, a repetition which eventually blinds one to all the world, even to the world of habit itself: "I have good reason to believe that a jog-trot life, the same from day to day, would reconcile one to anything. One don't see anything, one don't hear anything, one don't know anything; that's the fact. We go on taking everything for granted, and so we go on, until whatever we do, good, bad, or indifferent, we do from habit. . . . I [am] deaf, dumb, blind, and paralytic, to a million things, from habit." So, Florence lives "within the circle of her innocent pursuits and thoughts," as if "in a dream wherein the overflowing love of her young heart expended itself on airy forms, and in a real world where she had experienced little but the rolling back of that strong tide upon itself"; and so little Paul "saw things that no one else saw in the patterns [of the wallpaper]; found out miniature tigers and lions running up the bedroom walls, and squinting faces leering in the squares and diamonds of the floor-cloth," and "lived on, surrounded by this arabesque work of his musing fancy, and no one understood him"; and so Captain Cuttle's mental world is "an odd sort of romance, perfectly unimaginative, yet perfectly unreal." Such characters define themselves by negation, by their power to say "no" to everything which is not themselves. Thus Susan Nipper sets herself against everyone with the negations of her characteristic form of expression: "I may be very fond of pennywinkles, . . . but it don't follow that I'm to have 'em for tea." If Miss Tox, Mrs. Pipchin, Major Bagstock, and Mrs. Skewton are upperclass grotesques, walling out other people with their peculiar eccentricities and their obedience to stale conventions, and if Mr. Dombey "shut[s] out all the world as with a double door of gold," Captain Cuttle is no less isolated within his impenetrable linguistic wall of clichés and inapt quotations, madly askew, and Captain Bunsby is a striking example of a comic disjunction between spirit and body. The subjective life of Bunsby is hidden behind a face and a body which are stolidly inexpressive and opaque. His gaze is never directed at the people around him, and his speech is accompanied by no change of expression. His gestures seem to have no relation to any conscious intention, but to be made of their own accord by limbs which are animated by a mysterious and unconscious life of their own: "A deep, gruff, husky utterance, which seemed to have no connection with Bunsby, and certainly had not the least effect upon his face, replied, 'Ay, ay, shipmet, how goes it!' At the same time Bunsby's right hand and arm, emerging from a pocket, shook the Captain's, and went back again. . . . The stolid commander appeared, by a very slight vibration in his elbows, to express some satisfaction . . . ; but if his face had been as distant as his gaze was, it could hardly have enlightened the beholders less in reference to anything that was passing in his thoughts."

The central problem of *Dombey and Son*, a problem faced by all the characters, is how to break through the barriers separating one from the world and from other people. For here what is outside each person is alien and unfriendly; the protagonists differ from the other characters only in the completeness of their isolation. So little Paul lives "with an aching void in his young heart, and all outside so cold, and bare, and strange," and so Florence "live[s] alone in the great dreary house, . . . and the blank walls [look] down upon her with a vacant stare, as if they had a Gorgon-like mind to stare her youth and beauty into stone."

But this novel is in one way far more open than its predecessors, in spite of the isolation of each character and each scene. For all these characters expand outward from their private centers, and come into collisions with other characters and other milieus: "Like a heavy body dropped into water . . . it was in the nature of things that Sir Barnet must spread an everwidening circle about him, until there was no room left. Or, like a sound in air, the vibration of which, according to the speculation of an ingenious modern philosopher, may go on travelling for ever through the interminable fields of space, nothing but coming to the end of his moral tether could stop Sir Barnet Skettles in his voyage of discovery through the social system." Not merely do characters from widely different social levels continually meet and interact; the contact between characters is much more immediate and intimate than it was in *Martin Chuzzlewit*. *Dombey and Son* contains a much more elaborate and subtle treatment of direct psychological conflicts. Here other people no longer exist either as comic spectacle, beheld at a distance, or as directly possessed in the naïve immediacy of festival celebrations within the family circle. We have rather the long evolution of relationships between people who are opposed, but nevertheless deeply implicated in one another's lives. There is a movement from mere passive perception to psychological interaction. This is strikingly apparent in the central action itself, the relations of Florence, her father, Edith, and Mr. Carker. The relations between Edith and Mr. Dombey dramatize a bitter conflict of two personalities, each determined to dominate the other, and finding in the other a solid resistant object which altogether escapes his will. Mr. Dombey, whose pride centers on his "power of bending and binding human wills," finds that "a marble rock could not have stood more obdurately in his way than [Edith]," as she sets herself against his boast that he "will have submission," that his "will is law." She takes the extreme step of asserting the freedom of her spirit by letting him believe she has dishonored herself and him by running away with Mr. Carker. And in the treatment of the relations between Carker and Edith, one might add, we find a new delicacy, for Dickens, in the perception of nuances of intersubjectivity.

The real center of the novel, however, is parent-child relations, a theme which connects *Dombey and Son*, back through *The Old Curiosity Shop*, with *Oliver Twist*. This is the last of Dickens' novels in which the establishment of satisfactory relations with one's parents can be an escape from isolation. But here again there is a shift toward the direct representation of relations between person and person. For Oliver it was enough to find his parents or substitutes for them, and to enter into a paradisiacal state recalling the unity of child and parent in earliest infancy. But the tragedy of the lives of little Paul and Florence is that they have a parent, possess him in flesh and blood, and yet are, for different reasons, infinitely divided from him. The central passage of *Dombey and Son* is that in which Dickens asserts that "not an orphan in the wide world can be so deserted as the child who is an outcast from a living parent's love." *Dombey and Son* shows us people apparently living with all that Oliver wanted— money, family, and status—and yet enduring exactly Oliver's state of forlorn alienation from all about them. The death of little Paul reiterates the deaths of Oliver's avatars in *Oliver Twist* and the death of Nell in *The Old Curiosity Shop*, but Paul is inexorably destroyed by a mistaken, selfish, and all-devouring love rather than by the complete absence of love. And Florence wins her father's love only when his selfish pride has been subdued and the barriers between them have been broken down at last.

But how can the walls of pride, or simply of the innate

uniqueness of each character, be demolished, and direct contact between persons be established? What is the concept of love in *Dombey and Son?*

Here we must recognize an authentic religious motif in the novel, the apprehension of a transcendent spirit, present in nature and reached through death, but apparently unattainable in this world. If the everyday social world of *Dombey and Son* is a realm of self-enclosed milieus, of the impossibility of communication between people, of triumphant solitude, the sea of death, with its "wild waves" (which have caused so much unneccessary embarrassment to Dickens' readers), is the authentic symbol of a nonhuman power whose chief characteristics are reconciliation and continuity. The sea is a place of the incessant repetition of a murmuring speech which no human ears can understand: "The sea, Floy, what is it that it keeps on saying?"; "always saying—always saying!" The sea is the place of origin and ending, the place from which all things come and to which they go, "[w]here those wild birds lived, that were always hovering out at sea in troubled weather; where the clouds rose and first began; whence the wind issued on its rushing flight, and where it stopped." Toward this sea the rushing river carries Paul when he dies. But, most important, the sea is the symbol of that realm beyond this earth where the seemingly inescapable separation between people will be transcended and the reciprocity of love will be possible: "The golden water she remembered on the wall, appeared to Florence, in the light of such reflections, only as a current flowing on to rest, and to a region where the dear ones, gone before, were waiting, hand in hand; and often when she looked upon the darker river rippling at her feet, she thought with awful wonder, but not terror, of that river which her brother had so often said was bearing him away." But the ocean is, precisely, transcendent. Its message cannot be understood by mortal ears, and its fluidity, breaking up the solid and enclosed and putting every thing and person in contact with every other thing and person, cannot, it seems, be attained in this world. And yet it is satisfactory existence within this world which Dickens' characters always seek.

There is, though, an immediate, immanent form of this fluidity: human feeling, an undifferentiated current of sympathy, potentially existing in anyone's heart as the same presence, and flowing out through the prisons of language and inalterable peculiarities to bathe all those around in a warm glow of love. This unintellectualized feeling derives from the divine sea, and makes its qualities available in the human world: "And the voices in the waves are always whispering to Florence, in their ceaseless murmuring, of love—of love, eternal and illimitable, not bounded by the confines of this world, or by the end of time, but ranging still, beyond the sea, beyond the sky, to the invisible country far away!" The human form of this ubiquitous spiritual force is spontaneous and nonrational feeling, everywhere the same. When it is shared in a reciprocal interchange, this outgoing feeling puts the characters of *Dombey and Son* in contact with one another, in spite of the apparently unbreakable barriers between them, and solves the fundamental problem of the novel:

. . . he fairly overflowed with compassion and gentleness.

There was a glory and delight within the Captain that spread itself over his whole visage, and made a perfect illumination there. . . . But the fulness of the glow he shed around him could only have been engendered in his contemplation of the two together, and in all the fancies springing out of that association, that came sparking and beaming into his head, and danced about it.

In the beating of that heart for her, and in the beating of her own for him, all harsher music was unheard, all stern unloving hearts forgotten. Fragile and delicate she was, but with a might of love within her that could, and did, create a world to fly to, and to rest in, out of his one image.

ANGUS WILSON: 1960

Charles Dickens: A Haunting

I HAD hoped, free of any creative nag, to prepare an objective, documented assessment of Dickens' significance for the modern novelist. A novel of my own has refused to give me either the time or the detachment required; yet the itch to analyse, if only in outline, the constant and haunting pressure of Dickens' created world upon my imgination has persisted despite all the pull of my own fantasy. I make, then, only a half apology for offering the following short "thinking aloud"; it is I suspect the only sort of critical contribution that a novelist, untrained in literary scholarship, can make which may justify his amateur intrusion—a contribution unashamedly subjective.

Dickens first exerted a strong hold over me when I was a somewhat sophisticated boy of eleven. I had already laughed at but failed to understand *Pickwick Papers.* I had felt the pursuing breath of Quilp upon Nell's innocent neck and the awful eyes of Fagin intruding into Oliver's illusory rural safety, as too terrible to bear. But now at eleven I was enough detached from the terrors of childhood to support such horrors and yet still to feel the full force of their reality. Dickens already had the power of "taking me back" in emotion; he also hinted, as obscurely as my then sophistication could support, at hidden adult sins. I remember par-

Critical Quarterly, II (1960), 101–108.

ticularly the double force of the passage describing the luring of poor Florence Dombey by Good Mrs. Brown. It was a terror familiar from nurses' lips to me as to all children of comfortably off families; and, I suppose, in the earlier 'twenties, there was still the possibility of lost well dressed children being brutally robbed by old hags. But then came the old woman's mention of her harlot daughter, Alice Marwood, and all its hints of a mysterious adult world of sex and crime. In the combination of fading childhood fears and impinging adolescent knowledge it was the right passage at the right age. But the intense haunting of my imagination by scenes and characters from Dickens' novels has continued and developed into my middle age; nor has some experience of the craft of novel writing exorcised this possession, although it has often increased my admiration for his technical powers and on occasion explained my dissatisfaction with some of his weaker artistic devices.

Jane Austen, too, possesses and haunts me for many hours every week; as do other writers. But although I can feel the sad, rather hypochondriacal piety of Fanny putting up so gallant a fight against the lively, tough desperation of Mary Crawford's will; or again can participate with Emma in her struggle to accept with good grace the humiliations her spoiled vanity has brought upon her; I can always step out of Miss Price or Miss Woodhouse, can leave Mansfield's lawns and Hartfield's shrubberies to see the novels from outside as total works, as significant invented tales; —and this I can do without losing the emotions I have particpated in. With Dickens it is, more often than not, quite otherwise. As I pull myself away from the gales and the waves and from Steerforth's dead head leaning upon his arm as in his schooldays, other images may take its place—of Daniel Peggotty's neat London lodging ready for Emily as he tramps the ports of Europe to find her, or of Mrs. Steerforth and Rosa alone in their Highgate garden looking down over London's lights in hatred and misery —but the "inside" feeling obstinately refuses to give place to an outside view. There are novels of Dickens, as I shall suggest, that on various serious levels seem to me wholly satisfactory works of art. But their obsessive power does not derive from their total statements; it seems to come impressionistically from atmosphere and scene which are always determinedly fragmentary.

That this places him—save for a work like *Hard Times* that has been equally shaped and impoverished by discipline—outside the significant tradition suggested by Dr. Leavis is a matter of regret, I think, for both sides. It is no assistance to Dickens' reputation to pretend that could he have married his genius to a more completely disciplined artistry without reducing its force, we should not all be the richer. It is also disturbing that the most suggestive and sincere literary criticism of our time should have to guard its moral health so desperately that it can find no place for the heterodoxy of Dickens' masterpieces. Perhaps the misuse of such brilliance may qualify him for the place of Lucifer—but a serious literary criticism should not be able to fall so easily into theological parody.

Nor can it surely be right that *Hard Times*, beautifully though Dr. Leavis analyses the moral structure of its fable, should be Dickens' contribution to the rich treasure house that contains *Emma* and *Middlemarch*. The structure may be present in Coketown as in no other of his novels. Indeed Bounderby, Mrs. Sparsit and above all James Harthouse offer more flesh to the skeleton than has usually been recognised; but the novel remains a skeleton. I suspect that those of us who feed regularly on Dickens are too prone to an indigestible diet; but we do know from experience what is one of his feasts and what merely a menu card. *Hard Times* is a menu.

Great Expectations surely has more claim to greatness as a work of art. Only the most puritan of critics cannot readjust the ending so unfortunately imposed by Lord Lytton's worldly sentimentality. Yet for all the rare artistry of the ironic "I" narrative so excellently sustained, there is a certain two dimensional quality about the novel compared for example with *Little Dorrit* or *Our Mutual Friend*. The narrative, and the symbol, only seem to merge in order to create that totally significant atmosphere which is Dickens' greatest achievement in a few scenes—with Magwitch on the marshes, with Magwitch escaping on the Thames, and at Mr. Jaggers' sinister dinner party for Pip and his new grand friends. I believe, as I shall suggest, that there is a definite reason for this. Connected with this, to my feeling, is a certain ordinariness or timidity about the odder characters. For all Miss Havisham's insanity she lacks the great test of divine madness in Dickens' world—the use of the English language to express a solitary cutoff universe, the mark of Mrs. Gamp or Flora Finching or Mrs. Nickleby. Miss Havisham, in fact, is too conventionally mad. The minor humors of the novel—Mr. Pumblechook, Mr. Wopsle, or Mrs. Pocket—are a regression and belong to the feeble, journalistic facetiousness that on the whole had died away from his work by that time. There is a feeling of feebler Crummles or of Mrs. Wititterly in the air. Irony and economy are the marks of artistry laid upon the novelist by the followers of Flaubert and Henry James. *Great Expectations* has them as no other Dickens novel. Yet, if this is what we are after, we cannot really be after Dickens.

David Copperfield, I suppose, has a claim to be his best work of art if we look for unity of narration, development and, above all, that sense of intermingled comedy and tragedy, laughter and tears, and so on, that Tolstoy has set up as the norm of great realism. Yet I cannot really think that *David Copperfield* for all its excellencies is great in the sense of *Anna Karenina*. This sort of vivid, life acceptant realism has always the danger of flattering that somewhat smug acceptance of life that is called "middlebrow." I think that in *David Copperfield* after the childhood scenes, and especially in the character of David himself, Dickens comes nearer to this sort of complacency, so much more adult than his sentimentalism yet to my mind so much less immediate and effective. *David Copperfield* on the whole avoids melodramatics, but it does not entirely avoid the awful "sweet wisdom" that can be so nauseating in Thackeray; indeed the character of David is dangerously close to that of Arthur Pendennis. The fabricated nostalgia that hangs around happy memories of Dr. Strong's academy, though less "embarrassing" to the sophisticated reader than much about Little Nell or Tom Pinch, is, I believe, less sincere and therefore finally more embarrassing than the obsessive preoccupation with innocence. Steerforth alone and all the scenes that concern him seem to break through the padded comfort of the book. Again, I think that this can be explained.

These three more "successful" novels have been selected by various critics, who untouched by Dickens' magic, have yet wished to find him a place in Olympus. The purpose is laudable, but it cannot succeed. He is either great in a way that can defy these conventional canons of greatness, or he has written three competent, but imperfect, and many highly incompetent novels.

Like most people of my generation, in their forties, I have been influenced at a deep level by the ideas of Freud and Marx, largely, I suppose, at second hand. I have no doubt that some of the serious examination of Dickens since 1930 or so is due to the possibility of making such an examination along Freudian or Marxist lines. Of course, all attempts—and there have been a number—strictly to interpret him in either of these ways break down badly. Nevertheless he was an undereducated man of genius, and as such was free and open to intuitive responses to the facts of his age which a better conventional education might have refused; it is not surprising then that he had certain presciences which seem to anticipate his time. Such figures as Rosa Dartle, Miss Wade, Bradley Headstone, Mrs. Clennam, or the Doll's Dressmaker are clinical studies that must demand the Freudian's admiration; as the analyses of the class structure of *Little Dorrit* or *Our Mutual Friend* fascinate the Marxist. But neither can explain the power of his novels any more than the prefiguration of Joycean linguistic experiments with the dialogue of Jingle, Mrs. Gamp, or Flora. That he should have spoken so directly to our age is evidence, I think, of his exceptionally sensitive response to the depths of his own time: for he undoubtedly heard overtones that were not to be commonly received for half a century. But prophecy, even intuitive prophecy, is not literary greatness; and our harping upon these prophetic excellencies seems a little provincial.

I used the word "heard" purposely because Dickens' greatest natural gift was his ear. Those who think that his ear was a naturally distorting one, have only to be referred to Mayhew to see how authentic was the working class note which Dickens caught. Nevertheless to dismiss him as a great mime is one of the least satisfactory attacks made by his detractors. Indeed he was incapable of the sustained mime required for an "I" narration that went outside himself, as the disastrous voice of Esther Summerson all too clearly announces. Nevertheless he had a marvellous ear; but, I believe, an only just less marvellous eye. Certainly a combination of the two that is possibly unique in the English novel. Jane Austen had as good an ear, so for some voices had George Eliot; but Jane Austen's eye appears to have been no more than adequate, while George Eliot's vision, so naturally clear, is too often dissipated in discursive thought.

In his early works, of course, his eye and his ear both desert him when the wealthier classes cease to be objects of irony and are intended to suffer real emotions. From Sir Mulberry Hawk and Lord Frederick onwards passion in the nobility or the upper middle classes is bad theatrical melodrama. But just as *Dombey and Son* saw the first really well observed relics of the Regency upper class in Cousin Feenix and Mrs. Skewton; so the same book said farewell to ranting in the last, stilted words with which Edith turned upon the man who had wronged her. The Dedlocks in their tragic hours have an altogether greater realism.

Apart from this limited failure in the early novels, it is difficult to see when Dickens' eye and ear ever failed him. The people whom we hear and see may not always be to our taste as they were to the taste of Victorian readers; but I do not doubt the authenticity of, for example, either Dora's playfulness or Agnes' moralising.

Is this all—a miraculous eye and ear—that accounts for the atmospheric genius, the encircling magic of Dickens? I do not think so. Edmund Wilson and Lionel Trilling have at various times traced through the symbolic unities of individual novels. I have no doubt at all that if we must assess Dickens' greatness on the basis of any artistic unity, it is to this deeper level rather than to the more conventional technical or moral surfaces that we must go. *Little Dorrit* in its working out of symbol and in its unity of atmosphere is surely the most perfect of his books. It is here rather than in the more conventionally unified novels that Dickens competes with *Emma* or *Middlemarch* or *The Secret Agent*. To seek his greatness in *Hard Times*, *David Copperfield*, or *Great Expectations*, is to judge him by as alien a measure as to assess Lawrence's greatness by *Sons and Lovers* —the conventional mistake of all who fail to see the point of Lawrence.

Yet this great unity of symbolism which, infusing the realism of speech and vision, creates that unspoken "atmosphere" which is Dickens' form of communication, is not to be found only in individual novels. There are certain situations, images, and symbols that recur throughout his work. These, it is, that account to me for the haunting quality of his world; their obsessive power over him finds an equally obsessive need in that large number of serious contemporary readers who are so possessed by him.

These situations, images and symbols, changing their relationships as he grew older, may be found in nearly all his work, great, ordinary or feeble. So comparatively poor a book as *Pictures from Italy* illustrates this excellently. Mr. Sacheverell Sitwell, who contributes the preface to the New Oxford Edition of this work, points to a characteristic piece of humor as the link between the improbable subjects of Vesuvius, Leonardo, Papal ceremonies etc. and Dickens, the familiar novelist. It is a good example of his humor: an English gentleman tourist at the back of a huge crowd that watches the Pope's Feeding of the Poor who calls out, "Can any gentleman, in front there, see mustard on the table? Sir, will you oblige me? Do you see a mustard pot?" It is indeed a fine piece of Mr. Podsnap, or, to be kinder, Mr. Meagles abroad. Yet to see only this as a characteristic in the book is to allow only for Dickens' ear. There are indeed a hundred examples as excellent of his eye's power. More striking than either, however, is the journey he makes around Northern Italy on a winter visit from Genoa (or home with Kate, Georgina and the children) on his way to England (home, conviviality, boon companions, the Inimitable at his liveliest, etc.). It is one of the haunting passages of Dickens, with coaches at night, strange alighting passengers, stranger inns and towns seen through night's darkness, and so on. Here in these somewhat ordinary essays of a tourist-novelist we are brought into the heart of Dickens' atmosphere. Why?

The answer lies, I believe, in the fundamental and complex meanings of "travelling" and "home" that lie deep in Dickens' world. Only Mr. Jack Lindsay, to my knowledge, has traced the importance of the wanderer in Dickens' work; and he has limited his analysis by confining it to the lost boys or children of the early works who tie up so conveniently with the blacking factory trauma. To extend the search over the whole of Dickens' work may tell us a little more of his obsessive strength.

We must begin surely with *Pickwick Papers*. In *Oliver Twist*, *The Old Curiosity Shop*, *Dombey*, and *David Copperfield*, he relived his childhood terrors, but *Pickwick Papers* is something deeper connected with his youth. This masterpiece which changed by the outpouring of his vision of life from a hack writer's notes to the English *Don Quixote* surely represents the ideal world as his youthful heart conceived it, before even child-hood terrors had been allowed to mar it, let alone the despairing vision of his middle years. Of course evil is there in Dodson and Fogg, but it isn't very serious; like Jingle, one feels, these lawyers might have been changed by true virtue. That true virtue surely is the ethic of the New Testament personified in Mr. Pickwick, and exemplified by the feasts and social occasion which through-out Dickens' work may stand for the reign of love on earth. This sort of New Testament Christianity, with its hostility to dogma and ceremony, and its dislike of ostentatious piety and works, is far away from any religion now revered, whether Catholic or Quaker. Nor can it be assimilated to any humanism though it may seem akin to it; for, in fact, the Redemption was central to Dickens' belief. As a humanist without transcen-dental beliefs, I cannot share it, but I agree with Mr. Fielding in believing it to be vital to our understanding of Dickens' work.

The whole history of Dickens' novels is the story of the at-tempt, often near to despair but never wholly forsaken, to retain something of the vision of *Pickwick Papers* against the inflow of the knowledge of evil's power. It centres around and is at its most powerful in scenes that concern the wanderer, "home," the feast of fellowship. As Dickens grew more complex, each of these essential symbols came to be filled with ambiguities which alone sufficed to reflect the subtle interaction of good and evil which he observed. By fusing them with such moral subtlety, he was able to maintain a more conscious simplicity on the surface of his books, and so retain the "humors" of his characters that were his great means of popular appeal.

Some examples must suffice to illustrate what I mean. After *Pickwick Papers* and the power of love, he regressed, as I have said into childhood. There "home," the ideal world of love, may be either the family party or the rural retreat. Into such perfect happiness Fagin's, or Squeers's, or Ralph's, or Quilp's menacing, jovial, hideousness may suddenly be thrust. Quilp's arrival at the ladies' fish tea is a kind of humorous parody of the awful invasion. Stagg, the sinister blind man (with his blackmailing secret), forerunner of Rogue Riderhood, finds Mrs. Rudge in sweetest rural seclusion. The wanderers seek a home: Oliver and Nell. Yet Nell looks forward to later works, because she also leaves what home she has because it is menaced. The picaresque wanderings of Nicholas and Martin need less of our attention, they are derivative; indeed not a little of the weakness of these two books comes I think from the fact that this important symbol is lost in the conventional figures of the 18th century picaresque hero. Nevertheless in Jonas' flight we have the precursor, though in an unsubtle form, of the murderer in flight. At the time of *Martin Chuzzlewit* we may see that though Dickens could already identify himself with the murderer, he had not yet realized that the murderer was also the victim, nor had he associated this fugitive figure with "home."

The pattern may be found in all his middle books. What, one wonders, would he have made of Walter Gay, had he but kept to his resolution of making that young wanderer a "bad" person? Would he have been a sort of Pip or a Charlie Hexam, and had such a figure been tied to the concept of "wandering" and of Florence's "prison" home and Uncle Sol's "home of love" might not something more potent and subtle than Mr. Carker's Jonaslike flight have been given to us? Perhaps Dickens was not yet ready for it. Steerforth, the Stavrogin angel-devil whose charm so dominates the novel, first ties the murderer (seducer) wanderer to the "home." Peggotty's boat is the exact type of the house of fellowship and love, so different from the prison world of Rosa and his mother who had smothered James Steerforth. The first visit of Steerforth chez Peggotty brings him to exactly one of those evenings of fellowship and feasting that are central to Dickens' gospel kingdom. Fleeing from the smothering fires of Highgate, Steerforth must destroy the Peggottys' world. Everything in the novel, I think, that connects with this has an extra force. For example how horrifying is the entrance of Littimer upon exactly another such love feast of innocents, the party of David for Traddles and the Micawbers. We have to go forward to *Great Expectations* to see the feast so horribly blasphemed, but by then it is not an intrusion of evil among the innocents, but the demonstration of evil in youth and innocence themselves by the cynical Mr. Jaggers. The last profanation of the innocents' feast follows the pattern of that of Jaggers very exactly. But Jasper's motives seem more evil than those of Jaggers who only used the occasion to try to point a moral lesson to Pip.

To enumerate every example of the conjunction of these themes would only be tedious for the ardent Dickens reader. Lady Dedlock runs from a prison home, thinking herself to be suspected of murder; and in so doing, she kills herself and to all intents and purposes destroys Sir Leicester. Yet the most powerful ambiguities of home and prison, murderer and victim, love and hatred, occur in *Little Dorrit* and *Our Mutual Friend*, and in my opinion it is in these two last completed novels that Dickens makes a more haunting and subtle communication than in any of his work. In *Little Dorrit* indeed the central figure of the wanderer Arthur Clennam who returns to his prison home gives the novel a unity of mood which makes it the most impressive of all Dickens' work.

It would be easy to ally this pursuit-flight and home-prison theme solely to our modern dilemma. Dickens like many of his contemporaries came almost to despair of social progress in his own age. However, he never wholly rejected the idea of progress; he never sought a religion that consigned this world to vanity or to the evil one; though nostalgic about his childhood, he never romanticised the past to compensate for his disillusionment with the present. He would have been unhappy with the social views of Mr. Eliot or Professor Lewis today. On the other hand in his last novels his refusal to renounce man's achievement permitted him no progressive complacency; I suspect that he would have found even the moral stoicism of C. P. Snow too determinedly unregarding of the power of evil. Dickens' dilemma —that of a simple New Testament Christian who found little evidence of the Kingdom around him—is in great degree that of the modern humanist who sees man's nature lagging behind his achievements. The parallel may well be an underlying cause of the revival of his reputation today. Yet the fugitive-wanderer, the prison house, the blazing log and the convivial feast seem subtle enough symbols of the human dilemma to give his spell of lasting power.

Bibliography

THE following bibliography is a selection from the impossibly enormous body of material written about Dickens and the fiction of Dickens before 1960. We have singled out those articles, essays, and books that seem to us to be, in whole or in part, "criticism"—as generally conceived and as defined in the opening essay in this collection. The bibliography includes a selection of published doctoral dissertations; for a full list of dissertations (published and unpublished) the reader may consult R. D. Altick and W. R. Mathews, *Guide to Doctoral Dissertations in Victorian Literature, 1886–1958* (Urbana, 1960), items 964–1045. For noncritical writings about Dickens the reader may consult the customary general and special bibliographies, some listed under (A) below.

A. Some Special Bibliographical Sources

Kitton, Frederick George. Dickensiana. London, 1886.

The Dickensian. London, 1905 to date.

DeLattre, Floris. Dickens et la France. Paris, 1927.

Gummer, Ellis N. Dickens' Works in Germany. Oxford, 1940.

Miller, William. The Dickens Student and Collector. Cambridge, Mass., 1946. Extensive but inept, inaccurate, and incomplete. See the next item.

Calhoun, Philo, and Heaney, Howell J. "Dickensiana in the Rough," Papers of the Bibliographical Society of America, XLI (1947), 293–320. Appendix I, A List of Some Sources to Be Consulted in

Compiling a Bibliography of Dickensiana; Appendix II, Some Special Sources of Dickensiana and Dickens Bibliography Not Included in the Bibliographical Section of Miller's Book.

Ford, George H. Dickens and His Readers. Princeton, 1955.

B. A Checklist of Dickens Criticism (1840–1960)

Anonymous. "Charles Dickens," London Quarterly Review, January 1871, pp. 265–286.

———. "*David Copperfield* and *Pendennis*," Prospective Review, VII (1851), 157–191.

———. "Two English Novelists: Dickens and Thackeray," Dublin Review, April 1871, pp. 315–350.

———. "Christmas Books: The Submerged Dickens," Times Literary Supplement, 25 December 1937, pp. 969–970.

Adrian, Arthur A. "*David Copperfield*: A Century of Critical and Popular Acclaim," Modern Language Quarterly, XI (1950), 325–331.

"Alain" (Emile Chartier). "Le fantastique et le réel d'après les 'Contes de Nöel' de Dickens," Nouvelle revue francaise, LIII (1939), 817–823. Reprinted in *En lisant Dickens*.

———. "L'imagination dans le roman," Revue de Paris, 1 March 1940, pp. 47–52. Reprinted in *En lisant Dickens*.

———. En lisant Dickens. Paris, 1945.

Aldington, Richard. "The Underworld of Young Dickens," Four English Portraits. London, 1948.

Allen, Walter. The English Novel. London, 1954.

Anderson, Kate. "Scenery and the Weather in Dickens," The Dial, 16 February 1912, pp. 115–116.

Apostoloi, Nikolay. "Tolstoy and Dickens," Family Views of Tolstoy. London, 1926.

Aronstein, Phillipp. "Charles Dickens's Weltanschauung," Anglia, XVIII (1896), 218–262.

Atkins, Stuart. "A Possible Dickens Influence in Zola," Modern Language Quarterly, VIII (1947), 302–308.

Auden, W. H. "Huck and Oliver," The Listener, 1 October 1953, pp. 540–541.

Austin, Alfred. "Charles Dickens," Temple Bar, July 1870, pp. 554–562.

Aydelotte, William O. "The England of Marx and Mill as Reflected in Fiction," The Tasks of Economic History, VIII (1948), 42–58.

Bagehot, Walter. "Charles Dickens," National Review, VII (1858), 458–486. Reprinted in Literary Studies. London, 1879.

Baker, Ernest A. The History of the English Novel, VII. New York, 1936.

Baker, Richard M. The Drood Murder Case. Berkeley, 1951. Reprinted from Nineteenth-Century Fiction.

Ball, Adolph. "Dickens und seine Hauptwerke," Archiv für das Studien des neuren Sprachen und Litterateuren, LXXIII (1885), 325–370, LXXIV, 129–180, 369–446.

Barlow, George. "The Genius of Dickens," Contemporary Review, November 1908, pp. 542–562.

Beach, Joseph Warren. The Twentieth-Century Novel. New York, 1932.

Belloc, Hilaire. "Dickens Revisited," New Statesman, 22 January 1927, pp. 444–445.

Benjamin, Edward B. "The Structure of Martin Chuzzlewit," Philological Quarterly, XXXIV (1955), 39–47.

Benson, Arthur C. "Fiction and Romance," Contemporary Review, December 1911, pp. 792–805.

——. "Charles Dickens," North American Review, March 1912, pp. 382–391.

——. Introduction to Oliver Twist. London, 1912.

Bentley, Eric. "Pickwick in Love," New Republic, 6 October 1952, pp. 30–31.

Bergler, Edmund. "Little Dorrit and Dickens' Intuitive Knowledge of Psychic Masochism," American Imago, XIV (1957), 371–388.

Biron, H. C. "The Plots of Dickens," National Review, May 1912, pp. 514–523.

Bishop, Jonathan. "The Hero-Villain of Oliver Twist," Victorian Newsletter, Spring 1959, pp. 14–16.

Bland, D. S. "The 'Lost' Sentence in Dombey and Son Once More," The Dickensian, LII (1956), 142–143. See Kathleen Tillotson, below.

Bleifuss, William W. "A Re-examination of *Edwin Drood*," The Dickensian, L (1954), 110–115, 176–186, LI, 24–29.

Bodelsen, Carl A. Dickens og hans bøger. Copenhagen, 1957.

——. "Some Notes on Dickens' Symbolism," English Studies, XL (1959), 420–431.

Boege, Fred W. "Point of View in Dickens," PMLA, LXV (1950), 90–105.

——. "Recent Criticism of Dickens," Nineteenth-Century Fiction, VIII (1953), 171–187.

Boll, Theophilus Ernest M. "*Great Expectations*," Times Literary Supplement, 15 August 1935, p. 513.

——. "Charles Dickens and Washington Irving," Modern Language Quarterly, V (1944), 453–467. See Christof Wegelin below.

——. "The Plotting of *Our Mutual Friend*," Modern Philology, XLII (1944), 96–122.

Booth, Bradford E. "Form and Technique in the Novel," The Reinterpretation of Victorian Literature. Ed. Joseph E. Baker. Princeton, 1950.

Bowen, C. M. "*Dead Souls* and *Pickwick Papers*," Athenaeum, June 1916, pp. 269–270.

Boyd, Ernest. "A New Way with Old Masterpieces," Harper's, June 1925, pp. 96–104. Reprinted in *Literary Blasphemies*. New York, 1927.

Bradby, M. K. "An Explanation of George Silverman's Explanation," The Dickensian, XXXVI (1940), 13–18.

Brimley, George. "Dickens's *Bleak House*," The Spectator, 24 September 1853, pp. 923–925. Reprinted in *Essays*. London, 1858.

Brink, Jan Ten. "De Erste Romans van Charles Dickens," Litterarische Schitsen en Kriticken. Leiden, 1883.

Broderick, James H., and Grant, John E. "The Identity of Esther Summerson," Modern Philology, LV (1958), 252–258.

Brogan, Colin. "*Oliver Twist* Re-examined," The Listener, 26 August 1948, pp. 310–311.

Brown, E. K. "*David Copperfield*," Yale Review, XXXVII (1948), 651–666.

"Browne, Matthew" (William Brighty Rands). "From Faust to Mr. Pickwick," Contemporary Review, July 1880, pp. 162–176.

Brumleigh, T. Kent. "Autoplagiarism," The Dickensian, XXXIX (1943), 115–118, 169–173, XL, 9–11.

Brunetière, Ferdinand. "A propos de Charles Dickens," Revue des deux mondes, 1 April 1889, pp. 695–706.

Brush, Lillian Hatfield. "A Psychological Study of Barnaby Rudge," The Dickensian, XXXI (1935), 24–30.

Buchanan, Robert W. "The 'Good Genie' of Fiction (Charles Dickens)," St. Paul's Magazine, February 1872, pp. 130–148. Reprinted in *Master-Spirits*. London, 1873.

Büchner, A. "Charles Dickens," Revue des cours littéraires, 6 August 1870, pp. 566–574.

Burns, Wayne. "The Genuine and the Counterfeit: A Study in Victorian and Modern Fiction," College English, XVIII (1956–1957), 143–150.

Bush, Douglas. "A Note on Dickens' Humor," From Jane Austen to Joseph Conrad. Ed. Robert C. Rathburn and Martin Steinmann, Jr. Minneapolis, 1958.

Butt, John. "Dickens at Work," Durham University Journal, IX (1948), 65–77.

——. "Dickens's Plan for the Conclusion of *Great Expectations*," The Dickensian, XLV (1949), 78–80.

——. "Dickens's Notes for His Serial Parts," The Dickensian, XLV (1949), 129–138.

——. "The Composition of *David Copperfield*," The Dickensian, XLVI (1950), 90–94, 128–135, 176–180, XLVII, 33–38.

——. "*David Copperfield* from Manuscript to Print," Review of English Studies, New Series, I (1950), 247–251.

——. "New Light on Charles Dickens," The Listener, 28 February 1952, pp. 341–342.

——. "*Bleak House* in the Context of 1851," Nineteenth-Century Fiction, X (1955), 1–21.

——. "*Bleak House* Once More," Critical Quarterly, I (1959), 302–307.

——. "The Topicality of *Little Dorrit*," University of Toronto Quarterly, XXIX (1959–1960), 1–10.

——, and Tillotson, Kathleen. "Dickens at Work on *Dombey and Son*," Essays and Studies. London, 1951.

Butt, John, and Tillotson, Kathleen. Dickens at Work. Fair Lawn, 1958. Contains much of the material of the preceding entries.

Camerini, Eugenio. "Carlo Dickens," Nuovi profili letterari. Milan, 1875.

Cammaerts, Émile. "Dickens and Balzac," Contemporary Review, March 1929, pp. 331–339.

Cary, Joyce. "Introducing Mr. Micawber," New York Times Book Review Section, 15 April 1951, pp. 4, 21.

Cazamian, Louis. Le roman social en Angleterre. Paris, 1903.

Cecil, Lord David. Early Victorian Novelists. London, 1934.

Chancellor, E. Beresford. "Charles Dickens—Novelist," "The Pathos of Dickens (A Note)," Literary Types. London, 1895.

Chesterton, G. K. Charles Dickens. London, 1906.

——. Appreciation and Criticism of Charles Dickens. New York, 1911. Collected introductions to the Everyman Edition of Dickens' Works.

——. The Victorian Age in Literature. London, 1913.

——. "Charles Dickens," The Bookman Extra Number (1914), pp. 7–11

——. "The Great Gusto," The Great Victorians. Ed. H. J. and Hugh Massingham. London, 1932. Reprinted in A Handful of Authors.. London, 1953.

Christian, Mildred G. "Carlyle's Influence upon the Social Theory of Dickens," The Trollopian, March 1947, pp. 27–35, June 1947, pp. 11–26. Now Nineteenth-Century Fiction.

Churchill, R. C. "Dickens, Drama, and Tradition," Scrutiny, X (1942), 358–375. Reprinted in The Importance of Scrutiny. Ed. Eric Bentley. New York, 1948.

——. "Charles Dickens," From Dickens to Hardy. Ed. Boris Ford. London, 1958.

Clark, William R. "The Rationale of Dickens' Death Rate," Boston University Studies in English, II (1956), 125–139.

Clarke, George H. "Dickens Now," Queen's Quarterly, LII (1945), 280–287.

Clutton-Brock, A. "Dickens," Times Literary Supplement, 8 February 1912, pp. 48–49. Reprinted in Essays on Books. London, 1920.

Cockshut, A. O. J. "Sentimentality in Fiction," Twentieth Century, April 1957, pp. 354–364.

Colburn, William E. "Dickens and the 'Life-Illusion,'" The Dickensian, LIV (1958), 110–118.

Connolly, Thomas E. "Technique in *Great Expectations*," Philological Quarterly, XXXIV (1955), 48–55.

Cor, Raphael. "Charles Dickens," Mercure de France, 1 July 1920, pp. 82–121. Reprinted in *Un romancier de la vertu et un peintre du vice (Charles Dickens—Marcel Proust)*. Paris, 1928.

Corelli, Marie. "Why Dickens Is Popular," The Book Monthly, February 1920, p. 87.

Coveney, Peter. Poor Monkey: The Child in Literature. London, 1957.

Cox, C. B. "In Defence of Dickens," Essays and Studies. London, 1958.

——. "Comic Viewpoints in *Sketches by Boz*," English, XII (1959), 132–135.

"Cranfield, Lionel" (Edward Sackville-West). "Books in General," New Statesman, 10 February 1945, pp. 95–96. On *Oliver Twist* and *The Old Curiosity Shop*. Reprinted as part of "Dickens and the World of Childhood," *Inclinations*. London, 1949.

——. "Books in General," New Statesman, 3 November 1945, pp. 301–302. On *Dombey and Son*. Reprinted as part of "Dickens and the World of Childhood," *Inclinations*. London, 1949.

Crompton, Louis. "Satire and Symbolism in *Bleak House*," Nineteenth-Century Fiction, XII (1958), 284–303.

Cross, Wilbur L. "The Return to Dickens," Yale Review, II (1912), 142–162.

Crotch, W. Walter. Charles Dickens, Social Reformer. London, 1913.

——. The Pageant of Dickens. London, 1915.

——. The Soul of Dickens. London, 1916.

Crothers, Samuel McCord. "The Obviousness of Dickens," Century Magazine, February 1912, pp. 560–574.

Cruikshank, R. J. Charles Dickens and Early Victorian England. New York, 1949.

Cruse, Amy. The Victorians and Their Reading. Boston, 1936.

Danzel, Wilhelm. "Über Dickens' Romane," Blätter fur litërarische Unterhaltung, Nos. 221–225, 9–13 August 1845. Reprinted in *Gesammelte Aufsatze*. Leipzig, 1855.

Darwin, Bernard. "A Little Dickens," Life Is Sweet Brother. London, 1940.

Davis, Earle R. "Dickens and the Evolution of Caricature," PMLA, LV (1940), 231–240.

——. "The Creation of Dickens's *David Copperfield*," University of Wichita Studies, No. 9. Wichita, 1941.

——. "Charles Dickens and Wilkie Collins," University of Wichita Studies, No. 16. Wichita, 1945.

DeLattre, Floris. "La centenaire de Charles Dickens," Revue pedagogique, 15 January 1912, pp. 45–63.

——. Dickens et la France. Paris, 1927.

De Morgan, William. Introduction to *Our Mutual Friend*. London, 1912. Reprinted in *The Bookman Extra Number* (1914), pp. 84–89.

Depret, Louis. Charles Dickens. Lille, 1874.

Dibelius, Wilhelm. Englische Romankunst. Berlin, 1910.

——. Charles Dickens. Berlin, 1916.

Drew, Arnold P. "Structure in *Great Expectations*," The Dickensian, LII (1956), 123–127.

Drinkwater, John. "The Grand Manner: Thoughts upon *A Tale of Two Cities*," Essays of the Year. London, 1930.

Dudley, Arthur. "Charles Dickens. *Dombey and Son*," Revue des deux mondes, 1 March 1848, pp. 901–922.

Duffield, Howard. "The Macbeth Motif in 'Edwin Drood,'" The Dickensian, XXX (1934), 263–271.

Dybowski, Roman. Charles Dickens. Warsaw, 1936.

Eliot, T. S. "Wilkie Collins and Dickens," Times Literary Supplement, 4 August 1927, pp. 825–826. Reprinted in *Selected Essays*. New York, 1932.

Elton, Oliver. "Dickens," A Survey of English Literature (1830–1880), II. London, 1920. Expanded into *Dickens and Thackeray*. London, 1925.

Engel, Monroe. "Dickens on Art," Modern Philology, LIII (1955), 25–38.

———. "The Politics of Dickens' Novels," PMLA, LXXI (1956), 945–974.

———. The Maturity of Dickens. Cambridge, Mass., 1959. Includes the two preceding essays.

Fadiman, Clifton. "Pickwick Lives Forever," Atlantic Monthly, December 1949, pp. 23–29. Introduction to Pickwick Papers.. Reprinted in Party of One. New York, 1955.

Fiedler, Leslie. "What Can We Do about Fagin?" Commentary, May 1949, pp. 411–418.

———. "William Faulkner: An American Dickens," Commentary, October 1950, pp. 384–387.

———. "Good Good Girl and Good Bad Boy," "From Redemption to Initiation," New Leader, 14 April 1958, pp. 22–25, 26 May, pp. 20–23. Reprinted in No! in Thunder. Boston, 1960.

Fielding, Kenneth J. Charles Dickens. London, 1953.

———. "The Monthly Serialization of Dickens's Novels," The Dickensian, LIV (1958), 4–11.

———. "The Weekly Serialization of Dickens's Novels," The Dickensian, LIV (1958), 134–141.

———. Charles Dickens: A Critical Introduction. London, 1958.

Figgis, Darrell. "Charles Dickens," Nineteenth Century, February 1912, pp. 274–284. Reprinted in Studies and Appreciations. London, 1912.

Fisher, James. "Reform as a Dickens Background," The Dickensian, XXXIII (1937), 181–186.

Folland, Harold F. "The Doer and the Deed: Theme and Pattern in Barnaby Rudge," PMLA, LXXIV (1959), 406–417.

Ford, George H. Dickens and His Readers. Princeton, 1955.

———. "Self-Help and the Helpless in Bleak House," From Jane Austen to Joseph Conrad. Ed. Robert C. Rathburn and Martin Steinmann, Jr. Minneapolis, 1958.

———. Introduction to David Copperfield. Boston, 1958.

Forster, E. M. Aspects of the Novel. New York, 1927.

Forster, John. The Life of Charles Dickens. London, 1872–1874.

Fox, Ralph. The Novel and the People. New York, 1937.

Franklyn, Julian. The Cockney. London, 1953.

Friedman, Norman. "Versions of Form in Fiction—Great Expecta-

tions and *The Great Gatsby*," Accent, XIV (1954), 246–264.
——. "The Shadow and the Sun: Notes toward a Reading of *Bleak House*," Boston University Studies in English, III (1957), 147–166.
Futrell, Michael A. "Gogol and Dickens," Slavonic and East European Review, XXXIV (1956), 443–459.
——. "Dickens and Dostoevsky," English Miscellany, VII (1956), 48–89.
Galsworthy, John. Introduction to *Bleak House*. London, 1912.
Gibson, Frank A. "The Love Interest in *Barnaby Rudge*," The Dickensian, LIV (1958), 21–23.
Gibson, Priscilla. "Dickens's Use of Animism," Nineteenth-Century Fiction, VII (1953), 283–291.
Gissing, George. Charles Dickens. London, 1898.
——. Critical Studies of the Works of Charles Dickens. New York, 1924.
Goodheart, Eugene. "Dickens's Method of Characterisation," The Dickensian, LIV (1958), 35–37.
Gordon, Elizabeth Hope. The Naming of Characters in the Works of Charles Dickens. University of Nebraska Studies in Language, Literature, and Criticism, No. 1. Lincoln, 1917.
Gourdault, Jules. "Les privilégiés et les pauvres gens dans les romans de Charles Dickens," Revue des cours littéraires, 22 April 1865, pp. 333–341.
Greene, Graham. Introduction to *Oliver Twist*. London, 1950. Reprinted as "The Young Dickens," *The Lost Childhood and Other Essays*. London, 1951.
Greenhalgh, Mollie. "*Edwin Drood*: The Twilight of a God," The Dickensian, LV (1959), 68–75.
Grenander, M. E. "The Mystery and the Moral: Point of View in Dickens's *Bleak House*," Nineteenth-Century Fiction, X (1956), 301–305.
Griffin, Montague. "An Estimate of Dickens as an Artist," Irish Monthly, September–October 1896, pp. 490–498, 539–549.
Grubb, Gerald G. "Dickens' Pattern of Weekly Serialization," ELH, IX (1942), 141–156.
Gummer, Ellis N. Dickens' Works in Germany. Oxford, 1940.

Hagan, John H., Jr. "Structural Patterns in Dickens's *Great Expectations*," ELH, XXI (1954), 54–66.

———. "The Poor Labyrinth: The Theme of Social Injustice in Dickens's *Great Expectations*," Nineteenth-Century Fiction, IX (1954), 169–178.

Hagberg, Knut. "Samuel Pickwick," Personalities and Powers. London, 1930.

Harder, Kelsie B. "Charles Dickens Names His Characters," Names, VII (1959), 35–42.

Harrison, Frederick. "Charles Dickens," The Forum, January 1895, pp. 545–553. Reprinted in *Studies in Early Victorian Literature*. London, 1895.

Harrison, Lewis. "Dickens's Shadow Show," The Dickensian, XXXIX (1943), 187–191. On *Hard Times*.

Heichen, Paul Hermann. Charles Dickens. Naumberg, 1898.

Heilman, Robert B. "The New World in Charles Dickens's Writings," The Trollopian, September 1946, pp. 25–43, March 1947, pp. 11–26. Now *Nineteenth-Century Fiction*.

Henley, William Ernest. "Some Notes on Charles Dickens," Pall Mall Magazine, August 1899, pp. 573–579.

Hennequin, Émile. "Charles Dickens. Étude analytique," Nouvelle revue, 15 November 1887, pp. 314–378. Reprinted in *Écrivains Francisés*. Paris, 1889.

Heur, Hermann. Romaneske Elemente im Realismus von Charles Dickens. Marburg, 1927.

Highet, Gilbert. "Dickens as a Dramatist," People, Places, and Books. New York, 1949.

Hill, Thomas W. "The Poetic Instinct of Dickens," The Dickensian, XII (1916), 272–274, 293–296.

Holst, Henriëtte Roland. Romankunst als Levensschool (Tolstoi, Balzac en Dickens). Arnheim, 1950.

Horne, R. H., ed. A New Spirit of the Age. London, 1844.

House, Humphry. The Dickens World. London, 1941.

———. "The Macabre Dickens," All in Due Time. London, 1955.

———. Introduction to *Oliver Twist*. Oxford, 1949. Reprinted in *All in Due Time*. London, 1955.

House, Humphry. "G. B. S. on *Great Expectations*," All in Due Time. London, 1955.

Howells, William Dean. Criticism and Fiction. New York, 1891.

——. My Literary Passions. New York, 1895.

——. Heroines of Fiction. New York, 1901.

Hunt, Theodore W. "The Prose Style of Charles Dickens," Representative English Prose and Prose Writers. New York, 1887.

Hutton, Richard Holt. "The Dispute about the Genius of Dickens," The Spectator, 7 February 1874, pp. 169–170. Reprinted as "The Genius of Dickens," *Criticism on Contemporary Thought and Thinkers*. London, 1894.

——. "The Genius of Dickens," The Spectator, 18 June 1870. Reprinted in *Brief Literary Criticisms*. London, 1906.

Huxley, Aldous. Vulgarity in Literature. London, 1930. On *The Old Curiosity Shop*.

Innes, Michael. Introduction to *Edwin Drood*. London, 1952.

Jackson, Thomas A. Charles Dickens. New York, 1938.

James, G. Ingli. "Dickens: An Essay in Christian Evaluation," Blackfriars, November 1957, pp. 466–473.

James, Henry. "*Our Mutual Friend*," The Nation, I (1865), 786–787. Reprinted as "The Limitations of Dickens," *Views and Reviews*. Boston, 1908.

Jansonius, H. Some Aspects of Business Life in Early Victorian Fiction. Amsterdam, 1926.

Jeffreason, J. Cordy. Novels and Novelists from Elizabeth to Victoria. London, 1858.

Johnson, Edgar. "Dickens, Fagin, and Mr. Riah," Commentary, January 1950, pp. 47–50.

——. "*The Christmas Carol* and the Economic Man," American Scholar, XXI (1952), 91–98.

——. "*Bleak House*: The Anatomy of Society," Nineteenth-Century Fiction, VII (1952), 73–89.

——. "The Scope of Dickens," Saturday Review of Literature, 29 November 1952, pp. 13–14, 44–48.

——. Charles Dickens, His Tragedy and Triumph. New York, 1952. Contains much of the above material.

——. "The Paradox of Dickens," The Dickensian, L (1954), 149–158.

——. "Dickens and Shaw: Critics of Society," Virginia Quarterly Review, XXXIII (1957), 66–79.

Johnson, R. Brimley. "Dickens as Artist, or Genius and the Cry of 'Art for Art's Sake,'" Book Monthly, III (1906), 235.

Jones, Howard Mumford. "On Rereading *Great Expectations*," Southwest Review, XXXIX (1954), 328–335.

Katkov, George. "Steerforth and Stavrogin," Slavonic Review, XXVII (1949), 469–488.

Kettle, Arnold. "*Oliver Twist*," An Introduction to the English Novel, I. London, 1951.

Krutch, Joseph Wood. "Pickwick Redivivus," The Nation, 28 September 1927, p. 320.

Laird, John. "Philosophy in the Works of Dickens," Philosophical Incursions into English Literature. Cambridge, Eng., 1946.

Lane, Lauriat, Jr. "The Devil in *Oliver Twist*," The Dickensian, LII (1956), 132–136.

——. "Dickens' Archetypal Jew," PMLA, LXXIII (1958), 94–100.

——. "Dickens and the Double," The Dickensian, LV (1959), 47–55.

——. "Mr. Pickwick and *The Dance of Death*," Nineteenth-Century Fiction, XIV (1959), 171–172.

Lang, Andrew. Introductions to the Gadshill Edition of Charles Dickens's Works. London, 1897.

——. "Charles Dickens," Fortnightly Review, December 1898, pp. 944–960. General essay also contributed to the Gadshill Edition.

Leacock, Stephen. "Fiction and Reality: A Study of the Art of Charles Dickens," Essays and Literary Studies. London, 1916.

——. "Two Humorists: Charles Dickens and Mark Twain," Yale Review, XXIV (1934), 118–129.

Leavis, F. R. "The Novel as Dramatic Poem (I): *Hard Times*," Scrutiny, XIV (1947), 185–203. Reprinted in *The Great Tradition*. London, 1948.

Leavis, Q. D. "Dickens, George Eliot, Henry James," Hudson Review, Autumn 1955, pp. 423–428.

Lemonnier, Leon. "Actualité de Dickens," Mercure de France, 15 November 1936, pp. 70–91.

L'Estrange, Rev. A. G. History of English Humour. London, 1878.

Lewes, George Henry. "Dickens in Relation to Criticism," Fortnightly Review, February 1872, pp. 141–154.

Lewis, Cecil Day. Introduction to *The Mystery of Edwin Drood*. London, 1956.

Liddell, Robert. A Treatise on the Novel. London, 1947.

Lillishaw, A. M. "The Case of *Barnaby Rudge*," The Dickensian, XLIV (1948), 141–144.

Lilly, William Samuel. "Dickens. The Humourist as Democrat," Four English Humourists. London, 1895.

Lindsay, Jack. "*A Tale of Two Cities*," Life and Letters, September 1949, pp. 191–204.

——. Charles Dickens. New York, 1950.

——. "Charles Dickens and Women," Twentieth Century, November 1953, pp. 375–386.

Lord, Walter Frewen. "Charles Dickens," Nineteenth Century, November 1903, pp. 765–781.

Lubbock, Percy. The Craft of Fiction. London, 1929.

Lucas, Alec. "*Oliver Twist* and the Newgate Novel," Dalhousie Review, XXXIV (1954), 381–387.

Lucas, Audrey. "Some Dickens Women," Yale Review, XXX (1940), 706–728.

McCullough, Bruce. Representative English Novelists. New York, 1946.

Machen, Arthur. "The Art of Dickens," The Academy, 11 April 1908, pp. 664–666.

MacKenzie, Compton. "Charles Dickens," Irish Library Bulletin, April–May 1950.

McKenzie, Gordon. "Dickens and Daumier," University of California Studies in English, VIII (1942), 273–298.

MacLean, H. N. "Mr. Pickwick and the Seven Deadly Sins," Nineteenth-Century Fiction, VIII (1953), 198–212.

McMaster, Rowland D. "Dickens and the Horrific," Dalhousie Review, XXXVIII (1958), 18–28.

——. "Dickens, Jung, and Coleridge," Dalhousie Review, XXXVIII (1959), 512–516.

Magnus, Laurie. English Literature in the Nineteenth Century. London, 1909.

Manheim, Leonard F. "The Personal History of David Copperfield," American Imago, IX (1952), 21–43.

——. "The Law as Father," American Imago, XII (1955), 17–23.

Manning, John. Dickens on Education. Toronto, 1959.

Masson, David. "Pendennis and Copperfield: Thackeray and Dickens," North British Review, May 1851, pp. 57–89.

——. British Novelists and Their Styles. Cambridge, Eng., 1859.

Maugham, Somerset. "Charles Dickens," Atlantic Monthly, July 1948, pp. 50–56. Reprinted as preface to David Copperfield and in Ten Novels and Their Authors. London, 1954.

Maurois, André. "Dickens," Études anglaises. Paris, 1927. Translated as Dickens, His Life and Work. London, 1934.

——. "Dickens et nous," Nouvelles littéraires, 24 April 1937, p. 1.

Meynell, Alice. "Charles Dickens as a Man of Letters," Atlantic Monthly, January 1903, pp. 52–59.

——. "Dickens as a Man of Letters," Dublin Review, April 1912, pp. 370–384. Reprinted in Hearts of Controversy. London, 1917. Not the same as the essay listed above.

Miller, J. Hillis. Charles Dickens: The World of His Novels. Cambridge, Mass., 1958.

Miller, William, and Strange, E. H. A Centenary Bibliography of the Pickwick Papers. London, 1936. Contains a selection of contemporary criticism.

Moffatt, James. "Dickens and Meredith," Hibbert Journal, October 1922, pp. 107–120.

Monod, Sylvère. Dickens romancier. Paris, 1953.

——. "Alain, lecteur de Dickens," Mercure de France, CCCXXXI (1957), 108–121.

——. "L'expression dans Our Mutual Friend: Manière ou maniérisme?" Études anglaises, X (1957), 37–48.

——. Introduction to Oliver Twist. Paris, 1957.

More, Paul Elmer. "The Praise of Dickens," Shelbourne Essays, Fifth Series. New York, 1908.

Morris, Mowbray. "Charles Dickens," Fortnightly Review, December 1882, pp. 762–779.

Morse, Robert. "*Our Mutual Friend*," Partisan Review, XVI (1949), 277–289.

Moynahan, Julian. "The Hero's Guilt: The Case of *Great Expectations*," Essays in Criticism, X (1960), 60–79.

Munro, W. A. Charles Dickens et Alphonse Daudet. Toulouse, 1908.

Needham, Gwendolyn B. "The Undisciplined Heart of David Copperfield," Nineteenth-Century Fiction, IX (1954), 81–107.

Neill, S. Diana. A Short History of the English Novel. London, 1951.

Nisbet, Ada B. "The Mystery of *Martin Chuzzlewit*," Essays Dedicated to Lily B. Campbell. Los Angeles, 1950.

——. "The Autobiographical Matrix of *Great Expectations*," Victorian Newsletter, Spring 1959, pp. 10–13.

Noyes, Alfred. "Dickens and Mr. Chesterton," The Bookman Extra Number (1914), pp. 194–202.

O'Connor, Frank. The Mirror in the Roadway. New York, 1950.

O'Faolain, Sean. "Dickens and Thackeray," The English Novelists. Ed. Derek Verschoyle. London, 1936.

Orwell, George. "Charles Dickens," Inside the Whale. London, 1940.

Pattee, Fred Lewis. "The Shadow of Dickens," The Feminine Fifties. New York, 1940.

Paul, David. "The Novel Art: II," Twentieth Century, October 1953, pp. 294–301.

Pearson, Gabriel. "Dickens and His Readers," Universities and Left Review, I (1957), 52–56.

Phelps, William Lyon. "Dickens," Essays on Books. New York, 1914.

Phillips, Rev. T. M. "Life and Art in Dickens and Henry James," Manchester Quarterly, XLV (1919), 20–31.

Phillips, Walter C. Dickens, Reade and Collins. New York, 1919.

Poe, Edgar Allan. "*The Old Curiosity Shop*," Graham's Magazine, May 1841, pp. 248–251.

——. "*Barnaby Rudge*," Graham's Magazine, February 1842, pp. 124–129.

Pound, Louise. "The American Dialect of Charles Dickens," American Speech, XXII (1947), 124–130.

Powys, John Cooper. "Dickens," Visions and Revisions. London, 1915. With new preface, London, 1955.

Praz, Mario. La crisi dell'eroe nel romanzo vittoriano. Florence, 1952, Translated by Angus Davidson as *The Hero in Eclipse in Victorian Fiction*. London, 1956.

Priestley, J. B. "The Secret of Dickens," Saturday Review, 26 September 1925, p. 342.

——. English Humour. London, 1929.

——. The English Comic Characters. London, 1937.

——. "New Judgment," The Dickensian, XL (1944), 61–63.

Pritchett, V. S. "*Edwin Drood*," New Statesman, 26 February 1944, p. 143. Reprinted in *The Living Novel*. London, 1946.

——. "*Oliver Twist*," New Statesman, 25 March 1950, pp. 344–345. Reprinted in *Books in General*. London, 1953.

——. "The Humour of Dickens," The Listener, 3 June 1954, pp. 970–973. Reprinted as "The Comic World of Dickens," in *The Avon Book of Modern Writing*. New York, 1955.

Pugh, Edwin. Charles Dickens: The Apostle of the People. London, 1909.

Quennell, Peter. "Books in General," New Statesman, 13 September 1941, p. 257. Reprinted as "*Our Mutual Friend*" in *The Singular Preference*. London, 1952.

Quiller-Couch, Sir Arthur. Charles Dickens and Other Victorians. Cambridge, Eng., 1925.

Quirk, Randolph. Charles Dickens and Appropriate Language. Durham, 1959.

Raleigh, John Henry. "Dickens and the Sense of Time," Nineteenth-Century Fiction, XIII (1958), 127–137.

Rantavaara, Irma. Dickens in the Light of English Criticism. Helsinki, 1944.

Reed, James. "The Fulfillment of Pip's Expectations," The Dickensian, LV (1959), 12–18.

Rérat, A. "Le romanesque dans *L'ami commun*," Les langues modernes, LII (1958), 238–244.

Richardson, Joanna. "Dickens and *Hard Times*," afternote to Hard Times. London, 1954. Everyman edition.

Rickett, Arthur. "Charles Dickens," Personal Forces in Modern Literature. London, 1906.

Rooke, Eleanor. "Fathers and Sons in Dickens," Essays and Studies 1951. London, 1951.

Rouse, H. Blair. "Charles Dickens and Henry James," Nineteenth-Century Fiction, V (1950), 151–157.

Ruckmini, M. A. "The Didactic in the Art of Dickens," The Aryan Path, November 1946, pp. 419–422.

Ruskin, John. Footnote on *Hard Times*, Cornhill Magazine, II (1860), 159. Reprinted in *Unto This Last*. London, 1862.

Saintsbury, George. "Charles Dickens," Corrected Impressions. London, 1895.

——. "Dickens," Cambridge History of English Literature, vol. XIII, part II. New York, 1916.

Santayana, George. "Dickens," The Dial, LXXI (1921), 537–549. Reprinted in *Soliloquies in England*. London, 1922.

Schilling, Bernard S. Introduction to Comic Scenes from Dickens. Hamden, 1955.

Schmidt, Julian. "Studien über Dickens und den Humor," Westermanns Monatshefte, April–July 1870. Reprinted in *Bilder aus den geistigen Leben unserer Zeit*, Neue Folge. Leipzig, 1871.

Schmidt-Hidding, Wolfgang. Sieben Meister des literarischen Humor in England und Amerika. Heidelberg, 1959.

Scudder, Vida D. "Social Pictures: Dickens and Thackeray," Social Ideals in English Letters. Boston, 1898.

Sennewald, Charlotte, Die Namengebung bei Dickens, eine Studie über Lautsymbolik. Leipzig, 1936.

Shaw, George Bernard. Introduction to *Hard Times*. London, 1912.

——. "On Dickens," The Dickensian, X (1914), 150–151.

——. "On Dickens," The Bookman Extra Number (1914), pp. 103–104.

——. Introduction to *Great Expectations*. Edinburgh, 1937. London, 1947. Reprinted in *Majority, 1931–52*. Ed. Hamish Hamilton. London, 1952.

Shelton, F. W. "On the Genius of Dickens," The Knickerbocker, May 1852, pp. 421–431.

Sibbald, William A. "Charles Dickens Revisited," Westminster Review, January 1907, pp. 62–73.

Simpson, Evelyn. "Jonson and Dickens: A Study in the Comic Genius of London," Essays and Studies, XXIX (1944), 82–92.

Sitwell, Osbert. "A Note on Charles Dickens," Week-End Review, 21 November 1931.

——. Dickens. London, 1932.

——. "Dickens and the Modern Novel," Trio. London, 1938.

Sorensen, Knut. "Subjective Narration in *Bleak House*," English Studies, XL (1959), 431–439.

Spaventi-Filippi, Silvio. Carlo Dickens. Rome, 1924.

Spedding, James. "Dickens's *American Notes*," Edinburgh Review, January 1843, pp. 270–276. Reprinted in *Reviews and Discussions*. London, 1879.

Spielhagen, Friedrich. "Dickens und Thackeray," Europa, 1859, No. 19, cols. 641–652.

Spilka, Mark. "'Amerika': Its Genesis," Franz Kafka Today. Ed. Angel Flores and Homer Swander. Madison, 1958.

——. "*David Copperfield* as Psychological Fiction," Critical Quarterly, I (1959), 292–301.

——. "Little Nell Revisited," Papers of the Michigan Academy of Science, Arts, and Letters, XLV (1960), 427–437.

Stange, G. Robert. "Expectations Well Lost: Dickens' Fable for His Time," College English, XVI (1954–1955), 9–17.

——. "Dickens and the Fiery Past: *A Tale of Two Cities* Reconsidered," English Journal, XLVI (1957), 381–396.

Starrett, Vincent. Introduction to *Edwin Drood*. New York, 1941.

Stearns, Frank Preston. Modern English Prose Writers. New York, 1897.

Stephen, Sir James Fitz-James. "*A Tale of Two Cities*," Saturday Review, 17 December 1859, pp. 741–743.

Stevenson, Lionel. "Names in *Pickwick*," The Dickensian, XXXII (1936), 241–244.

——. "Dickens's Dark Novels," Sewanee Review, LI (1943), 398–409.

——. "The Second Birth of the English Novel," University of Toronto Quarterly, XIV (1945), 366–374.

Stevenson, Robert Louis. "Some Gentlemen in Fiction," Scribner's Magazine, III (1888), 764–768.

Stewart, James T. "Miss Havisham and Miss Grierson," Furman Studies, VI (1958), 21–23.

Stoll, Elmer Edgar. "Dickens's Villains," From Shakespeare to Joyce. New York, 1944.

Stone, Harry. "Dickens' Use of His American Experiences in *Martin Chuzzlewit*," PMLA, LXXII (1957), 464–478.

——. "Dickens's Tragic Universe: 'George Silverman's Explanation,'" Studies in Philology, LV (1958), 86–97.

——. "Dickens and Interior Monologue," Philological Quarterly, XXXVIII (1959), 52–65.

——. "Dickens and the Jews," Victorian Studies, II (1958–1959), 222–253.

Stott, George. "Charles Dickens," Contemporary Review, February 1869, pp. 203–225.

Strong, L. A. G. "*David Copperfield*," Personal Remarks. London, 1953.

Swinburne, Algernon Charles. "Charles Dickens," Quarterly Review, July 1902, pp. 20–39.

——. Charles Dickens. London, 1913. Additional material, especially on *Oliver Twist*.

Symons, Arthur. "*Oliver Twist*," Essays of the Year. London, 1930.

Symons, Julian. Charles Dickens. London, 1951.

Taine, Hippolyte. "Charles Dickens. Son talent et ses oeuvres," Revue des deux mondes, 1 February 1856, pp. 618–647. Reprinted in *Histoire de la littérature anglaise*. Paris, 1863–1864. Translated into English, Edinburgh, 1871.

Talbot, G. F. "The Genius of Charles Dickens," Putnam's Monthly Magazine, March 1855, pp. 263–272.

Tedlock, E. W., Jr. "Kafka's Imitation of *David Copperfield*," Comparative Literature, VII (1955), 52–62.

Thalmann, Liselotte. Charles Dickens in seinen Beziehungen zum Ausland. Zurich, 1956.

Tillotson, Kathleen. "A Lost Sentence in *Dombey and Son*," The Dickensian, XLVII (1951), 81–82. See Bland, D. S., above.

——. "*Dombey and Son*," Novels of the Eighteen-Forties. Oxford, 1954.

——. "*Oliver Twist*," Essays and Studies, New Series. London, 1959.

See also under Butt, John, above.

Topp, St. John. "Dickens," The Melbourne Review, July 1881, pp. 265–282.

Trilling, Lionel. "The Dickens of Our Day," A Gathering of Fugitives. Boston, 1956. Originally a review of Edgar Johnson, *Charles Dickens, His Tragedy and Triumph* (1952).

——. Introduction to *Little Dorrit*. London, 1953. Reprinted in *The Opposing Self*. London, 1955.

Trollope, Anthony. "Charles Dickens," St. Paul's Magazine, VI (1870), 370–375.

——. "Novel-Reading," Nineteenth Century, January 1879, pp. 24–43.

——. Autobiography. London, 1882.

Van Amerongen, J. B. The Actor in Dickens. London, 1926.

Van Dyke, Henry. "The Good Enchantment of Charles Dickens," Scribner's, June 1912, pp. 656–665. Reprinted in *Companionable Books and Their Authors*. New York, 1927.

Van Ghent, Dorothy. "The Dickens World," Sewanee Review, LVIII (1950), 419–438.

——. "On *Great Expectations*," The English Novel. New York, 1953.

Vasata, Rudolph. "'Amerika' and Charles Dickens," The Kafka Problem. Ed. Angel Flores. New York, 1946.

Vooys, S. De. The Psychological Element in the English Sociological Novel of the Nineteenth Century. Amsterdam, 1927. On *Hard Times*.

Wagenknecht, Edward. "White Magic," Cavalcade of the English Novel. New York, 1947.

Waldock, A. J. A. "The Status of *Hard Times*," Southerly, IX (1948), 33–39.

Walker, Saxon. "The Artistry of Dickens as an English Novelist," The Dickensian, LI (1955), 102–108.

Walters, J. Cuming. Phases of Dickens. London, 1911.

——. The Complete Mystery of Edwin Drood. London, 1912.

——. "The Place of *Pickwick* in Literature," The Dickensian, XXIII (1927), 93–99, 149–151.

Ward, Adolphus W. Dickens. London, 1882.

Ward, Mrs. Wilfrid. "The Realism of Dickens," Dublin Review, October 1907, pp. 285–295.

Warner, Rex. "On Reading Dickens," The Cult of Power. New York, 1947.

Waugh, Alec. Introduction to *Pickwick Papers*. London, 1956.

Wegelin, Christof. "Dickens and Irving: The Problem of Influence," Modern Language Quarterly, VII (1946), 83–91. See Boll, Ernest, above.

Wenger, Jared. "Character-Types of Scott, Balzac, Dickens, and Zola," PMLA, LXII (1947), 213–232.

Weygandt, Cornelius. "Dickens and the Folk-Imagination," A Century of the English Novel. New York, 1925.

Whibley, Charles. "A Study of Charles Dickens," The Dickensian, XIX (1923), 65–70.

Whipple, Edwin P. "Novels and Novelists. Charles Dickens," North American Review, October 1849, pp. 383–406. Delivered before the Boston Mercantile Library Association, December 1844. Reprinted in *Literature and Life*. Boston, 1850.

——. "The Genius of Dickens," Atlantic Monthly, May 1867, pp. 546–554. Reprinted in *Success and Its Conditions*. Boston, 1877.

——. Prefaces to the Works of Charles Dickens. Boston, 1878. Reprinted as *Charles Dickens*. Boston, 1912. Prefaces to *Pickwick Papers, Oliver Twist, Hard Times, Great Expectations*, and *Little Dorrit* also published in the Atlantic Monthly, 1876–1877.

Whitman, Walt. "Boz and Democracy," Brother Jonathan, 26 February 1842. Reprinted in *Rivulets of Prose.* New York, 1928.

Wickhardt, Wolfgang. Die Formen die Perspektiv in Charles Dickens Romanen. Berlin, 1933.

Wierstra, F. D. Smollett and Dickens. Amsterdam, 1928.

Williams, Orlo. "*Martin Chuzzlewit*," Some Great English Novels. London, 1926.

Williamson, Claude C. H. "The Humour of Dickens," Writers of Three Centuries. London, 1920.

Wilson, Angus. "Dickens and the Divided Conscience," The Month, May 1950, pp. 349–360.

Wilson, Arthur Herman. "The Great Theme in Charles Dickens," Susquehanna University Studies, VI, iii (1959), 422–457.

Wilson, Edmund. "Dickens: The Two Scrooges," The Wound and the Bow. Boston, 1941. First published in part in the *New Republic*, CII (1940), 297–300, 339–342, 463–467.

Winter, Warrington. "Dickens and the Psychology of Dreams," PMLA, LXIII (1948), 984–1006.

Woolf, Virginia. "*David Copperfield*," The Nation and Athenaeum, 22 August 1925, pp. 620–621. Reprinted in *The Moment and Other Essays*. London, 1949.

Wrigg, William. "Dickens' Message of Christmas," English Journal, XLVIII (1959), 537–539.

Yamamoto, Tadao. Growth and System of the Language of Dickens. Osaka, 1950.

——. Dickens's English. Tokyo, 1951.

Zabel, Morton Dauwen. "A Pickwick Holiday," Commonweal, 8 June 1927, pp. 122–123.

——. "Dickens as Historian and Reformer," The Nation, 11 April 1942, pp. 434–437. Reprinted in the next item.

——. "The Reputation Revised," Craft and Character in Modern Fiction. New York, 1957. Reprinted from *The Nation*, 17 September 1949, pp. 279–281; with additional material from *The Nation*, 11 April 1942, cited above.

——. Introduction to *Bleak House*. Boston, 1956. Reprinted as "The Undivided Imagination" in *Craft and Character in Modern Fiction*. New York, 1957.

Zabel, Morton Dauwen. Introduction to *A Tale of Two Cities*. New York, 1958. Included as "The Revolutionary Fate" in *Craft and Character in Modern Fiction*. New York, 1957.

Zweig, Stefan. "Charles Dickens," The Dial, January 1923, pp. 1–24, translated by Kenneth Burke. Reprinted in *Master Builders*. New York, 1939.

Index

Titles of Dickens' Writings and Names of Characters